AFRICAN NATIONALIST POETRY AND PROSE

AFRICAN NATIONALIST POETRY AND PROSE

FREDERICK MONDERSON

SUMON PUBLISHERS

FREDERICK MONDERSON

ISBN - 978-1-61023-061-2
LCCN – 201790822

African Nationalist Poetry and Prose Photo. At the "Tribute to Professor George Simmonds," Dr. Fred Monderson sat at the feet of his heroes, Professor George Simmonds, Dr. Yosef Ben-Jochannan, Brother X, Michael Carter, Elombe Brathe, Dr. Lewis, Sister Camille Yarbrough, etc.

ABOUT THE AUTHOR

Dr. Frederick Monderson is a retired College Professor and public-school teacher who taught African History in the City University of New York and American History and Government in the New York public schools. He has written some 1000

AFRICAN NATIONALIST POETRY AND PROSE

articles in the "New York Black Press," *Daily Challenge*, *Afro Times* and *New American* newspapers. In this venture, Monderson lends his expertise as a historian, Egyptologist, journalist and author of several books including *Ladies in the House*; *Michael Jackson: The Last Dance*; *50 on Point*; *Barack Obama: Ready, Fit to Lead*; *Barack Obama: Master of Washington D.C.*; *Obama: Master and Commander and Obama: The Journey Completed*; *Sonny Carson: The Final Triumph (5 Volumes)*; *Black Nationalism: Alive and Well*; *Black Nationalism: Still Alive and Well*; *Guyana: Land of Beauty and Many Waters*; and on Ancient Egypt, *Seven Letters to Mike Tyson on Egyptian Temples*; *10 Poems Praising Great Blacks for Mike Tyson*; *Research Essays on Ancient Egypt*; *Temple of Karnak: The Majestic Architecture of Ancient Kemet*; *Where are the Kamite Kings?*; *Abydos and Osiris*; *Temple of Luxor*; *Medinet Habu: Mortuary Temple of Rameses III*; *The Quintessential Book on Ancient Egypt: "Holy Land"* (A Tour Guide Novel on Egypt); *Hatshepsut's Temple at Deir el Bahari*; *Intrigue Through Time*; *An Egyptian Resurrection*, (A Novel on Ancient Egypt); *The Majesty of Egyptian Gods and Temples* (A book of Egyptian Poems); *Egypt Essays on Ancient Kemet*; *The Ramesseum: Mortuary Temple of Rameses II*; *The Colonnade: Then and Now*; *Reflections on Ancient Kemet*; *The Hypostyle Hall*; *Grassroots View of Ancient Egypt*; *Glory of the Ancestors: 19 Letters to O.J. Simpson on Ancient African History*; *Celebrating Dr. Ben-Jochannan*; *Black History Extravaganza: Honoring Dr. Ben*

FREDERICK MONDERSON

Jochannan; *Let's Liberate the Temple*; *More Woman, More Power*; *Reflections on Ancient Egypt - Book One*; *Reflections on Ancient Egypt - Book Two*; *Black History Everyday - Part One*; *Black History Everyday - Part Two*; and more. A student of the esteemed Dr. Yosef ben-Jochannan, Dr. Monderson conducts tours to Egypt.

Tour Contact Orleane Brooks-Williams, Nostrand Travel, 730 Nostrand Avenue, Brooklyn, New York 11216. Phone 718-756-5300.
Follow me on Utube; Book s of Amazon.com

fredsegypt.com@fredsegypt.com
sumonpublishers.com@sumonpublishers.com
blackegyptbooks.com@blackegyptbooks.com
blackfolksbooks.com@blackfolksbooks.com

African Nationalist Poetry and Prose Photo. Mama Parsela and the Master Drummer Chendo.

AFRICAN NATIONALIST POETRY AND PROSE

Very often the issue of names arises regarding modern man's description of the ancient Egyptians and this seems a predetermined pattern. As such, one has to wonder whether this has been part of the systematic attempt to estrange Egypt from Africa and solidify Egypt's place in Europe. After all, every book on contemporary European civilization begins with a chapter on Egypt, whereas in earlier times the history began with Greece and Rome. However, today we cannot ignore the persistent insistence and must dismiss claims of a "Caucasian Egypt!" That is, the theory of a migrating people originating in Southwest Asia, who, for "some unknown reason" left their homeland to settle in Egypt. Arriving there, sometime during the Old Kingdom these people brought a "superior mental attitude" which "added an impetus to the indigenous culture." As a result, Egyptian civilization was able to achieve the great glory the world is so familiar with. Such a late 18th and 19th Century view begun by German scholars beginning with Hegel and others predominated throughout the 20th Century and stubbornly persists into the 21st Century. However, there are problems with this "model" and it is being vigorously challenged by Afrocentrists among other peoples. The interesting thing is, the anti-Afrocentrists are vehemently fighting back, particularly from an *ad hominem* perspective, dismissing credible scholarship, even ignoring the contradictions in the Egyptian corpus that mitigates especially against a "Caucasian Egypt." Nonetheless, this latter view, remains stubbornly consistent with the "Hamitic

FREDERICK MONDERSON

Hypothesis" position that argues essentially, "Any evidence of a high culture found in Africa was brought there by people of a white morphology." Naturally, this now discredited theory is racist in its intent for it sought to project "White over Black" intellectual, cultural, social and even scientific frames of endowment in human development. Nevertheless, some of the contradictions as pointed out below, exposes the realities of the situation and asks how could intellectual and lay minds in face of credible evidence that argue against such positions, still allow the perpetuation of the myth of a "White Egypt?"

African Nationalist Poetry and Prose Photo. Jose, Chendo, Florencio, Joselina.

1.   Though similar arguments were put forward by others, the theory of a "migrating superior race" gained credence through the efforts of W. Flinders Petrie, "the father of modern archaeology," but was dismissed upon critical scrutiny because racist machinations drove his model! That migrating

AFRICAN NATIONALIST POETRY AND PROSE

peoples populated the earth and helped assist in the diffusion and development of culture and ultimately civilization is not altogether far-fetched but to outright argue from a superior-inferior, white over black, relationship questions the validity of this line of reasoning particularly in an age when the Slave Trade perpetuated under "naked imperialism," Europe was undergoing its nationalist assertion and consolidation and the Germans especially sought to foster Nordic-Aryan superiority over other peoples, white and non-white, particularly Africans being victimized by the horrible institution of slavery!

African Nationalist Poetry and Prose Photo. Dr. **Yosef ben-Jochannan** gets the Harlem Community's recognition he assuredly deserves.

2. Since man originated in Africa and migrated to people the earth, it is not inconceivable to associate Africans with migration. Brophy and Bauval in their *Black Genesis* argue a black African people from a

FREDERICK MONDERSON

region Southwest of Upper Egypt were the earliest astronomers who created a calendar based on observations of movements of the heavenly bodies. They mapped the heavens, initiated a religious "bovine mother goddess" worship and were farmers who practiced pastoralism. They did artwork utilizing the "predominant red" to represent people and animals. They even traveled great distances in the inhospitable desert navigating by star positioning. All this occurred thousands of years ago from perhaps approximately 7500-3,500 years Before Christ. By the latter age, this area was no longer regularly watered by torrential rains which gathered in catch basins allowing practices of farming and cattle rearing or pastoralism. Thus, about 3,500 B.C. as the rains became sparse these peoples migrated east towards the Nile River in the vicinity of Aswan where they settled. As a result of their extensive travels in the desert, they knew of the existence of the Nile; much unlike the Southwest Asians who "for some unknown reason" left their homeland.

African Nationalist Poetry and Prose Photo.
The Message is clear, culture paves the way.

AFRICAN NATIONALIST POETRY AND PROSE

African Nationalist Poetry and Prose Photo. Harlem pays tribute to a great one, visibly represented.

Possessing millennia of accumulated scientific knowledge developed in observation and charting movements in the heavens, as Bauval and Brophy argued, the inhabitants of **Nabta Playa** laid the foundation for pharaonic Egypt! Their arrival in Upper Egypt at about 3500 B.C. is very contemporary with Bruce Williams' discovery of the earliest monarchy at Qustol dated c. 3400 B.C. Evidently not the entire Nabta Playa community migrated for at least one Old Kingdom cartouche has been found in the vicinity, perhaps indicating pharaonic attempts to establish contacts with "ancestral beginnings."

3. Many arguments were advanced to support the "Caucasian Egypt" theory particularly those explaining how the "Dynastic Race" arrived in Egypt, even though these visitors are credited with arriving during the Old Kingdom. That is, after a thriving southern kingdom had galvanized a powerful fighting force, employing the wherewithal of military logistics and ordinance ramifications, mastered the descent of the river, conquered an equally viable northern kingdom, began building temples and initiating religious practices, established a monarchical form of government, possessed a numerical system numbering in the millions, even establishing a calendar and begun the orientation and construction of the Step, then True Pyramid and so much more. Dr. ben-Jochannan argued the "Silt Pyramid" of Nubia predated these two forms. Still, all were antedated by the wind-shaped phenomenon that created the natural pyramids over millennia in the hostile desert environment.

Nevertheless, as the story goes, after all of these accomplishments, the Caucasian, "for some unknown reason" who left his native Southwest Asia environment and migrated to Egypt, arrived with his "superior mental attitude" after the native African had done all of the above. There was no evidence of comparative accomplishments in the Caucasian home base, and he arrived with nothing but a "white skin and superior intellect," just as "for some

AFRICAN NATIONALIST POETRY AND PROSE

unknown" reason he left. No one knows if he actually knew where his final destination would be! Since the route is generally desert-like, we could well imagine the hardships of the journey, a struggle for existence, arriving thirsty, weary, desert whipped but with that "superior mental attitude," looking upon the accomplishments they encountered, they immediately set about reinventing Narmer's wheel!

4. The ancient Egyptians often painted themselves red and as the many theories of Egyptian origins collapsed, those leading the charge of a "Caucasian Egypt" offered the Egyptians were a Caucasian red race! Thus, there were "white Caucasian Egyptians," even "black Caucasian Egyptians" and now "red Caucasian Egyptians." Nevertheless, filterings or survivals of Egyptians painted black in statuary, paintings and even papyrus demanded examination of other possibilities. As it turned out, in his tremendously erudite *African Origins of Civilization: Myth or Reality* (1974) Cheikh Anta Diop argued the ancient Egyptians painted themselves red! Dr. Yosef ben-Jochannan equally affirmed the ancient Egyptians painted themselves red and also pointed out young Nubian brides were colored red with the Henna plant and sees this as a continuation of the ancient culture.

As a young student of ancient history this writer's professor, now seen as misguided, once stated the ancient Egyptians were painted red because they went into the sun and that their women who were

FREDERICK MONDERSON

painted a lighter color did not go in the sun but stayed at home. Yet, during the 20th Dynasty, Rameses III reported how safe he had made the country that women could come and go as they pleased and not be assaulted or molested in the street!

African Nationalist Poetry and Prose Photo. Tribute to the Ancestors Images 2019.

The Frenchman Henri L'Hote in his "Tassili Frescoes" in the Sahara and Mary Leakey in "Bushman Art" of East and Southern Africa and who chronicled some 2000 Stone Age sites therein mention the "predominant red" used by the artists. Recently, *The New York Times* reported finding a paint factory with red remains in Southern Africa dated at 107,000 years old. This factory "find" provided evidence of mixing paint from extracted iron ore. Similar sites dated to 150,000 years have also been found but there the clear evidence of "predominant red" has not been found. The southern

AFRICAN NATIONALIST POETRY AND PROSE

African "paint factory" provided clear cut evidence of the process of extraction and mixing which not only indicated red was a form of cultural coloring but seems to push back the age of early man's thinking by several millennia before the time its believed complex social thought processes actually began! With this "find" we could also associate a 1973 *New York Times* article chronicling discovery of an iron ore mine in South Africa carbon dated at 43,000 Before Present. It is reasonable to assume iron ore extracts were available and could have been mixed and used by local artists though evidence of paint had not survived.

African Nationalist Poetry and Prose Photo. Revered Dr. John Henrik Clarke, Hunter College CUNY Professor, poet, author, teacher, friend, a true son of Harlem.

Dr. Ivan Van Sertima argued in a lecture, a prevailing view entertained in Europe is that while scientists accept that man originated in Africa, the view is after migrating to people the world, and the African stagnated. The Caucasian man, after he had conquered the harsh realities of the ice environment returned to Africa to civilize the African. Now, the paint factory discovery with evidence of paint extraction process that extended man's thinking practices beyond accepted time frames certainly makes obsolete the above claim.

Dr. Diop argued the African who evades the issue of Egypt is either an educated fool or a neurotic and Prof. John H. Clarke who pointed out "the people who preached racism colonized history" and "when Europe colonized the world it colonized the world's knowledge," insisted African history must be written by African historians! Maulana Karenga in his work *Maat* (2006: 16) reiterates Diop's contention "that enduring attempts to deny the African character of ancient Egypt and recent claims that the racial or ethnic identity of the ancient Egyptians is irrelevant (Yurco 1989), although it is relevant for the rest of Africa and the world, are both products of an ideological "scholarship" which grew out of an age of racism and imperialist expansion and the resultant "need" for a justificatory ideology. This, he states, "led to a concerted effort to discredit dominated peoples through the manipulation of science and the falsification of human history, a falsification which in Africa's case involved depriving it of its most important classical civilization. The thrust seemed to have been one of taking Africans out of Egypt, Egypt of Africa, and then Africa out of human history. Such a project and view reaffirmed Hegel's and others' Eurocentric claims that Africa was a non-historical continent aided in justifying centuries of oppression

AFRICAN NATIONALIST POETRY AND PROSE

and denial of African history and humanity. (Mudimbe 1988; Amin 1989)"

African Nationalist Poetry and Prose Photo. Chendo and drummers being "Called" to do their thing.

Further, Karenga reinforces the significance of the task ahead by revisiting Diop's "necessary condition" to achieve his "three basic goals": 1) "to reconcile African civilization and history;" 2) "to build a (new) body of modern human sciences;" and 3) "to renew African culture." Thus, he insists, in a new and systematic study of new paradigms posed by the body of knowledge, "Egypt will play in a reconceived and renewed African culture the same role that the Greco-Roman ancient past plays in western culture."

These admonitions mean we must vigorously challenge falsity and misconceptions and strongly aid African historiographic reconstruction so that the

FREDERICK MONDERSON

record is corrected to properly reflect the role of Africans in Egypt and in human progress.

African Nationalist Poetry and Prose Photo. The Great One, Paul Robeson, finally at Rest!

African Nationalist Poetry and Prose Photo. Tribute to the Ancestors Image 2019

AFRICAN NATIONALIST POETRY AND PROSE

African Nationalist Poetry and Prose Photo. Dr. Yosef A.A. Ben-Jochannan, "Man of many words, books and moods."

FREDERICK MONDERSON

African Nationalist Poetry and Prose Photo. **Crispus Attucks**, America's first and truest hero, "For he gave his life for his country and to etch a place at the American table of brotherhood for his people, who will not relinquish their place, responsibilities and entitlements."

AFRICAN NATIONALIST POETRY AND PROSE

African Nationalist Poetry and Prose Photo. "Liberty, Progress and Justice for My People!"

African Nationalist Poetry and Prose Photo. The "Great Liberator" **Harriet Tubman**, has found her place in Harlem, New York, USA.

FREDERICK MONDERSON

African Nationalist Poetry and Prose Photo. Tribute to the Ancestors Images 2019.

African Nationalist Poetry and Prose Photo. Tribute to the Ancestors Images 2019.

African Nationalist Poetry and Prose Photo. Tribute to the Ancestors Images 2019.

AFRICAN NATIONALIST POETRY AND PROSE

African Nationalist Poetry and Prose Photo. Two young ladies "mug for the camera" standing before Dr. Martin Luther King's image as a "Stone of Hope" from the "Mountain of Despair" at the Martin Luther King Jr., Memorial in the nation's capitol, Washington, DC.

FREDERICK MONDERSON

African Nationalist Poetry and Prose Photo. "**I LOVE BLACK PEOPLE!**"

African Nationalist Poetry and Prose Photo. "**BLACK LIVES MATTER!**" Without a doubt!

AFRICAN NATIONALIST POETRY AND PROSE

TABLE OF CONTENTS

1. LIFT EVERY VOICE AND SING — 31
2. REMEMBERING THE ANCESTORS — 33
3. "SPEAK TO THE ROCK" – OH KANYE! — 48
4. DINKINS AND OBAMA AND RUDY AND DONALD — 62
5. DON'T FORGET US DOWN HERE, SONNY CARSON — 73
6. THE CHOICE — 95
7. NAN CONVENTION – 2018 — 113
8. ASANTE AT CEMOTAP – 2018 — 120
9. IDPAD 2018 SUMMIT – GUYANA — 133
10. ROSA PARKS – CHAMPION — 146
11. ARC OF THE MORAL UNIVERSE — 157
12. POEM TO AMON-RA — 167
13. SPIRITUALITY IN ANCIENT EGYPTIAN TEMPLES — 175
14. POEM TO RA - THE SUN GOD — 193
15. BLACK GENESIS — 19
16. POEM TO PTAH — 219

FREDERICK MONDERSON

17. **MILLION MAN MARCH –** 233
    Substance and Significance
18. **BLACK HISTORY** 243
    REFLECTIONS – Making
    of a Revolutionary
19. **COME BACK, SONNY CARSON** 274
20. **SONNY CARSON:** 285
    AT THE GATES
21. **SONNY CARSON -** 299
    REVERED ANCESTOR
22. **POEM TO OSIRIS** 314
23. **BLACK HISTORY:** 325
    CULTURE FOR LIBERATION
24. **MA'AT VERSUS ISFIT IN** 339
    PRESIDENTIAL POLITICS
25. **SPIRITUAL VALES VERSUS** 350
    SECULAR MATERIALISM
26. **Dr. YOSEF A. A. BEN-**
    JOCHANNAN: A TRIBUTE 358
27. **DR. BEN, "OUR FATHER"** 381
28. **CELEBRATING** 391
    DR. BEN-JOCHANNAN
29. **CELEBRATION for** 396
    "DR. BEN" - Part I
30. **POEM TO GODDESS ISIS** 407
31. **HORUS:** 415
    THE FALCON OF EDFU

AFRICAN NATIONALIST POETRY AND PROSE

32. CELEBRATION for DR BEN PART II. — 422
33. MAJOR OWENS: Reflection — 438
34. SENMUT'S PRAISE OF QUEEN HATSHEPSUT — 448
35. BOB LAW'S TRIBUTE TO NELSON MANDELA — 455
36. KWANZAA AT CEMOTAP — 471
37. POEM TO THOTH — 477
38. AL SHARPTON AND BENJAMIN CRUMP'S "MARCH ON WASHINGTON" — 484
39. BLACK INFLUENCE ON THE SUPREME COURT — 487
40. POEM TO GODDESS HATHOR — 520
41. LEGACY OF MICHAEL JACKSON — 526
42. UNROLLING THE MUMMY OF RAMESES THE GREAT — 541
43. LIFE IN DEATH – MEDGAR EVERS — 547
44. "SOUTHERN SHERIFFS" — 564
45. MORE THAN TEN IMPORTANT SUPREME COURT DECISIONS IN BLACK HISTORY — 572

FREDERICK MONDERSON

FROM DRED SCOTT TO AFFIRMATIVE ACTION

46.	STATEMENT OF PURPOSE	576
47.	CAN WE TRUST REPUBLICANS?	580
48.	ORIGINAL BOYS WEARING HOODS	598
49.	POEM TO IMHOTEP	611
50.	VOTING RIGHTS AND REDISTRICTING	615
51.	LAWMAKERS IN HOODIES	621
52.	POEM OR ODE TO QUEEN-TIY	625
53.	BARACK OBAMA AND THE POWER OF SYMBOLISM	628
54.	OBAMA: "FAITH IN THE FACE OF DOUBT"	638
55.	YOU CAN DO MORE QUEEN AAHMES-NEFERTARI	649
56.	OBAMA AND THE SUPREME COURT	653
57.	POEM TO GODDESS NEPHTHYS	661
58.	"THE AMERICA WE KNOW!"	663
59.	POEM TO GOD MIN	671
60.	CONSPIRACY AGAINST OBAMA	674

AFRICAN NATIONALIST POETRY AND PROSE

61.	POEM TO GOD SETH	681
62.	NO TO THAT "NO-BEL" PRIZE	686
63.	A CONSEQUENTIAL ELECTION	695
64.	POEM OR ODE TO KWAME TURE (STOKELY CARMICHAEL)	709
65.	THE RISING TIDE OF COLOR	712
66	ABOUT THAT 96 PERCENT	727
68.	STAND STILL ...	739
69.	JAMES BROWN – A PERSONAL VIEW	760

African Nationalist Poetry and Prose Photo.
Tribute to the Ancestors - Images, 2019.

FREDERICK MONDERSON

African Nationalist Poetry and Prose Photo. Beloved, Caring Thoughtful and Courageous Wife.

AFRICAN NATIONALIST POETRY AND PROSE

BLESSED
with Charm, With and Graciousness

BELOVED
Your Loving Ways are Unlike the Rest

African Nationalist Poetry and Prose Photo.
Beloved – Your Loving Ways are Unlike the Rest.

FREDERICK MONDERSON

African Nationalist Poetry and Prose Photo. Rev. Al Sharpton with Rev. Herbert Daughtry (left) and Attorney Michael Hardy (right) with others, at the **Podium,** at "This Week's **Rally** at the House of Justice," May 5, 2018.

"Beware when you take on the Church of God. Others have tried and have bitten the dust." **Archbishop Desmond Tutu** (Remark, April, 1987)

African Nationalist Poetry and Prose Photo. Cherise Maloney of Brooklyn (left), with radio personality Bernard White, unknown lady and Dr. Len Jeffries at **CEMOTAP**, 2018.

AFRICAN NATIONALIST POETRY AND PROSE

"Women, we need you to give us back our faith in humanity." Archbishop Desmond Tutu. (*The Words of Desmond Tutu*, Naomi Tutu, ed. 1989).

1. THE BLACK NATIONAL ANTHEM! "LIFT EVERY VOICE AND SING" – JAMES WELDON JOHNSON

1. Lift every voice and sing till earth and heaven ring,
ring with the harmonies of liberty;
let our rejoicing rise high as the listening skies,
let it resound loud as the rolling sea.
Sing a song full of the faith that the dark past has taught us,
sing a song full of the hope that the present has brought us;
facing the rising sun of our ne day begun,
let us march on till victory is won.

2. Stony the road we trod, bitter the chastening rod,
felt in the days when hope unborn had died;
yet with a steady beat, have not our weary feet
come to the place for which our people sighed?
We have come over a way that with tears has been watered;
We have come, treating our path through the blood of the slaughtered,
out from the gloomy past, till now we stand to last
where the white gleam of our bright star is cast.

FREDERICK MONDERSON

3. God of our weary years, God of our silent tears,
thou who has brought us thus far on the way;
thou who has, by thy might, led us into the light,
keep us forever in the path, we pray.
Lest our feet stray from the places, our god, where we met thee,
lest, our hearts drunk with the wine of the world, we forget thee;
shadowed beneath thy hand, may we forever stand,
True to our God, true to our native land.

African Nationalist Poetry and Prose Photo. Two "Great Africans" whose contributions are immeasurable, Harlem Congressman; and Composer of Music, "The Black National Anthem."

AFRICAN NATIONALIST POETRY AND PROSE

African Nationalist Poetry and Prose Photo. The **Roots Revisited** Logo!

"No Justice, No Peace." Rev. Al Sharpton.

"Whose Streets? Our Streets." Rev. Al Sharpton.

2. "REMEMBERING THE ANCESTORS" BY DR. FRED MONDERSON

In their ongoing enlightening and informative dynamic presentations, **CEMOTAP** presented a memorable memorial this Memorial Day-weekend, 2018. More particularly, befitting the meaning of African Liberation Day, the program sought to and effectively did Commemorate the life and work of Dr. Jack Felder, TV Personality **Gil Noble** of **Like It Is** fame, Poet Brother Edward Taitt and cultural

FREDERICK MONDERSON

visionary Sister Kefa Nephthys who founded the First World Alliance. Speakers at this auspicious occasion included Nova Felder, Chris Noble, poets Tony Mitchelson and Lading Kaliba and significantly Nana Camille Yarbrough. The drummer Majetu provided scintillating melodies as the tributes unfolded in a wonderful cultural, spiritual and informative crescendo befitting those who worked for the betterment of African condition at home and abroad. These four heroes were the principal recipients were the we can, did and will never forget. They stood in place of and on the shoulders of giants and simple folks who were the victims of Slave Trade and American slavery, racism, discrimination, murder, lunchings, terrorism, suspicions, unspeakable horrors, even unjust incarceration. Still, the possessed the wherewithal and imbued their progeny and provide the torch and light as these ancestors have done so we can our progeny like the poet will be able to boast now and int eh future, despite all adversity, "Still I Rise."

African Nationalist Poetry and Prose Photo. Tribute to the Ancestors – Images, 2019.

Dr. James McIntosh entitled the day's proceedings "Remembering the Ancestors" and pointed out "Our

AFRICAN NATIONALIST POETRY AND PROSE

community is very blest with its complexity. These ancestors being honored did just what they had to do to improve the lot of African people who were berated, enslaved and ill-treated in their experiences in this country."

Even in programs such as the one outlined here or elsewhere, there is generally unintended outcomes that add greater meaning and significance culturally, spiritually, even symbolically. In this case, besides the distinguished individuals on the Dais and in the audience, a number of individuals, males and females, were identified, given African belief holds, though an individual may now reside in collective immortality, echoing their names, resurrects their spirits to pour forth blessings, spiritual power and symbolic inspiration that empowers those who invoke the African spirits of such revered ancestors. After all, "If you embrace the community, the community will embrace you."

With that, Dr. James McIntosh, **Co-Chair** of **CEMOTAP** and **Master of Ceremonies**, introduced the now deceased Dr. Jack Felder as teacher and educator who was not in the system to miseducate. In the classroom he put students first; helped reinforce teachers' knowledge of Africa and African people's history; in the community he defended their interests against blatant misinformation and oppression; and on the world

FREDERICK MONDERSON

stage he put Africa and things Africa first. For such unabashed blackness some referred to him as **Dr. Black Felder**. The **Master of Ceremonies** remembered Dr. Amos Wilson who correctly identified three areas where African people are under serious assault: socially, psychologically and intellectually. Such areas are - health, corrections and importantly the Education Department for this area has life-long influence and implications, psychologically and socially on the mind and social status of the individual. Thus, given his personality, conviction and destiny Dr. Jack Felder was not in the school system to miseducate as Dr. Carter G. Woodson pointed out in his books *The Miseducation of the Negro* and the corrective *The Education of the Negro*. Using his years in education wisely, Dr. Felder made his students very aware of historical issues and about Africa culture. He taught, "Columbus was lost and did not discover anything." As such, and as this commemoration has sought to underscore and reinforce, "if you teach them right; if you support our community right; they will remember you."

So, to set the program in progress "Dr. Mac" called upon Nova Felder, whose brother Quasar was in attendance, to speak on behalf of their father, Dr. Jack Felder, "a faithful fighter" whose image and contributions will surely be missed.

Nova began his presentation by quoting Frederick Douglass the abolitionist who reminded, "Power concedes nothing without a struggle. It never did and

AFRICAN NATIONALIST POETRY AND PROSE

it never will." This admonition as presented by Nova is aimed at African people insisting, only in challenge will the system concede, curb its oppression and usher in necessary and constructive reforms. This can be in the form of the ballot box; peacefully taking to the streets in manner of the Civil Rights Movement; or outright in economic boycott as proved successful similarly challenging the system as did A. Philip Randolph in threat of a "March on Washington" in 1941; even a **Million Man March** and **Million Woman March** as Minister Farrakhan's call and inspiration has cultivated and empowered with a potent vision toward the future in activism. Then Nova chronicled his father's early years, college education, work as a bio-chemist, migration to New York, visit by the FEDS accusing him of being a draft dodger, his military service while stationed in Germany where he met his first Africans who would profoundly impact his life and Blackness. Then this dutiful son was a bit more specific about the things his family had to endure.

African Nationalist Poetry and Prose Photo. The "Drums" is one of African People's powerful means of communicating musically and spiritually.

FREDERICK MONDERSON

Next, young Felder focused on some of the literary works his father produced, particularly:

1. **AIDS**: *US Germ Warfare*;
2. *From the Statue of Liberty to the Statue of Bigotry*;
3. *Who really Assassinated Malcolm X*;
4. *Who really Assassinated Martin Luther King*;

Then he went into the holidays insisting, "We have to know the origins of the holidays we celebrate" because they bolster the white man's culture but berate and downplay the African's. Don't celebrate anything you're not a part of." So:

5. *Should African People Celebrate Columbus Day?*
6. *Should African People Celebrate Halloween?*
7. *Should African People Celebrate George Washington's Birthday?*
8. *Should African People Celebrate Misgiving (Thanksgiving) Day?*
9. *True and Accurate Moments in African People's Holidays and Culture.*

What was interesting about Nova Felder's presentation in praise of his father Dr. Jack Felder, was the profound electric, educational and emotional relationship the two enjoyed. Everyone knew it was Jack and Nova as Booksellers, at the **United African Movement**, the African Street Festival,

AFRICAN NATIONALIST POETRY AND PROSE

at the Washington, D.C. Protest, the **Million Man March** and at any of **CEMOTAP's** celebrations. That is why, the loss of the father had such a profound effect on the son. Conversely, however, what the father imparted the son in his life's lesson, not simply enabled him to meet and overcome the emotional and psychological challenges and drama in losing a beloved one; so much so, it strengthened his resolve to continue support for his community. More important, the relationship demonstrated the efforts of a cherished and adored father whose imprint was manifested in upbringing of two well-adjusted young citizens successfully raised in "The Felder Method of Child-Rearing."

African Nationalist Poetry and Prose Photo. Tribute to the Ancestors – Images, 2019.

FREDERICK MONDERSON

1. EDUCATE THEM YOURSELF. Keep them next to you. Teach them yourself. Teach them the purpose of education. Prepare them to understand the system, economically, socially and politically.

2. DISCIPLINE THEM WITH COMPASSION. Here Nova repeated the old adage, "Spare the rod and spoil the child." In truthfully modesty he confessed, "I was not spoiled!" Enough!

3. BOOST THEIR SELF-ESTEEM. Expose them to such cultural institutions as **CEMOTAP**, Sister Kefa's **First World Alliance**, **United African Movement**, and **National Action Network**. Build their confidence and teach them to say 'Thank You' to our Community. Significantly, you must teach them, "The African family is the most important thing we have."

4. Most important, **INSIST YOUR CHILDREN BELONG TO THEMSELVES**. They are the owners of their own destiny. Saying his father, Dr. Jack Felder was a man of compassion, he possessed tremendous compassion for his people. Finally, and quoting Willie Johnson, Nova Felder called upon his brother Quasar Felder to relay the message Dr. Jack (Black) Felder had for Black People:

AFRICAN NATIONALIST POETRY AND PROSE

STAY BLACK!
STAY STRONG!

Brother Tony Mitchelson and Brother Lading Kaliba sang praises in poetry to Brother G.E. Taitt. Brother Mitchelson explained, "Brother Taitt gave me more information than I could ever imagine." Most important Brother Taitt emphasized we understand politics and appreciate culture. He would say a prayer for anyone on his birthday. His mind was a computer index machine. He insisted we be dignified and maintain the concept of dignity. He went to schools, churches, libraries in his mission to unify the African Community. He founded the Tamberry Temple and invited "36 Healers" who contributed intellectually and culturally to reinforce a positive model of behavior and thinking he envisioned. "We as a people should keep and practice his model."

Lading Kaliba, who met Mr. Taitt in the 1960, quoted something Arthur Ashe, the tennis phenomenon told him: "The only thing worse than having the AIDS virus (which he contracted through a blood transfusion) was being a Black man in America."

Next Dr. McIntosh introduced Nana Camille Yarbrough, a cultural Scientist, author and actress; who, in her presentation of praise for Sister Kefa Nephthys spanned accomplishments from Banneker to Baldwin and from John Clark to Ben-Jochannan to

FREDERICK MONDERSON

Ivan Van Sertima. In her praise of Sister Kefa and the **CEMOTAP** community Sister Yarbrough asked that we:

"Honor our Elders
Honor or our Children
Honor the African might
Honor the sacred womb of the African woman."

African Nationalist Poetry and Prose Photo. Tribute to the Ancestors – Images, 2019.

After the customary **Hotep** and **Asante Sana**, she spoke of the words and spirit of this great Ancestor, Sister Kefa and her husband Bill who formed the **First World Alliance** on 145th Street in Harlem. Sister Kefa brought a whole lot of speakers such as Dr. Len Jeffreys, Asa Hillard, Maulana Karenga, Molefi Asante, Leonard James to present and culturally enrichen minds. People were there because there was something mission in their African lives.

Nana insisted we praise our Gods; Praise our Elders; praise our great African teachers. Then she

AFRICAN NATIONALIST POETRY AND PROSE

admonished elders, children, sisters, we must Honor African life.

We must start our day in praise. We must be praise worthy. Each organization such as **First World Alliance** has its own spirit. We were taken from Africa but we have a great hunger, wanting, for Africa. All this despite they downgrade us, not our intention; face us down on the ground in order to demean us; insist we 'Don't tell that story;' "Why you keep talking about that." First World Alliance brought out the healers, Dr. Ben-Jochannan, Elombe Brathe, Bill Lynch, Jitu Weusi, Sonny Carson, Alton Maddox, Khalid Mohammed, Ben Chavis, Jitu Weusi, Sonny Carson, Rev. Daughtry to tell our story. Dr. John Clarke, "The People's Historian," reminded, "A people who cannot exercise their culture cannot survive." Though we come together at **CEMOTAP** we recognize, "A great tree or organization always has a bitter fruit." "Your story is your power. Our story is our power." "Once our children know who they are, they will act and be dignified, respectful. We still have the pain from the separation from Africa."

Praising Sister Viola Plummer, present in the audience, Arthur Ashe, Barbara Justice, Imhotep Gary Byrd and Betty Dopson, Camille Yarbrough insisted "We create our own freedom. We must be vigilant in our defense. We must be creative in our

FREDERICK MONDERSON

thoughts and protests. We must be artistic in our creations. Most important, we must recognize and advocate Our destiny rests in our own hands and actions."

African Nationalist Poetry and Prose Photo. The "Batey Church" at New Year's Day's Festival Celebration, showing Thiesel, Parsela, the High Priest "Bienvenido" and Carmen, place of "Re-visit 'Mountain View of African Spirituality.'"

Finally, Gilbert Christopher Noble was called upon to speak on behalf of his father Gil Noble, the host of **Like It Is** of ABC TV 7.

Most often known as Chris not Gilbert as his father, Noble felt it "An honor to be here. Without you I will be nothing." He began by thanking Viola Plummer, Brother Mac, Sister Betty all "beautiful people." Then he mentioned in praise Noble Drew Ali, Elijah Mohammed, Marcus Garvey, whose Philosophy and

AFRICAN NATIONALIST POETRY AND PROSE

Opinions was and is still relevant. Stokely Carmichael (Kwame Ture) (Black Power), Maurice Bishop, Fidel Castro, Bill Lynch, Nelson and Winnie Mandela, Elombe Brathe, Dr. John Henrik Clarke, Marimba Ani, Sekou Touré, Dr. Ben-Jochannan and others. Insisting he was "working tirelessly to reverse European doctrination," he offered a "shout out" to Bill Cosby because this whole thing is about "his money."

To have a true understanding of our situation, we must analyze our people through the context of history. Bill Cosby's case is about justice! However, where is the justice for Fernando Castile, Eric Garner, Trayvon Martin, and so many others? When we arrived here Europeans knew they had to de-Africanize and Europeanize us. Slavery disrupted our ability to share information. Like It Is deals with healing the "Slave Virus," "Slave Syndrome." We are suffering from the slave virus. They are coming at us 24/7."

There are no more programs such as **Like It Is**, **Tony Brown's Journal**, **Positively Black**, **The McCreary Report**. What are they doing to us? We get Basketball Wives and Love and Hip Hop. These programs emphasize destructive behaviors which portray Black people in a tremendously negative manner. Those shows are a proliferation of straight garbage. The messages from the enemy is

FREDERICK MONDERSON

Gucci bags and name brand clothing. There are no more Dr. Ben-Jochannan, Julius Nyerere, Cheikh Anta Diop, Dr. Clarke, Ivan Van Sertima, W.E.B. DuBois and Booker T. Washington. Diop's associate Theophile Obenga is still holding it down! the great scholars whose teachings, lectures, writings enlightened, and empowered, and enabled patters of thought that praised Africa and African people. Sadly, however, all of the work of the great scholars is being forgotten. To counter this, contemporary researchers must resurrect and perpetuate the positive things about African people's history. They must create a body of knowledge that can inform and enlighten the young as we march forward in intellectual, cultural, political, economic, even educational empowerment. We must also be conscious of how and where we spend our dollars!

As an example of ongoing assaults on the psyche of African people, look at this new NFL ruling. The league is 70 percent black. Yet they insist, "We pay you a lot of money. Stand up, shut up and get paid." We have hypocrisy at the highest level of government. He is saying the most outrageous things and nothing happens. He is a pathological liar. It is the easiest thing to accuse a Black man of rape. Many of our people were killed, raped, lynched and nobody paid for the devastation and psychological and spiritual depravity our people experienced. Other groups got over at our expense. 'I am so proud to be my father's son.' "Make sure you learn from the experience. All black persons go through adversity. Let's not forget Leonard Jeffreys, Malcolm X, Paul

AFRICAN NATIONALIST POETRY AND PROSE

Robeson, Medgar Evers, Adam Clayton Powell and Fannie Lou Hamer, as well as the Scottsboro Boys and Emmitt Till. We are stronger. We must be wiser, more focused."

"My father guided me. I will continue to fight."

African Nationalist Poetry and Prose Photo. Brother Minister Hafeez Mohammed speaks at **CEMOTAP**.

African Nationalist Poetry and Prose Photo. Businessman, father, politician and humanitarian.

FREDERICK MONDERSON

African Nationalist Poetry and Prose Photo. Famous sculpture head from West Africa.

3. "SPEAK TO THE ROCK" – OH KANYE!
BY
DR. FRED MONDERSON

Speaking of the "spiritual journey African people are experiencing," Reverend Al Sharpton referenced Biblical **NUMBERS 20** in which **GOD** admonished Moses to "Speak to the Rock," as he

AFRICAN NATIONALIST POETRY AND PROSE

stood amongst the people in the desert thirsting for water. In his infinite wisdom and unbounded beneficence, **GOD** instructed Moses to "Speak to the Rock" over there from which refreshing thirst quenching waters would pour forth. Thus, in following exactly as admonished, would be demonstrated the power of what **GOD** could do in looking out for his people. However, and whether for his own agenda or showmanship, Moses chose not to speak to but tap the rock twice with his staff. This again, was not the nature of his instruction.

African Nationalist Poetry and Prose Photo. Standing on the side of **LOVE**!

Now, amongst the mounting challenges confronting the Rev's constituency; whether economic – in the form of joblessness, low wages for the working poor, rising rents, goods and services; need for Criminal Justice Reform – long sentences for minor offenses, wrongful prosecution and imprisonment; Police

FREDERICK MONDERSON

Misconduct – inordinate numbers of deaths at the hands of police officers; – Attorney Benjamin Crump mentioned at the recently concluded **National Action Network National Convention**, since 2015 to today there have been some 83 killings by the police officers in the USA, of which 80 have been people of color; on-going methods of disfranchisement of Black and Brown voters across the nation; the current administration using vile terms to describe African nations; Mr. Trump and subsequently his administration has fostered and his actions in many respects have enabled an inordinate rise in hate related crimes; when seen in sound-bite clips on Television, African-American are generally seen as guards or waiters; women are often sexually harassed or berated; racism and Ku Klux Klan white supremacy groups' activities are on the rise evidenced at Charleston and Charlottesville and elsewhere; gun violence is escalating across a wide spectrum and there's a whole lot more.

Thus, the tremendous need for the spiritual and refreshing potency God promises and can deliver to aid his people. Given all of that and speaking with a mountain of confidence in divine capability that come from earnest efforts and in good faith while "Speaking to the Rock," Reverend Sharpton confessed, "We are the people God uses to speak to the world."

AFRICAN NATIONALIST POETRY AND PROSE

African Nationalist Poetry and Prose Photo. Former Congressman Charlie Rangel converses with Medgar Evers College President, Dr. Rudy Crew.

African Nationalist Poetry and Prose Photo. Erik Michael Dyson and Erik Monderson at the 50th Anniversary March on Washington (1963), 2013.

FREDERICK MONDERSON

African Nationalist Poetry and Prose Photo. Art, Art and More Art in its most picturesque and detailed artistic expression.

African Nationalist Poetry and Prose Photo. Tribute to the Ancestors, - Images, 2019.

AFRICAN NATIONALIST POETRY AND PROSE

African Nationalist Poetry and Prose Photo. More Art, Art and More Art in its most picturesque, detail and artistic expression.

FREDERICK MONDERSON

African Nationalist Poetry and Prose Photo.
Famous African sculptured head.

African Nationalist Poetry and Prose Photo.
Tribute to the Ancestors – Images, 2019.

AFRICAN NATIONALIST POETRY AND PROSE

African Nationalist Poetry and Prose Photo. *Black Star News* Publisher Milton Allimadi at the mike announcing the names of recipients at the *Black Star News* Annual Awards in Harlem.

Next, the Reverend turned his attention to Kanye West who has been in the news lately in expressing his "Love for Donald Trump;" insisting Martin Luther King and Malcolm are essentially "obsolete" in today's world; and that "slavery was a choice." Well, first of all, with Rev. Herbert Daughtry, attorney Michael Hardy and Kirsten Foy, among others on the podium, Rev. Sharpton insisted we "Pray for Kanye." No less significant, "Kanye has a right to express his love for Donald Trump" but saying the struggles and martyrdom of Malcolm X and Martin Luther King and the ramifications of such a statement by one with a national and global

FREDERICK MONDERSON

platform is like going in the wrong direction on a super highway. Even more detrimental that Kanye could think or "not think" that slavery was a "choice" is on par with Ben Carson's Heritage Foundation blabber that "Obamacare was worse than slavery." At least, many believe, Carson got his "30 pieces of silver." Kanye, on the other hand, got a lot of people mad as he allowed himself to be "played like a fiddle" by Donald Trump.

Not only has Mr. West demonstrated an ignorance of the history and struggles of African people here in America, but his thoughts diminish the horrific nature of the oppression and the gallant resistance demonstrated in the hundreds of rebellious activities throughout the Americas. He certainly seems unaware of the more famous rebellions of Denmark Vesey, Gabriel Prosser and certainly that of Nat Turner. Clearly he is misguided about the work of Frederick Douglass, Harriet Tubman and even John Brown, but much more important and detrimental, the view from his ivory tower obscures the meaning and reach of the KKK, Knights of the White Camelia and Red Shirts' terrorism of the 19th Century, "Jim Crow" activism in the insidious work of disfranchisement particularly after the 13th, 14th, and 15th Amendments; the significance of the Dred Scott Decision, the "Grandfather Clause" trickery, and Plessy V. Ferguson ruling, and significantly the "White Primary;" Mr. West could now have a "white wife" and this tremendous turnaround in the nation's recognition and acceptance is partly why Malcolm X and Martin Luther fought and died. This is especially

AFRICAN NATIONALIST POETRY AND PROSE

and particularly noteworthy after Emmett Till and so many others were lynched and railroaded into prison for simply "looking" at or "whistling" at a white woman!

Sadly, perhaps Mr. West does not read, for on Thursday April 26, 2018, a Memorial and Museum, as *The New York Times* has indicated, "That gives voice to the targets of American white supremacy;" opened in Montgomery, Alabama to commemorate the nearly 4000 African-Americans lynched in the southern states, many of which were in rebellion against the union; today they continually fly the hated Confederate Flag. Even more important, and in his down-playing their significance it is clearly evident, Mr. West would be hard-pressed to peacefully stroll hand-in-hand with his "white wife" publicly in such places despite the sacrifices of Martin Luther King, Rev. Shuttlesworth, Rosa Parks, Thurgood Marshall, Adam Clayton Powell, and most certainly the "Four Little Girls" killed in the "Bombingham" church. Naturally we cannot forget Dylan Roof and the Mother Emanuel massacre; Charleston and Charlottesville; and Trump's pronouncement that "There were good people on both sides" as the KKK and White Supremacist or Alt-Right members marched in Virginia and continue their evil and insidious efforts.

FREDERICK MONDERSON

African Nationalist Poetry and Prose Photo. Radio Personality Gary Byrd and **Black Star Newspaper** Publisher Milton Allimadi.

It is still in the memory, when Kanye foolishly boasted that he and his wife were more culturally popular than Barack and Michelle Obama and today again, that he and his wife are globally the most popular spouses in contemporary times. In addition, and fudging on being African, Mr. West sought to portray himself as a universal icon, who is not Black. Well, whatever floats his boat. Nevertheless, and tremendously significant, like so many, or perhaps so few, Negroes who "Kiss Trump's Ring," despite his praise for the man, Mr. Trump did not see Kanye as a monumental global figure but simply, "There's my African-American." That is, Mr. Trump did not confirm Mr. West improved his "numbers" among

AFRICAN NATIONALIST POETRY AND PROSE

the global or American constituency Mr. West seeks to entertain and inadvertently messages a false narrative. The President simply stated, "Kanye improved my numbers among Blacks from 11 to 22 percent." This in itself is not correct though more correctly Mr. Trump sees this fiddler as "his Black to the Blacks!"

Thus, as the slave owners had their plantation overseers or foremen who harassed, harangued and even raped enslaved and free African Men and women; unknowing to him, Mr. West was simply reduced to being one of Donald Trump's Negroes. Now, Kanye West can consider himself a member of the club of Donald Trump and Rudy Giuliani - called "Brutaliani" while Mayor of New York City, an avowed racist with whom both Al Sharpton and Sonny Carson clashed repeatedly.

As Rev. Sharpton further pointed out, Kanye must understand Donald Trump will one day leave the White House and there will be another President. However, history and people of good faith and certainly activists will remind him of his words and action as so many continue to speak correctly to power.

FREDERICK MONDERSON

African Nationalist Poetry and Prose Photo. These ladies are just chilling and watching the people go by!

However, and having gotten off the train of his "spiritual journey" to throw some light on the West saga, the erudite and iconic Civil Rights leader returned the conversation back to "Speaking to the Rock" and how God uses Blacks in his message to the world. Underscoring this phenomenal experience, Rev. Sharpton pointed to the numerous negative portrayals of African-Americans nationally and internationally; but when Barack and Michelle Obama and their beautiful daughters Malia and Sasha stepped off the plane, their demeanor as a loving and respectful family, contradicted the false narrative. Therefore, and affirming it is his destiny and magnifying the power that God can do anything, Rev. Sharpton closed his rally by affirming an unending commitment to bring forth the "waters of salvation"

AFRICAN NATIONALIST POETRY AND PROSE

that will empower and protect those who have to live with the consequences of the new mood of the country in the "Age of Trump."

African Nationalist Poetry and Prose Photo. Cherise Maloney and Dr. Leonard Jeffries at **CEMOTAP**.

African Nationalist Poetry and Prose Photo. Two of the dishes being prepared on the awesome fire for the Festival.

FREDERICK MONDERSON

"History, I contend is the Present." James Baldwin (1924-1987, Quoted in *Emerge* January 1990)

African Nationalist Poetry and Prose Photo. David Dinkins, dapper as ever, at *Black Star News* Awards Ceremony, 2017.

4. DINKINS AND OBAMA AND RUDY AND DONALD
BY
DR. FRED MONDERSON

In 1993 David Dinkins, the first African-American Mayor of New York City, faced re-election against the Republican challenger Rudy Giuliani. The "ancient Malcolm X" often expounded, "History is a good teacher" and despite the "modern Kanye West's" ignorance of Malcolm's significance, the "old master's" insightful wisdom is ever-potent as a

AFRICAN NATIONALIST POETRY AND PROSE

tool for anyone seeking to understand the profound predicament America faces today.

Bubbling in "law and order propaganda palaver," the former federal prosecutor Rudy Giuliani deployed law enforcement related thugs who discombobulated the Dinking campaign through "storm trooper tactics" and racist behaviors that ultimately enabled him to seize the prize of becoming Mayor of New York City. Full of obfuscation and chicanery resulting in polarization of the city along black-white lines, through racial attitudes, actions and behaviors, destiny ultimately began sucking Mr. Giuliani into a negative downward spiral. In calamitous irony, the devastation of 9-11-2001 happened and with the blessings of the nation's and the world's goodwill, Mr. Giuliani was able to salvage his reputation, to become "America's Mayor," but only after earning the title "Brutaliani." However, rather than relinquish his term-limited position after two terms of service in 2001, the Mayor arrogantly argued he was "the only one" who could lead the city at that time. This insistence therefore necessitated he be given a third term of service which was rejected. As late as February 19, 2015, Giuliani voiced the following about President Obama: "The President does not love America. He was not brought up the way you and I were brought up to love this country." Asante. *Lynching Barack Obama.* (2016)

FREDERICK MONDERSON

As District Attorney for the Southern District in New York, before he became Mayor, sadly Rudy Giuliani did not hire "Black DAs" despite there being more than 100 slots. While there were many who did significant work in the "post-911 recovery," Giuliani hogged the media spotlight as often as possible whether as DA or as Mayor and this visibility contributed much to him being labeled "America's Mayor." David Dinkins once remarked, the portraits of himself and his wife Joyce to whom he was married for 42 years at the time, "depicted her hair jet black and his, all white." Word had it, as one iota of Giuliani's insidiousness, this portrait, hung in Gracie Mansion as a mayor's tribute, was removed by Giuliani when he took over as mayor.

Today, following the 2016 election, in which unfolding actions and evidence increasingly mirror "1984" the "Animal Farm" activists come to power. Then many of the new rulers began exhibiting "beams of political incorrectness." Such actions, in comparison are profoundly being manifested by the current administration. Yet, as we assess contemporary developments and look to the future, we see a special prosecutor methodologically and painstakingly sugaring "Molly" the white horse beside the fence as he seeks insider information in an effort to do destiny's work of dethroning animal rule."

Equally significantly, now that we are faced with Donald Trump and Rudy Giuliani back together in close relationship publicly, an interesting but

AFRICAN NATIONALIST POETRY AND PROSE

profound observation has emerged as we reflect on history. Yogi Berra, the well-known baseball icon, known for his entertaining wit, first offered, "You can see a lot from observing" and more appropriately, "Looks like its Déjà vu all over again."

Increasingly, as contemporary revealing evidence seems to indicate, the imagery of "1984" has returned and "Old Major" and his boys, having ousted the "humans" are now running the "farm." It is apparently interesting, as history reminded us, when Barack Obama, the first African-American President held the reins of leadership of the nation, a falsely concocted heavy cloud of racism and disrespect descended upon the efforts and personality of a man whose work ethic was exceptional; still, all because his race mattered. In that unfolding hostile age, many people and movements coalesced. There we say, Republicans, Blacks, Men of the Cloth, Evangelicals, Militias, and more than a gaggle of racists, white supremacists, "Tea Party" radicals and others as "Lipstick on a Pig" Sarah Palin; "Joe the Plumber" the "socialist" architect; not to exclude "Waterloo DeMint;" "Go for the Jugular" Billy Crystal; "You Lie" Joe Wilson; "Poison the Well" Rick Santorum; "Gangster Government," "God told me to run" Michele Bachmann; "I intend to make Barack Obama a one-term President;" and even Allen West, now gone like the Do Do bird, and more, all intensely focused on the "mole in the President's eye."

FREDERICK MONDERSON

African Nationalist Poetry and Prose Photo.
GYE NYAME – "Supremacy of God," an African symbol and spiritual expression displayed in the **African Burial Ground** in Manhattan, NY.

AFRICAN NATIONALIST POETRY AND PROSE

African Nationalist Poetry and Prose Photo. **Zimbabwe**. African sculpture on display at the Atlanta National Airport. Norbert Shamuyariri. "'How Can I Rise'" makes a strong statement about the inner strength that may overcome adversity."

So much so, they Caucused in the halls of legislatures; did TV advertising and "Robo Calls" to discredit him and his programs; the Devil was at work in Bible study gatherings; he was sent threatening gestures in Military style militia training camps; Obama's integrity became a campaign issue; one guy, half naked, kept jerking his middle finger up and down in front of the White House as the Secret

FREDERICK MONDERSON

Service helplessly watched; many others massed and protested on the Great Lawn and streets of Washington, D.C.; *The New York Times* reported some 20-odd NGO Presidents or Chief Operating Officers were involved in training operatives to fan-out across the nation and negatively portray the ACA falsely labeled "Obamacare;" while still others gathered, posturing on the steps of the Capital Building to focus on that speck magnified, in Mr. Obama's Demeanor; all such actions naturally ignoring his integrity, work ethic, elegance of mind and nobility of spirit. Today a mighty oak beam has fallen across the roadway in Ronald Reagan's "City on a Hill," yet and hypocritically, no one seems to notice. That is, the same Republican persons who hounded Mr. Obama for purportedly ethical issues which were never evident, have turned a blind eye to all transgressions particularly in the case, so far, of "Trump's 3401 lies to Obama's 18."

We see such questionable behaviors highlighted, manifesting in grabbing women's private parts; representative spokespersons who twist the fact and never listen to themselves as they spew distorted messages to the American people through the media platforms; high rates of personnel turnover in the current administration in association with abusive and unethical behaviors; associates pleading guilty to misconduct or being fired as public servants; "porn stars" now becoming respectable household names juxtaposed to "fixers" awash in questionable money, smelling of sleaze business, forcing investigators to follow the money into the swamp; Russian oligarchs

AFRICAN NATIONALIST POETRY AND PROSE

as players in American political and financial dealings. Many among the young can now ask their parents, "Can I now tell lies since the President does it?" Altogether these confluences of ethical and suspicious activities raise questions of conspiracy and issues of credibility; or, as one Fox News anchor called it, "Swamp stink!" In fact, administration apologists most vehemently defend the rotting log lying in the swamp. Strange, while Biblical lore holds, "If God be for you who could be against you;" today, many religious groups hold the position, "If the Devil is giving out goodies, then what do we care." What is clouding this alarming attitude and, importantly more compelling, according to an old African proverb. "A log can lie in water for any length of time, but it still will never become a crocodile." Yet, appropriately, however, "having lain in the water for some time, the log has begun to rot and stink."

As is becoming increasingly clear, now that Mr. Giuliani has joined Donald Trump's legal team, they seem to have rekindled many decades of friendship. Well, given the success of Mr. Giuliani's rambunctious discombobulation of the Dinkins campaign in 1993 which brought him success as candidate for mayor; and Trump was active then, so let's not forget the "Central park Five" and that unfortunate incident; is it now not so-farfetched that he instructed and encouraged his buddy to apply the same strategy against the first African-American

FREDERICK MONDERSON

President in which the "Birther" charade lie was born and perpetuated.

Men of wealth generally seem to want everything even possess aspirations to achieve high political office. Donald Trump rose to political prominence on the "Birther" falsity and whether supporting the charade, goaded on by admirers, or simply ignoring this travesty in silence; as Abraham Lincoln reminded, "Silence in face of wrongdoing embodies culpability" for which Republicans are guilty in condemning this wrong. So, "one lie grew into 3401 lies," the last count was at 4 720 and as the lying behemoth gets taller and taller, we are left to wonder, what's next? Assessing such behaviors has become tremendously important; for, given the previous high moral standard associated with being American as viewed on the world stage; and most assuredly the morality associated with the Office of the Presidency of the United States; in such a tumbling Humpty Dumpty world this reputation, high position and morality standards are fast becoming lusterless.

African Nationalist Poetry and Prose Photo. Jack Johnson Plaza is a fitting tribute to a Champ!

AFRICAN NATIONALIST POETRY AND PROSE

African Nationalist Poetry and Prose Photo. Image of iconic nationalist, educator, creative community activist and organization builder, Jitu Weusi.

African Nationalist Poetry and Prose Photo. Erik and Luis flank **NAN's** *Legal Eagle* Michael Hardy at a "Weekly Rally" in Harlem.

FREDERICK MONDERSON

African Nationalist Poetry and Prose Photo. Legendary activist Robert "Sonny" Carson, also dubbed "Mayor of Bed-Stuy," or "Abubadikaville," in a tremendously pensive mood.

African Nationalist Poetry and Prose Photo. Tribute to the Ancestors – Images, 2019.

AFRICAN NATIONALIST POETRY AND PROSE

"You cannot subjugate a man and recognize his humanity, his history, and his personality; so systematically, you must take this away from him. You begin by telling lies about this man's role in history." John Henrik Clarke. *Address to Jewish Currents Conference*, New York (February 15, 1969).

5. DON'T FORGET US DOWN HERE, SONNY CARSON! BY DR. FRED MONDERSON

While it is easy to imagine Robert "Sonny" Carson holding Court among the great heroes and heroines of the Black Pantheon of ancestors, in these challenging times, here on earth, we need the qualities he possessed: strength, insight, tenacity and wisdom.

Today is his birthday so I salute him.

He was courageous and resilient; he was an organizer, a builder and was adept at attracting men and women of vision and intellect capable of generating ideas to address social problems with reasonable outcome; we miss the input of that thinker and activist.

FREDERICK MONDERSON

African Nationalist Poetry and Prose Photo. Assata Shakur, "Revolutionary Woman."

Remembering Sonny on his Birthday May 18, 2018, one day before Malcolm X's, we recognize the world has changed in the 15-years since Sonny Carson made his transition to join the ancestors. However, one of his most consistent commitments has been the

AFRICAN NATIONALIST POETRY AND PROSE

challenge in keeping a focus on the Prison Industrial Complex that, on a daily basis entraps and psychologically and emotionally emasculates Black man and Black womanhood - languishing in the bowels of a system that instead of rehabilitating, debilitates.

In his day, Sonny would receive more than a hundred calls from prison inmates across the country complaining of ill-treatment, bad food, lack of quality reading materials, the need for constructive training in arts, crafts and educational and industrial skills, that not only assuages the rigors of prison life but could also be parlayed meaningfully upon release as a challenge and check to recidivism.

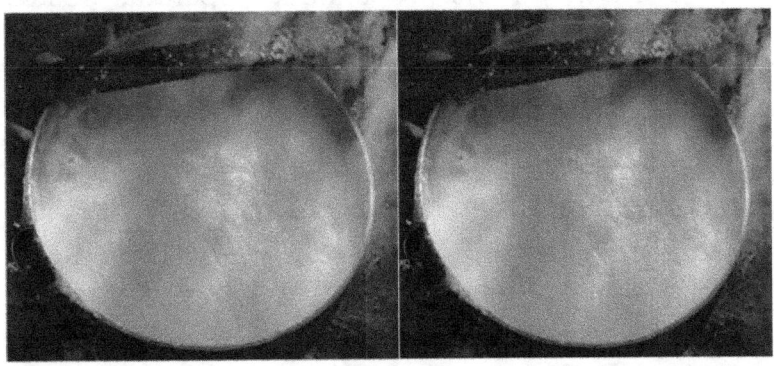

African Nationalist Poetry and Prose Photo. Still more of the wonderful dish being prepared for the Festival.

Many others either pleaded for assistance in securing bail or what measures to apply in pleading their cases in pending trials or even appeals.

FREDERICK MONDERSON

Clearly, Carson was engaged in an unending task but the nature of its disposition, given recent developments, attention to that singular task is even more pressing. Much has transpired in criminal justice since Sonny Carson's passing, but, in a way, he set in motion one idea whose ultimate consequences he did not live to see play out.

To understand Sonny Carson's monumental impact on New York I must comment on several other major players in this city's distant and recent history; but the story always comes bs

Very early in the Rudolph Giuliani administration -- after he helped orchestrate the defeat of David Dinkins through race-baiting and became Mayor of New York City - his propaganda apparatus posted signs in the Black Community such as "Rudy G. Fights Racism." In fact, Mayor Giuliani turned out to be the most polarizing leader and racist who ever held the chief executive office in New York City. He even earned the moniker, "Brutaliani!"

Rudy was on a downward spiral in the court of public opinion after his disastrous closing years, then "9-11" happened. In that enormous misfortune, the city, state and nation, even the world, rallied to offer New York City support.

In time, the obfuscating mayor milked the resources and moral support lavished on the city through unending media appearances, ultimately being recast

AFRICAN NATIONALIST POETRY AND PROSE

by image-makers, falsely, as "America's Mayor." As the Civil Rights activist Rev. Al Sharpton remarked during those sorrowful and challenging times: "Any leader responding to such a calamity given the forthcoming moral and material support would have performed in the same manner as Giuliani."

Now, if the "America's Mayor" title was really worthwhile, the next elevation would have been either governor or president. Fortunately, however, the American people recognized a sham when they saw one and twice rejected Giuliani's efforts in his 2012 and 2016 quest to become president. Unfortunately, Sonny did not live to see that well-deserved rejection; but he did, in the spirit of the "Million Movement" call for a "Million Voter Registration."

Significantly, five years after his passing, the "Million Voter Movement," must have played some role in helping to elect Barack Obama in 2008 and again in 2012.

African Nationalist Poetry and Prose Photo. Truly, a "Son of Harlem" and never to be forgotten.

FREDERICK MONDERSON

African Nationalist Poetry and Prose Photo. Radio Personality Bernard White and Dr. Leonard Jeffries at **CEMOTAP**.

African Nationalist Poetry and Prose Photo. Even more delicacies on the fire as the Festival time nears, expecting hundred at "Mama's Party."

AFRICAN NATIONALIST POETRY AND PROSE

African Nationalist Poetry and Prose Photo. Iconic African nationalist Malik "el-Hajj" Shabazz - Malcolm X, ever present, ever mindful, ever inspiring, "**Our Shining Black Prince**!"

FREDERICK MONDERSON

African Nationalist Poetry and Prose Photo. Colorful and smaller statues at the International African Arts Festival.

All this notwithstanding, in the years since Carson's death, there have been a number of developments in Criminal Justice reform. During the Obama administration, with Eric Holder as Attorney General, efforts were made to reform some aspects of the system, given America is considered the prison capital of the world and Black and Brown persons comprise nearly ninety percent of prison population. The Obama administration was successfully in getting judges to use discretion instead of the diabolical mandatory minimum sentence guidelines; Obama also worked to reverse the discriminatory sentencing regime whereby prison terms for 10 times more for crack convictions relative to powder cocaine, which is mostly abused by Whites.

AFRICAN NATIONALIST POETRY AND PROSE

Lil Nickelson writes: "Mass incarceration in the U.S. has grown; in 2012, the total of 2.23 million people was nearly seven times the number in 1972. The three levels of government together had expanded the nation's penal population by more than 1.9 million people since 1972. The U.S. incarceration rate is unsurpassed internationally; it accounts for about 23 percent of the world total."

As such, and to combat the inequity such numbers represent, a list of reforms was instituted under the Obama Administration.

Since the beginning of the Trump administration, steps have been taken to roll-back the Obama administration Criminal Justice Reforms, in this and many other areas, all as part of a hardline law and order propaganda mode of operation. Some believe, however, it's all part of a grand scheme to eliminate every achievement of the nation's first Black President. More precisely, as General Hayden, former CIA head diplomatically explained -- some of President Trump's efforts to "undo Obama's legacy," is a futile attempt to erase his record of having been "his predecessor." This is classic diplomatic speak for a vindictive mindset and associated actions.

At the recently concluded **National Action Network National Convention 2018**, a panel entitled "The State of American Justice in the

FREDERICK MONDERSON

Age of Trump" was moderated by Michael Hardy, Esq., with panelists Tahanie A. Aboushi, Benjamin Crump, Donna Lieberman and Joseph Tacopina. A great deal of facts and figures were supplied by these experts but Mr. Crump, who has been the "point Legal Eagle" representing families in the murders of Trayvon Martin, Eric Garner, Gurley, Michael Brown and the most recent case of Stephon Clarke in California was compelling.

Even more, Donna Lieberman's figures were very convincingly devastating about the "railroading business in American Criminal Justice." Still, Crump spoke to police misconduct in challenge to black and white persons suspected of being in breach of the law. In the case of blacks, who have no "kills" to their credit, the police shoot to kill and do just that. Now, with white suspects who do kill, the police generally apprehend them unharmed and alive. Some are treated to refreshments and one even taken to McDonald for a snack. In the recent Florida school killing, the police seemed to know the suspect patronized MacDonald's before he was apprehended unharmed. Even the most recent "Waffle House" killing; the suspect, though the Black hero disarmed him, he too was apprehended unharmed and fled, even though he had killed four and wounded several. More important, whites are apprehended alive while Blacks are shot dead because, in the encounter, the official line in most cases is, "cops fear for their lives." Still, the finest marksmen never shoot to wound, but ended up killing Black men and women.

AFRICAN NATIONALIST POETRY AND PROSE

Next Crump spoke about the roll back of Obama's Criminal Justice initiatives and the increasing numbers of For-profit prisons being built and managed across the country. This means its open season on Black and Brown men and women to fill the cells thus created, particularly in those towns upon which prison income is a significant means of support.

African Nationalist Poetry and Prose Photo. Workers and instruments to prepare the delicacies.

African Nationalist Poetry and Prose Photo. "We demand Equality for All" (**LULAC**).

FREDERICK MONDERSON

African Nationalist Poetry and Prose Photo. More colossal and colorful masks displayed at the **International African Arts Festival**.

AFRICAN NATIONALIST POETRY AND PROSE

African Nationalist Poetry and Prose Photo. Dr. Jack Felder (left) and Robert "Sonny" Carson (right) on a Middle School stage addressing young people.

Elsewhere, in a discussion on "David N. Dinkins' 21st Annual Leadership and Public Policy Forum" held at Columbia University's Miller Theater, Lil Nickelson in the *Harlem Community Newspaper* of May 3, 2018, p. 12, reported on the topic, "The Incarceration Crisis that Threatens America's Democracy."

There, Eric H. Holder, himself a Columbia University graduate and Attorney General in the Obama Administration, was the Keynote Speaker. Holder recounted, "The policies and practices we put into place during the Obama administration like our Smart on Crime initiatives are being rescinded by the current administration. The plan to rectify mass incarceration hasn't changed." These include:

1. Reduce mandatory sentences;

2. Give credit for good behavior for attending rehab programs;

3. Increase funding for alternative incarceration programs;

4. Eliminate sentencing disparities for uses of powder cocaine versus crack cocaine;

5. Financial support for re-entry programs.

Calling upon lawyers in general to render pro bono service to those grappling with challenges to the system, Mr. Holder continued, as Nickerson recounted: "Racial and gender disparities exist in the criminal justice system from a person's first interaction with police to sentencing through release and probation. Mass incarceration of our men means they are absent from their homes, children's lives, families and communities for long periods. Most women in the system have experienced sexual and/or physical abuse during their lives and every time they go through pat down traumatizes them. Women are also most likely to lose custody of their children during their incarceration. Men who are fathers leave prison at least $17,000 in debt for back child support which doesn't stop adding up while in jail."

AFRICAN NATIONALIST POETRY AND PROSE

African Nationalist Poetry and Prose Photo. West African symbol **NKISI SARABANDA** - "Signature of the Spirit."

African Nationalist Poetry and Prose Photo. Tribute to the Ancestors – Images, 2019.

FREDERICK MONDERSON

African Nationalist Poetry and Prose Photo. African Sculpture on Display at Atlanta International Airport. Zimbabwe. Lameck Bonjisi. In "Caring Mother" Bonjisi drew his ideas from both traditional and contemporary Shona sculpture."

AFRICAN NATIONALIST POETRY AND PROSE

"More should be done to rehabilitate and educate inmates to return them to society as productive members. When people serve their sentences, their past shouldn't label them present or forever; ex-felons should not be the term used to describe them the rest of their lives."

One item not mentioned in this report is the issue of disfranchisement of incarcerated individuals. Many states, particularly in the South, use prison as a mechanism to deprive persons of the fundamental right of being an American, the right to vote.

These were all issues that would have engaged the full support and participation of Sonny Carson.

Like most Black urban youth in the 1950s and 1960s, ran afoul of the law. He was incarcerated, then he served in the U.S. Army in Korea. He soon found his destiny; he became an activist. His first venture was in the economic arena. He advocated that Blacks were entitled to work where they shopped; the white-owned stores. Next, he insisted "Mom and Pop" shops be recognized and owned by Blacks. As a youth he belonged to the Bishops gang and even sold drugs, but this changed after his arrest and time served in prison.

The movie, "The Education of Sonny Carson" chronicled his early career. For long, especially after his death, there has been talk of a Sequel under the

FREDERICK MONDERSON

Title "Sonny Carson: The Final Triumph," after a book of that name.

Carson became involved in education issues, serving as President of the Brooklyn Branch of the Urban League. He was a key player in the famous Ocean-Hill/Brownsville School boycott, resulting in Community Control of School Boards in New York city.

In fact, the true purpose of that movement was to secure jobs for Black and Brown educators in a system overwhelmingly populated by Black and Latino stories: whereas the Superintendents, Principals, Assistant Principals and teachers were overwhelmingly White.

This was also a challenge to Whites educating Blacks and the cultural ramifications this form of employment represented. Les Campbell who changed his name to Jitu Weusi, was a principal associate of Sonny Carson and they both received bad press for their bold and uncompromising activism.

Sonny advocated for the founding, institutional recognition and four-year status for Medgar Evers College in Brooklyn as part of the City University of New York (CUNY) system. During the 1960s upheaval then New York City Mayor John Lindsay appealed to Sonny as a peacemaker. He was instrumental in helping to establish Bedford-Stuyvesant Restoration Corporation as an economic

AFRICAN NATIONALIST POETRY AND PROSE

revitalization engine for the Black Community in that region of Brooklyn.

Expressing an interest in tenant/landlord disputes and exploitation, Sonny then challenged the "Crack Epidemic" plaguing the Black Community, and in process he "attended too many funerals." In his office he kept posters of images of Black men-lynched and hanging by ropes from trees and other devices. Founding **Black Men Against Crack** and even more important **The Committee to Honor Black Heroes**, he advocated for and a number of streets and schools were successfully named in honor of Black Heroes in Brooklyn. Today there is Marcus Garvey Boulevard and Malcolm X Boulevard and Harriet Tubman Avenue. Malcolm X or Malik Shabazz School in Bed-Stuy and Toussaint L'Ouverture School in Crown Heights were some of his successes. Called the "Mayor of Bed Stuy," "Abubadika" (He who leads his people) and now the "Co-naming" "**Abubadikaville,**" for his efforts on that community's behalf; though Community Board 3 voted to name three blocks along Gates Avenue in his honor (Classon Avenue through Bedford Avenue, Nostrand avenue and Marcy's Avenue), sadly, the City Council under the Speakership of Christine Quinn voted down the measure.

FREDERICK MONDERSON

Sonny Carson's biggest and most important achievement was the repatriation of his ancestor Samuel Carson to Ghana, challenging the "Door of No Return" by opening the "Door of Return."

This extraordinary feat of Repatriation was successfully accomplished 20 years ago on August 1, 1998; the burial took place beside the river at a place called Assin Manso. There, he was buried beside an enslaved female named Crystal from Jamaica and this site serves as a place of Pilgrimage and point of departure for African-Americans seeking their roots on the African continent.

This return of the "Runaway Samuel Carson" became the symbol to inaugurate the First Emancipation Day Celebration in Ghana, that has now gained credence and credibility across Africa and the Black world.

This and much more we have to thank Sonny Carson for accomplishing. Not only must we educate our young about our heroes, but their leadership, courage, insightfulness, even daring must symbolically serve as inspiration to empower and propel African-Americans as we face the daily challenges so often manufactured as a mechanism of cultural, social and political stultification.

In that famous lyric "Dancing with My Father" Luther Vandross asked his father to return and so we too request of Sonny Carson, return that undaunting inspiration, courage and insightfulness so African

AFRICAN NATIONALIST POETRY AND PROSE

people down here on earth can boldly meet the challenges in these enormously challenging times.

African Nationalist Poetry and Prose Photo. The Black Heroes Collage.

FREDERICK MONDERSON

African Nationalist Poetry and Prose Photo. The "Shining Black Prince" Malcolm X, icon for all times, who remains a beacon of inspiration for African people worldwide.

AFRICAN NATIONALIST POETRY AND PROSE

"My intellectual debts are extensive in regards to the ideas in this book. I have read Thutmosis III, Ptahhotep, Amenomope, Ogotommeli, Delaney, Blyden, Garvey, DuBois, and groups of European thinkers such as Platonists, Aristotelians, and especially the Neo-Aristotelians, Hegelians, Marxists, and Wittgensteinians. However, I am most keenly a Diopian, believing essentially that Cheikh Anta Diop has said quite enough on the theories of culture and history to inform most of what I write. Those whose works I do not mention or whose names I do not call but to whom I am indebted are equally my teachers. Most particularly, of the contemporary theorists, I am most closely associated with the intellectual circle expounded by the philosopher Maulana Karenga and the scientist Wade Nobles whose works are essentially analytical and critical in much the say way as mine." Molefi Asante. *Kemet, Afrocentricity and Knowledge.* (1990) 1992.

6. THE CHOICE BY DR. FRED MONDERSON

The old adage about "An educated consumer," most appropriately applies to an "educated voter." A current dissatisfied view correctly expressed on television is that "Democrats take the Black vote for granted." Ironically, this view may be both correct and incorrect. It is mostly incorrect, however, and "educated voters" more fully understand the dynamics at play in the political process of what can be achieved within and between political parties. Still, before we examine events in the history of the vote, let us explain what is first the "Choice for Black voters." We either:

1. Vote Democrat

2. Vote Republican

3. Don't Vote

4. Our Vote don't count or matter

In order to exist, all organism must struggle! America is a nation of laws and no matter how some persons seem to bend the law, stretch the law, even break the law, the law is flexible and ultimately springs back to its unbiased legality. This is underscored in Dr. Martin Luther King's explanation: "The Arc of the Moral Universe is long but it bends towards justice."

The Congressional Black Caucus is an entity operating at the federal level of government in Washington, D.C. The effectiveness of such a body has encouraged state law makers to form similar groups, even forming coalitions to increase and strengthen the effectiveness of their representation. One such group is the Black and Puerto Rican Caucus functioning in the New York State Assembly. Such groupings also form on the city and county levels,

AFRICAN NATIONALIST POETRY AND PROSE

again forming coalitions to leverage political strength.

The late Congressman Major Owens, himself a member of the federal Congressional Black Caucus, at a forum organized in Brooklyn, New York, posed and answered his own question, "why we are, as members of the Congressional Black Caucus, in Congress?" To this he replied, "It is not so much the legislation that we propose or author, but the legislation we block because so much frivolous legislation is proposed on the floor of the House and Senate. It is only through the coalitions we form with liberals, progressives and like-minded persons that we are able to be effectively block such proposals particularly aimed at Blacks, Browns and the poor.

Now, this brings us to the Vote and Why we vote Democrat. But first.

There are 435 Congressional Districts across the country each with a representative seated in the House. The 50 states each elect 2 Senators for a total of 100. The House of Representatives is the principal legislation and finance-driven body that originates most legislation, particularly "money bills." The House can also bring impeachment charges against the President but he must be tried in the Senate which determines guilt or innocence. In the House of Representatives large states have greater representation based on population size more so than

FREDERICK MONDERSON

small states. In ratifying the Constitution of 1787, the "Connecticut Compromise" addressed this disparity of large against small states. So, a "Two House Chamber" was formed, giving each state equal representation in the Senate with two votes or Senators. This brings up the issue of "D.C. Statehood" which would essentially create "2 Black Senators" given the preponderance of predominant and permanent Black residents of the District of Columbia.

Still, before we answer the question as to why we vote Democrat, we must also have some understanding of the struggle to achieve the vote, before and after the Civil War from 1860 to 1865. Before and after "Declaration" and "War for Independence" (1776-1783) the vote belonged to the wealthy, whether land owners or merchants. A few Blacks enjoyed this privilege, even owning slaves themselves. The Civil War Amendments, the 13th abolished slavery; the 14th gave citizenship to persons born in the United States regardless of prior status or skin color; the 15th Amendment bestowed the right to vote on all able-bodied men over the age of 21. This for the most part, covered the African Freedman, emancipated in the 13th Amendment. That being so, with passage of the 15th Amendment nearly two million Blacks registered and were eligible to vote, particularly in the Southern States. They elected state and federal representatives to both the House and Senate. This was part of the Reconstruction movement which lasted, essentially from 1865 to 1877.

AFRICAN NATIONALIST POETRY AND PROSE

African Nationalist Poetry and Prose Photo. Michelle and Barack Obama, the "First Black First Couple" occupying the White House after the 2008 and 2012 Presidential elections.

FREDERICK MONDERSON

In the election of 1876, the "Southern Candidate," Rutherford B. Hayes succeeded to the Presidency in what many termed a "Union betrayal." This opened the floodwaters of Southern backlash that brought into existence terrorist groups and activities that ultimately changed the new status of the Freedman. The Ku Klux Klan was formed by General Forester and the Knights of the White Camellia was instituted as one of several terrorists, racist, organs to oppress Blacks as part of a disfranchisement movement that developed following the Civil War. They sought to short-change them economically with property ownership, jobs and wages and sharecropping fiasco. This meant, anytime a Black was observed and not "toeing the line" any action was possible even by the "lowest white man." Throughout, the federal government ignored the ongoing terrorism meted out to its black citizens.

Meanwhile, a more sinister and practical societal move was afoot to reinstitute "Southern Supremacy" and regain the political and economic clout the South had enjoyed before the War they lost. In the process, a systematic disfranchisement movement reduced Black voting strength from something like three million to less than ten thousand in a matter of decades. A good reason for this is because Blacks had, in appreciation of "Lincoln freeing the slaves," voted "the Party of Lincoln" spearheaded by its "Radical Republicans." As a good example, in discussing "constitutional disfranchisement of the Negroes," Joanne Grant in *Black Protest* (New York: Fawcett Books, 1968: 111) wrote: "In Louisiana in

AFRICAN NATIONALIST POETRY AND PROSE

1896 there were 164,088 whites registered and 130,344 Negroes. In 1900, the first registration year after a new constitution had been adopted, there were 125,437 white and 5,340 Negroes registered. By 1904 Negro registration had declined to 1,718, and white registration was 106,360. This represented a 96 percent decrease in Negro registration, and a four percent decrease in white."

"In Alabama, Mississippi and South Carolina disfranchisement began earlier. In 1883 in Alabama there were only 3,742 registered Negroes out of the 140,000 formerly registered. In South Carolina Negro registration decreased from 92,081 in 1876 to 2,823 in 1898. In Mississippi the decrease was from 52,705 in 1876 to 3,573 in 1898. Systematic exclusion continued up to through the present time [1968]. Between 1920 and 1930 about 10,000 Negroes voted in Georgia out of a potential Negro electorate of 369,511, and in Virginia the Negro vote at any time in that decade was 12,000 to 18,000 out of a voting-age-or-over and literate Negro population of 248,347."

All of a sudden, in this unfolding injustice voter registration officials insisted Blacks take "literacy tests," show proof of payment of property taxes, pay poll taxes, and in the southern backlash seeking "Southern Supremacy" the dreaded "Grandfather Clause" was invoked insisting only persons whose grandfather had voted previously could vote. This

FREDERICK MONDERSON

essentially covered almost 99 percent of Black voters. In addition, on the labor front, an unequal system called "share-cropping" became the principal form of wage earning for Blacks but this amounted to "economic peonage" for it trapped Blacks into working unending on white owned, but leased farms, and never coming out ahead. Though Blacks had technical skills from slavery days, they were paid pittances as employers robbed them blind. Meanwhile terrorism became the order of the day while practices of "Jim Crow" segregation became enshrined into law and practice aided by the *Plessy V. Ferguson* Supreme Court Ruling of 1896. These two, "Jim Crow" and the Supreme Court ruling were both significantly influenced by a prior ruling in the Dred Scott Decision of 1857 in which Scott sued for his freedom after being taken to a "Free State" then returned to a "Slave State" Missouri. In this historic ruling, the Supreme Court declared, as a slave, like the millions of other Africans held in perpetuity bondage, Scott was not a citizen and could not bring suit in an American Court. More important and significant, the ruling made it clear "a black man had no rights which a white man was bound to respect!" Here then, despite all that would later transpire, the Black man was stamped with the negatively pernicious visibility that would shape nefarious white views of him allowing all forms of prejudged behaviors, legal and otherwise.

Fortunately, the "Grandfather Clause" was outlawed by the Supreme Court in 1915, but it took nearly forty years before the court could muster the fairness to

AFRICAN NATIONALIST POETRY AND PROSE

outlaw segregation in *Brown V. Board of Education of Topeka, Kansas* in 1954. Ten years earlier, Thurgood Marshall, a young lawyer, had successfully pleaded his case before the Supreme Court in which the "White Primary" was outlawed. However, after the 1915 outlawing of the "Grandfather Clause" we must recognize a number of legal battles were being waged, some won, some lost, that began to gradually chip away at the legal second-class citizenship of Black-Americans. That is, de jure segregation and its nefarious actions supporting white supremacy and white privilege began to lose some of its legal standing but de facto segregation and related terrorism against Blacks was hard to kill and in fact it did kill. From 1870 to 1950, *The New York Times* reported recently, more than 4000 Blacks were murdered or lynched in 9 southern states. To show the mindset continued in the "New South," these are the states that essentially voted against Barack Obama for President in 2008 and 2012. Most, if not all, voted for Donald Trump in 2016. Talk of "birds of a feather" and "Ties that bind."

Recently, the Southern "legal eagle" who chronicled the nearly 4000 lynchings from 1878-1950; as racist white men intimidated Black American citizens and the federal government essentially remained silent; this courageous individual opened a Memorial and Museum in Montgomery Alabama. This new institution commemorates the horror and listed the names of the identified victims. The gentleman also

FREDERICK MONDERSON

wanted to place a "Tourist marker" on each and every site, but current property owners raised "Hue and Cry" for such a designation would associate them and their property with the heinous acts of lynching of Blacks by whites.

In the period after securing the vote in 1865 until 1930 Blacks essentially voted Republican but their plight was ignored by the party until the election of 1932 when Franklin Delano Roosevelt promised a "New Deal." Recognizing the significance of such a claim, Blacks then fled the Republican Party in droves and have voted Democrat since. Still, the door was opened so little it was difficult to get a shoe into it. In 1936 and again in 1940 they similarly voted Democrat. Throughout, A. Philip Randolph, a brilliant author and activist, protested treatment of Blacks and denial of getting meaningful jobs. This became highlighted as the nation inched towards World War II and Black citizens could not get meaningful jobs in the War industry. In the summer of 1941 Randolph proposed a "March on Washington" to put 100.000 Black men on the streets and Great Mall of Washington, D.C. This move was not just to protest prevailing conditions but to embarrass the American government and show the world, the cousin to the scourge of Nazism and white supremacy was alive in America. Recognizing the threat of a significant "March on Washington," would send the wrong message to the world, President Roosevelt issued an Executive Order opening the war industry to Blacks workers, but the struggle was far from over.

AFRICAN NATIONALIST POETRY AND PROSE

African Nationalist Poetry and Prose Photo. Langston Hughes and Alaine Locke, two of Harlem's greatest sons, literary giants and world renown.

This action did not, however, solve the problem that dragged on into the 1950s and 1960s witnessing Rosa Parks' incident on the bus and the resultant Montgomery Bus Boycott; the racist southern backlash that gave birth to the Civil Rights

FREDERICK MONDERSON

Movement; the bombing deaths of 4 little Black girls in a Birmingham Church; the historic "Selma to Montgomery" protest march to the Alabama state capital; within the ensuing creative protests, numbers of Blacks were registered to vote against the machinations of the "Bull Connors," "George Wallaces" and men of similar persuasions. In this movement, Dr. King emerged as an effective Civil Rights leader because he used non-violence as a tool that exposed American racism to the conscience of the world and as a result won concessions against de jure and de facto discrimination and segregation. Northern or liberal support that challenged the plight of Blacks ultimately led to the death of President John F. Kennedy in 1963; yet, as a show of "Continuity," President Lyndon Johnson, himself a Southerner, a Texan, forged through congress passage of the **Civil Rights Bill** in 1964. The **Voting Rights Act** was passed the next year in 1965 and Malcolm X was killed that same year. Because Negroes were "fed up and won't take it no more," and kept up their peaceful protests. Yet, by 1968 Medgar Evers, Bobby Kennedy and Martin Luther King were also killed for racist reasons. Nevertheless, the civil right struggle remained strong and effective under the leadership of Rev. Joseph Lowery, Andrew Young, Wyatt Tee Walker, Rev. Shuttlesworth, Jesse Jackson, Rev. Abernathy, Fannie Lou Hamer, Amelia Boynton Robinson (1911-2015), and many others including activist soldiers such as Stokely Carmichael, Harry Belafonte and even Sidney Poitier.

AFRICAN NATIONALIST POETRY AND PROSE

The fascinating development is that more and more blacks began registering and voting and more and more Black representatives were being elected to local, state and national positions. As the Black voting rolls increased Democrats consistently and effectively courted this enthused and empowered constituency, while Republicans orchestrated a multitude of efforts to nullify the Black vote.

African Nationalist Poetry and Prose Photo. Former New York City Mayor David Dinkins with young people at *Black Star News* Newspaper Awards.

African Nationalist Poetry and Prose Photo. Tribute to the Ancestors – Images, 2019.

FREDERICK MONDERSON

African Nationalist Poetry and Prose Photo. West African Symbol **NSOROMMA** – "Guardianship."

African Nationalist Poetry and Prose Photo. Tribute to the Ancestors – Images, 2019.

AFRICAN NATIONALIST POETRY AND PROSE

African Nationalist Poetry and Prose Photo. Atlanta Airport Walkway Art. Zimbabwe. Edronce Rukodzi. Woman showing Traditional Salute illustrates a respectful salutation to village elders.

FREDERICK MONDERSON

Now we come to the realization, the American political system supports two principal parties, Democrat and Republican. The "educated voter" knows, because elected officials represent constituencies with particular interests, it is sometimes difficult to get things done in the halls of legislatures unless the people take to the streets to force legislative action and this can be in the form of Initiative, Referendum, Recall or forced legislation, particularly at the ballot box, to address issues of concern. The government, in this case, federal, state and city or local, moves slowly if issues don't really benefit particular constituencies. So, it's a constant struggle "pushing the envelope" to bring about the necessary changes and social, educational and economic, even political rewards. Significantly, therefore, despite what may be said by the "uneducated voter," there are more than 50 Black elected Democrats at the Federal level in Washington, D.C. and 2 or 3 Black Republicans out of the 435 and 100. Similar disparities exist between the two parties at state and city or local levels. Nonetheless, and reinforcing this fact, we should always reflect on Major Owens' previously stated view. More important and unmistakable, while Democrats try to "get out the Black vote," Republicans try to suppress or disfranchise the Black voter.

During the 2008 election in which Barack Obama was the Democratic Party Standard-Bearer, in the presidential election and again in 2012 the problem

AFRICAN NATIONALIST POETRY AND PROSE

was acerbated. Fact is, all manner of chicanery and misleading propaganda was perpetuated from the Republican playbook to nullify the Black vote. Significantly, as late as this time, during the Obama Administration, Attorney General Eric Holder filed suit against many state legislatures who devised strategies to deny the Black vote after the 2010 Census count.

Fact is, if you don't vote you don't count. But people must understand to make a difference everyone must vote. People vote for themselves, their children and their children as well as their communities. Only then will voters be able to leverage their strength against lawmakers who only pay attention and disburse funds to people who vote or they have an affinity for. Either you vote or you don't count.

African Nationalist Poetry and Prose Photo. Rev. Al Sharpton addresses the audience at National Action Network's "Keeping the Dream Alive" **National Convention, 2018**.

FREDERICK MONDERSON

African Nationalist Poetry and Prose Photo. Tribute to the Ancestors - Images, 2019.

"The black culture is characterized by an oral tradition. Knowledge, attitudes, ideas, notions are traditionally transmitted orally, not through the written word. It is not unusual, then, that the natural leader among black people would be one with exceptional oratorical skills. He must be able to talk, to speak – to preach. Int eh black religious tradition, the successful black preacher is an expert orator. His role involves more, however, his relationship with his parishioners is reciprocal; he talks to them, and they talk back to him. That is expected. In many church-circles this talk-back during a sermon is a firm measure of the preacher's effectiveness." Molefi Asante. Quoted in *The Afrocentric Idea* (1987).

AFRICAN NATIONALIST POETRY AND PROSE

African Nationalist Poetry and Prose Photo. Getting down at **CEMOTAP's** 31st Celebration.

7. NAN CONVENTION 2018
BY
DR. FRED MONDERSON

Reverend Al Sharpton and the National Action Network celebrated their "Annual Keeping the Dream" Convention on the 50th Anniversary of the Assassination of Reverend Dr. Martin Luther King. Held April 18-21, 2018 at the New York Sheraton, Times Square, this year the Convention was bigger than ever, with more dynamic speakers, more penetrating presentations and analyses of important issues and larger numbers of attendees coming from all over the nation. Motivated as those attendees were, they packed the halls and corridors to receive the valuable information disseminated, network with academics, economic, political and technical

FREDERICK MONDERSON

administrators and entrepreneurs, thereby honing strategies of activism to apply in their own situations, in their respective towns, cities and states across the nation.

From big-time politicians seeking to embellish their records, returning representatives reporting to the people on their activities since the last convention and their planned activities going forward. This has now become a staple because Al Sharpton's movement, vocal in holding their feet to the proverbial fire. More important, however, has been the professionals, academics in the colleges who write books, and seek to guide young minds in choosing the proper way forward; the lawyers battling in the trenches of the criminal justice system in the "Age of Trump" and the epidemic of senseless killing of Black men, particularly those victimized by law enforcement officials. These factors help attest to the strength of the Movement spearheaded by Rev. Sharpton and his **National Action Network**, that truly networks in the interest of the people. Mothers whose sons and even daughters that have been killed senselessly, have in their right become a regular feature of Sharpton's events. The presence of these courageous women of indomitable spirits and tenacious determination in seeking justice for all womanhood. has been designed to showcase the tragic events of their plight and offer support to members of such a unique club of victimized mothers. They are also there to demonstrate revolutionary and activist fervor with which, having given all, these standard bearers serve as symbols of

AFRICAN NATIONALIST POETRY AND PROSE

resoluteness, exhibit a quiet and compelling dignity and steadfast resoluteness as mothers of martyrdom they belong on in a long list of courageous and innocent persons whose family members have had their lives cut short by senseless gun violence in America and the impact this tragedy has had on their lives.

Invaluable information was disseminated by individuals representing corporate entities seeking to help bridge the digital divide in black, brown and poor communities. This expertise provides tremendous insights as a way to educate individuals and entrepreneurs on the advantages and disadvantages posed in this rapidly expanding revolutionary technology and economic direction the world is rapidly moving within.

A hallmark of Reverend Sharpton's annual convention has been to invite and showcase Black executives, administrators, entrepreneurs and young people who share their experiences in a "teaching moment" that can make a difference if their advice is adhered to. These professionals offer wisdom gained in their respective arenas of expertise and in their appearance emphasize various facets of their engagement designed to serve as role models but also to highlight what they do. In such efforts, they point to positive and profitable opportunities enterprising individuals can pursue to enhance their situation and make a difference in their lives and the lives of others.

FREDERICK MONDERSON

In reflection on the Convention's purpose and intent, the President's Welcome Address Commemorating the 50th Anniversary of the assassination of Dr. Martin Luther King is signature recognition of the meaning and significance of this year's convention in the "Fight for Justice." In assessing the times, according to Rev. Sharpton: "We currently have a Commander-In-Chief in the White House who is actively working to undo all that Dr. King fought for. The administration's attacks on people of color, immigrants, women, poor people, marginalized communities and the disfranchisement should frighten us all."

"As we mourn Dr. King's assassination, the greatest challenge we face is to maintain his vision and all that he and others achieved after so much sacrifice – including sacrificing his own life. From the Voting Rights Act to the Civil Rights Act and more, everything is under renewed threat, and what we do today will have ramifications for years to come. It is not enough to just memorialize Dr. King; we must continue his work."

"The recent police killing of Stephon Clark, an unarmed Black man in Sacramento, CA, is evidence that we still need police and criminal justice reform. NAN has been on the frontlines fighting this battle for decades, and we continue to stand with the families of victims of police killing/police brutality. Fifty years after Dr. King's assassination, unfair police practices and the criminal justice system are

AFRICAN NATIONALIST POETRY AND PROSE

decimating families and entire communities. This is simply unacceptable."

NAN's President Dr. W. Franklyn Richardson's Welcome is also highly instructive; for, he states: "Our gathering takes on special significance this year in light of the 50 years global commemoration of the assassination of the Reverend Dr. Martin Luther King, Jr. The National Action Network has aligned its movement with the legacy of Dr. King, a nonviolent movement for justice and equality. This week we pay special tribute to his life and memory. Our objective is to further the cause for which he died."

Some of the "Heavyweights" in attendance at this year's convention include former Attorney General Eric H. Holder, attorneys Michael Hardy and Benjamin Crump; New York's Governor Andrew Cuomo; Ras Baraka, Mayor, Newark, New Jersey; Chirlane McCray, First Lady of New York City; Senator Bernie Sanders; Honorable Jim Clyburn, Honorable Joseph Kennedy, Honorable Cedric Richmond, Chairman, Congressional Black Caucus; Chris Matthews, host, "Hardball," MSNBC; the intellectuals, Dr. Eddie Glaude, Dr. Christina Greer, Dr. Obery Hendricks, Dr. Marc Lamont Hill, Dr. Tricia Rose; New York State Comptroller Thomas P. DiNapoli and New York City's Comptroller, Scott M. Stringer.

FREDERICK MONDERSON

Topic at this Convention included: "What is the State of the Union Under Trump;" "The State of American Justice in the Age of Trump;" "How do we deal with the Digital Divide;" "Sharing Our Stories: Mental Health and Blacks in New York City;" "Daughters of the Movement;" "Black Intellectuals;" "Delivering on the Black Economic Agenda: Guarding Against Economic Erosion in Our Communities;" "Truth to Power Revival;" "Advancing Equal Education in the Era of Trump;" and a whole lot more.

It is interesting, "Out of Evil Cometh Good." Despite his nefarious behavior, as in all such adverse time of the past, Donald Trump has helped unite and strengthen the Black Community who will be here long after he is history, albeit a sorrowful experience.

One of the interesting issues of serious thought raised by Rev. Sharpton had to do with Pension Funds investment. He pointed out; Black folks pay money into Pension Funds that lend to investors. These investors build housing and help perpetuate Gentrification. In a strange, seemingly contradictory twist, according to Rev. Sharpton, "Black folks are paying for their own Gentrification victimization!"

AFRICAN NATIONALIST POETRY AND PROSE

African Nationalist Poetry and Prose Photo. Dr. Leonard Jeffries and Dr. Molefi Asante are joined by a number of Beautiful African women at **CEMOTAP's** 31st Anniversary Celebration, 2018.

African Nationalist Poetry and Prose Photo. Master Drummer Chendo and his assistant at the festival in San Juan de la Maguana, Dominican Republic.

FREDERICK MONDERSON

"I am certain that the Indians did not believe they had sold Manhattan Island for twenty-three dollars' worth of trinkets, no matter what the Dutch thought. Native Americans revered the land in much the same way as Africans. No king or clan leader could sell what did not belong to him. On the basis of European contractual custom, the Dutch may have actually though they were purchasing the island from the Indians, but this was obviously a view based on their own commercial traditions." *The Afrocentric Idea.* Molefi Asante (1987).

8. ASANTE AT CEMOTAP - 2018 BY DR. FRED MODNERSON

As a prelude to the appearance of Dr. Len Jeffries, Dr. Molefi Asante gave his Keynote Address as the gathering awaited the old master, always off somewhere taking care of business for African people.

In his presentation regarding "Embracing Who We Are," Dr. Molefi Asante made two powerful statements as the Keynote Speaker at **CEMOTAP's** 31st Anniversary Celebration on April 21, 2018. After a significant laudatory introduction by **CEMOTAP's** Co-Chair Dr. James McIntosh, Dr. Asante took to the microphone and said, first and foremost; that is, after thanking the Master of

AFRICAN NATIONALIST POETRY AND PROSE

Ceremonies for the wonderful introduction and recognizing Nana Queen Mother Camille Yarbrough, whose "spirit made us greater people by translating our own substance into significance." Thus, in "Embracing who we are," he insisted we always give honor to the great ancestors who have defined and shaped the destiny of African people. Then he began a roll-call of Africans of substance throughout history who have not simply shaped the destiny of African people but whose impact on the world in general has been extraordinary.

The Keynoter began his Roll Call by listing great heroes in the African Experience and supplying an understanding of why "African People must Embrace Who We Are!"

Imhotep – Earliest personality recorded in history who dealt with questions of space, time, volume, the nature of illness, physical and mental disease, and immortality. There was no situation during his lifetime that did not cause Imhotep to reflect on the meaning and significance of its origin, development, and conclusion. He was the first philosopher in human history. In this sense, he is the true father of medicine, architecture, politics, and philosophy. The world's first multi-genius, he built the Step-Pyramid at Sakkara for Pharaoh Zoser of the Third Egyptian Dynasty.

FREDERICK MONDERSON

Ptahhotep – Old Kingdom Philosopher, who, among his writings instructed, "Do not be arrogant because of your learning. Converse with the learned as well as the ignorant for who knows where wisdom will be found.

Duauf – Accepted as the master of protocol. The philosophy of Duauf is concerned with the protocols of living in society. In that he urged youth to read books, he may be called the first intellectual in philosophic history. His was a remarkable testimony of the ancient African emphasis on learning. Reading was promoted as the best way to train the mind and to reveal the secrets of the hiding things.

All the philosophers of the Egyptian experience

Akhenaten – Called the "father of monotheism." Akhenaton believed that Aton was the one God. Akhenaton's choice of the small priesthood of Aton as the national religion created a massive crisis in Kemet. Soon after he moved the capital to Tell el Amarna, he was overthrown and the power reclaimed at Waset (Thebes). He not simply rebelled against contemporary religious practices but ushered a new view of art and explanation of science.

Amenhotep, Son of Hapu – Architect of Amenhotep III of the 18th Dynasty and whose architectural accomplishments made his king Amenhotep a memorable figure for he built at Karnak, Luxor, across the River at Thebes, also a

AFRICAN NATIONALIST POETRY AND PROSE

palace at Malcata for Queen Tiy and in Nubia, among other places.

Hatshepsut – 18th Dynasty ruler who built her mortuary temple at Deir el Bahari, erected 4 obelisks at Karnak temple and dispatched an expedition to Punt in Central East Africa that successfully returned as graphically represented at the temple.

Thutmose III - greatest military strategist – Neither Alexander the great nor Napoleon did what he did. During the early 18th Dynasty, he led his armies in 17 campaigns and returned victorious every time. Alexander did it 7 times. Thutmose set a model as a pattern.

Next, he mentioned 3 Nubian queens who checked the Roman ascent on the Nile.

Yaninga of Burkino Faso – a caring ruler and fierce fighter.

Recognizing and relating to African womanhood had dignity, Asante then mentioned -

Queen Yaa Asantewaa – Ghanaian warrior Queen who led an army against and defeated British forces threatening her nation.

FREDERICK MONDERSON

Queen Asmal in the 19th Century taught Muslim women it was all right to learn to read.

Sundiata Keita – His name reverberated all over West Africa.

Mansa Musa – one of the greatest kings of West African lineage.

Jomo Kenyatta wrote *Facing Mount Kenya*, the story of the **Mau Mau**.

There was incredible, outstanding work done by **Shaka the Zulu** in Southern Africa.

W.E.B. DuBois – African-American intellection who dominated the literary and activist world of the Twentieth Century. He initiated and carried the mantle of "Father of Pan Africanism" for nearly half a century. He began the Encyclopedia of Africa while living and working in Ghana where he died and is today buried.

Dr. John H. Clarke – Unequaled African scholar and African sovereignist who is well-revered in the African American experience.

Dr. Yosef Ben-Jochannan – Egyptologist, historian, publisher and nationalist activist.

AFRICAN NATIONALIST POETRY AND PROSE

The educational work of **Yanga** of Mexico – was instrumental in furthering literacy in that nation.

Dessalines of Haiti - Revolutionary who helped establish and solidify the State of Haiti, the first Black Republic, even as America and the West perpetuated their system enslaving the African in the New World.

After which Dr. Asante reminded, "There is no history in the world that is greater than African history. This is who we are. How can we not embrace who we are?"

James West invented the Telephone.

Charles Just – Known as the "Black Apollo of Science" he was the first science to demonstrate the cancerous nature of ultra-violet rays.

Marcus Garvey – Great organize, orator and architect of global African unification and

Malcolm X – Restless young African-American whose life was transformed after a term in prison, acceptance of the Islamic faith and national spokesman for the Nation of Islam, from which he later rebelled. Having traveled abroad to mecca and

FREDERICK MONDERSON

acquiring a new view of the world, he was killed in the Audubon Ballroom in Harlem in 1968.

Martin Luther King – No violent civil rights icon who changed America in more ways than one. Finally, he was killed because forces arrayed against African-Americans sought to stem the tide of history.

Frederick Douglass – Runaway slave who became a mighty voice as an abolitionist, publisher of the North Star newspaper and father of African-American nationalism who decried the meaning of the 4th of July

Despite being a mighty people, we were sleeping. **CEMOTAP IS AWAKE**. A consistent theme of Dr. Ben-Jochannan has been "**Wake Up Dead Man**."

We can give a thousand, ten thousand names. There is a lengthy list of so many geniuses. We must salute the mother of our creativity Sister Camille Yarbrough. We are an artistic people. We understand creativity. This is who we are.

Trump is an aberration. He is more than that. He is a liar. We must think things through. We must be rational. Then he posed his next significant question.

AFRICAN NATIONALIST POETRY AND PROSE

"When did Europeans begin to dominate African minds?"

Afrocentricity teaches us what's at work.

African culture – We must return to and appreciate traditional African culture. In Nigeria we have Ebo, Ibib, Yoruba, etc. All these cultures relate back to the Nile Valley civilization.

What this Nile Valley experience has taught us, Africans had a solar view of the Universe. There was an epistemology of agriculture, color, and our understand of cosmic orientation was acute. The divine relates to the solar principle.

Thus, "when did we have a devolution, not an evolution, in our connection to the solar principle?

In response, Dr. Asante suggested the occupation by the Greeks, Romans and later Arabs. The enslavement and finally the colonial experience. In seeking to analyze these three experiences, he again asked: "When did we slip to a material universe the Europeans and Arabs gave us?" In this, he disagreed with Ali Mazrui who argued "Africa had three heritages." Asante said, "No. Africa had one heritage and two invasions."

FREDERICK MONDERSON

Then he returned to the Nile Valley experience by identifying Amon as the Hidden One. The four basic names our people gave to the divine one was Ra, Atum, Ptah and Amon. While he argued "Ra is the divine symbol of the sun, the Sun is not Ra." That is, "Not that the sun is god, but that the sun symbolizes the divine."

The reflection of the sun (African male/female principle) Sun (Heru). The Sun and Earth gave us the Moon (Heru). That is, added to a symbol. Everything is everything. We are star dust. We return to dust when everything is over.

In coming to America, when we landed here, we still had understanding of the solar symbol. This was taken from us.

He then took issue with the consistent refrain that: "Christianity brought us through slavery!" In fact, Africans came through slavery by virtue of the solar experience. Less than 10 percent of Africans were Christians by slavery's end in 1860. About that time there were about 4 million enslaved Africans in this country. That would make 400,000 Africans were Christians.

AFRICAN NATIONALIST POETRY AND PROSE

African Nationalist Poetry and Prose Photo. Sporting the colors with Malcolm, Mandela and Martin, while he says "I Love Black People."

African Nationalist Poetry and Prose Photo. Two outstanding Africans, recognized in Harlem and worldwide!

FREDERICK MONDERSON

African Nationalist Poetry and Prose Photo.
ASASE YE DURU – African Symbolism - "Divinity of Mother Earth."

Interestingly enough, it was the 1870s, 1880s, and 1890s, that Africans became Christian wholesale. To which he answered, "If we embrace who we are, we will realize who we are."

AFRICAN NATIONALIST POETRY AND PROSE

Next, he visited the 1788 invasion of Australia by English convicts who mistreated and brutalized the indigenous Africans they met there. Had this sorrowful experience not taken place, then two continents of the world would have belonged to people of African ancestry. We must come to realize all European history is brutal. English, French, Portuguese, Spanish - No enslaved African got better treatment by any of the European conquerors.

Ending a well-structured and enlightening presentation, Dr. Molefi Asante recited the last stanza of the Black National Anthem by James Weldon Johnson, Lift Every Voice and Sing.

Stony the road we trod, bitter the chastening rod,
felt in the days when hope unborn had died;
yet with a steady beat, have not our weary feet
come to the place for which our people sighed?
We have come over a way that with tears has been watered;
We have come, treating our path through the blood of the slaughtered,
out from the gloomy past, till now we stand to last
where the white gleam of our bright star is cast.

Thus, stimulated and energized, the collective consciousness was now ready for Dr. Leonard Jeffries presentation after which **CEMOTAP's** Co-Chairs, Dr. McIntosh and Betty Dopson brought the

FREDERICK MONDERSON

celebration to an end. What a wonderful evening of intellectual thought, cultural inspiration and colorful attire that is so characteristic of the Committee to Eliminate Media Offensive to African People as it has in its 31 years of successful activist history.

From his work on *The Egyptian Philosophers* (2000) Molefi Kete Asante quotes Ptahhotep, the Egyptian philosopher.

"May old age serve me as a staff
So that I may repeat the words of those who heard
The words of the ancestors
Who listened to the gods.
I want the same thing done for you
So that strife may disappear from among the people
And the people of both banks of the river serve you!
The majestic God said, therefore,
Instruct him in the words of the past
That he may become a model for posterity
May he be obedient
May he be devoted to the one who speaks to him
Because no one is born with wisdom. (Translation is author's.)

AFRICAN NATIONALIST POETRY AND PROSE

African Nationalist Poetry and Prose Photo. Another group who answered Rev. Al Sharpton's "We Shall Not Be Moved" March on Washington, January 2017.

9. IDPAD 2018 SUMMIT – GUYANA
BY
DR. FRED MONDERSON

African Nationalist Poetry and Prose Photo. The International Decade for People of African Descent (2015-2024) held its 2018 **IDPAD** Summit in Georgetown, Guyana, at the Marriott Hotel on March 8-11, 2018.

FREDERICK MONDERSON

While Dr. Norman Ng-A-Qui, the Summit's Director of Communications gave the Welcome Address he also introduced the Opening Ceremony's Master of Ceremonies Mr. Vincent Alexander. Mr. Alexander in turn introduced Honorable Dr. Carl Greenidge, Member of Parliament and Vice-President of the Republic of Guyana who gave the Opening Remarks and representing President David Granger, on a visit to India attending matters of state.

Mr. Greenidge emphasized the role of the IDPAD Assembly in Guyana is to coordinate the work of African organizations in Guyana for an interface with the government. Together they seek to promote and protect the diverse heritage, culture and contribution of African people and work for the elimination of all forms of racial discrimination. As such, African people must speak for themselves, for as "Elder wisdom" has held, "Until lions get their share, historians will always favor the hunter."

African Nationalist Poetry and Prose Photo. The Message is clear. "Love One Another."

AFRICAN NATIONALIST POETRY AND PROSE

African Nationalist Poetry and Prose Photo. Professor Joycelyn Loncke and members of the Pan-African Movement – Guyana Branch in attendance.

Dr. Hillary Brown stressed the need for a "concrete program of action" to work for the elimination of racism. There has been a blatant disregard for the humanity of African people. Tremendous crimes have been perpetuated against people of African descent.

The first two days, of which this writer was in attendance featured the Opening Ceremony and the first full day. These were followed by two additional days of Keynote Address on such matters as "Business and Finance;" "Health and Wellness;" Education and Culture;" "Human Rights and Geopolitics;" and "Information and Technology." There were "Subject Matter Experts" and "Open

FREDERICK MONDERSON

Session Round Tables" that further explored the issues. A gifted young Faith Harding recited a moving Spoken Word quoting Bob Marley that the Conference "Get Together and Be All Right!"

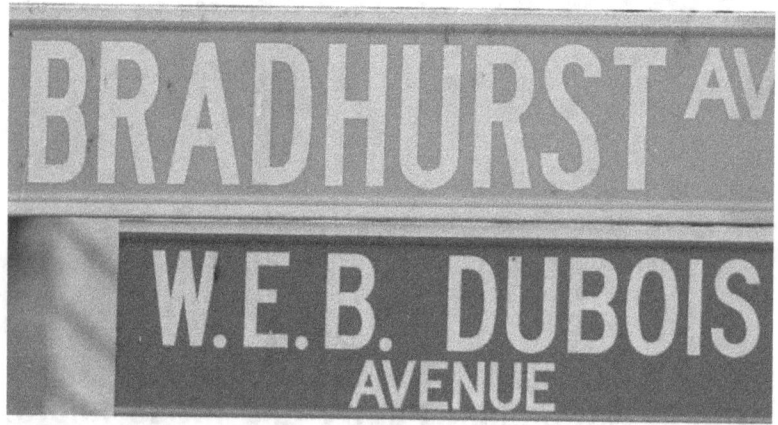

African Nationalist Poetry and Prose Photo. W.E.B. DuBois, "father of Pan-Africanism," is recognized in Harlem.

While a number of speakers had their say including Dr. Hillary Brown, Program Manager of Culture and Community Development – Caribbean Secretariat; Dr. William Adu-Krow, PAHO/WHO Representative; Ms. Brigit Gerstenberg, Senior Human Rights Advisor United Nations, Jamaica; and Dr. Melissa Varysyk, Chairperson IDPAD Summit 2018 Committee member, compelling presentations were made by Panel members who addressed the overall theme of the Conference, "Where We Are, Where We Need to Be, and How Do We Get There!" Additional summits are scheduled for 2020 and 2022 before the final culmination in 2024.

AFRICAN NATIONALIST POETRY AND PROSE

It was generally agreed, there is need to seek Reparative Justice within the framework of the 10-Point Action Plan adopted by Caribbean heads of government, recognizing there are 200 million Africans in the Western Hemisphere. Given there are some 200 million Africans in the Western Hemisphere, the Movement is International and thus, the Action Plan agenda is doable.

The Coordinator for the Morning Panel for the Theme: "Where We Ought To Be" was Ms. Ambolike Belle: She first introduced:

Dr. William Adu-Krow was the first Black to head a hospital. He reminded Kwame Nkrumah's dictum, "The independence of Ghana is meaningless not only of the African continent, but also the African minds" must be liberated. In recognition and support of International Women's Day, he reiterated elder African wisdom, "When you teach a man you have taught an individual. If you teach a woman, you teach a nation." He descried "Pushback" he experienced when he became Executive Director of his Hospital. Many responded questioning who is he, a black to head a hospital? The sad fact, the most vocal of such persons were Blacks. These people fell into what a later speaker described herself as a "former" but now "Recovering White Supremacist." That is to say, she once believed that White People were superior and were more beautiful, wiser and could do anything.

FREDERICK MONDERSON

Fortunately, her mother gave her a Black Doll and reminded her how beautiful she truly was.

Nevertheless, Dr. Adu-Krow then offered an analogy to view the current situation, vis-à-vis, "Inequalities and Ethnicity." He stated: Take for example, Cervical Cancer Screening which is open to all. This is universal. But, if one group is more prevalent, the universal screening is not necessarily effective. Intercultural approaches are important. If a malady affects 1 in 8, then we have to ask why this one. Therefore, a number of things must be considered. (1) support the production of data; (2) consider comparative studies; (3) social factors must be taken into consideration; (3) credence must be given to ancestral knowledge of medicinal properties; etc. He further described an injury he suffered on his knee and how despite the best doctors he could not bend his knee. His father then took him to a Ghanaian "traditional Doctor" who mixed a potion, administered it and within three days his knee was able to be bent.

Next, Dr. Anthony Browder spoke of "forbidden knowledge" kept from the African people particularly in the work of two Guyanese authors, George G.M. James and Ivan Van Sertima who wrote, *Stolen Legacy* and *They Came Before Columbus*, respectively.

There are emerging new concepts and ideas that will allow us to free our minds. We must redefine what education is. What culture is.

AFRICAN NATIONALIST POETRY AND PROSE

"The idea we were born in sin is a false idea." I have learned never say anything in public unless you can back it up with at least four sources. No one died for your sins.

We must center ourselves in an education that is Africa based. We must share with people who need to know. Times are shifting. Times are changing. A new consciousness is emerging. We live for the future. We live for our children.

The new museum in Washington, DC cost 15 Million dollars. It articulates the history of African people.

200,000 years ago, African people roamed East Africa. 60,000 years ago, people left Africa to migrate to Asia and Europe. That meant, the first people in both Asia and Europe were Africans. 35,000 years ago, people began crossing the Bering Straits. Recently scholars have found the genes in Africans that mutated 8-7000 years ago to become Europeans. So, Africans had a head start of 192,000 years. That is to say, for 192,000 years Africans were the only people on the earth.

African history and African education are the earliest.

We must debunk the myth about African Reality. Finally, he promised to discuss the new movie, Black Panther, at a later setting.

FREDERICK MONDERSON

Next and importantly, in introducing Dr. Julius Garvey, the Moderator Ms. Ambolika Belle pointed out, "Amy Jacques Garvey told Julius Garvey who his father Marcus Garvey was!"

Dr. Julius Garvey then addressed the gathering and felt it "Good to see so many intelligent and warm faces."

Africans were the only human being on earth for 150,000 years. From then on it was a negative experience.

Everything is in Egypt. We have gone in the wrong direction.

The Honorable Marcus Garvey reminded, "A people without a knowledge of their history is a people without roots." He also, "Inspired Africans to redeem Africa."

He pointed out; Marcus Garvey had a Six-Point Plan:

1. The Unity of all Africans;
2. Development of a nation state in Africa;
3. Self-reliance on the part of African people.
4. Economic policies and procedures to favor Africans;
5. Education to emancipate Africans from mental slavery;

AFRICAN NATIONALIST POETRY AND PROSE

6. Culture as the milieu instrument of change – encompassing titles, symbols, propaganda, parades.

Garvey made it clear there is a difference between a vision and a Dream. African minds have been conditioned by 500 years of European oppression.

We must recognize what we must do to reach the promised land. We face extinction. God in nature. Out of our own creative genius we make ourselves what we are.

We are equipped with spiritual purity. Amon, Ptah, Ra – Spiritual Unity

These ideas and cosmology that existed at least 4000 B.C.

The African mind has been awakened.

We must have a clear purpose in life, a strong sense of purpose. Wisdom. Know oneself.

The ANKH is a mirror of the mind.

Heru - We become the change we want to be.

A way of life.

Harmony with ourselves.

FREDERICK MONDERSON

Lead by example, working little people, settle example.

We the people must rise up.

We must decide what we want to accomplish.

We must have a vision and implement it. This the true revolution.

There must be a revolution in consciousness and spirit. In fulfillment we must have:

ONE GOD, DESTINY, LOVE, AIM. EACHNG HAS TO BE PURPOSEFUL.

African Nationalist Poetry and Prose Photo. Dr. Anthony Browder (white shirt) among part of the audience listening intently to presentation on the issues at the 2018 **IDPAD** Summit in Georgetown, Guyana.

AFRICAN NATIONALIST POETRY AND PROSE

The civil rights activist Ms. Faya Ora Rose Toure acknowledged, "Where we should be today, is not where we are."

"We face the problem of mid-education. We must tell the children about who we are. There has been a lynching of the mind, in addition to the neck."

Ms. Toure claimed to be "Recovering white supremacist." She insisted, "I never thought white people were smarter than I am. I thought they were more beautiful. Neither the civil war nor the civil rights movement but only Marcus Garvey challenged white supremacy."

The white race is the most important, smart, most beautiful. The most dangerous white supremacist are black people who believe white people are superior.

We are not where we ought to be because of white supremacy. There has been that lynching of the mind. We are still sick from white supremacy. We are still choosing white dolls.

Where we should be?

1. In every school.

2. There are prisons that exploit Africans.

FREDERICK MONDERSON

3. I know Africans will be saved.

4. Black Lives will matter.

5. Reparations.

African Nationalist Poetry and Prose Photo. Bob Marley and Haile Selaisse.

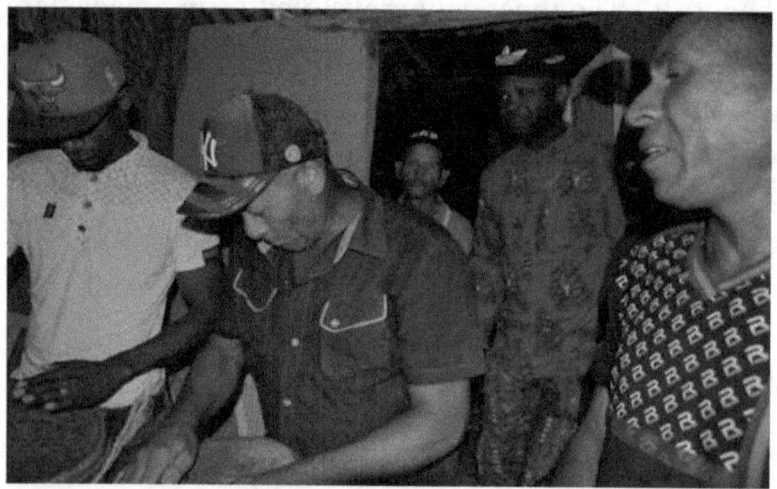

African Nationalist Poetry and Prose Photo. "Getting the Drummers on" with Chendo in the lead!

AFRICAN NATIONALIST POETRY AND PROSE

Regarding Obama: "As much as he tried, he could not escape the negativity of many white citizens who would push and pull him into as many crevices as they could. In a profoundly courageous expression of dignity and elegance, worthy of the vest presidents, he lived above the fray in ways that many of us would not have been able to do. Indeed, this was almost necessary given the fact that he was the first African-American president in the nation's history. His plate had to be clean; is responses had to be measured; and his rhetoric had to be couched within the framework of history. As a student of Constitutional Law and history he was able to disregard the trivial even when it must have hurt, but he knew also that he was a symbolic figure for millions of Africans around the world. He could not break; he could not demonstrate anger; he had to show patience and wisdom. No other president had to undergo as many attacks on his person as Barack Obama. While some may have disagreed with policies of other presidents, they did not necessarily attack them personally or wish their deaths. Obama's tenure as president, consequently, had to teach him that the idealism of his youth was corralled into the enlightened fringes of the nation while the central trunk of the American nation was still racist at its core. I am convinced had Obama responded in kind to the like of the Italian immigrant Rudy Giuliani or the racist tweets and email of

Ferguson, Missouri police, he would have been reduced to an ordinary man and he wanted most of all for the nation and for African-Americans to be seen as good citizens. But why should the President have to entertain the idea of image of African-Americans when no white president has ever had to cover for white people in this way?" Molefi Kete Asante. *Lynching Barack Obama: How Whites Tried to string Up the President.* 2016.

10.   ROSA PARKS
BY
DR. FRED MONDERSON

As a woman of African descent and without question, Rosa Parks was and is an icon in the American, global as well as Women Movement for change in both human relations and social systems.

It has been affirmed, one person's views can become a majority if their truths are immutable and they remain steadfast in belief and action. Ms. Park's action on a bus in time of the emerging civil rights movement was not necessarily about belief or ideology.

AFRICAN NATIONALIST POETRY AND PROSE

African Nationalist Poetry and Prose Photo. Erik Monderson at the 50th Anniversary "March on Washington" August, 2013.

African Nationalist Poetry and Prose Photo. Rosa Parks in a very pensive mood.

FREDERICK MONDERSON

African Nationalist Poetry and Prose Photo. Rosa Parks receives a Citation of Honor.

The de jure or legal and de facto or standard practice in the American South especially was that Black people, people of African descent, sit or stand in the back of the bus. That meant whether or not there was a vacant seat in the front section it was reserved for

AFRICAN NATIONALIST POETRY AND PROSE

whites. In addition, if a white person boarded the bus, a black had to get up and relinquish that seat.

In Ms. Park's case, it was not ideology or protest. It was really necessity. She had worked all day, was dog tired and seeing an empty seat, sat down. Told to get up, she refused. The police were called. I don't really know if she had agreed to get up by that time. However, the die was cast, the egg fell to the ground and was now broken. She had broken the cardinal rule. That was the white folks view!

In the eyes of Black folks Rosa Parks was a hero, a symbol, an icon. She became the straw that broke the camel's back. The beast had been overburdened with the inhuman savagery slave trade and slavery's legacy; the resulting institution gave way to share-crop peonage, terrorism on part of white supremacy group such as the Ku Klux Klan, Knights of the white Camelia, and despite the Civil War's 13th, 14th, and 15th Amendments, concerted disfranchisement stripped the African of the 15th Amendments inherent right to participate in the political process. More than two million Black men had won the right to vote under the 15th Amendment and within two decades, this number was radically diminished to no more than ten thousand still eligible.

This onslaught against the Black man was reinforced by 19th Century terrorism through lynchings, tar-and-feather, denial of meaningful jobs, but encouraged through share-crop peonage. This saw the emergence of Jim Crow segregation, Separate but Equal which was in fact, separate but unequal participation in allocation of economic resources, viz., funds, books, facilities, teaching mechanisms, etc.

While Abe Lincoln issued the Emancipation Proclamation that freed the enslaved African in 1863, and as a result Blacks flocked to the "Radical" Republican Party. Amidst all the machinations and such creations as the "White Primary" and active "Jim Crow," "Grandfather Clause," by the end of Reconstruction which lasted from 1865-1877, the defeated South reasserted itself and sought to drive the freed Black back into the subservient position devoid of the protections of the Constitution. As the Republican Party ignored the plight of Blacks amidst lynchings, joblessness, poor or denial of education privileges, and more, Blacks flocked to the Democratic Party because FDR promised of a "New Deal" in response to the **Great Depression** of 1929.

Two things need to be considered across a broad stretch of time. First, spear-heading the mechanism of Black oppression was the harsh reality of lynching. A Black legal eagle identified and chronicled some 3875 instances of black lynchings in 9 southern states from 1870-1950. He proposed to set up a marker to identify such places of brutal murders to highlight this heritage. Naturally such an idea is not received since the location of such evens on the properties of today's prominent individuals ties them to such

AFRICAN NATIONALIST POETRY AND PROSE

atrocities. Second, amidst the unfolding and systematic oppression committed against Africa people the significance of joblessness was key.

As the world and nation edged towards World War II American industry geared for the impending calamity. However, Black were systematically denied jobs in such war industries. The seasoned activist A. Philip Randolph was first invited to the White House by President Roosevelt and he made a compelling case of Black unemployment among other social ills perpetuated against African people. The president listened intently and essentially said, "Mr. Randolph, your case was well made. Now go out there and make me do it!" Now, seeing no redress, Mr. Randolph threatened to "March on Washington!" In response, the president passed an Executive Action opening up the war industries to black workers. That threat to "March on Washington," finally culminated in the historic 1963 march in which Martin Luther King gave his famous "I have a Dream" speech. This speech was really about the plight of the poor, black and white, but reports centered on the idea of his "Dream" that Americans should be viewed, not by the color of their skin, but by the content of their character.

In *Black Protest* (1968: 391) Joanne Grant reported on Roy Wilkin, urging Congress not simply to support Congressman Celler's bill which, as executive Director of the *National Association for the*

FREDERICK MONDERSON

Advancement of Colored People (**NAACP**) in collaboration with the **Leadership Conference on Civil Rights** that asked for strengthening the bill in the following respects:

1. The total elimination of the poll tax as a restriction on voting in state and local elections as well as in federal elections.

2. The elimination in the bill that a prospective registrant must first go before the state official to attempt to register before going to the Federal register or examiner. The perspective registrant ought not to be put to the delays, the hardships, and the indignity of attempting to satisfy hostile state officials before he can come to the Federal register.

3. Extended coverage of the register or examiner provisions of the bill, so that persons who have been wrongfully denied the right to vote, regardless of their geographical location, will have the benefits of these provisions of the legislation.

4. Further and maximum protection of registrants and voters, both those who will be registered under the bill and those already registered, and prospective registrants, from all economic and political intimidation and coercion. In extending such protection, the Federal Government should use the full range of its powers, criminal, civil and economic, to protect the citizens from the beginning of registration process until his vote has been cast and

AFRICAN NATIONALIST POETRY AND PROSE

counted." These requirements were necessary, particularly in the South for though one may be able to vote in Presidential elections, local officials made it difficult for voters and registrants to vote in state and local elections. Such events were a backdrop in the age in which Rosa parks and so many others "existed."

Thus, Rosa Parks sitting down to stand up had helped galvanize a movement suffering under a long train of abuse. They first began to boycott the Montgomery, Alabama buses until legislators changed the status quo. However, the hard-won success of the bus boycott, spread to other social areas seeking redress which resulted in untold suffering on part of African people. The racist police sought to turn back the cascading avalanche of social protest through the use of dogs, water hoses and all forms of intimidation including bombings and other forms of murder, intimidation.

The sixties decade saw the bombing of church in Alabama in which four little girls then three civil rights workers were also killed. In response people like Stokely Carmichael (Kwame Ture) formed **SNCC** (Student Non-violent Coordinating Committee) and began a **Freedom Riders** campaigns of registering voters and providing systematic push-back against white aggression. Dr. King helped organize the "March" from "Selma to

FREDERICK MONDERSON

Montgomery," Alabama, in which they had to cross the Edmond Pettus Bridge. This was the big confrontation with police who used horses, water-hoses, night-sticks, riot police and much more. The marchers prevailed because many ethnic groups and religious denominations took a stand. The President sent in federal troops to protect the marchers; despite Governor Wallace insistence they will not meet Montgomery.

Besides the loss of four little girls' lives in the bombing, the civil right workers, the movement saw Medgar Evers being killed, then Dr. King and Malcom X as well as a systematic assault made on the Black Panthers who stood up to all forms including police brutality.

African Nationalist Poetry and Prose Photo. "The Message" is "**JUSTICE FOR ALL!**"

AFRICAN NATIONALIST POETRY AND PROSE

African Nationalist Poetry and Prose Photo.
HYE WON HYE – "Imperishability and Endurance."

FREDERICK MONDERSON

African Nationalist Poetry and Prose Photo. Zimbabwe. Sylvester Mubayi. "Exercising Man" – Made out of Springstone and with its highly polished finish, the fluid figure in "Exercising Man is bending and stretching."

AFRICAN NATIONALIST POETRY AND PROSE

"Racial oppression of black people in America has done what neither class oppression nor sexual oppression, with all their perniciousness, has ever done: destroyed an entire people and their culture." Eleanor Holmes Norton – For Sadie and Maude – *Sisterhood is Powerful* (Robin Morgan, Ed. 1970)

11. ARC OF THE MORAL UNIVERSE
By
Dr. Fred Monderson

"Being a Negro in America means trying to smile when you want to cry. It means trying to hold on to physical life amid psychological death. It means the pain of watching your children grow up with clouds of inferiority in their mental skies. It means having your legs cut off, and then being condemned for being a cripple. Martin Luther King – *Where do we go from Here - Chaos or Community* (1967)

Dr. Martin Luther King exhorted, "The arc of the moral universe is long, but it bends towards justice!" Even further, "The measure of a man is not where he stands in times of comfort and convenience, but where he stands is times of challenge and controversy."

FREDERICK MONDERSON

At his 2005 Inaugural, the Republican President George W. Bush decried the prevalence of racism in the country up to that date, one hundred and fifty years after the Emancipation Proclamation and subsequently the Civil War Amendments. Through "Jim Crow" (1865-1890), *Plessey v. Ferguson* (1896), *Brown v. Board of Education of Topeka, Kansas*, (1954), the **Civil Rights Act** (1964) and the **Voting Rights Act** (1965) in response to the **Civil Rights Movement** demonstrated positive advances in the American social and political order. The 1965 Voting Rights Act empowered African-Americans to gain political representation across the different states, culminating in the 2008 election of Barack Obama as the first African-American President. In response, the then Mayor of Newark, New Jersey, Cory Booker characterized Mr. Obama's election victory as ushering in a new post-racial America. Naturally, there was a difference of opinion on both sides of the issue, from Black and White perspectives.

Then along came Mr. Mitch McConnell (R. Kentucky), Minority Leader in the Democratic Controlled Senate of the United States Congress. First, Mr. McConnell made a publicly advertised statement, "I intend to make Barack Obama a one-term president."

This statement, Mr. Morgan Freeman, the Academy Award winning actor, on Piers Morgan's CNN program, characterized as "blatantly racist!" Mr.

AFRICAN NATIONALIST POETRY AND PROSE

McConnell's next ground-breaking and outrageous statement was, after an important round of negotiations with the president, where bright-eyed and bushy tailed, the smiling McConnell gave that now infamous "thumbs up" signal to like-minded cohorts on television who were probably in the treasonous gathering. Observers with penetrating vision saw this for what it was, a "signal to his handlers" that "I got that Nigger in the White House!" Some five years later in October 2013, *The New York Times* newspaper published a "big write-up" indicating in the run-up to the 2012 election, a group of influential Republicans and their backers met and strategized on how to deny Mr. Obama a second term. The article named individuals and the CEOs of some 20 Republican affiliated non-governmental organization, many of whom were trained or involved in training propaganda programs designed to propagandize falsity and generate opposition to Mr. Obama's **Affordable Care Act**. Many characterized the gathering as a treasonous conspiracy to subvert the legally elected representative of the United States Government.

Because Mr. Obama is African-American with the audacity to declare for the presidency, beat back his democratic challengers and be chosen to represent his party, a number of racial cross-currents began to emerge directed at Barack Obama. While Blacks accused him of not being black enough, Whites accused him of being "too black." As a result, whole

FREDERICK MONDERSON

flurry of activity mobilized to denounce Mr. Obama's quest. Republican propaganda helped spread false notions Mr. Obama would change the Constitution and this fueled right-wing militias to purchase and stock up on enormous armaments for the coming "race riots" which, up to this date, have yet to materialize.

African Nationalist Poetry and Prose Photo. "Blackness" in all its resplendent beauty.

AFRICAN NATIONALIST POETRY AND PROSE

African Nationalist Poetry and Prose Photo.
ANKH – "Egyptian Symbol of Life."

An unregistered plumber named "Joe the Plumber" accused Mr. Obama of promoting socialism and this garnered him enormous but short-lived fame. "I can see Russia from my front porch" "Lipstick on a pig" Sarah Palin accused Mr. Obama of "Palling around with terrorists." Questions of his patriotism, ability to effectively lead and lack of foreign policy experience proved enormous capital for the Anti-Obamaites. When Ted Nugent called president Obama "The Nigger in the White House," Sarah Palin was later seen hobnobbing with him in the Trump White House under George Washington photo-image. Talk about "Birds of a feather!" Still, as President, Mr. Obama forged ahead with an effective organizational strategy, a tremendous work ethic and an unfailing desire to be successful while not paying much attention to nay-Sayers. Yet, along plodded the "Birther" movement with its queen and king Trump on their "fools' errand" and while this embolden anti-Obama forces, it also gave birth to the "Tea Party" formation in a cauldron of hatred for the Black man. Through all this, Mitch McConnell's parallel quest remained in full stride. All the while, the Republican "Party of No's" obstructionist agenda blocked every legislative effort proposed by Mr. Obama that was designed to improve the condition and advance the cause of the American people. Meanwhile, Senator McConnell, having been issued his charge, set about plowing the path of opposition as part of the grand scheme we could come to learn of later. Today, the loud voice of "I intend to make Barack Obama a one term President" and "I looked the President in the eye and said, Mr. President you will not have a Supreme Court pick" is silent on the **SEVEN INVESTIGATIONS INTO HIS GOLDEN**

AFRICAN NATIONALIST POETRY AND PROSE

BOY PRESIDENT DONALD J. TRUMP!

Talk about "Be careful of what you pray for Mr. Speaker!"

Undaunted, President Obama continue to repair the faltering auto industry; lending money to banks and to bail out Wall Street; assessing the nation's crumbling infrastructure and providing for "shovel ready" jobs, despite the Republican controlled House of Representatives' refusal to pass his "Jobs Bill." Next Mr. Obama sought to overhaul the nation's economic and financial systems; and expressed concern about the environment, energy supplies and research and development of future resources. Nevertheless, Republicans turned up the heat on the President. As a result, a climate of racial hatred and disrespect pervaded against Mr. Obama. Surprisingly, as Republicans and their allies peppered Mr. Obama, un-mindful that Edmund Burke wrote, "The only thing necessary for evil to triumph is for good men to do or say nothing;" among the higher echelon of Republican leadership nothing was said or done against such mis-characterization. Nothing!

Despite their failure to achieve anything but block the President's every move and falsely characterize the man and his work, nefarious individuals continued to hood-winked the American people, and the Republicans made gains in the 2010 and 2014 mid-tern elections. Later they won both houses of

FREDERICK MONDERSON

Congress and the Presidency in 2016. Nonetheless, and despite the vituperative Republican mischief, President Obama continued his efforts to scale down the wars in Iraq and Afghanistan, contend with Somali pirates and pursuit of Osama Bin Laden and his Al Qaeda affiliates. As this unfolded, Obama continued his responsibilities as Chief Executive and Commander-in-Chief. Meanwhile the Republicans convened, in a tunnel vision focus on how their new Congressional majority will hamstrung Mr. Obama in the incoming Congress. Throughout it all, as Mr. Obama played it cool, in response to unfolding events, the Grand Jury decision happened more than once and this galvanized protests. Eric Garner, Michael Brown, Gurley, and today Stephon Clark. All followed Trayvon Martin, Black men shot down in the prime of their lives. These deaths matched the spate of killings of Black men across the nation. Many were killed by cops, exonerated at trial; many were killed senselessly in gang related violence. Strang and rather alarming, after the death of Stephon Clark, the Civil Rights Attorney Benjamin Crump, in calling attention to "Cop Killings," noted the alarming figure of 73 men killed by police since 2015 and 70 of them were Black! The times saw the birth of Colin Caperton's "take a knee" in protest of police killing of unarmed Black men! Many interpreted this as "disrespect for the flag" in not standing when the anthem was being played at football games. Though the Supreme Court has upheld Americans' right to burn the American flag, sometimes in contentions demonstrations, many still see the silent "Take a

AFRICAN NATIONALIST POETRY AND PROSE

Knee" as more sinister than the senseless violence that ends a sacred American life.

Nonetheless, in wake of such senseless and wrong killings, the Arc of the Moral Universe swung back when people of goodwill, young and old, across all ethnic spectrums took, to the streets in city after city. The "Chickens had come home!" Republicans were caught off-guard. They said nothing and had nothing to say as the people staged numerous "Die-Ins" across the various cities and states. Activists protested, demonstrated and chanted "Justice for Michael Brown," "I am Michael Brown" and "Hands-Up, Don't Shoot!" In New York and as far away as California protesters chanted Eric Garner's last words, "I Can't breathe!" and "Justice for Eric Garner!" as well as "Black Lives Matter!" Prominent Athletes in the NFL and NBA joined the fray with "Hands Raised" in a "Hands Up, Don't Shoot" gesture. One year after Garner's death, State Assemblyman Nick Perry began his presentation in a New York protest, "I can't breathe' eleven times. To this day, his killer Panatela

Again, Republicans, caught bent over with their pants below the knee and the people at their rear, were in a quandary. The hatred and disrespect they have sowed was now being called into question by young people who want an America with justice for all.

FREDERICK MONDERSON

African Nationalist Poetry and Prose Photo. The Message is clear, "We Out." So said Harriet Tubman.

African Nationalist Poetry and Prose Photo. Beautiful ladies at **CEMOTAP's** Anniversary Celebration.

AFRICAN NATIONALIST POETRY AND PROSE

African Nationalist Poetry and Prose Photo. Ms. Hill **CEMOTAP's** Secretary.

"We Can never be satisfied as long as a Negro in Mississippi cannot vote and a Negro in New York believes he has nothing for which to vote.... We will not be satisfied until justice rolls down like waters and righteous like a mighty stream." Martin Luther King, Jr., August 28, 1963. Speech at civil rights march in Washington, D.C., *The New York Times* (August 29, 1963)

12. POEM TO AMON-RA

O mighty Amon, the Greatest of the Black African deities, ithyphallic, you were from primeval times, Lord of Gods.
Your creativity radiated over an age, father of the gods, when worshippers praised your hidden nature.

FREDERICK MONDERSON

Conquering peoples and places, they brought light and civility to the world, in your immortal name, multitudinous, more numerous, not known. The vanquished contributed wealth filling your treasury and your subjects, victorious in their imperial exploits, erected mansions in glory and praise of your being, Chief of the Great Ennead of the Gods, Self-Begotten, Lord of Heaven, Lord of Earth.

O Dweller in Anu, the Gods ascribe praise to you, maker of things celestial and things terrestrial, for you illuminate Egypt, President of the Apts.

Beautiful child of Love, from relative obscurity you emerged in the Middle Kingdom and sat on your Sacred Mound of Creation.

That first time, seeking to complete the task of previous gods fallen short, you Created Brilliant Rays, Thunder in Heaven.

Black African rulers of that age imbibed in your inspiration, Lord of the Two Lands.

Mighty in Power, Lord of Awe-inspiring terror, they similarly manifested resolute courage, wisdom, intellect, and creative prowess.

They therefore gained success as Warrior Pharaohs, with mighty souls, all in your name, Fashioner of the Beauty of Kings, Priests and Artisans, O Lord of the Throne of Egypt.

All the Gods are three, Amen, Ra and Ptah and none like thee. Amen is his hidden name; Ra is his face, Ptah his body.

AFRICAN NATIONALIST POETRY AND PROSE

Power made by Ptah, Bull of Heliopolis, kings' architects shaped a society whose blueprint you encouraged in manifold attributes.
Lord of Scepter and Ankh, Frog, and Uraeus, Couchant Lion, your symbols include Beautiful Tiaras, Lofty Plumes, and Ureret, War, Nemes and Atef Crowns.
The prosperity you endowed your adherents generated artistic, scientific and linguistic creations, Lord of the Apts.
These first beneficiaries of your generosity toward mankind, erected temples as chapels simply to glorify your great name, Amon Lord of Thebes, Lord of the Two Lands, Lord of Might, Lord of Food, Bull of Offerings, Kamutef at the head of his Fields.
Lord of Victuals, Bull of Provisions, the gods beg their sustenance from you, Lord of Fields, banks and plots of ground.

Lord of Truth, Father of the Gods, Maker of Men, Creator of all animals, Black African kings, men of vision, fortitude and tenacity, benefited from an earlier age of African creativity. They synthesized, experimented and with vision and bellicosity bequeathed a creative era where craftsmen, philosophers, priests and kings, were motivated to extol your name to greater heights.
Lord of Radiant Light, you Exist into Eternity as Lord of Heaven, Lord of Earth, Lord of the Gods, Lord of

FREDERICK MONDERSON

the High Lands and Mountains, Lord of the Joy of Heart, Mighty One of Crowns.
Your Loveliness is in the Southern Sky and Your Graciousness is in the Northern Sky.
Your name is strong; your will is heavy.
Mountains of ore cannot withstand your might, for you set in order the kingdom of eternity unto eternity.

Lord of eternity, creator of everlastingness, you arise in the eastern horizon and set in the western horizon. Born early every day, you overthrew your enemies, steering oar, pilot who knows the water, Lord of the ship of the morning and ship of the evening, master of two stems. Beautiful form fashioned by Ptah, Ox with strong arm who loves strength; you are first in Upper Egypt, Lord of the Land of the Matoi and Prince of Punt.
Lord of Perception who speaks with authority, Lord of the Gods whose shrine is hidden, you are Lord of the Double Crown, Great Hawk who makes festive the body, fair body that makes festive the breast.

Beneficent God, you presided over a world as King of Kings.
Lord of the Thrones of the Two Lands, Bull of your Mother, New Kingdom monarchs competed trying to out-do predecessors praising Amon, Greater than Great of the Primordial Deities, who continues to bless his champions.
Chief of Egypt, territorial conquests, ensuing wealth, architectural constructions, and religious and

AFRICAN NATIONALIST POETRY AND PROSE

philosophical sonnets, extolled the name of Amon Presider of Karnak, who dwells in the Most Select of Places, in Power and Glory, Invisible and Creative.
As Chief of all the Gods, you fashion the deities, One in his actions as with the Gods.
Stablisher of all things, Lord of things that are, you Create all Life, Lord of the Sektet Boat and of the Antet Boat.

First Born Son of the Earth, Chief of Mankind, your Sanctuary at Karnak is a splendid piece of divinely inspired architecture.
Master of the Double Crown, you receive the Ames Scepter.
Lord of the Makes Scepter and whip, your precinct, befits the Eternal Spirits of the Theban Triad, Amon, Mut, Khonsu, whose reigns encompassed millennia.
Priests manifested political and theological power from this sacred abode, constructed in stone while similar 'Mansions of Millions of Years' profess Amon's august name, as Source of all Light in Heaven.
Lord of Karnak, King of the South and North, Lord of Things Which Exist, Stablisher of All Creation, You Last Forever, equips all lands, fashioner of all that exists, Just One, Lord of Thebes.

Beautiful boy whom the gods praise, maker of men and stars who illuminates the two lands, you are great of strength, Lord of Might, Chief who made the two lands, the Gods rejoice in your beauty, Amen-Ra, venerated in Karnak.

Lord of the Deeds Case who holds the flail, you are the Heliopolitan, first of his Ennead, who lives daily on truth.

The gods love to gaze at you when the Double Crown rests upon your brow, hawk in the midst of the horizon; you are beloved in the Southern Sky, and pleasant in the Northern Sky, possessor of praise, the Sun of Heaven.

Lord of Things that are, acting as Judge, Vizier of the Poor Who Takes No Bribes, your intellectual majesty enlightened the world in knowledge of arts and medicine.

Your inspiration pioneered astronomy, quarrying, navigation, stone-transportation, agriculture, mathematics, and all gifts of the African mind. Generations of black men and women worship and praise you mighty Amon, King of the Gods, First Born, and Resting upon Ma'at. Amenmeses, Sesostris, then Ahmose, Amenhotep, Thutmose, Hatshepsut, Seti, Rameses, Merenptah and Piankhy, Shabaka, Shabataka, Taharka, were greatest adherents, physical father of these kings, Power of the Gods.

Amen-Ra the Justified, you give your hands to those you love and assign those you hate to fire.

The Gods love to behold you and they rejoice in your beautiful acts. These divinities acclaim you the Great House and Crown you with Crowns in the House of Fire.

AFRICAN NATIONALIST POETRY AND PROSE

Homage to you, Dweller in Peace for you are Successor to Ra.

Fashioner of Kings and Queens, sole king among the gods, your collective wisdom schooled the Greeks and Romans, the newest converts.

They immersed in your wonderful cultural heritage, praising you with equal zeal and vigor.

Chief of all the Beings of the Underworld, Lord of the Nubians, Governor of Punt, King of Heaven, Amon the great African God, we beseech you, Lord of Eternity, today continue to make enlightening the Black culture of Kemet/Egypt, land of the ancestors.

Pour forth your salvation and ingenuity to inspire our people even more as they meet challenges in a new Millennium.

African Nationalist Poetry and Prose Photo. The message is clear: "Stop the Prison Pipeline" "End Poverty."

FREDERICK MONDERSON

African Nationalist Poetry and Prose Photo. Luis, Erik and Erismelle at the African International Arts Festival, 2017.

African Nationalist Poetry and Prose Photo. Tribute to the Ancestors – Images, 2019.

AFRICAN NATIONALIST POETRY AND PROSE

African Nationalist Poetry and Prose Photo. Mama Parsela calls the "Drummers to Order" and Chendo and his assistant responds.

"I have a dream that one day on the red hills of Georgia the sons of former slaves and sons of former slaveowners will be able to sit down together at the table of brotherhood… I have a dread that my four little children will one day live in a nation where they will not be judged by the color of their skin but the content of their character." Martin Luther King, Jr. August 28, 1963. Speech civil rights march in Washington, D.C. New York Times August 29, 1963.

13. SPIRITUALITY IN ANCIENT EGYPTIAN TEMPLES
BY
DR. FRED MONDERSON

The well-known elder and master teacher Dr. Yosef ben-Jochannan has taught this writer and scholar

FREDERICK MONDERSON

principally three things, listed as follows: "Monderson, there are fifty countries in Africa [at the time], choose one and specialize in it. Become a specialist not a generalist;" and though my first Masters' Degree from Hunter College of CUNY was as an African Historian; I chose to specialize in Egyptian studies.

After buying and reading his books in first edition in the 1970s, when I first traveled with Dr. Ben in the 1980s, he issued his dictum, "Now that you have come to Egypt, seen what you have seen and secured the knowledge, what are you going to do with it?"

Third and most important, when doing research on Egypt and Africa "Get the oldest material you can find and work from there!"

Now, in an interesting article entitled "Egyptian Mummy" among Antiquarian and Philosophical Studies in *The Gentleman's Magazine* of October 1820, pp. 349-350, in describing a mummy donated by Mr. Joshua Heywood to the Hunterian Museum at Glasgow, the writer states: "The body, shrouded in from fifty to sixty folds of coarse pale brick-red colored linen, is deposited in a strong wooden coffin, fashioned so as to bear a rude resemblance to the human shape. At the upper extremity is carved a face, the features of which (as in the case with all Egyptian sculpture) are very much of the Negro cast." We know the Egyptians loved the color red because they associated it with the sun, a solar and special phenomenon. They considered themselves special!

AFRICAN NATIONALIST POETRY AND PROSE

Still, it seems this particular mummy was colored or stained with red coloring so the linen could not be "brick-red colored" from rubbing off the red-Egyptian color." Even Dr. Ben has often said, "The Egyptians painted themselves red with the Henna plant. Even young brides were painted red with Henna." Going back to the most ancient African "Bushman Art" and even art among the "Tassili Frescoes," predominant red was the favorite color, again like gold, considered to be of a divine nature!

The article continued, "Though the features were very much collapsed, the face was nowhere divested of skin. The skin itself was of a chestnut-brown color. The brow was well shaped, though, if any way defective, narrow; and to some it may be interesting to learn, the organ of music was prominent. The nose, though slightly compressed, retained enough of its original shape to be recognized as Roman." Even further, the gentleman wrote, "One circumstance must have struck all who had an opportunity of seeing the above interesting examination; namely, the dissimilarity of the features to what we are taught to believe were those of the inhabitants of Egypt [The present writer's emphasis], at the remote period at which the custom of embalming existed in that country. A moment's reflection will suffice to convince us that this circumstance can in no way throw discredit on the antiquity of the genuine character of the mummy."

FREDERICK MONDERSON

The writer goes on to say, "Mr. Millar, portrait painter in Glasgow, is at present finishing a likeness in oil of the face and surrounding parts. As they appeared immediately after they were exposed; and was completely successful in the accuracy of the likeness before the exposure to the air had converted the face from a brown to a sable hue, which it did in the short period of three hours."

The above is quoted because, in contrast, John David Wortham in The Genesis of British Egyptology: 1549-1906 (University of Oklahoma Press, Norman, Oklahoma, 1971: 93) has written: "Great progress was made during the nineteenth century in the study of Egyptian mummification. Augustus Bozzi Granville, a physician and a student of Coptic, undertook the earliest nineteenth-century dissection of a mummy at his London home in 1825. From his detailed dissection he correctly concluded that the ancient Egyptians were Caucasians. He also succeeded in clearing up many erroneous ideas about the embalming process. Among other things, he proved the correctness of Herodotus' assertion that the ancient Egyptians had, when preparing a cadaver for burial, extracted the pituitary through the nostrils." We can confidently assume Herodotus never visited a mummy factory but was told this by priests, which Wortham believes. However, Herodotus' description that "The Colchians, Egyptians and Ethiopians have broad noses, thick lips and are burnt of skin" was an observed fact that this and other writers dismiss. Now, one can ask the reader "you do the math!" If Egyptians as late as the

AFRICAN NATIONALIST POETRY AND PROSE

time of the Romans, after 30 B.C., could have "brown skin," particularly after admixture with Persians, Assyrians, Greeks and Romans themselves, since these soldiers do not carry their women when on expedition but mix with the local females, how then can we still believe they were Caucasians with white skins!" This is why, as Dr. John Henrik Clarke has said, "Europe's claim to Egypt is not based on logic" and "African history must be written by African people!"

Now, the purpose of this essay. The Egyptian temple has been a sacred place and a bastion of spirituality from its inception at the "first occasion" when the "god arose" from the waters of chaos and his aura created the protective space the temple came to represent. Of this act, Gaston Maspero has written, "the temple is molded on the principle of the Egyptian conception of the universe" and as such, it's constructed and regulated on the same principles as the heavens. The only difference, the temple is in close proximity to humans, as opposed to the distant realm, and the human function and responsibility is to guard the portals and administer to the resident deity in hopes he or she would bring good fortune to the domain and society in general. However, while the Egyptian temple was unlike any other religious structure, whether Jewish Temple, Christian Cathedral or Muslim Mosque, because people never came there to worship; nevertheless, the creation,

FREDERICK MONDERSON

guarding and maintaining of these sacred spaces were very similar to that of the Egyptian temple.

African Nationalist Poetry and Prose Photo. Dr. Fred Monderson and son Erik flank Dr. Len Jeffries at **Medgar Evers' Black Writers Conference** 2017.

African Nationalist Poetry and Prose Photo. "The Boys," "Malcolm X Warriors," at **CEMOTAP** Celebration, sandwiching an esteemed **Elder**.

AFRICAN NATIONALIST POETRY AND PROSE

African Nationalist Poetry and Prose Photo. Joe Mutasa. Zimbabwe. "Protected family." – For Mutasa, family relationships and their role in transforming Shona are the focus of this narrative style."

FREDERICK MONDERSON

In respect to this experience, Byron E. Shafer in *Temples of Ancient Egypt* (1998: 2) has supplied an interesting description of cosmological forces at work when he says: "Temples and rituals were loci for the creative interplay of sacred space and sacred time. Sacred space is 'a place of clarification (a focusing lens) where men and gods are held to be transparent to one another' and 'a point of communication,' the 'paradoxical point of passage from one mode of being to another.' In sacred space one is oriented to the cosmos and immersed in primordial order; there one experiences truth and renews life. Over time, such space appears unchanged and unchanging, 'stable enough to endure without growing old or losing any of its parts.'"

Even further, Shafer (1998: 2) continued: "What has been said of sacred place can, for the most part, be said of sacred time as well. It is a moment, or season, or cycle of such clarification and communication, orientation and immersion, experience and renewal. Time, however, is not so stable a dimension of order as space. Egyptians experienced time as a spiral of patterned repetitions, a coil of countless rebirths. The purest moment of sacred time was the first, the moment of creation, when the existent and its order emerged from the nonexistent and its aspect of disorder. Subsequently, time, as a component of order, proved vulnerable to chaos. So, for example, the intervals between sunrise and sunset came to change from day to day and season to season, and the beginning of each new 365-day year came to rotate

AFRICAN NATIONALIST POETRY AND PROSE

slowly backward relative to the seasons and the helical rising of the star Sirius. Because of order's ongoing vulnerability to chaos, Egyptians needed to conceive of creation not as a single past event but as a series of 'first times,' of sacred regenerative moments recurring regularly within the sacred space of temples through the media of rituals and architecture." Thus, according to Egyptian beliefs and because evil and demonic persons and forces existed, to combat such required priests be kept busy protecting their sacred space in unending ritual and prayer so the god's safety can be assured and he maintain harmony or Ma'at in the universe.

All this notwithstanding, while there is a religious, theosophical or spiritual aspect to the temple, this survivability equally depended on an economic incentive that nevertheless supported the sustainability of the sacred space. While early theorists have postulated the view, priests were the earliest architects, in their other worldly connection with the divine who instructed them psychically as to the dimensions and arrangement of the principal features of the sacred space; temples were generally gifts of monarchs who actually built them. Having done so, they next created economic endowments to sustain their creation as an obligation to their father, being sons of the god in the divine lineage with its attendant obligations, responsibilities and benefits. However, having been endowed with the structure and "seed money," the caretakers of the temple sought to economically increase their largess by initiating a number of strategies such as the manufacture of crafts and creation of building and decorative skills that beautified their residence but also became trade commodities. Agricultural produce was grown to feed residents and surplus food exported in trade, to which crafts were added. Gardens grew flowers that were an essential part of the daily ritual of lustration of the god. All this involved an untold number of individuals working in harmony depending on the size of the temple and the prominence of the god relative to the age in which he was worshipped.

In addition, the temples became schools that trained members of the government bureaucracy, produced medical and dental professionals, catered to mortuary needs of high and low and became literary help-centers for the majority of the population who were illiterate and needed documents such as letters, contracts, wills, etc. Even more important, as the god and priests conspired to instill an imperialist mentality in vigorous warrior pharaohs, who went forth to conquer, significant portions of their captured spoils were in turn donated to the temple as endowments for the deity who had brought good fortune to these kings.

This increased wealth enabled the god's domain to be significantly beautified and expanded; so much so, the Middle Kingdom and New Kingdom capital temple at Karnak, home of the Empire God Amun, experienced 2000 years of "vegetative growth" as

AFRICAN NATIONALIST POETRY AND PROSE

untold numbers of pharaohs vied with each other to reward the good fortune the god granted them. In all this, as a result of their ever-expanding roles, the priests who formed a confederated body called the Priesthood, came to wield significant power and influence, becoming, in their own right, king makers and king breakers. They became so powerful by the Late Period priests represented themselves in art on a footing with the pharaoh. In all such developing dynamics, weak pharaohs trembled at the prospect of the priests' material power and their presumed spiritual power gained through a divine connection with the god, which the king himself lacked.

While the strong kings manipulated the priests through endowments, buildings and the threat of their military prowess, their weak counterparts stood in awe of the priests because, though they claimed to be gods on earth, the priests as "true god intermediaries" knew their weaknesses while they themselves were unsure how much the priests knew or how much power and influence these "men of the cloth" could wield with the god. This growing power of the Priesthood materialized and by the 22nd Dynasty priests challenged the established order and declared themselves kings beginning with the High Priest Herihor. Such an action began a long journey of the ultimate demise of Egyptian culture along with its inherent power and divine inspiration gained in adherence to the principles of religious practice. Nevertheless, though the nation declined in its material and military power, its religious beliefs and spirituality remained a potent force even though conquerors came, destroyed much and even tried to inculcate and emulate what Egyptians had been doing for the three thousand years of pharaonic rule. Still, thousands of years later, the power and force of this spirituality is still evident when one visits the temple. That is, providing one's mind and body is in the right place to experience this spiritual phenomenon.

The architecture created in the sacred space is a fascinating subject that challenges the imagination, excites the intellect and titillates the art appreciation sensitivities. The well-known Dr. Yosef ben-Jochannan has always emphasized the principal architectural features of the temple and instructed his students to visit, for example, the Hypostyle Hall at Karnak five or six times so as to comprehend what the magnificent hall stands for, as a "forest at creation." Equally too, Mann in his profound work *Sacred Architecture* (1993: 14) has supplied a very penetrating view in describing several ways in which the symbolic or the spiritual is expressed through sacred architecture manifesting in sacred space. These, he lists as: "First, sacred architecture reflects the structure of the cosmos. Before there were buildings, humanity worshipped the stars and planets, the four elements, the earth, and its animals and plants, as gods. In our progression from caves to modern buildings, the symbolism of this early integration with the cosmos has been central, and still activates the deepest essence within us, the core of our psyche. Initially, sacred monuments were

AFRICAN NATIONALIST POETRY AND PROSE

associated with a particular god, goddess, or the natural or supernatural powers they represented. They were aligned by or with the stars of planets in the sky, which represented the god or goddess. They were also geographically oriented and located in places significant to the gods. Some monuments were used by priests or priestesses as observatories to measure the movements of the planets or heavenly bodies they worshipped, while others were sited in accordance with planetary motions. Most megalithic monuments echoed some or all of these functions in their siting, design and function."

"Second, sacred monuments were organized using primary geometric shapes and proportions, described by number symbolism. Mathematical mysticism or sacred geometry is a profound part of sacred architecture, and it's often mentioned in relation to the Egyptians and Pythagoreans. Pythagoras created a humanistic philosophy which utilized mathematical harmony and proportion as primary tools in daily life, including art, architecture, music, morality and history. He believed that the order inherent in numbers, a number symbolism, creates specific effects on the observer, both psychologically and spiritually. The discovery of the innate meaning of numbers is therefore a primary creative legacy of sacred architecture. The exploration of the numbers and proportions of the sacred brings a higher understanding to architecture."

FREDERICK MONDERSON

"Third, the sacred lives in buildings or monuments in which the structure and decoration follow clear and basic patterns derived from the ancient conception of the four elements, earth, water, air, and fire, the forms of nature and from living energies and the geometries derived from them. Proportion systems amplifying natural rhythms and patterns bring a natural and organic energy and spirituality to sacred architecture – the building contains an elemental as well as a human quality evoking the spiritual."

As a result, Mann (1993: 106-07) concludes: "The creation of sacred buildings echoes the creation of the universe, and both seek to follow similar mathematical laws. Therefore, the Golden Section (phi) is found to govern the growth of plants and animals and is also the primary proportion found in sacred buildings and monuments. In their use of numbers as a symbolic language, the Egyptians predate and influence Pythagoras and Plato. The Egyptians communicated symbolic astrological and astronomical concepts beyond the actual form of the buildings. Similarly, their hieroglyphic language used symbols instead of mere signs. A sign has a limited meaning, while a symbol evokes correspondences and widens understanding. The Egyptians used their mythology to further understanding because it was more than simple history. Their gods came from the stars, beginning wisdom, understanding and power. Their myths were cosmic myths, describing planetary movements, and brought the mathematic reality of the stars to humanity."

AFRICAN NATIONALIST POETRY AND PROSE

Justly, let us not forget the layout of the temple is significant and, in many ways, mirrors the design of the home of a noble or king. When the king visited the temple for a festival, to dedicate some new part of the temple, participate in temple ritual or offer some tribute, more important to be crowned, there is a particular protocol he participates in. The geography of the landscape and the Nile River played a significant role in not only in the architecture but every aspect of the society whether science, art, philosophy, trade, craftsmanship, religion, theosophy or economics. As such, it was also the principal highway of travel and on a visit to the temple the king arrived by boat at a pier. The temple generally was approached through a canal and he then entered an Avenue of Sphinxes that brought him to the First Pylon entrance. Here he was introduced to the three principal parts of the temple. Just as the private home is considered to have three principal parts, the temple also does. The roadway brings the visitor to the home where a fence and walkway introduces him to the entrance door. This is comparable to the Egyptian Pylon entrance into the Great Court often decorated with colonnades, altars, statues, and even shrines. The second part of the home is the living room where guests are entertained that sometimes even doubles as a dining room. Beyond the Great Court, the Hypostyle Hall is described as a forest as at creation where a number of ceremonies are performed and only certain individuals are allowed there. The third part of the home is the bedroom area where no visitors are allowed and only the master and his family are permitted. Behind the Hypostyle Hall lies the "Holy of Holies" where the god resides and only the High Priest or King and their entourage for the ritual are permitted in this most sacred location. In the room where the god dwells in complete darkness, a door shuts him off from all external activities and forces. When the King of High Priest visits the god, after their encounter, the door is locked until the next visit whether to bathe, feed or praise the deity. Therefore, while the Open Court is filled with sunshine, the "Holy of Holies" is in complete darkness; and it is interesting, from front to rear, whether through pylons or building walls, the light penetrating back towards the "Holy of Holies," particularly in an open temple like Karnak, is regulated and become less and less at day's end. At the beginning of the day, however, the rising sun is encouraged to bathe the god's image to invigorate its solar force. Some temples have a small shrine, on the roof at Dendera, for example, where the god is taken for the solar encounter. Ancillary to this spot were adjacent rooms that housed liquid and solid offerings, a library for the temple ritual, vestments of the god and the High Priest and such things as incense and other utilities used in the ritual. Other gods associated with the temple are also housed nearby.

Nonetheless, an important feature of the temple layout is as one ascends into the deep recesses, the floor rises and the roof lowers. This allows the "Holy of Holies" to rest on the highest point in the sacred

AFRICAN NATIONALIST POETRY AND PROSE

space mirroring the rise of the god from the waters of chaos at creation. A Sacred Lake is also an essential part of the temple where priests wash themselves, sometimes three times or more per day, before administering to the god. These ancient Africans lived the notion, "Cleanliness is next to godliness." On certain festival or feast days, the Ark or boats of the gods are allowed to sail on the Sacred Lake. Naturally, there are residences nearby within the enclosure for the god's servants to be housed. A nearby garden provided for flowers that adorned the sanctuary and other pivotal places in the temple. Interesting, too while incense with its spiritual and esoteric potentialities, was burned in the temple ritual as part of worshipping the god, banishing evil, it was never burned on an altar. An incense burner was generally placed in a nearby corner and once lit, the incense was placed within. Many illustrations depict the pharaoh about to incense the god but he generally holds the incenser in his hand.

So here we are! The temple meant many things to the ancient Egyptian but we need a different way of seeking to understand what they did in the time which they lived. Remember, everything they did was original because they had not one to imitate. They were writing on their own Tabula Rasa or clean slate.

FREDERICK MONDERSON

African Nationalist Poetry and Prose Photo. Sign indicating the "Ancestral Shrine" at the International African Arts Festival.

African Nationalist Poetry and Prose Photo. The Great Educator, Mary McLeod Bethune Place.

"The true worth of a race must be measured by the character of its womanhood." Mary McLeod Bethune. Address to **Chicago Women's Federation** (June 13, 1933) quoted in *Black Women in White America*. 1972.

AFRICAN NATIONALIST POETRY AND PROSE

14. POEM TO RA - THE SUN GOD

O Ra, King of the Gods, you enjoyed a prominence matched by few divinities. You emerged at Heliopolis, and once absorbed, you extended your significance throughout dynastic times. Father of the Gods whose souls are exalted in the hidden place, your symbols are the Disk of the Sun, encircled by the serpent Khut, as well as Ankh, with scepter and tail from your waist. Self-begotten and Self-born creative vigor, Power of Powers with two uraei, you are a doubly hidden and secret god. Lord of Eternity, Sovereign of the Gods, you exist forever, Lord of Souls. You possess **14 Kas or life force**, as strength, might, prosperity, food, veneration, eternity, radiance, glory, fame, magic, authority, sight, and hearing and perception, Lord of Heliopolis, Supreme Power.

Sekhem, begetter of his gods, from Heliopolis, your priests influenced political developments in the Old Kingdom when Pyramid builders incorporated your name into theirs, becoming Son of the Sun, hence the title Son of Ra. These kings-built sun temples with names as 'Favorite Place of Ra' and 'Satisfaction of Ra' all in Praise of you Lord of Rays. Self-Created, King of Heaven, Great Duration of Life, Lord who advances, you are the Soul that do good to the body. Governor of his Eye, Lord of Generation, invisible and secret, you are Governor of the Tuat, Double

FREDERICK MONDERSON

Obelisk God, Lord of the Eastern Bend, and Supporter of the Heavens who dwells in Darkness. Born as the all-surrounding universe, you send forth the plants in their season, Eternal Essence.

Maker of the Gods, Governor of your circle, Aged One of Forms, Memphis received endowments in the Middle Kingdom in Praise of thee, King of the World. The Priesthood of local gods linked their deity to the Sun God's name Ra, Mighty in Majesty, Vivifier of Bodies. The Theban triumph merged Amon with Ra assuming all of the ancient god's attributes as Maker of Heaven where you are firmly established. God One from the beginning of time, Mighty One of myriad forms and aspects, Creator of Laws Unchangeable and Unalterable, Lord of Truth your shrine is hidden. You are the Soul, which give names to his limbs, Body of Khepera, God of Souls who is in the Obelisk. You are Master of the Spheres who cause the Principles to arise.

Chief of the Earth, Lord of the Gods, Judge of Words, and the glory of Ra manifested in Amon at the Temple of Karnak. During the New Kingdom, Thebes gloried in the imperial age, and you were Opener of Roads in the Hidden Place, who confers his crown on Pharaoh. The Ruler of all the Gods, more strong of heart than all those who are in your following, you are maker of gods and men, Creator of Heaven, Earth and the Underworld. Divine Man-Child, Heir of Eternity, you are Chief of the Gods, Supreme in their Districts, being Crowned King of the Gods, Ram, Mightiest of Created Things. You

AFRICAN NATIONALIST POETRY AND PROSE

Provide the Breath out of your Throat for the Nostrils of Mankind, Fashioner of Himself, and Tonen who produces his members, Supremely Great One.

Provider of the Sovereign Chiefs, Governor of the Holy Circle, re as Amon brought victory and fame to those who followed his teachings and praised his name, as Crowner of Pharaoh. Proclaimed King of Earth, Prince of the Tuat, Governor of the Regions of Aukert, Souls in their Circles ascribe your Praises. Beautiful Being, Rays of Turquoise Light, you are Personification of Right, Truth and Goodness, O Mighty One of Journeys, Lord of the Gods, light of the lock of hair. Your Emblems secure entrance of the Dead Man into the Kingdom of Osiris. Chief of the Great Cycle of the Gods, your principles have become your manifestation. Chief of the Powers inhabiting the holy sphere, you raise your soul, hide your body, shine and see your mysteries.

Creator of Hidden Things, Lord of Heaven, Lord of Earth, for untold ages men praise the Exalted of Souls. The Maker of Eternity, Ra you sail a Boat of Millions of Years. In all your glory, you emerge in a Morning Boat Matet, becoming strong at Midday. The day's work done, and weak, you ride the Evening Boat Semktet. Confronting your mortal enemy Apep, fishes Abtu and Ant swim before the Boat of Ra with its defenders at the ready. United in Numbers, Destroyer of Darkness, Night, Wickedness and Evil, on the dawn of a new day, there are

FREDERICK MONDERSON

Acclamations of your Rising in the Horizon of Heaven, Only One. Soul that speaks, rests, creates the developed hidden intellects, you shine in your sphere and hide what it contains, moving luminary.

Ra, Lord of Truth, Lord of the Horizon, Horus of the East, Lord of Fetters of your enemy, protector of hidden spirits, you conquer the fiends of the underworld. Souls of the East follow and Souls of the West praise you, while you get Support of the Circle of Amenta. God of Life, King of Right and Truth, you are the World Soul that rested on his High Place. The Soul who moves onward, Opener of the roads in the Hidden Place, One Alone with many hands, Ra, you are the Great God who lifted up his two eyes. You address your eye and speak to your head, the spirit that walks, that destroys its enemies, that sends pain to the rebels, you impart the breath of life to the souls that are in their place, Brilliant One who shines in the Waters of the Inundation.

Hidden Face, Glorious Creator of Eternity, you make beings come into existence in your creations in the Tuat. You rise like unto Gold, Great Light Shining in the Heavens illuminating darkness. Oldest One, Great One, you are Self-begotten, Self-created and Self-produced, the Soul Who Departs at his Appointed Time. You existed forever and would exist for Eternity, Illuminer of Light into his Circle. Source of Life and Light, Glorious by reason of thy Splendors, you are Joy of Heart within your Splendor. Mighty One of Victories, Ra, how wonderful was your manifestation among early

AFRICAN NATIONALIST POETRY AND PROSE

Africans, initiating laudable moral, spiritual and intellectual standards of creative genius, Mighty one whose body is so large it hides its shape, Double Luminary.

Generator of Bodies, True Creative Power of Divine attributes, Sender of Light into his Circle, Ra you rise in the Horizon, and are Beautiful. So too, Rat, Mistress of the Gods, your female counterpart, Lady of Heaven, Mistress of Heliopolis. Hathor and Isis are also your companions. Mightier than the Gods, Glorious Being, Lord of Love, Double Sphinx god, you are Ruler of Everlastingness. God of Motion, God of Light, Lord of Might, you send destruction, fire into the place of destruction and destroy your enemies, Light that is in the Infernal Regions. Protector of hidden spirits, the Souls that Mourns, the God that Cries, you are the Soul One who avenges his children and who calls his gods to life when he arrives in the hidden sphere.

Aged one of the Pupil of the Utchait, Ra, Lord of the hidden circles, creative force who gathers together all seed, you are manifold in your holy house. Great One, who rules what is in him, you send forth the stars and make the night light, in the sphere of hidden essences. Master of the Light, Only One who names the earth by his intelligence, the vessel of heaven, Powerful, Ra in his disk with Brilliant Rays, Lord of Wisdom your precepts are wise. Lord of Mercy, at whose coming men live, you make strong your

FREDERICK MONDERSON

double with Divine Food. Creator of Hidden Things and Generator of Bodies, Enlightener of the Earth, Lord of the Gods who lights the bodies on the horizon, Africans need your continued illumination and Blessings now more than ever.

African Nationalist Poetry and Prose Photo. **NUBIAN FATHERHOOD** depicts Malcolm X and Mohammed Ali and their families.

"I wake up in the morning
Just befo' the break of day.
I was bitter, blue and black; Lawd.
There ain't nothing else to say." Lerone Bennett, Jr. *Blues and Bitterness*, 1964.

15.   BLACK GENESIS
BY
DR. FRED MONDERSON

BLACK GENESIS: *The Prehistoric Origins of Ancient Egypt* is not for the faint of heart for it strikes at and shatters the racially charged and falsely

AFRICAN NATIONALIST POETRY AND PROSE

propagated theory that the ancient Egyptians were Caucasian migrants from South West Asia who entered Egypt from different points. Significantly, upon close scrutiny each point of entry betrays the "straw man" nature of the argument since it was designed to falsely portray Caucasian supremacy in a scheme offering no logic and despite overwhelming evidence to the contrary of that stated position. We must remember, "The existential data contradicts the symbolic representation," for as Dr. John H. Clarke has competently argued, "Europe's claim to Egypt uses no logic." However, he incisively recognized and pointed out, "The people who preached racism colonized history" and "When Europe colonized the world, she colonized the world's knowledge." As such then, "she cut the feet to fit the slippers in the Caucasian Egypt falsity.

The authors, Robert Bauval and Thomas Brophy of *Black Genesis*: *The Prehistoric Origins of Ancient Egypt* (Rochester: Bear and Company, 2011) apply state of the art scientific investigatory techniques to trace the prehistoric origins of the ancient Egyptians emanating from the Saharan region, far in the west of Southern Egypt at a time when the desert area was teeming with vegetation that supported a zoological horde of wildlife including cattle. This time was contemporary with freezing temperatures in the Caucasian region when the astronomical, architectural and artistic accomplishments of the desert dwellers could not have been duplicated in the South-West Asia environment.

It is interesting how, when in analogy, the architectural structure of Zimbabwe was first discovered by westerners, it was "Expertly" determined "Shipwrecked Chinese" or even "Phoenician sailors" found themselves in the heart of Southern Africa and built these architectural marvels. In the same way, origins of the Egyptians were ascribed to the Caucus region in South-West Asia but the point of the entrance into Africa became a question of contention in the 19th Century white supremacy escapade because emerging new information made each theory obsolete. First, the Isthmus of Suez was thought as the point of entry, thence an ascent of the Nile River to the southern capital that emerged as the center of most prominence of the culture from the Middle Kingdom onward.

Another argument held, "for some unknown reason," a migrating group left South-West Asia, following a path during the Old Kingdom that brought them to the Horn of Africa, entering Egypt from the Red Sea, traversing the Wady Hammamat and arriving at the Nile in the region of Koptos. Once there, they sailed down the Nile conquering the indigenous peoples, who, incidentally had already built the foundations of a cultural civilization unheard of in the place of origin of these wanderers. The significance of this contact is that though these individuals did not bring the units of culture then manifesting in the Nile Valley, they brought a "superior mental attitude" that gave an

AFRICAN NATIONALIST POETRY AND PROSE

added impetus to the civilization they found. Unfortunately, this "superior" mentality never created the rudiments of any comparative culture in their place of origin. Sir Gaston Maspero of "Negroid not Negro" fame, proposed people from the Sahara region migrated to the Nile Valley when that region had begun to desiccate. Unfortunately, he claimed these were Caucasians who had crossed over from Southern Europe and inhabited North Africa. Then they migrated into the Nile Valley. Notwithstanding, however, argument for a North-African entry into the Valley of the Nile differs from an entry from the Sahara. Evidence indicates Black Africans in occupation of the Sahara from time immemorial. Even Henri L'Hote found among the Tassili Frescoes and elsewhere Black Africans were in the Sahara and left their mark, thousands of years before the dynasties began.

We all know, there are times researchers have a tendency to construct a theory and then set out to find data that supports such, irrespective of how off base it may be. Nevertheless, all arguments for a "Caucasian," "European," "Semitic," "South West Asian" origin of the Egyptians is based on speculation whether through language borrowings. Nonetheless, such evidence is scant, if any at all, substantive information in support, more likely smoke and mirrors.

FREDERICK MONDERSON

The notion of a cow, goddess of nourishment, is an integral part of the drama in the heavens as she is tended to by these divinities. The question this raises is simply this - How dissimilar is this idea from that articulated by Brophy and Bauval in Black Genesis that the people of Nabta Playa were earliest astronomers who initiated the idea of the "Cow Goddess" or great mother worship given she nourished mankind as pastoralists and that they were the precursors to the pharaohs!

African Nationalist Poetry and Prose Photo. Zimbabwe. Gladman Zinyeka – "Who will Raise the Child" - The mother, father and child in 'Who will raise the Child' laments the **AIDS** epidemic that leaves many children without parents."

AFRICAN NATIONALIST POETRY AND PROSE

African Nationalist Poetry and Prose Photo. Dr. Len Jeffries and Erik Monderson give the "Power Salute."

For example, the Louvre Scribe, purportedly from the Old Kingdom, resides in a prominent position in that French Institution. One of its more prominent features is that it has blue eyes! As such, gullible yet ill-informed particularly European visitors buy into the theory, "See, the ancient Egyptians had blue eyes." No one entertains the fact, ancient Egyptians utilized inlaid eyes of whatever color in their statuary decoration. Another example is that of Wortham in *The Genesis of British Egyptology*, Norman, Oklahoma: wherein he states, Augustus Bozzi conducted an autopsy on a mummy in his London home in 1825 and correctly concluded the Egyptians were Caucasians. Both examples go from a specific to the general, using deductive rather than inductive logic, a sort of "one sparrow so its summer," syndrome. Nonetheless, all arguments for an alien origin of the Egyptians recognize the pivotal nature of Upper Egypt, yet circuitously seek to inculcate this region into their scheme but to no avail.

It is interesting how the obstinacy of white racial intellectual arrogance can perpetuate, and, in defiance of credible evidence, cling to outdated and outmoded positions on the origins of the culture of ancient Egypt and the role of Africa and Africans in that North-East African, Nile Valley culture. Many people have commented on the statement by Zahi Hawass as he oversaw the Supreme Council of Antiquities in its never-ending work to rescue, recover and revitalize the culture of ancient Egypt. He was quoted as saying the ancient Egyptians were not White, Black, Africans. They certainly were not Arabs though Arabs claim ancient Egypt as their ancestral culture! We do know; however, the Arabs were a long line of invaders who conquered Egypt but generally added little to the culture complex that developed there. In fact, in their marauding through any territory, conquerors are too busy destroying rather than preserving and when they do settle down for the long haul, their efforts at preservation fall short having destroyed much. Still, it is interesting to read what Dr. Hawass has to say about Robert Bauval and Thomas Brophy's *Black Genesis*: *The Prehistoric Origins of Ancient Egypt* (Vermont: Bear and Company, 2011) that not only provides evidence

AFRICAN NATIONALIST POETRY AND PROSE

for the foundation of Egypt but also shatters much of the myths of a Caucasian Egypt.

Montesquieu, the French philosophe, admonished, people act, think, and write as if their behaviors can become a universal law. Universal laws are unalterable! Much of the conclusions about the ancient Egyptians, particularly of the 19th and 20th Centuries have now been proven not to be universal laws. Georges Foucart indicated, "the early Egyptologists made errors." Dr. Leonard James, on the other hand, argued, "Those mistakes were purposeful." For instance, Europeans on exploration love to name places and things and the proliferation of British heroes' names in geographical features of Canada is a remarkable example of this. Nevertheless, in Egypt as Europeans began ascending the Nile, they began naming landmarks and other features, perhaps "unconsciously" to change the culture or even as part of the grand strategy of remaking Egypt. Nonetheless, and using the "king and queen metaphor" they named the large room in the pyramid of **Khufu** (Chufu), the "king's chamber" and the next sized one, the "queen's chamber." At Amarna this was also repeated, only to find out the large room was in fact the queen's not the king's chamber! Equally too, at Aswan the cataract encountered there was described as the "first" and the "sixth" at the river's source in Central Africa. Whereas, the river flowed south to north, the first cataract should be where the sixth is stated to be and the sixth is where the first has been identified in this scheme of reckoning. These disparities have not been corrected.

One incontrovertible fact no naming could tamper with is the situation of the Nomes. The first Nome began at Elephantine Island in the Aswan vicinity and the 22 Nomes of the South stretched all the way towards the apex of the Delta below Memphis. The 20 Nomes of the North began in the Memphis vicinity and is numbered out towards the Mediterranean Sea. How the significance of the first Nome this far towards inner Africa has escaped so many is a surprise among the many caveats that point to the "Black Genesis" of ancient Egypt!

While Bauval and Brophy mention Cheikh Anta Diop's work, one of the recommendations the revered ancestor has insisted upon is group research or partnerships to which these two scholars so wonderfully excel in this fascinating new book as well as Diop himself and Theophile Obenga have masterfully stated their cases. The back-cover description of *Black Genesis* notes, "uncovering compelling new evidence Egyptologist Robert Bauval and astrophysicist Thomas Brophy present the anthropological, climatological, archaeological, geological and genetic research supporting this highly debated theory of the Black African origin of Egyptian civilization."

This book should be read by as wide an audience as possible.

AFRICAN NATIONALIST POETRY AND PROSE

In essence, Robert Bauval and Thomas Brophy's *Black Genesis: The Prehistoric Origins of Ancient Egypt* is a thought-provoking and methodologically laid out treatise that uses state of the art scientific techniques investigating established contemporary and especially new data that convincingly traces the beginnings and routes of Black People from the Sahara region who migrated to Southern Egypt armed with a surprisingly sophisticated astronomical knowledge that ultimately laid the foundation for science and other practices upon which pharaonic Egypt later built.

Showing that these Blacks were the progenitors of ancient Egyptian culture, they came with a scientific sophistication developed over several millennia associated with early stargazing of the clear skies of the western desert of Upper Egypt. Nabta Plays is a place the monsoon rains of that time had made fertile for several months of the year in which the occupants were able to raise a cattle culture, making them early pastoralists. This may have formed the basis for the religious myths of Hathor, the cow goddess, generally ascribed to being of Sudanese origin.

The significance of *Black Genesis* rests in its systematic examination of the calendar through use of astroarchaeological data that bring to life the later prehistoric years of the last Precession measured at some 26,000 years, a time of early scientific innovations that make these years very real. The archaeoastronomical sleuthing of the authors vividly highlight the tangible features of Nabta Playa creations, viz., stone carvings, placement and astronomical orientation of stones, creation of a calendar, together with cave paintings depicting "red persons" even though the people were black! Added to this is the significance of the monsoon rains and development of agriculture and pastoral culture that influenced religious beliefs. Equally, location of principal sites that encouraged early desert movement to extensively traverse a hostile environment; that, in the latter years, rapidly desiccated and forced these original inhabitants to migrate to the Nile arriving in the Aswan, Elephantine region. Here they brought their extensive and long developed early scientific knowledge and techniques then providing a profound impetus to pharaonic civilization that clearly left evidence of its connection to these early desert-dwelling Africans.

The book also recounts early pharaonic efforts at connecting with these desert dwellers at Nabta Playa, the "Land of Yam," reaching out to them as if recognizing their ancestral heritage as precursors to their own cultural manifestation. At least one Old Kingdom cartouche was found in the region.

1. The desert-dwellers, in heading east, first entered the Nile in the Aswan vicinity and their traveling knowledge seems to have manifested in a temple of Satet at Elephantine where astronomy, magic and religion may have percolated to create the powerful

AFRICAN NATIONALIST POETRY AND PROSE

generator that set-in motion significant features of Egyptian culture.

A number of happenings of significance can be associated with the people of Nabta Playa whose presence in the region range from approximately 7500-3500 B.C. and who arrived at the Nile in the Upper Egyptian region, somewhere between Aswan and Abu Simbel anywhere between 3500 B.C.E. and the start of dynastic rule variously given as 3100-3000 B.C.

First, Bruce Williams' discovery from Qustol in Nubia, proximate to Upper Egypt, where pharaonic symbols such as enthroned pharaoh, white crown, Nile boat, palace serekh facade, incense burner, cattle, etc., were associated with such paraphernalia emerging in Southern Egypt some two centuries later.

The "Great Mother" is often represented as a cow that suckles the monarch and Society to bring good fortune. Hathor the "Nubian" is also shown as a cow-goddess and this may be related to the black Africans of Nabta Playa who initiated the "Cow Goddess" worship and equally were considered the precursors to the Pharaohs.

Second and tremendously significant, the First Egyptian Nome encompasses the Elephantine vicinity and since we generally associate one or first with beginnings, it is conceivable this is the point of origination, from whence, following the river, Egyptian civilization developed as the culture evolved. Thus, the whole notion of South-Western Asiatics bringing civilization is nothing but mythology founded on falsity.

African Nationalist Poetry and Prose Photo. Rev. Sharpton poses with young people after a "Weekly Rally."

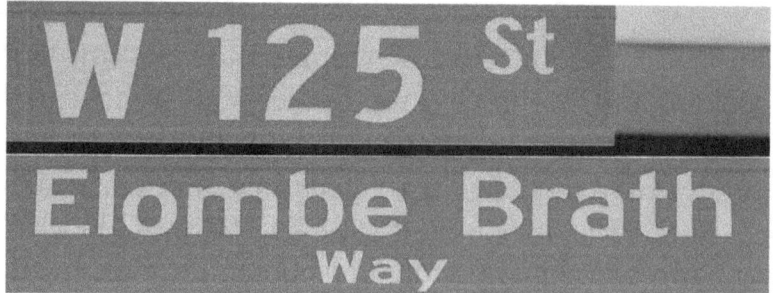

African Nationalist Poetry and Prose Photo. The "Little Giant" and great Nationalist Elombe Brathe on 125th Street, a place in Harlem where he belongs.

AFRICAN NATIONALIST POETRY AND PROSE

African Nationalist Poetry and Prose Photo. **Zimbabwe.** Nicholas Mukomberanwa – Buying tons of Serpentine and Sprintstone from a mountain quarry near Tengenenge, Mukomberanwa sculpts with hand tools in a spontaneous reflective process.

Let us not forget, in the spurious claims of the origin of the ancient Egyptians, migration was considered a significant factor by Flinders Petrie author of the theory. However, as the Delta entry into Africa turned out to be a "straw man," the "Horn of Africa" was offered as a viable alternative in which these wanderers crossed over to the Nile through the Wady Hammamat arriving at the Nile in the vicinity of

FREDERICK MONDERSON

Koptos, home of god Min, who despite efforts to link him to Mesopotamia, origin of these migrants, Min has been determined to be Black and linked to Black Africans. So, if these people could arrive at Upper Egypt, the key to Egypt, and sail down the Nile, why can't the original inhabitants with their demonstrated scientific and social underpinnings not do same?

Third, despite what may be said about antecedents in the north, Narmer, from the south whether Abydos or Thebes, was able to muster a significant military force that sailed north, defeated the region's elements and began the process of unification at a time when, as the slate palettes and early Abydos burials indicate Egyptian culture was just coming into credible vogue. Notwithstanding, social theorizing and administrative practicalities were sufficiently "advanced," Narmer was able to lay the social, administrative, political, military, scientific and religious parameters that served as foundation pillars of the society for the three thousand years' duration of dynastic rule. To have had the wherewithal to institute such developments means they had to have existed prior to Narmer's expedition down the Nile. Incidentally, Cheikh Anta Diop identifies Narmer as Theban.

Fourth, Bauval and Brophy have connected prehistoric scientific observation with dynastic architectural developments that locate both the Step Pyramid at Sakkara and the "True Pyramids" at Gizeh with astronomical happenings as the dynamics of the heavens unfolded and the Egyptians not only

AFRICAN NATIONALIST POETRY AND PROSE

observed, built structures, but also formulated cosmic myths that regulated their society through interconnected religious practices.

The authors have shown an astral relationship to the calendar and how this social register has had the most significant impact on the totality of Egyptian culture, cultivated from a profound and long-standing observation of the heavens.

It is interesting how persons of questionable knowledge and intent have made statements about Egyptian culture that lead the masses, far afield in the wrong or opposite direction. Case in point!

a. For some unknown reason, a group of migrants left South-West-Asia following the sun and, well, ended up in Egypt. This myth was articulated as tangible fact. After all that Narmer and his Southern administrators had accomplished, and particularly given the antecedents of such developments. What could wandering migrants coming out of the desert actually bring except racial prejudice especially as perceived and articulated by the emerging 19th Century white supremacy mind-set.

b. The Egyptian gods came from the skies; they myths came from the skies. That is to say, they very early believed events of the heavens influenced human and earthly developments. Thus, the gods were born in the sky, they lived there and this is

FREDERICK MONDERSON

where heaven existed eternally. Nonetheless, misunderstood pronouncement has engaged the creativity of Hollywood to produce "Battle Star Galactica," the "Fifth Element," associated mummy movies; and even indulged the creativity of the falsity of Van Deniken and his "Chariot of the Gods" syndrome. Of course, let us not forget Charleston Heston and Cecil de Mille's epic **Ten Commandments** shown thousands upon thousands of thousand times ingraining a false reality in the minds of the world's peoples, even shaping their beliefs.

Fifth, **Black Genesis** connects panels of the Step-Pyramid built by Imhotep with the Sothic Cycle of 1461 or 1459 years showing knowledge of the shifting nature of this solar phenomenon. Everyone is familiar with the attributes of Imhotep as priest, astronomer, administrator, physician and poet. He has been called the world's first multi-genius and a "Poet of the Ages" for his now famous admonition, "Eat, drink and be merry, for tomorrow you die!" However, his architectural, astronomical and medical knowledge is more renown.

It is well known that knowledge and skill in ancient Egypt was generally a family trait, closely guarded and handed down, secretly from generation to generation. We know Imhotep descended from a long line of architects whose heritage may reach back to Narmer's age. As Black Genesis connects the Step-Pyramid, its panels with Imhotep's architectural and

AFRICAN NATIONALIST POETRY AND PROSE

astronomy skills at a time not too distant from the emergence of the desert people with their astronomy observational accomplishments, these authors have articulated a powerful thesis that flies in the face of the innumerable falsities about ancient Egypt by 19th, 20th and 21st Century writers. Let us not forget, the palace façade of Ta-Seti at Qustol is not dissimilar as an architectural feature akin to such accomplishments at Sakkara's Step-Pyramid built for Zoser by Imhotep. Equally too, we must remember, while Georges Foucart admitted, "The early Egyptologists made mistakes," Dr. Leonard James very rightly argued, "many of these mistakes were purposeful." Thus, as Egyptian archaeology science struggled to be born under its architect Flinders Petrie, many significant discoveries were also being made. However, the problem with the age was the interpretation of the data in a mad-dash climate to discover and rapidly publish at a time when no African stood at the bar of discussion to critique the various interpretations as for example, the various times Henri Frankfort in Kingship and the Gods point out mistakes made by Herman Junker who chose, among other mistakes limit the "Appearance of the Negroes in the Nile Valley. Lacking serious critical scrutiny, egotistical gents prognosticated at great length to an audience yearning to be influenced by these experts who ossified the false interpretation of ancient Egypt in impressionable Western, European and American minds who ate it all up.

FREDERICK MONDERSON

One of the arguments for the origin of the Egyptians has been that they were a "boat people." So, we are to believe, either these mythical migrants of South-West-Asia dragged their boats across the unknown desert passage or upon arrival in Africa, Egypt, on the Nile, made boats on which they descended the river. To accept such, we must disregard the existence or incapacity of the Nile dwellers of central Africa, Nubia, and Upper Egypt, particularly from the Aswan area to make boats and descend the Nile. It is absurdity when we realize not only that these Africans live on the Nile as their principal means of transportation highway, the Qustol discovery depicts sailing boats and Narmer marshalled a military armada to sail down the Nile before the visitors arrived. Let us also and equally not forget, the size of Narmer's military force at unification was also capable of projecting Egyptian power abroad and was very capable of repelling any group of visitors who crossed the hostile terrain, more than likely, tired, hungry, desert whipped who came to demonstrate "Their superior mental faculty."

In the evolution of Egyptian boat culture, particularly as sketched in Baines and Malek's *Cultural Atlas of Egypt* (1980), boat building developed from age to age as greater mastery of the craft and river were demonstrated. We know in the earliest times the sun god sailed across the sky in a solar barge and this certainly connects this myth with the earliest stargazers since religious beliefs and practices go back millennia before dynastic rule and continued as a powerful force in many different aspects. In the Old

AFRICAN NATIONALIST POETRY AND PROSE

Kingdom, pharaohs had boat pits dug and boats buried adjacent to their pyramids. Hence, boat culture pervaded every aspect of the culture even to this day.

Another attribute of the ancient Egyptians is that they were a pastoral people for without some doubt cattle played a significant role in the cultural and religious practices. Bauval and Brophy have demonstrated the significance of "cow culture" among the desert dwelling Black people who left drawing of cows and were the genesis of the Egyptian genius. The goddess Hathor of Sudani or Upper Egyptian origin played a tremendous role in Egyptian religion that permeated every aspect of the culture and the general belief is that Hathor, the cow goddess, was a manifestation of every female deity in whichever pantheon.

African Nationalist Poetry and Prose Photo. Iconic Malcolm X on equally iconic Lenox Avenue.

FREDERICK MONDERSON

African Nationalist Poetry and Prose Photo. The Beautiful and resplendent Carmen Monderson.

African Nationalist Poetry and Prose Photo. Dr. Rev. Herbert Daughtry poses with a friend and admirer at National Action Network's "Weekly Rally."

AFRICAN NATIONALIST POETRY AND PROSE

"Down South where I come from you don't go around hitting too many white keys." Eubie Blake. When asked why his compositions contained so many sharps and flats.

16. POEM TO PTAH BY DR. FRED MONDERSON

Ptah, Great Architect of the Universe, you were among the earliest African Gods. At Unification of Kemet, Narmer founded the White Wall at Memphis, as his capital in Aneb-Hetch, the first Nome of the Lower Kingdom. Lord of the White Wall, the King built a temple, Hat-Ke Ptah at Khut-Taui, Horizon of the Two Lands and established worship of your triad Ptah-Sakhet-Nefertum, later worshipped at Thebes. While the fortunes of other gods rose and fell, yours as Patron of Artists, Artisans and Artificers remained not paramount, but consistent, and your festival was celebrated on March 21, Lord of Truth, Great Chief of the Axe.

Lord of the Hidden Throne, whose hidden form is unknown, Powerful One, at Memphis, your High Priest, Great One, Commander of Workmen, was the Chief Artist of the Court. From here, the Great Chief of Artists played a prominent role in state politics, as you Ptah established Ma'at throughout the Two Lands. Father of Fathers, Power of Powers, you are the Master Architect and Designer of Everything which exist in the World and was employed in the Construction of the Heavens and the Earth, Great of Handicrafts.

Ptah, Disk of Heaven, you illuminate the Two Lands with the Fire of your Two Eyes. The Theban triad dominated the Middle and New Kingdoms and you, Great Chief of the Hammer resided in the palace of their abode, with a temple at Karnak. Father of the Gods, the emblem of your Majesty is a close-fitting garment, and from an opening in front project your two hands with Scepter, Ankh, and Tet representing power, life, stability. The Menat, symbol of pleasure and happiness hangs from the back of your neck.

Lord of Thebes, Fire God, while little evidence of Middle Kingdom temples remain; the 18th Dynasty embellished your Sanctuary at Karnak and Memphis, the City of Walls. Ramesside kings were your most ardent champions, O God Who Stands upon the Ma'at Pedestal. Rameses II erected two great sandstone statues at Memphis, one over 10 feet high, in your name. God of the Beautiful Face in Thebes who Created his own Image, and Fashioned his own Body, you oversaw the Construction of that great city, being Chief of All Handicraftsmen and of all Workers in Metal and Stone, God of Wisdom, you understood things before Creation.

AFRICAN NATIONALIST POETRY AND PROSE

Very Great God who came into existence in the earliest time, you are the Blue-Collar God, Master-workman of the Universal Workshop, the Supreme Mind. Mind and Tongue of the Gods, all things proceeded from you Ptah, Lord of Ma'at, King of the Two Lands. As a form of the Sun God, Father of Beginnings, you are the Creator of the Eggs of the Sun and Moon. In this you are the Personification of the Rising Sun, Artificer in metals, smelter, caster, sculptor, great Celestial Workman and Architect, preparing the primeval elements of earth and water.

God the Father and Son, Lord of Justice, Divine Sculptor, you gave and still give forms to all things and beings on earth. Opener of the Ways, you fashion the Souls of the Dead to live in the Underworld. As Ptah-Seker, with crook, whip, scepter, crown of disk, plumes, horns and uraei with disks on their heads, the Office of your High Priest existed form the time of the Second Dynasty. Great God who came into being in the beginning with two feathers of Ma'at, Lofty Plumes, you rested upon the darkness as King of Eternity, Everlastingness and Lord of Life. You bring the Nile from its source to make flourish the staff of life and to make grain come forth aged one of Nu. In same manner you make fertile the watery mass of heaven.

Ptah-Tanen, Disk of Heaven, in peace you light up the world with your brilliant rays. Ready Plumes, of multitudinous forms, with the Sun and Moon as your

FREDERICK MONDERSON

eyes, you pass through eternity and everlastingness. Builder of your own limbs, maker of your own body, your upper part is heaven; the lower part is the Tuat. Maker of the Tuat with all of its arrangements, you make to come forth the water on the mountains to give life to all men and women in your name Ari-Ankh, Lord of Justice. Aged one traversing Eternity, Prince of Annu, you judge the dead and give them access to the Field of Peace, Field of Reeds, Field of Grasshoppers.

Ptah, you make all land and all countries. As you mold gods, men and everything produced Great God who stretched out the heavens; you make your disk to revolve in the body of Nut as you fashion yourself without the help of any other being. Fully equipped you came forth fully equipped. The Company of Gods of your Supreme Company praises you, one with many companions.

Ptah-Seker-Asar, Triune God of Resurrection, you Dwell in a Secret Place. Lord Ta-Tchesetet, pygmy with large baldhead and thick limbs, beetle and plumes, you are the Governor of Everlastingness. Begetter of Men, Maker of their lives, Creator of all the Gods, you are the Father of the Father of the Gods. Ptah-Tanen, Babe Born Daily, Aged One on the Borders of Eternity, Lord of Life, Giver of Life at Will, you hear the prayers men make to you.

The Hapi or Apis Bull, incarnate of Ptah, emerged as the Ptolemaic Serapis in the Memphis Mausoleum or Serapeum of the Greeks, where the great Imhotep

AFRICAN NATIONALIST POETRY AND PROSE

was recognized as your son. From this House of the Aged One, your temple Aneb-Abt in Memphis, Men-Nefer, the House of the Beautiful Face, you maintain the Balance of the Two Lands.

In this City of White Wall, Persea and Acacia trees bloom and here reside your female counterpart Sekhet, sister and wife, mother of your son Nefertum, later Imhotep. This great African Goddess, the Great Lady, Lady of Sa, Queen of Ant, is mighty, strong and violent. O Holy One, the Lady of Flame, Mighty Lady, Greatly Beloved of Ptah, Lady of Heaven, is Mistress of the Two Lands. You Gods of Holiness, Bless and Protect African people in the many challenges they face, O Divine Artificer of Creation, Lord of Life of the Two Lands.

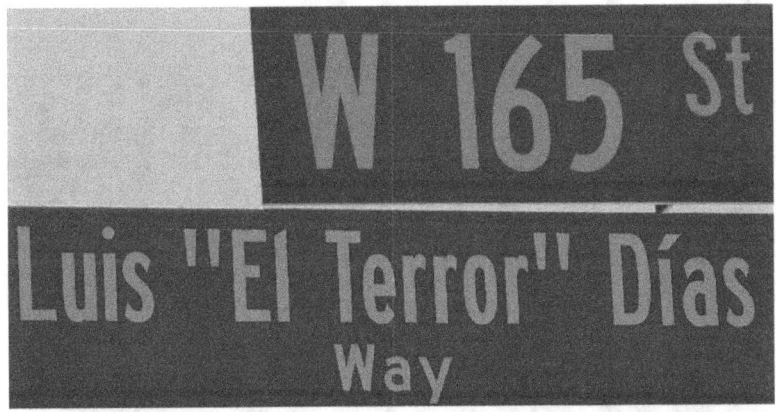

African Nationalist Poetry and Prose Photo. Luis "El Terror" Dias Way in Washington Heights, New York City.

FREDERICK MONDERSON

African Nationalist Poetry and Prose Photo.
MEDICINE WHEEL – "Native American Circle of Life."

African Nationalist Poetry and Prose Photo.
Minister Hafeez Mohammed and associates greet Dr. Tyrene Wright.

AFRICAN NATIONALIST POETRY AND PROSE

African Nationalist Poetry and Prose Photo. Zimbabwe. Nicholas Mukonberanwa. "'Madora (Mupani Work)' Mukonberanwa found inspiration in his Shona heritage and respect for the natural and spiritual worlds."

African Nationalist Poetry and Prose Photo. Douglass and Garvey.

FREDERICK MONDERSON

African Nationalist Poetry and Prose Photo. Harriet Tubman has arrived.

African Nationalist Poetry and Prose Photo. Rev. Al Sharpton shakes the hand of the author, Dr. Fred Monderson.

AFRICAN NATIONALIST POETRY AND PROSE

African Nationalist Poetry and Prose Photo. Rev. Al Sharpton's "Weekly Rally" with Rev. Daughtry, Mr. Foy and Attorney Mike Hardy seated.

African Nationalist Poetry and Prose Photo. Members of the **Pan-African Movement – Guyana Branch** in attendance at the United Nation's sponsored **International Decade of People of African Ancestry**, held in Guyana in 2017.

FREDERICK MONDERSON

African Nationalist Poetry and Prose Photo. Dr. Fred Monderson poses with Dr. Len Jeffries at **Medgar Evers' Black Writers Conference**, 2017.

African Nationalism Poetry and Prose Photo. Dr. Rudy Crew, President of Medgar Evers College, **CUNY**, at *Black Star News* Award Ceremony.

AFRICAN NATIONALIST POETRY AND PROSE

African Nationalist Poetry and Prose Photo. Honorable Marcus Moziah Garvey President General of Africa and founder of the Universal Negro Improvement Association, **UNIA**, in his resplendently colorful Red, Black and Green.

FREDERICK MONDERSON

African nationalist Poetry and Prose Photo. Luis, Nova, Dr. Felder and Erik on 125th Street in Harlem.

African Nationalist Poetry and Prose Photo. Congressman "Charlie" Rangel at **Black Star News** Award Ceremony.

AFRICAN NATIONALIST POETRY AND PROSE

African Nationalist Poetry and Prose Photo.
Frederick Douglass Boulevard, honored in Harlem.

African Nationalist Poetry and Prose Photo.
Prince of "Purple Rain" fame.

African Nationalist Poetry and Prose Photo.
Adam Clayton Powell, Jr. Boulevard.

FREDERICK MONDERSON

African Nationalist Poetry and Prose Photo.
Tribute to the Ancestors – Images, 2019.

AFRICAN NATIONALIST POETRY AND PROSE

"The evidence that Barack Obama is a natural-born U.S. citizen is so overwhelming that disputing this fact constitutes a form of venal denialism, rather than a mere conspiracy theory. As his birth certificate showed, the President was born in Honolulu, Hawaii at Kapiolani Hospital, on August 4, 1961, the child of an immigrant Kenyan father (Barack Obama, Sr.) and an American mother (S. Anne Dunham). Yet, the smears continued until finally the Obama campaign created a website called *Fight the Smears* which showed a short form of Obama's birth certificate. Obama also allowed factcheck.org to distribute information about his birth. Some conservatives said this was not enough. The State of Hawaii then came out with the long form of Obama's birth certificate just before Election Day in 2008 as an indication that Obama was born in Hawaii and was thus a natural-born citizen as required by the Constitution." Molefi Kete Asante. *Lynching Barack Obama*. 2016.

17. MILLION MAN MARCH: Substance and Significance
By
Dr. Fred Monderson

Riding in a District of Columbia cab the day after the March, the driver wanted to know the "Numbers! - A Million or so?" I responded, "Two million or more," based on my own unscientific observations looking out at the stretched-out masses of people within the barricades lining the Great Lawn, on adjacent streets,

FREDERICK MONDERSON

and the continuing streams entering from north and south conduits. Equally significant, even when leaving early, the late throngs of people pouring in and heading to the Mall certainly adds to an elevated assessment of how many people were there. I'm reminded 20 years ago of the controversy over the number of people who attended that first March. While Minister Farrakhan called for and acknowledged a million in attendance, the government downplayed this number offering no more than 400,000 to 500,000. On the other hand, others gave a figure of more than a million! However, while some folks may have arrived late, such as my daughter Keisha traveling with her family, who incidentally were in attendance at the Million Family March in 2000, the 2,000,000 number seems a real possibility.

African Nationalist Poetry and Prose Photo. Minister Louis Farrakhan and former District of Columbia Mayor Marion Barry hold a Press Conference to discuss the upcoming "Million Man March" in 1995.

AFRICAN NATIONALIST POETRY AND PROSE

African Nationalist Poetry and Prose Photo. Dr. Leonard Jeffries holds Amos N. Wilson's book **Blueprint for Black Power** at a Bedford Stuyvesant Restoration gathering in Brooklyn, New York, some years ago.

Continuing the dialogue with the driver, he remarked, "I have been in this town 40 years. This town belonged to African-Americans but this has changed." I did observe a fair amount of destitute people on the streets and made contributions. On Sunday morning at McDonalds, to several of the persons nearby I asked, and answered the question, "Did you have your coffee this morning, brother?" To which several resounding "Thank yous" were heartfelt responses to my actions.

Notwithstanding, as the driver said, my mind reflected on a photograph at the Meridian Park, now renamed Malcolm X Park, showing a tremendous

FREDERICK MONDERSON

gathering of Marching African-Americans streaming out onto the street on **Black Solidarity Day** in 1972. Gathered in what appeared a military formation, an individual in "fatigues" led and directed persons in prominent Afro hairstyles and wearing dashiki shirts. This was a classic Black Nationalism moment! Perhaps this was the "golden age" the driver referred to.

Nevertheless, though the "stomach may appear a bit soft," the stalwarts at the far reaches of the "Empire" are "no ways tired," because the substance and significance of the gathering inherent in the ideology of the March attracting the numbers in attendance as reflected in the many who announced their presence two decades ago, broadening of the multi-ethnic flavor of the gathering to include Whites, Native Americans, Asians, Latinos, LGBTs, in addition to those Black stalwarts who brought their sons and daughters, even wives, those who brought youngsters and those returning to assert their manhood in support of the call, the need for, and the demands for Justice or Else going forward. Such is the essence of Substance and Significance of this most potent idea.

Consequently, and without question, we must give praise and thanks to Minister Louis Farrakhan of the **Nation of Islam** for conceiving, executing and contributing to the "Million" idea. We know there are "forty something" million African Americans in this country. They spend one million-million (Trillion) dollars annually and there are perhaps a million

AFRICAN NATIONALIST POETRY AND PROSE

Brothers and Sisters incarcerated, but Farrakhan's idea is different, tremendously revolutionary, and with continuous tweaking will remain a potent beacon of consciousness, soul searching and demands on government, all ripe for activism in nationalist assertion as a reminder to the powers that be, "We will not go quietly.". Its crystal clear, in the most vital organ of the American system, Washington, DC, this genius planted a profound idea whose time has not only come but will endure for eons because of the power, substance and significance contained in the message.

The numbers, quality and receptivity of those who answered the call and as they return to their widespread areas of operation, the trees of this forest will in turn generate forests of their own who will creatively experiment with, carry forward, and sustain the message of **Justice or Else**, while making their own significant contributions not simply to advance the cause of Blackness but equally continue to make America a better place for all.

Living the legacy decades later, when One Million will become Twenty and Minister Farrakhan finally joins the revered ancestral pantheon; that is, among Jitu Weusi, Sonny Carson, Reverend Jones, Elombe Brathe, Dr. Ben-Jochannan, Professor Clarke, Bill Lynch, and the oldsters Malcolm X, Martin Luther King, Mary McLeod Bethune, Fannie Lou Hamer, Reverend Shuttlesworth, Dorothy Height, W.E.B.

FREDERICK MONDERSON

Dubois, Marcus Garvey, Elijah Mohammed, Kwame Ture, Herman Ferguson, Queen Mother Moore, Nelson Mandela, Langston Hughes, Kwame Nkrumah, Sekou Touré, Patrice Lumumba, Claude McKay, Forbes Burnham, Mitta Monderson, Ollie McClean, on the fiftieth anniversary and after, these will rejoice over the success of their efforts added to the Million Man March ideology and program's harvest of fruitful political, economic, educational, and social empowerment outcomes.

Naturally much was said, but a most powerful theme Mr. Farrakhan evoked was the call for an economic boycott especially at holiday time. Investing in Black Enterprise is always an equally potent idea. However, for the longest our leaders have emphasized the importance of the economic boycott. They cite the successes of the Montgomery Bus Boycott and the concurrent Boycott of Birmingham stores that brought that city's white supremacy to its knees! Equally, many features of early Black Solidarity Day Boycott were successful but for whatever reason that movement lost its way, as only a few groups across the country see the need for and continue the tradition.

When Sean Bell, on the eve of his wedding, was shot many times in Queens, New York, Reverend Al Sharpton called for an economic march along Fifth Ave on December 16th of that year, entering 50th Street in Manhattan and passing through the "Heart of Christmas," the intent was to "Shop for Justice."

AFRICAN NATIONALIST POETRY AND PROSE

The theme was, "Hold your Money, Don't Shop this holiday!" That is an equally significant theme Minister Farrakhan emphasized on this 20th Anniversary of the Million Man March under the shibboleth "Justice or Else!"

Again, Bob Law and Reverend Calvin Butts in New York have proposed and are currently pursuing a national economic boycott to redirect the One Trillion Dollars African-Americans spend annually. Echoing Adam Clayton Powell's "Don't shop where you can't work" boycott dictum, down through the ages, leaders have emphasized the same idea. Thus, Bob Law, also emphasizing the prevalence of "fast food" establishments in the Black community and the implications for long-term health concerns, has advised "redirect your burger and fries money," not necessarily your big spending habits. He emphasized, in these "fast food joints" that don't hire Blacks or support any nationalist initiatives that concern African-Americans, they should not shop there. However, when shopping they should ask proprietors of such establishments, "Where are the Black people who work here since we're shopping in your place of business?" Without question, "our dollars represent the margin of profit" for these businesses as Bob Law expressed, particularly so the big chains with their ubiquitous presence in or serving the Black Community. More specific, only about "8 percent of Blacks" need to withhold such spending to make a difference and these enterprises will recognize Black

FREDERICK MONDERSON

aspirations because Black Lives Matter in all of its manifestations! One sign at the march even advocated, "Make the Black Dollar circulate more in the Black Community!"

African Nationalist Poetry and Prose Photo. Tribute to the Ancestors – Images, 2019.

A classic case was once observed in Maryland, famous for crabs. One Asian establishment selling crabs but not employing Blacks was servicing a line that stretched around the corner, "Because they make good crabs!" How foolish and counterproductive!

More importantly, however, in his two-hour presentation one pointedly important assertion Minister Farrakhan posed, "I know you all think I killed Malcolm! If I killed Malcolm, do you think I would be here? See who was giving him mouth to mouth resuscitation? It was an FBI agent!" The idea elicits a Hollywood analogy in the movie **Shooter** starring Mark Walberg and Danny Glover. When the hero and the FBI agent went seeking "Wisdom" from the old shooting expert, to the question, "Who killed Kennedy?" he responded, "Those boys on the grassy knoll were dead within hours." The FBI agent

AFRICAN NATIONALIST POETRY AND PROSE

responded, "You know this for sure?" To which the expert responded, "I still have the shovels in the back!" This sort of lends credence to the Minister's denial. Notwithstanding, Sonny Carson and Herman Ferguson both thought he did it! However, he may not have been at the Audubon to pull the trigger but to feign ignorance of the "climate around Malcolm" and "the hit going down" is not a tenable position.

Nevertheless, the Minister pointed out the Honorable Gentleman in question had married the ladies and took care of his children, "not like some of you players out there." He equally criticized the many women who "let the players play" and not hold them accountable for their behaviors. He also made special note of black-on-black crime and killings as well police killing of blacks. Others gave a litany of names of victims of such violence. Nonetheless, with these issues and the substance and significance of the March recognized in the numbers who came and the seeds they will plant to creatively organize and continue to demand Justice or Else then return at this idea of anniversary in five years to the **Million Family** in 2020; all the while the **Million Woman** in 2018 and **Million Youth** anniversaries in Harlem and Brooklyn, remain on deck, certainly underscores the significance of the idea of the Black Community thinking in the millions as a tool of social and nationalist activism for enforcement.

FREDERICK MONDERSON

Whatever, we must still acknowledge, praise and give thanks for Minister Farrakhan's vision in seeing the need, inspiring Millions to think in such mega proportions while participating in structured recurring like decimal anniversaries to encourage future youth to build on the multifaceted platforms of social activism he bequeathed them. Thus, the Million Man March idea, its history as ultimately will materialize in creative epic proportions is a self-help movement to uplift African people here and abroad; and, we have Minister Louis Farrakhan and his cadre to thank for the creatively brilliant concept.

African Nationalist Poetry and Prose Photo. Portrait image of Rev. Al Sharpton in the "We Shall Not Be Moved" March in Washington, January 2017.

AFRICAN NATIONALIST POETRY AND PROSE

"The Egyptians believed that the search for *Maat* was the ultimate justification for human life. We do not need some greater insight, some deeper thought, some mystical endarkenment to understand the creation of this will *Maat* in all of its characteristics. Whether we speak of language, architecture, art, politics, religion, or mathematics, we are speaking of the majesty of the search for *Maat* in society. Without Egyptian cultural concepts, ritual forms, and ethical ideals we would not be speaking of the possibility of an African renaissance. This much Cheikh Anta Diop understood in *Civilization or Barbarism*." Molefi Kete Asante. *An Afrocentric Manifesto*. 2007.

18. BLACK HISTORY REFLECTIONS
Making of a Revolutionary
BY
DR. FRED MONDERSON

The election of Barack Obama to the United States Presidency in 2008 was probably the greatest revolution of modern times. Possessing political, social, economic, and military and foreign policy ramifications, he not simply changed but equally rescued his nation from a perdition that was essentially caused by years of arrogance and greed manifesting from its political citadels especially that under Republican leadership and control. Sadly, the

FREDERICK MONDERSON

many revolutionary and far-reaching accomplishments and transformations of Obama's tenure in office, standing proudly on the altar of justice are being challenged particularly by purveyors of bigotry and racial hatred. Surprisingly, however, people of goodwill, enthused with equally revolutionary fervor, will fight and challenge the evil this represents for the nation's moral fiber and its spine is at stake as we compete in a fast-changing modern world.

African Nationalist Poetry and Prose Photo.
LATIN CROSS – "Christian Faith."

AFRICAN NATIONALIST POETRY AND PROSE

Revolutionaries are people, often called reformers, who struggle to change inequities, whether political, social, artistic, economic or educational, in social systems, institutions or society. Conditions that motivate such individuals are generally ripe with oppression necessitating extended activism, much negotiation and even armed struggle. The process involves blood, sweat, tears, isolation, character assassination, and sometimes even death and dishonor. However, because those sincere individuals oftentimes have right and truth on their side, history's pendulum of equity, Dr. King's "Arc of the Moral Universe," eventually swings in their direction justifying their efforts and crowning their hard earned, richly deserved glory. I should add, in today world with its technological developments, armed struggle is not as viable an option as previously particularly thought in an organized societal context. As within the United States, organize, organize, organize, join organizations, form alliances, and effectuate unending creative protests are some of the best and most effective strategies to bring change! A good example is the movement that coalesced after Eric Garner, Michael Brown, and so many more wrongfully and needlessly murdered especially in 2015. However, since persistence and consistency are mandatory, remember Lerone Bennett advised: "Don't expect to win by Monday afternoon." The more potent and effective tool is that used by Dr. Martin Luther King in creative non-violence, civil disobedience and

FREDERICK MONDERSON

incessant activism. Surely, they took his life but he brought our people a long way! Looking back with today understanding, he was truly a remarkable American ahead of his time.

African Nationalist Poetry and Prose Photo. The "Great One" gets his street name in Harlem.

We could equally assign the term to revolutionary to religious reformers of which Akhenaton, the 18th Dynasty pharaoh (Amenhotep) is considered a religious revolutionary who in his contribution initiated new ideas in religion, science, art and architecture. However, he tried violence and this worked against his ideas because the oppressor always finds justifications to silence legitimate opposition once it is undergirded by indiscriminate actions and especially violence. Contrast this with Mahatma Gandhi and Dr. M.L. King's non-violent creative protests that proved effective. Also, in ancient times, Imhotep was a genius and architectural revolutionary who built the Step-Pyramid at Sakkara for the Pharaoh Zoser, 3rd Dynasty, 2600 B.C., that still stands today which is a triumph of his innovative

AFRICAN NATIONALIST POETRY AND PROSE

building techniques. Mentuhotep II of the 11th Dynasty was certainly revolutionary in enclosing mortuary structural paraphernalia in his worship temple building at Deir el Bahari. Senmut the architect who helped Queen Hatshepsut seize pharaonic power in a male dominated world and ruled for two decades, was obviously involved in a revolutionary process. His building of the Queen's temple at Deir el Bahari, next to and patterned on 500 years after Mentuhotep's Middle Kingdom structure, to which he innovated with many new architectural features, classifies him as revolutionary in thinking and building construction. However, this essay attempts to focus on revolutionary action that addresses oppression and people's attempts to change their societal norms and the political landscape of their nation in more contemporary times. More important, African-Americans and all people of goodwill must reject and struggle against the spurious claim "Man is made in the image of God, God is white. White is superior, black is inferior. So, in the natural order, so in the social order.

Equally and significantly, for the Black African race, the first revolutionary struggle against injustice has been the one to combat the "Curse of Ham" in the Bible. There are no other people on earth who has been cursed and despite the passage of time, the notions of the ages of "political" and even "religious correction" this problem has not been addressed. Remarkably the struggle must continue unless some people accept the merits of the situation and live in perpetuity in the belief that Blacks are cursed! Imagine all the unspeakable atrocities committed by other peoples and races, yet they are not cursed! However, but a Black man, actually a white man turned Black, who looked at his "drunk and naked father," must bear the animosity of that supposed curse and degradation for all time. While this notion is alien to Africa, imagine what form of cruelty this, myth made tangible in fact, really is? Let us also remember, in the Pre-Biblical world, the "paint factory" discovered in South Africa truly reminds us the African was pursuing Complex thinking" before any other people at the remote time of 107,000 years ago.

However, in particular regard to slavery and other forms of injustice, we first learn of large scale and systematic resistance to tyranny and oppression in the tale of a Roman slave named Spartacus who led a great force against that mighty Empire. But, though crushed, the memory of his actions put tyrants on notice. Slaves will rebel, causing great dislocation to society's order as they seek to right the wrongs of their conditions and set their people free. The African-American Historian Herbert Aptheker chronicled more than 100 slave rebellions in the Americas, and though many did not succeed and get positive press, they remain on the books and have been inspirational to many revolutionaries since that time.

AFRICAN NATIONALIST POETRY AND PROSE

The enslaved Cuffy led a rebellion in Guyana as early as 1763, a date which incidentally set in motion conditions that similarly led to the American Revolution to which that Great American statesman Patrick Henry proclaimed: "Give me liberty or give me death!" However, it was Crispus Attucks who has been the first revolutionary to lay down his life and also Peter Salem and Salem Po who were out there with George Washington and the Green Mountain Boys struggling to free this nation. Cuffy's struggle and aims were inspirational in the fight for Guyana's independence two centuries later in 1966. In the early 1800s, a Black-American ship captain of the same name, Paul Cuffe, repatriated Blacks back to Africa in his own vessel so they would escape the challenges and miseries facing free and enslaved Blacks in early 19th Century America.

The American people's revolutionary fight for freedom against tyranny, oppression, "taxation without representation" and the unjust nature of colonialism created several significant developments with long-lasting impact on the historical landscape. First, it produced the **Declaration of Independence**, **Articles of Confederation** and **United States Constitution** that challenged and inspired the French, Haitian and Latin American revolutionaries, as well as later peoples to be successful in their struggles for equality and independence. At that

FREDERICK MONDERSON

time, Benjamin Banneker's intellectual and architectural contributions in planning America's foundation surveying was equally revolutionary for an African-American possessing such tenacious skills. Sadly, on the day of his burial, arsonists destroyed his papers, his life's work and property seemingly to erase his name and contributions from history. On the other hand, the actions of Toussaint L'Ouverture, Henry Christophe and Jacques Dessalines were certainly revolutionary, emerging from slavery to struggle, free and found the First Black Republic in the New World comprising the state of Haiti. Unfortunately, the pressure brought on Haiti by slave holding nations and interests discouraged these great leaders' progeny from remaining true to the revolutionary spirit and this has helped contribute to the mess poor Haiti experiences continuously.

African Nationalist Poetry and Prose Photo. Tribute to the Ancestors – Images, 2019.

AFRICAN NATIONALIST POETRY AND PROSE

The second important thing about that American spirit exposed the underbelly of the horrible institution of slavery that not only later tore this nation apart but ingrained its tentacles and ugliness in an institutionalized system of *de jure* and *de facto* injustice. Sadly, this in turn gave birth to Jim Crowism, lynchings, racial discrimination, great economic disparity across the nation among haves and have-nots, Share Crop economic peonage, and the workings and essential features of the second generation off-springs represented in "James Crow, Jr. Esq.," and his *modus operandi*. The end result is racial profiling, institutional racism, police brutality, an organized and institutional incarceration system that today's activists, even legislators see the need for Prison Reform. But there is so much more, beyond despair feeding an ingrained hatred and self-hatred on the part of the victim and victimizer of the cruel malady.

Jean Baptiste Pointe du Sable and the founding of the site that became the City of Chicago were certainly revolutionary acts! Equally, this pioneering spirit followed in the footsteps of Estavanico who challenged the wilderness and blazed a trail across this country, opening trails that encouraged settlement.

Nonetheless, in the dictum of "a majority of one," Black and White American men and women of good

FREDERICK MONDERSON

conscience have risen up to challenge slavery's system of oppression, defusing it in all its institutionalized rancor and odiousness. We see the same cooperation and coalescing of opposition as acts of horror against African-American as they have unfolded. Significantly, in this quest, these activists were bruised and battered, giving and even having their lives threatened, even taken, by unjust and inhumane, heartless individuals. The roots and seeds of that resistance began on the shores of Africa resisting the slave catchers. It continued aboard the slaving vessels resisting the cruelty and inhuman conditions and made manifest in the likes of the Amistad and Gabriel Prosser's revolt, where in their minds, men refused to accept a man-made and unjust system imposed upon them. Yet, the truly revolutionary struggle began in earnest on the spiritual front when Revs. Absalom Jones and Richard Allen walked away from their Methodist Episcopal Church Christian brothers and sisters and founded their own African Methodist Episcopalian Zion Church in 1816. Equally too, by this time, Christian slave owners had effectively closed the strategic and tactical Christian conversion "salvation route" to African emancipation. Nonetheless, the use of the word African was revolutionary in itself for it kept the light shining in those dark days when the ugliness of an unjust legal system justified reversing god-created man into a beast, chattel! In fact, the tenacious cement-like resilient nature of African spirituality, to this day, has meant salvation and survival even to those who have not been or are in the

AFRICAN NATIONALIST POETRY AND PROSE

revolutionary struggle challenging the spiritual warfare directed against the sons and daughters of Africa.

Gabriel Prosser and Jack Bowler led a revolt in 1800 and this response sent a strong and significant warning to the bastions of oppression. Captured and bound, in his challenge in face of this tyranny, Prosser compared himself to George Washington. He said, essentially, according to Norman Hodges' *Black History*, Monarch Notes, (1974: 77), "I have nothing more to offer than what General Washington would have had to offer, had he been taken by the British officers and put to trial by them. I have ventured my life in endeavoring to obtain the liberty of my countrymen and am willing to sacrifice to their cause.... I beg as a favor that I may be immediately led to execution. I know that you have predetermined to shed my blood. Why, then, all this mockery of a trial?" Again, revolutionary action was followed in 1822 by the Denmark Vesey conspiracy in Charleston, South Carolina. Vesey's insurrection, however, was betrayed by a "house (Negro) slave" infected with the Judas Iscariot syndrome. This was Malcolm X's "We sick boss" realization. Nevertheless, the message kept being sent, "You may oppress us, even kill our leaders," but as the Calypsonian Black Stalin so eloquently sang, 'The more Africans they gun down, the more Africans keep coming.'

FREDERICK MONDERSON

Significantly, resistance triumphed in the literary masterpiece of David Walker's **Appeal to Colored Men** in 1926 imploring rise up and overthrow oppression as a God given right. A few years later, Nat Turner's 1931 blitzkrieg **Slave Rebellion** with its bone chilling seriousness killed 45 whites in Virginia. This revolutionary resistance was a rude wake-up call, even though he was betrayed and executed. This action also sent a powerful message, "Don't sleep too sound, Black Power will get you!"

Strange enough, oppression is its own enemy for it gives birth to fearless individuals who emerge and challenge its injustice. A decade after Nat Turner, Samuel Carson ("**The Runaway**") ran away from slavery in South Carolina. He joined the US Navy, fought and died in the Mexican War and was buried in the Brooklyn Navy Yard. Resurrected a century and a half later, he created a significant impact by opening the "Door of Return" creating a site of pilgrimage for African-Americans beginning the search for roots beginning in Ghana, West Africa. Henry Highland Garnett, a great abolitionist gave voice to activism and resistance about mid-Nineteenth Century. In his own right, Garnett's contemporary Dred Scott stood up and allowed Chief Justice Roger Taney to use the power of the state, the

AFRICAN NATIONALIST POETRY AND PROSE

US Constitution and the Supreme Court in the most oppressive and humiliating manner to sit him down.

Conversely, a century later, in an age of passionate activism, when Rosa Parks sat down, the Supreme Court stood up to fight the prevailing wrong having done so a decade earlier in the *Brown v. Board* ruling. From there on, the courts followed a "Domino Theory" reversing previous odious rulings by helping the Black man to stand up and at least putting the oppressor on notice America no long sanctions your type of behavior. Still, there are "die hards" who must yet learn this lesson.

Interestingly enough, Roger Taney's historic ruling actually exposed and expressed the inherent contradiction of the **Declaration of Independence**, enforcing it in law. In the cornerstone of its historic affirmation, the Declaration of Independence declared: "We hold these truths to be self-evident that all men are created equal and are endowed by their creator with the inalienable rights to life, liberty and the pursuit of happiness," meaning right to own property.

At that time Blacks were enslaved and thus had none of those rights, because they were property, chattel. One hundred years later Chief Justice Taney so

FREDERICK MONDERSON

emphatically and essentially pointed it out! "Blacks were property and neither men nor citizens of the United States." This came about because, upon capture in Africa and trans-shipment across the Atlantic for purposes of transforming the "New World," colonialism used the force and power and armament aided by man-made law to deprive Africans of their humanity, reversing the process of evolution, depriving them of their manhood, and making them less than a man! The **3/5 Compromise Law** of the U.S. Constitution, upholding the reversal still advanced the African to 3/5 of a man! Imagine being a man from the feet up to just below the shoulders; headless, therefore brainless! The "Super-masculine menial!" syndrome is what Blacks were reduced to in that existence. Equally, slavery was so cruel it never sanctioned marriage. It never permitted families that basic, human, nurturing, social unit that all humans were entitled to.

As an example, when Coleman Sharpton was sent from South Carolina to Florida to pay a debt of the Thurmond family, it was some feat to keep his wife and two kids together. Mr. Coleman Sharpton could not complain. The law did not protect him. He had no guarantees of life, liberty or pursuit of happiness. He was chattel, same as a sheep, a bale of cotton, a pig, goat, or horse, property! This state of affair, a "house divided" between "slave and free" coined by Lincoln, is what tore the Union apart in the Civil War. It's what John Brown rose against and gave his life to

AFRICAN NATIONALIST POETRY AND PROSE

end. John Brown was a true revolutionary who gave his all for the cause. It's the same issue metamorphosed, or "Old wines in new wine skins" the new oppressive strategy of joblessness, mis-education, incarceration, disfranchisement, police brutality, and most important a cultivated viciousness in which, through ingrained self-hatred, Blacks senselessly kill Blacks, and this is just a part of overall senseless violence Blacks are equally and perennially victims of.

It's the same issues abolitionists like Frederick Douglass, Harriet Tubman, Martin Delaney, Sojourner Truth and the Black regiments in the Civil War fought, worked against and hoped to change, yet saw its reality in which he pointed to names as slow in coming. But there were other Black Abolitionists in the struggle as indicated in Benjamin Quarles' book by the same name including William Wells Brown, Charles Lenox Remond, James Forten, Lensford Land and Prince Saunders who were very active in efforts "fighting the system." Their white counterparts in the abolitionist struggle included William Lloyd Garrison, Arthur and Lewis Tappan, Theodore Weld, and James G. Burney who put their money and effort into the struggle against this form of oppression. Theirs was a continuation of the struggle begun by the English abolitionists Granville Sharpe, Wilberforce, Buxton, Clarkson and so many others who worked to end the Slave Trade in Africans as the first step to eradicate that institutionalized

FREDERICK MONDERSON

"crime against humanity" represented by internal and external slave trade, "slave farms" in the "deep south," the "home of prolific lynching," and slavery. The Underground Railroad and its agents were also part of the radical revolutionary spirit transforming America at a time when Harriet Tubman (1820-1913) boldly declared: "I never lost a passenger and I never ran my train off the track."

The rights, privileges and advantages gained in Reconstruction following the Civil War produced significant Black southern political power in the persons of Robert Smalls and Blanche K. Bruce as Senators from Mississippi and a number of Congressmen including Robert Smalls of South Carolina; John W. Maynard of Louisiana; John R. Lynch of Mississippi; Benjamin Turner of Alabama; Robert C. DE Large, South Carolina; Josiah T. Walls, Florida; and Joseph H. Rainey and Robert Brown Elliot of South Carolina. Their white allies Thaddeus Stevens and Charles Sumner soon passed on after their work on the **Reconstruction Acts of 1861** and the **Civil Rights Act of 1875** were accomplished. Important also, betrayal in the shameful and political sell-out in the **Election of 1876** spelt doom for Blacks in the South and nationwide in curtailment of the emerging political power. Shamefully, for showing such courageous effort, Charles Sumner was attacked on the floor of the House of Representatives, that "Holy Grail," where more than a century later, Joe Wilson's

AFRICAN NATIONALIST POETRY AND PROSE

disrespectful pliant "You Lie" to Barack Obama echoed far and wide!

African nationalist Poetry and Prose Photo. Adam Clayton Powell and Clyde Frazier together is fantastic.

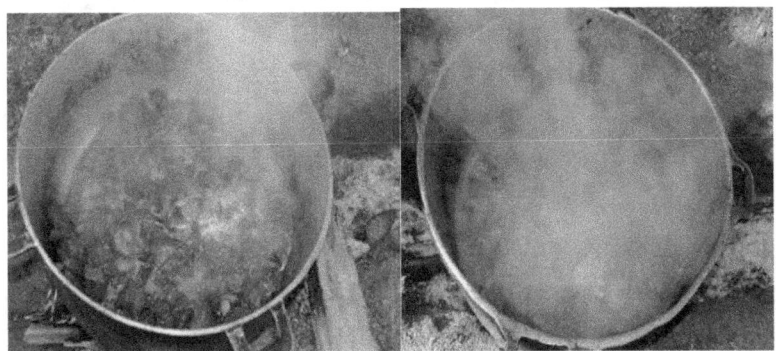

African Nationalist Poetry and Prose Photo. How deliciously luscious these meats look on the fire.

In the developing Post-Civil War and Reconstruction new reality, Black gains were snatched by the "Elder Crow" and his associates the Ku Klux Klan, Knights of the White Camelia, Knights of the Rising Sun, the White Line, The Palefaces, all with their intimidation

FREDERICK MONDERSON

of Blacks through lynchings, tar and feathers and as co-conspirators enforcing poll taxes, property taxes, literacy tests and the "Grand Father Clause" ramifications, all of which undergirded Share-Cropping and economic peonage. Later White Citizens groups holding "White Primaries" equally tried to stop black progress, political and otherwise. But the way forward was already established and such terrorism did not stop churchmen from Republican activism during the age of Reconstruction, Rev. Hiram H. Wells of Mississippi; Rev. Richard R. Cain of South Carolina; and Bishop Henry M. Turner of Georgia who played major roles in unfolding 19th Century politics in a nation confronted by ongoing racial terrorism. In the southern white backlash, Congressman George A. White of North Carolina remained a single voice against spreading Jim Crow.

Out of this mayhem emerged Booker T. Washington and his contemporary George Washington Carver who began revolutionizing farming techniques advancing the southern economy from his base at Tuskegee Institute. In this nightmarish age for Black people, "Booker T" preached "Do for Self," and founded Tuskegee Institute to teach Blacks industrial skills for self-sufficiency as a way to create economic independence. In that age, Elijah McCoy, the "real McCoy," and Granville Woods were industrial engineers, contemporary with Machinist Frank J. Farrell in the Knights of Labor, whose pathways were followed by such eminent scientists as Charles

AFRICAN NATIONALIST POETRY AND PROSE

Richard Drew, Ernest Everett Just, James Latimore and Percy Julien in establishing themselves as geniuses of creativity. Nevertheless, "men of devil like aspirations" later infiltrated Tuskegee Institute and perpetrated the "Tuskegee Syphilis Experiment" that maimed and disfigured many Blacks for decades. By the last two decades of the 19th Century, conditions of terrorism were such that 3 Blacks were being lynched per week! This forced women such as Ida B. Wells, a protest leader in the 1890s, to challenge Pres. William McKinley in the statement: "We refuse to believe this country, so powerful to defend its citizens abroad, is unable to protect its citizens at home."

In those days of unspeakable horrors perpetrated against Blacks, two revolutionary giants emerged. Much like the tides, strong Black men kept coming! W.E.B. DuBois was a literary and intellectual giant whose writings, activism and pronouncements dominated the 20th Century, long after his death in Ghana in 1963. The first Black Harvard University Ph.D. in 1896, author of *Reconstruction, The Slave Trade To America*: 1638 to 1878, *The Negro, Souls of Black Folks, Black Folks Then and Now, The Gift of Black Folks, The World and Africa* and more, particularly as Editor of *The Crisis* newspaper. His interests were manifold, for he was the "Father of Pan-Africanism" and a vocal voice for the oppressed African. His counterpart in the first decades of the

FREDERICK MONDERSON

20th Century, though they differed in strategy, was Marcus Moziah Garvey whose mass movement under the banner of the Red, Black and Green's Universal Negro Improvement Association and Universal Communities League upliftment efforts mobilized millions of Blacks worldwide and essentially foreshadowed James Brown's 'Say it Loud, I'm Black and Proud' acclimation for Garvey made the Black man believe in himself! His saying "Up you mighty Race, You can accomplish what you will" almost has cultural status with James Weldon Johnson's "Lift Every Voice and Sing" the **Black National Anthem**. A third revolutionary was William Monroe Trotter, who at the turn of the 20th Century demanded "Full equality in all things governmental, political, civil and judicial." J. Thomas Fortune advocated and set up "Protection Leagues" in many states.

Paralleling DuBois' activism and literary expression, Drusilla Dungee, John Huggins, Arthur Schomberg and Carter G. Woodson opened an intellectual front in publishing and archiving. A journalist for Garvey's newspaper *The Negro World*, Woodson published *The Mis-Education of the Negro* and *The Education of the Negro*, as well as *The African Background Outlined*. He is considered the "Father of Black History Month" celebrations. Thank God, this cultural breakthrough has had long lasting and positive ramifications!

AFRICAN NATIONALIST POETRY AND PROSE

It's reasonable to assume these intellectual revolutionaries operating within the minefield of American social injustice influenced Paul Robeson as they probably equally influenced the educator Mary McLeod Bethune. In that age as the world shrank by events of the devastation of World War I and World War II, Langston Hughes carried the torch in the **Harlem Renaissance** while Claude McKay's powerful poem "If We Must Die" was really far reaching in its notifying implications. Equally too, the emergence of unionization in the colonies of Africa and the West Indies, faster trans-Atlantic travels, Blacks coming of age recognizing limitations and potentials, and contemporary decolonization in the colonies, all fueled a new movement to put human rights and civil liberties on the crucible of America's conscience. This was the Civil Rights Movement! It gave birth to "Sit-ins," formation of the Southern Christian Leadership Council (**SCLC**), "Freedom Rides," creatively effective protests and other forms of activism that led to the March on Washington in 1963, and the deaths of 3 civil rights workers, Andrew Goodman, James Chaney, and Michael Schwerner. The 4 little girls killed in a church bombing in Birmingham, Alabama, were part of 14 such bombings in "Bombingham" that year. Then there were assassinations of Black leaders in the persons of Malcolm X, Martin Luther King, Medgar Evers, James Meredith, and several others. These

FREDERICK MONDERSON

events of mobilization resulting in legislation at national and state levels.

Men with military service, an eye opener for Harry Belafonte, Rev Shuttlesworth, and Thurgood Marshall as legal counsel for the **NAACP** who won a historic **Brown v. Board of Education of Topeka, Kansas** in 1954; a decision that had fueled the challenges to white supremacy, racial segregation and discrimination, possessed an audacity to tell "Bull Connor" and his types, "Bring it on!" Don't get me started with Martin Luther King and John Lewis' historic stance at the Edmund Pettis Bridge on the march from Selma to Montgomery, Alabama. Then there's Huey Newton, Bobby Seale, George Jackson, Angela Davis, Eldridge Cleaver before salvation and Fred Hampton of the Black Panther Party rising up fearlessly.

AFRICAN NATIONALIST POETRY AND PROSE

African Nationalist Poetry and Prose Photo.
TANIT - "Islamic Faith."

African Nationalist Poetry and Prose Photo.
The message is clear.

FREDERICK MONDERSON

African Nationalist Poetry and Prose Photo. **Zimbabwe. Gladman Zinyeka**. "'At One with Nature.' Centering on the environment, 'At One with Nature' depicts a man embracing an eagle."

As these events unfolded revolutionary Black men and women began to spring up in the States, in Africa and the Caribbean. The persons of Martin Luther King, Malcolm X, Stokeley Carmichael (Kwame Ture), Elijah Mohammed and the Black Muslims, James Meredith and Medgar Evers, Andrew Young, Rosa Parks, Rev. Joseph Lowery, Jesse Jackson, and Fannie Lou Hamer, that staunch Civil Rights activist in the U.S. ; in Africa, Kwame Nkrumah, Namdi Azikwe, Tafawa Balewa, Julius Nyerere, Chief Luthuli, Patrice Lumumba, Sekou Toure, and Nelson and Winnie Mandela all followed in the footsteps of Bishop Crowder, the West African missionary and activist; and, in the Caribbean Forbes Burnham; in Jamaica, Norman then Michael Manley; and in

AFRICAN NATIONALIST POETRY AND PROSE

Trinidad and Tobago George Padmore, Jeremiah Butler and Eric Williams. This latter personage particularly, who blended political insight and acumen with intellectual fervor and academic excellence began chronicling many significant events in the African experience including *Capitalism and Slavery* and *From Columbus to Castro*.

Joel A. Rogers opened new intellectual frontiers with his books *Sex and Race* (3 volumes) and *World's Great Men of Color* (2 volumes); the Guyanese George G.M. James in *Stolen Legacy*, and Chancellor Williams in *Destruction of Black Civilization: Great Issues of a Race*, while Dr. John Henry Clarke, Dr. John Jackson, and Dr. Yosef Ben-Jochannan in the United States all challenged literary backwaters, academic distortion and omission while becoming prolific authors emphasizing roles of African people in creating historical accomplishments of unparalleled magnitude. Dr. Clarke emphasized the United States' role of Blacks and Africa particularly; Dr. Jackson explained about African Civilizations; and Dr. Yosef Ben-Jochannan researched Nile Valley cultural and religious history. Chief Anta Diop and his associate Theophile Obenga deconstructed and reconstructed the role of Blacks in ancient Egypt. Diop published several important works including *African Origins of Civilization: Myth or Reality*, *Cultural Unity of Black Africa*, *Civilization or Barbarism* and with Obenga he wrote "The Peopling

FREDERICK MONDERSON

of Ancient Egypt and the Decipherment of the Meroitic Script" at **UNESCO's** 1974 Conference on Egypt. Obenga wrote among other things, *Ancient Egypt and Black Africa* and the profound *African Philosophy: The Pharaonic Period: 2780-300 B.C.*

By this time, the great Black revolutionaries in the fields of science, agriculture, stage and screen, education and literary and intellectual output emerged successful in beating back the specter of Black illiteracy and fear. They secured and cleared new ground upon which they built citadels of Black integrity, industriousness, artistic creativity and intellectual and educational creative daring. They were the dynamos representing their people's social and human progress along the right path of human development, experimentation, advancement and empowerment.

On another front, the political struggle was hard fought, sometimes bitter but it had sweet results in the election of Black mayors Richard Hatcher, in Gary, Indiana; Coleman Young, in Detroit, Michigan; Charles Evers in Fayette, Mississippi; Carl Stokes in Cleveland, Ohio, and later Andrew Young and Maynard in Atlanta, Georgia. Such progress was the result of Black enfranchisement granted by the Civil Rights Acts and the Voting Rights Acts passed as a result of the fearlessness of creative protests with a revolutionary fervor developed in the Civil Rights Movement.

AFRICAN NATIONALIST POETRY AND PROSE

These fathers and mothers paved the way for revolutionary progress of Blacks in music, business, radio, screen and television and particularly in medicine and in education and business administration. Louis Satchmo Armstrong, Nat King Cole, The Drifters, Ben E. King, Otis Redding and Carla Thomas, as well as Dizzy Gillespie, Charlie Byrd Parker, James Brown, Marvin Gaye, Michael Jackson and the Motown sounds began to sing away the veils of the blues. Lorraine Hansberry's *A Raisin in the Sun*; James Baldwin's prolific pen wrote *Nobody Knows My Name* and *The Fire Next Time* among others; Richard Wright's *Black Boy*; Ralph Ellison's *Invisible Man*, Claude Brown's *Manchild in the Promised Land*; and Leroi Jones' (Amiri Baraka) *The Dutchman* and *The Slave* were not simply ground-breaking literary expressions but they told several stories with a message   The suave and signification of Sidney Poitier and Harry Belafonte on the screen and musically aided every civil rights cause in their own low-key but effective manner of creative protest. Equally, such revolutionary groups as **The Last Poets**, the multi-talented Rashaan Roland Kirk, and Comedian Dick Gregory coupled their musical expressions and comic performances with messages of social consciousness and political activism. Let us not forget James Farmer of **CORE** as well as W.E.B. Dubois' role in founding the Niagara Movement and the **NAACP** in the early

FREDERICK MONDERSON

days of the 20th Century and Whitney Young of the **National Urban League**. We must recount the contributions of A. Philip Randolph heading the **Sleeping Car Porters Union**; Jackie Robinson, Satchel Paige and Jack Johnson in sports as well as Jessie Owens in track who were all blazing trails in their respective fields lifting and polishing the Black image. As such, they not simply helped to raise the people's consciousness but had begun to challenge and beat back the citadels of Jim Crowism in its many guises, racism, overt and covert and institutional, even manifesting in the machinations of the prison industrial complex. In this way, they began opening doors and paving the way for the next generation of activists.

Out of this legacy emerged Robert Sonny "Abubadika" Carson as activists in education along with Jitu Weusi (Les Campbell); the pens of Molefi Asante, James Amos and Maulana Karenga, Dr. Jacob Carruthers and Conrad Worrill; Chief James Parker, Rev. Herbert Daughtry, Rev. William Jones, Attorneys Alton Maddox, Mason and Colin Moore, Michael Warren and Michael Hardy and even such icons as Jeanette Gadsen and certainly Carlos Lazama who added the carnival cultural flavor to Black expression, all count as illustrious ancestors. Jimmy Cliff, Mighty Sparrow and Lord Kitchener certainly lent their share of party music to make the challenges and suffering go down easier.

AFRICAN NATIONALIST POETRY AND PROSE

The new revelation that the Rev. Al Sharpton's ancestors were enslaved by the ancestors of the most vocal and intractable racist and slavery apologist, Strom Thurmond; who incidentally loved Black women as did Thomas Jefferson; underscored the view that people who probably abhorred slavery produced progeny who were/are foremost revolutionaries and activists. Samuel Carson ran away from slavery, and his time in the U.S. Navy added to the myth of "**The Runaway**," until discovered by the Navy in 1996. Resurrected and galvanizing many activists, he was repatriated and buried in Ghana by his revolutionary great-nephew Sonny Carson. His going home to Africa was certainly revolutionary for it was the first time that any African who came through the "**Door of No Return**" ever returned to the mother continent to create the "**Door of Return**." This Samuel and Sonny Carson did and sent a multi-faceted message.

The moral of this story is that though many spurious and misleading allegations were made about the benefits of slavery, a rather accurate and not much discussed pronouncement is that some descendants of the slaves became revolutionaries in their own right blazing trails in different fields and fighting the powers that be. After all, in the heyday of the French Revolution, the Englishman Edmund Burke's *Reflections on the Revolution in France* (1792-93) affirmed: "The only thing necessary for evil to

FREDERICK MONDERSON

triumph is for good men to say nothing." In our case, not that there is an exception to the rule but that the exception proves the rule for, without question good people will rise up to challenge oppression and injustice, whether it was in the past, contemporary times and in the future. Martin Luther King in his "I have a Dream" speech spoke of a 'stone of hope from a mountain of despair' and while Jesus, who incidentally was a Black man, spoke of a 'mustard seed of faith,' so we must recognize there were millions of slaves lost to Africa, in which W.E.B. Dubois gave 100 million. Nevertheless, the few, yet significant revolutionaries mentioned here have shouldered the burden and advanced the cause of their people, mountains of challenges notwithstanding, their actions were secured the benefit of all humanity. Thus, we know without question, any gains made by Blacks benefits all Americans and America as well.

African Nationalist Poetry and Prose Photo. NAACP "March to end Racial Profiling" and call to "Unite Here."

AFRICAN NATIONALIST POETRY AND PROSE

African Nationalist Poetry and Prose Photo.
"The Right to Vote! Use It or Lose It."

African Nationalist Poetry and Prose Photo.
Tribute to the Ancestors – Images, 2019.

FREDERICK MONDERSON

"The antiquity of Egypt creates problems of understanding because of the numerous breaks in the chain of dynasties, coups, foreign invasions and regional intrigues. Changes in religion, politics and art happened frequently enough to force Africanists and Africologists to create their own perioizations. Large blocks of Egyptian history have been designated the Old Kingdom, Middle Kingdom, Empire, Ethiopian Period, Persian Period, and the Saitic Revival. I have renamed these periods: *United Kingdom, Middle Kingdom, Majestic Period, Grand Empire, Persian Period*, Saitic Revival, and *Ptolemaic Rule*. Despite the modifications suggested by these periods the constancy and continuity of Egypt are remarkable for a country. The Egyptians retained their essential African outlook in terms of myths, symbolisms, and ethos throughout the history of the country. Only with the arrival of the Greeks, and later in 639 A.D., with the arrival of the Arabs in force did the mythopoeic pattern of Egypt undergo changes that have impacted the historiography of the region to this day." Molefi Kete Asante. *African Pyramids of Knowledge*. 2015.

19. COME BACK, SONNY CARSON
BY
DR. FRED MONDERSON

It's been fifteen years since the passing of a giant of the human spirit, Sonny Abubadika Carson and notwithstanding efforts of others; no one has been

AFRICAN NATIONALIST POETRY AND PROSE

able to take the place of the redoubtable, educational activist and nationalist leader. The live presence of Mr. Carson caused all with negatively disposed intentions towards the Black and Spanish communities in New York especially, to pause and think carefully before they acted. This is because he was able to bring these two important groups together and stand to represent their combined interests. Oftentimes malcontent individuals won out in their intended misgivings but Sonny was quick to let them know he was keeping score. The symbolism of the man was significant across the political, educational, law-enforcement, economic, cultural and even religious spheres of social existence. That is why in these critical and troubling times we pray his indomitable spirit continue to guide, strengthen, embolden and empower their leaders and the people for whom he fought so un-relentlessly, for so long. He challenged the Prison Industrial Complex that perennially emasculated the psychological and moral nature of African-Americans. So much so, today a wide spectrum of people of conscience recognize the injustice in the system and insist on the need for change.

FREDERICK MONDERSON

African Nationalist Poetry and Prose Photo. In rare form and in all smiles, Sonny Carson sits at Akbar's funeral.

In his efforts, Sonny's symbolism was unmatched as a beacon among those incarcerated; those about to be incarcerated and those in training for incarceration. By challenging the prison industrial complex behemoth that daily eviscerated the emotional and psychological manhood of young Black and Spanish persons, he was a beacon to which these persons within its clutches could reach seeking help to address their predicaments. Even more significant, however, his influence particularly manifested among the young, creative artists in the music and entertainment industry, who, with encouragement, have produced wonderfully spectacular cultural lyrics. However, when, in this new and modern musical upsurge, the lyrics had embraced a negative and seemingly destructive tone, Sonny was quick to

AFRICAN NATIONALIST POETRY AND PROSE

insist the artists, who actually listened to him, "tone it down" and so helping to shape a more constructively creative expression of the cultural phenomenon.

African Nationalist Poetry and Prose Photo. Sonny Carson stands with his son, Lumumba Carson (left), Prof. James Small (rear right). His Chief of Staff Atiem Ferguson (right) and others in this photo at 'Allah You Akbar' funeral.

Still, Sonny Carson was more than an advocate for those in trouble with the law and purveyors of good and bad music. He was an avid education activist, a principal in the Ocean-Hill-Brownsville challenge to the New York City Board of Education displacement of resources, human and material, and an advocate for the voiceless in conflict with landlords and social agencies, and he played a crucial role in movements, institutions and organization building. He despaired of the many funerals he attended and never forgot that devastation of lynchings showing black men hanging, and even burning, across America as avid reminders of the underbelly of racial animosity in the nation when Black men had no rights which a white man was bound to respect. Within the realm of maladies affecting the Black Community, Sonny formed **Black Men's Movement for Social Betterment** and **Black Men Against Crack**, to combat the scourge that decimated so many. He was instrumental in helping found Medgar Evers College and actively involved in moving the institution into permanence as a 4-year institution with an African cultural orientation, since it served a predominantly African-American population.

African Nationalist Poetry and Prose Photo. **UNIA-ACL** (United Negro Improvement Association and African Communities League).

African Nationalist Poetry and Prose Photo. Tribute to the Ancestors – Images, 2019.

AFRICAN NATIONALIST POETRY AND PROSE

African Nationalist Poetry and Prose Photo. Sonny Carson speaks to his son Lumumba Carson also known as "Professor X."

As a founding member of the **Restoration Corporation** with a mission to economically revitalize the Bedford Stuyvesant and neighboring communities, Sonny's involvement in community's economic revitalization yet antedated formation of Restoration. In fact, like most young black men of his time, coming of age in post-World War II urban America, shaped by civil rights activism, Mr. Carson was imprisoned for conduct unbecoming. Upon his release, he began advocating for jobs for blacks,

FREDERICK MONDERSON

shaping the relationship between businesses in the black community and the residents they served, even finally insisting on black ownership of "Mom and Pop" stores and even larger entities. Next, he advocated for jobs in the broader "downtown" business community and in construction enterprises.

African Nationalist Poetry and Prose Photo. Sonny Carson - Nationalist, civil rights activist, father and friend of many.

One of his most significant accomplishments was formation of **The Committee to Honor Black Heroes**. Such a creation was a stroke of

AFRICAN NATIONALIST POETRY AND PROSE

genius! He had despaired over the absence of any recognition of Black heroes, particularly in black communities, especially in Brooklyn. He was quick to recognize there were roadways named after Martin Luther King, but these had come at a tremendous price. Sure, Harlem had Malcolm X and Frederick Douglass Boulevards but they too were hard won. Gazing at the cornice and face of the Brooklyn Museum, Columbia University's Paley Library and the Department of Health's building at 125 Worth Street in downtown Manhattan, even the sidewalk along lower Broadway emblazoned with the names of western, European and American literary and scientific heroes, even foreign visitors, Sonny soon realized no more modern buildings were so decorated.

To wait to see black heroes so honored is like waiting to see the cows come home and they never do. As such, Sonny, in forming the Committee to Honor Black Heroes quickly pushed for recognition, passage and implementation of streets honoring **Marcus Garvey** and **Malcolm X** with Boulevards. He named **Malcolm X** and **Toussaint L'Ouverture Schools** and laid the foundation to rename Fulton Street after **Harriet Ross Tubman**. Had he lived longer in general things may have been better.

FREDERICK MONDERSON

However, as "systems" could be reactionary, when it was time to name 3 blocks along Gates Avenue in Bedford-Stuyvesant section of Brooklyn, Abubadikaville, the Speaker of the City Council and several elements therein castigated him and voted against such a measure. Sadly, this denial, despite the local community through its local, local government, the Community Board, that voted overwhelmingly to recognize Sonny Carson as a local hero; their hero, deserving this honor; and not let their heroes be chosen or dictated to by people who use their power for selfish ends! Mindful that some such individuals were accused of City Council financial inappropriateness, the spirit of Sonny Carson hovers, having come back, crying for change, decrying the foul odor generated therein by the little Caesars who though him unworthy! Even more sadly, while he fought for his community, they sought empowerment recognition and enrichment at the expense of the community.

Sonny Carson was not simply a local hero; he had national standing and this he took to the international stage by creating the "Door of Return" in Ghana, West Africa. For decades, the Carson family retold the "Myth of the Runaway" only to have in 1996, the US Navy contact Sonny Carson informing that his ancestor Samuel Carson, an ex-slave who served and died in the Mexican War of 1845 was buried in Brooklyn Navy Yard, at that time a segregated cemetery. Forming the "Bones Committee" that met for 2 years, the decision was finally to reinter this

AFRICAN NATIONALIST POETRY AND PROSE

hero in Ghana as the highlight of the **First Emancipation Day Ceremony** on August 1, 1998, inaugurated by President Gerry Rawlings. Strange, this significant happening was given worldwide media exposure but went unreported in this United States of America. Nevertheless, the *Daily Challenge* and *Afro Times* did wonderful centerfold exposures of the Prospect Park Ceremony honoring the runaway's departure entitled "Brooklyn Remembers Runaway Slave Samuel Carson." Signed by the photographer and author on the day of the burial establishing a philosophic and spiritual connection to the Ghanaian burial, this colorful centerfold expose is now a respected artwork in the Library of Congress, Washington, DC. Unfortunately, no one in America, black or white, rich or poor, museum or household, possesses a copy of this masterpiece of historical significance. All part of the legacy of Sonny Robert Carson, insightful leader, theorist, activist, nationalist and local hero, equally a revered ancestor forever remembered in personal and collective immortality.

FREDERICK MONDERSON

African Nationalist Poetry and Prose Photo. The Message is clear – as part of the "We will not be moved" march, "I stand with Planned Parenthood."

African Nationalist Poetry and Prose Photo. Print mural of Black Heroes.

African Nationalist Poetry and Prose Photo. Tribute to the Ancestors – Images, 2019.

AFRICAN NATIONALIST POETRY AND PROSE

"Most Afrocentrists have a transcontinental African consciousness about research so that the entire African world and all of its phenomena and penumbrations are open to this dynamic historiography. Scholars are eager to engage Africa that suggest agency and centrality, that is, Africa as subject and actor in its own sphere of the world. New discoveries made by Afrocentrists and non-Afrocentrists in Ghana, Nigeria, Benin, Cameroon, South Africa, Malagasy are just as interesting as those made in Egypt and Nubia. But why should we leave out the study of Egypt. Should Afrocentrists abandon their interest in Algeria and Morocco before Islam? Shall we not encourage our students to conceive a history of Africa written from an African point of view? The meaning of such appoint of view, is, of course, Afrocentric." Molefi Kete Asante and Ama Mazama. 2002. *Egypt vs. Greece - and the American Academy. The debate over the birth of civilization.*"

20. SONNY CARSON: 'AT THE GATES' BY DR. FRED MONDERSON

Reflecting, one could well imagine Robert Sonny "**Abubadika**" Carson's arrival at the "Pearly Gates" of heaven and Saint Peter beginning questioning him as to his credentials for admittance

FREDERICK MONDERSON

into the joys of this wonderful existence. Before answering, the observant Carson looked past the gate to a gathering of anxiously awaiting friendly faces who, informed he was on his way and in protest mood, kept shouting "Welcome, Welcome," "Let him in! Let him in!" In this crowd, he could make out the "Runaway Slave" Samuel Carson, Harriet Tubman, Nat Turner, Martin Luther King, Junior and Senior, Thurgood Marshall, Alex Haley, Adam Clayton Powell, Langston Hughes, Rosa Parks, Charles Richard Drew, George Washington and George Washington Carver, "Allah You Akbar" Bramwell, Benjamin Banneker, Marcus Garvey, Percy Julian, Paul Robeson and Mary McLeod Bethune. Across from these he saw ancestors who had survived the Slave Trade and some ex-slaves still in rags but with their chains tossed to the side. Behind these all, he heard the most melodious singing coming from an orchestra composed of singers Michael Jackson, Teddy Pendergrass, Luther Vandross, Mahalia Jackson, Marvin Gaye and Bob Marley, while Miles Davis, Dizzy Gillespie, Charlie Parker, "Satchmo" Louis Armstrong and Count Basie played unbelievable and melodious sounds on their instruments.

Embolden by such familiarity Sonny Carson moved toward the questioning table at the gate to begin the process. He stated; he came from a poor South Carolina family who moved to Brooklyn in a significant population migration in the World War II era. Coming of age in Post-World War II America,

AFRICAN NATIONALIST POETRY AND PROSE

Sonny, like so many Black Urban youth were "troublesome," indulged in drugs and all forms of illegal behavior including gang membership that landed him in prison and was forced to enroll to fight in the Korean War of the 1950s. After one stint in prison, perhaps becoming socially transformed by his experiences, Sonny Carson became a social activist.

The **Fulton Street Corridor** in the Bedford-Stuyvesant section, for the longest, had been the economic mainstream of that community. In that era of the Civil Rights Movement, all such businesses and their employees were white in a black community. Sonny began advocating if Blacks shop and spend their money in these stores, then they should be able to work there. Here began his notion of the economic boycott that had gained so much for organized black movements. As this idea caught on, in an era when "Black is Beautiful" was a meaningful mantra, Sonny began the long and arduous voyage of social transformation of himself and his community. As the good of this new idea caught on, Sonny began calling for "Black ownership."

FREDERICK MONDERSON

African Nationalist Poetry and Prose Photo. At the funeral of 'Allah U Akbar,' Bramfield, Lumumba Carson (far left), "Shamgod" (partially obscured), unknown in hat, Sonny Carson, Atiem Ferguson and Jeanette Gadson, formerly Deputy Brooklyn Borough President.

African Nationalist Poetry and Prose Photo. Sonny Carson reads a "Proclamation" at Akbar's funeral.

AFRICAN NATIONALIST POETRY AND PROSE

This novel idea led to opening of "Mom and Pop Stores" that sprang up in many places in the black community, across the country. Thus, Sonny Carson had arrived as a civil rights/social activist, and soon he evolved into a nationalist activist who teamed up with the Republic of New Africa demanding nation status for blacks. Such respectful advocacy did not preclude him being implicated and charged with kidnapping and labeled a rabble rouser as well as garnering the enmity of many.

From this time on Sonny Carson emerged as a leader who challenged the establishment because he was not satisfied with the condition of blacks in this country and reactions to black protest to address civil and human rights issues, all being fueled by the significance of the African decolonization movement sweeping that continent in the 1960s. As America blazed with the new activism, Sonny became an admirer of Malcolm X, the fiery Black Muslim Minister who wanted radical change for blacks in America and he was particularly moved by his assassination, never accepting nor forgiving those who committed the despicable act. With a number of others, he held high Betty Shabazz because she had to raise those children, but most important she was considered the queen of a fallen battlefield general. Nevertheless, at first, Carson was lukewarm towards Martin Luther King, Jr., who believed in non-violent social protest. Thus, with the assassination of first Malcolm X and then Dr. Martin Luther King, Sonny

FREDERICK MONDERSON

intensified his efforts for social change, extended his interest beyond America and raised his profile as a black-nationalist leader with international standing.

In broadening his interests, Sonny became an education activist and equally involved in institution building, advocating for the dispossessed, speaking up for many falsely accused and brutalized by law enforcement as well as becoming a voice for many languishing and being psychologically emasculated daily in the prison industrial complex system. With such a resume of involvement; a visiting king of Ghana, West Africa, touring Brooklyn, New York, anointed Sonny Carson "Abubadika," which means "he who leads his people." For those who found the name difficult to pronounce, Sonny simply became "AB." From here on, Mr. Carson began "earning his stripes."

African Nationalist Poetry and Prose Photo. Tribute to the Ancestors – Images, 2019.

AFRICAN NATIONALIST POETRY AND PROSE

African Nationalist Poetry and Prose Photo.
MANMAN BRIGITTE – "Female Cemetery Guardian."

FREDERICK MONDERSON

African Nationalist Poetry and Prose Photo. Zimbabwe. Tapfuma Gutsa. "'Galactic Dancer' – Gutsa's sculptures reflect an embrace of technique and a desire to speak of both historic and present-day Zimbabwean culture."

Carson appeared in court to show support for those "falsely accused" of a crime by police. He also appeared in court to support tenants victimized by unscrupulous landlords. He attended funerals to show

AFRICAN NATIONALIST POETRY AND PROSE

dislike for "Black on Black Crime." Like all good generals, Sonny passed on and had a parade from the Brooklyn Bridge and up Fulton Street and a wonderful "home going." As Sonny recounted such involvements, Saint Peter checked his books and replied: "These things I'm familiar with but what else have you done?" Thereafter, in that usually assertive manner Sonny Carson reminded the Saint he was a founding member of Restoration Corporation on Fulton Street in Brooklyn, designed to economically revitalize the Bed-Stuy community. He was a principal advocate for the four-year status of Medgar Evers College of the City University of New York and was highly critical of its administration when he attended graduation ceremonies, finding no drums or other such African cultural motifs, and thought he was in Greece rather than in Africa. Sonny founded **Black Men Against Crack** to fight the scourge that was plaguing the Black Community and took to the streets to actively protest against the drug. When merchants acted improperly in the black community, "AB" led boycotts on Fulton Street and Church Avenue. Through all these developments, Mr. Carson testified and spoke out at Congressional Hearings and other such forums as at Medgar Evers College and other venues.

Still not satisfied and appearing somewhat sarcastic, St. Peter challenged Sonny Carson. Meanwhile his cheering section among the Black Pantheon within the "Gates of Glory" became more active as their

FREDERICK MONDERSON

champion was being put through the questioning rigors. Just then Sam Cook backed by Baby Huey broke into song: "A change is going to come" and this was followed by Brooke Benton who blurted out, "I who have nothing, I who have no one, adore you and want you so." As Hasan Roland Kirk, Charlie Parker, Gillespie and Miles blew their horns, the whole company burst into chorus emboldening Sonny, much to Saint Peter's surprise. The Saint felt those people were interfering with the interrogation and selection process and should stay out of it.

The singing and instrumental music seemed to revitalize Sonny even further as he started St. Peter down "a dusty road." He blurted out, "I led the Ocean-Hill-Brownsville educational challenge to the New York City Board of Education that resulted in community control and a disproportionate number of black and Puerto Rican teachers and administrators being hired in a school system disproportionately minority. For this action they branded me an extreme radical and a racist. But all I did was to enhance the condition of my people, as Malcolm X would say, 'By Any Means Necessary.'"

African Nationalist Poetry and Prose Photo. Tribute to the Ancestors – Images, 2019.

AFRICAN NATIONALIST POETRY AND PROSE

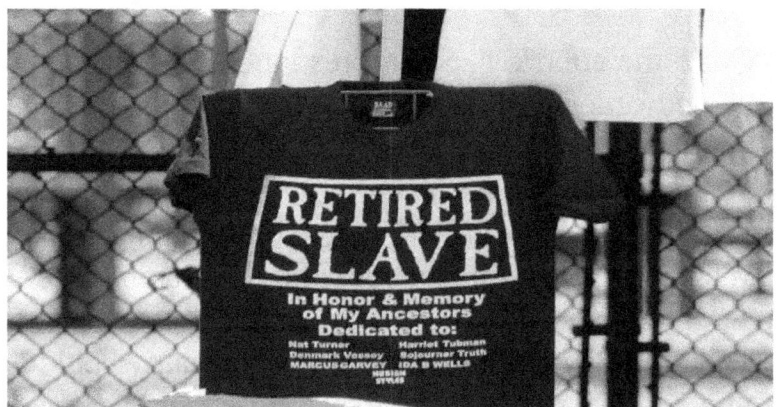

African Nationalist Poetry and Prose Photo. RETIRED SLAVE, Not funny!

African Nationalist Poetry and Prose Photo. "Shamgod," Sonny Carson and Atiem Ferguson at Abkar's funeral.

FREDERICK MONDERSON

Saint Peter asked: "Does this mean you had no respect for law and order?"

"Quite the contrary" Sonny responded. "I respected law and order but disdained racists and all forms of exploitation and discrimination and disrespect for the community the police were sworn to serve." "Never mind, just go on" Saint Peter, baiting sonny asked, "What more can you add about hour miserable life?"

"Thinking, 'What's with this M…?'" Sonny held his tongue but continued. He exclaimed, "Dr. Newman described a path similar to mine: 'After the fever of life; after weariness, sicknesses, fighting and despondings, languor and fretfulness, struggling and failing, struggling and succeeding; after all the changes and chances of this troubled and unhealthy state, at length comes death, - at length the white throne of God, - at length the beatific vision." Even more he added, "I attended funerals, stood up to uppity politicians, challenged Sony over 'Gangsta Rap,' and founded **The Committee to Honor Black Heroes**. This enabled me to change streets as **Malcolm X** and **Marcus Garvey Boulevards** and lay the foundation for **Harriet Ross Tubman Avenue**, all in Brooklyn; I also changed the names of schools to **Malcolm X** and **Toussaint L'Ouverture**."

"Sounds impressive to me" chimed Saint Peter.

AFRICAN NATIONALIST POETRY AND PROSE

Still Sonny continued, "But that's not all I did. I retrieved the Bones of my ancestor Samuel Carson, that fellow over there behind the "Gates of Heavenly Bliss," from his U.S. Navy burial site in Brooklyn and transported it back to Ghana, West Africa, to inaugurate the **First Emancipation Day Ceremony** on August 1, 1998 and create a site of pilgrimage for African Americans seeking roots in Africa. In this I was able to create the "**Door of Return**" opposing the "**Door of No Return**." As he continued to pour out his heart, Sonny Carson could hear the orchestra break out in chant, "We Shall Overcome, We shall Overcome" and even more, "We're gonna study this war some more, we're gonna study this war some more."

"Even in my passing on transition to these 'Pearly Gates' the Community I fought for so hard for so long, chose to honor my name in a section of **Gates Avenue** in Brooklyn as **Sonny Carson Avenue**. Yet, despite wide and demonstrated community support on the day of the vote, the reactionaries in the New York City Council voted to deny such. In turn, the Community named Linden Park on Linden Boulevard in my honor and even put up their own sign which the Parks Department removed. Similarly, on Gates Avenue they put up their own sign at Nostrand Avenue which was also taken down by officialdom. Finally, the good people

FREDERICK MONDERSON

of Bedford-Stuyvesant, Bed-Stuy, renamed that section of Brooklyn, "**Abubadikaville**!" The rest you know.

With that Saint Peter responded, "Mr. Carson, you have done well but you must understand my position, to fully examine every entrant. You deserve to enter this 'Company of Blessed Souls.' God be with you!"

The Orchestra, patiently awaiting the results of the inquisition, broke out in thunderous applause and began singing, "We're gonna walk these streets of gold" before beginning to welcome and brief Sonny on extant conditions in heaven and on earth.

African Nationalist Poetry and Prose Photo. Rev. Al Sharpton recognizes an attendee at his "Saturday Rally" who had a photo of them both in younger days.

AFRICAN NATIONALIST POETRY AND PROSE

"The work of Albert Churchward was in the tradition of the researches of Gerald Massey, Leo Weiner, and other Egyptologists. In his response to critics he maintained that all signs and symbols originated from the African's stellar, lunar, and solar mythos. Indeed, the original Australians were part of the African exodus. Churchward argues that the Egyptian Book of the Dead is the key to the door and without it one cannot 'trace back the history of the world – the history of all religions, and the history of all mankind, and that which is attached thereto."

21. SONNY CARSON – REVERED ANCESTOR BY DR. FRED MONDERSON

As a revered ancestor, Sonny Carson has left an imprint in the United States as well as in Ghana, West Africa, that always reminds us of the merits of working for the people which in itself is a great reward as real time events are challenged. On this Sonny's birthday, May 18, juxtaposed to Malcolm X's birthday May 19, we are reminded of one indisputable fact that bucks the modern trend, especially in New York City.

For some time, New York City has honored deserving individuals by having some edifice named after them. As an example, even streets were named

FREDERICK MONDERSON

to honor these individuals. For that matter, sometimes an entire street was named after such personalities. However, New York City politics is always changing, sometimes even for the worse.

As Mayor, and in his run on the people, Rudy Giuliani restricted the naming of streets to co-naming and then to a block or two. This became the standard from his time onwards. Sonny Carson, as a thinking activist and realizing the significance of motifs and the cultural and philosophic consciousness of historical personalities soon realized there was no visible public evidence of noteworthy black figures in Brooklyn, New York, especially. So, therefore, he created an organization called **The Committee to Honor Black Heroes**. He further realized old style building techniques engraved the names of significant historic personalities on the cornice of façade of buildings and even on lower Broadway in New York City, the names of distinguished visitors to the city were engraved on the sidewalk indicating the dates of their visit.

Amidst his activist activities, Sonny "Abubadika" Carson, through his novel organization and demands was able to quickly change street names that read **Malcolm X Boulevard** and **Marcus Garvey Boulevard** in the Bedford Stuyvesant section of Brooklyn. He successfully lobbied for a school named **Malcolm X** and one for **Toussaint L'Ouverture**, the great Haitian

AFRICAN NATIONALIST POETRY AND PROSE

liberator. In this vein, however, the most significant accomplishment he initiated was laying the foundation to name Fulton Street in Brooklyn, after **Harriet Tubman**, the great African American liberator. Strange, but not one block but many. Practically the entire Fulton Street in Brooklyn, was named for Harriet Tubman.

Only recently and again, it became apparent to this writer, instead of the customary block or two named after an individual, Harriet Tubman Avenue stretches from Flatbush Avenue to Utica Avenue. This achievement was significant because of the now operational law limiting the naming of such streets as implemented by Mayor Giuliani. Clearly the work of Robert "Sonny" Carson was quietly behind this co-naming. It's as if he had said, "I may not be there but we can still beat the system," if we remain active and vigilant.

Equally, let us not underestimate the role Sonny Carson has played in institution building in the establishment of Bed-Stuy Restoration Corporation to revitalize that community, the achieved 4-year status of Medgar Evers College and significantly, the repatriation of the Bones of Runaway Slave Samuel Carson to Ghana, West Africa, to create a site of pilgrimage and departure for African Americans seeking their roots in **Mother Africa**. In this gallant and triumphant act Sonny Carson had created

FREDERICK MONDERSON

the "**Door of Return**" contradicting the "**Door of No Return**" of the horrendous slave trade experience. Collectively, these achievements, despite whatever minor indiscretions, have earned Sonny Carson, the indubitable title of revered ancestor. More important, Sonny Carson's tenacity, daring and resilience coupled with the untold numbers of African and African-American heroes whose demonstrated courage and concern for their people's welfare not simply represents the new age and reality but resolutely affirms we will not go quietly into the night!

African Nationalist Poetry and Prose Photo. Even more of the luscious stew prepared for participants at the Festival.

"Afrocentricity maintains intellectual vigilance as the proper posture toward all scholarship which ignores

AFRICAN NATIONALIST POETRY AND PROSE

the origin of civilization in the highlands of East Africa. Our need is to advance the theory of Afrocentricity through critical attention to what is written and spoken by those who profess knowledge regardless of their ancestry. Arnold Toynbee, for example, wrote that whites founded four ancient civilization while blacks found none. This I not merely Eurocentricity; it is malicious racism of the type we have confronted and exposed for the last two hundred years. We know because our Afrocentric consciousness that only once ancient civilization could be considered European in origin, Greece. And Greece itself is a product of its interaction with African civilizations. Among ancient civilizations Africans gave the world, Ethiopia, Nubia, Egypt, Cush, Axum, Ghana, Mali, and Songhay. These ancient civilizations are responsible for medicine, science, the concept of monarchies and divine-kingships and an Almighty God. Afrocentricity establishes a profound movement in critical readings as well as critical thinking. To the degree that we begin to examine the literary perspectives of black and white writers we will understand the power of symbols." Molefi Kete Asante. *Afrocentricity*. (1988) 1989.

"Frederick Douglass once said that the African had to speak with the front of his head rather than the back in order to achieve true victory. What he meant was that our objective had to remain constant while we changed means. All our philosophers have

FREDERICK MONDERSON

understood the distinction between tactics and strategy. A profound sense of the collective imperative carries us toward our strategy. In the process of achieving social, political, and economic victory over the negatives within us, we shall arrive at our objective through various tactics. A strategy is a long-term plan for achieving an objective while tactics are the science of arranging and managing the details of human behavior. Afrocentricity does not negate strategies nor tactics; it recognizes their individual places in the overall thrust toward victory. In this respect, it may be tactically wise to perform some task, make some pledge; or carry out some action. This is permissible so long as the profound objective remains the overall strategy for achieving the objective." Molefi Kete Asante. *Afrocentricity*. (1988) 1989.

African Nationalist Poetry and Prose Photo. Finally, another "Great One" gets his just reward in Harlem, USA.

AFRICAN NATIONALIST POETRY AND PROSE

African Nationalist Poetry and Prose Photo. Music and Art has their place, on the Streets of Harlem.

FREDERICK MONDERSON

African Nationalist Poetry and Prose Photo. Even more evidence of Music and Art on 125th Street in Harlem.

AFRICAN NATIONALIST POETRY AND PROSE

African Nationalist Poetry and Prose Photo. Still more evidence of Music and Art on 125th Street in Harlem.

African Nationalist Poetry and Prose Photo. Tribute to the Ancestors – Images, 2019.

FREDERICK MONDERSON

African Nationalist Poetry and Prose Photo. Still More evidence of Music and Art on 125th Street in Harem, New York.

AFRICAN NATIONALIST POETRY AND PROSE

African Nationalist Poetry and Prose Photo.
"Mother Africa" in her resplendent glory.

African Nationalist Poetry and Prose Photo.
Message from the People of Harlem.

FREDERICK MONDERSON

African Nationalist Poetry and Prose Photo.
"Harlem welcomes the world!"

African Nationalist Poetry and Prose Photo.
Image of the People of Harlem.

AFRICAN NATIONALIST POETRY AND PROSE

African Nationalist Poetry and Prose Photo. Still more Music and Art on 125th Street in Harlem.

FREDERICK MONDERSON

African Nationalist Poetry and Prose Photo. Again, evidence of Music and Art on 125th Street in Harlem.

African Nationalist Poetry and Prose Photo. Adam Clayton Powell Jr. Boulevard in Harlem.

AFRICAN NATIONALIST POETRY AND PROSE

African Nationalist Poetry and Prose Photo. Two Giants for the price of One.

African Nationalist Poetry and Prose. The "Great Educator" gets her recognition.

African Nationalist Poetry and Prose Photo. This is the "House of Justice" Headquarters.

FREDERICK MONDERSON

African Nationalist Poetry and Prose Photo. James Brown and Adam Clayton Powell meet at Allah and Justice Square.

22. POEM TO OSIRIS
BY
DR. FRED MONDERSON

O Osiris, great immortal with attributes part divine and part human, you are Lord of Being with many names.

Great God, you are the promise of eternity, for the just and those who live by Ma'at's law of right and truth.

Lord of Abydos, you suffered the indignity of death and decapitation, being victimized by conspirators filled with envy.

When the righteousness of your cause reached to heaven, father god Ra dispatched his emissaries to rescue you from the perdition you did not deserve.

They came to shed light on the First among the Westerners, the One God Living in Truth.

You are the Father and Mother of Mankind, Everlasting Soul.

AFRICAN NATIONALIST POETRY AND PROSE

Lord of the Horns with tall Atef-Crown, of good memory in the God's Palace.

Presider over the West, your brother Seth and his evil cohorts plotted your death to seize your throne and legacy, Glorious, Good God!
They entrapped your body through guile and trickery, and into the Nile they discarded your coffin.
The dastard deed done, the doers of iniquity rejoiced, claiming your legacy, mummy, crown, scepter and whip, great warrior, King of Upper and Lower Kemet/Egypt, King of All the Gods.
When Ra rises every day and comes to the Underworld, in order to survey this land and also the Countries, you sit there also as he.
The Majesty of Thoth stands near unto you, in order to execute the commands, which proceed from your mouth.
You are king of the Illuminated, prototype of the Dead man, King of Eternity.

Lord of Rosta, greatly loved on earth, Isis the faithful and loving wife searched the land untiring, for your remains out of honor and duty.
With her sister Nephthys, their lamentations echoed throughout and reached the heavens, triumphant.
Thoth, the personification of intelligence and scribe of the gods, with Anubis assisted the search, Great One contained in Sokhen.

FREDERICK MONDERSON

You were great of strength when you overthrow the adversary, Powerful of arms when you slew the foe. Shining noble at the head of nobles, permanent in high rank, stablished in your sovereignty, you are the beneficent power of the company of the gods, the Lord to whom praises are sung.

You put your fear in the enemy and reached the boundaries of them that plotted mischief. Out of fear of reprisal, Seth decapitated and scattered your body in thirteen locations; Beneficent Spirit in the Land of Spirits.
O Noble One with mysterious ceremonies in the temples, the Celestial Ocean Nun offered you water and the sky created air for your nose for contentment of your heart.
Source of the Nile, the north wind journeys southward to you, the plants grow according to your desire and the fields created its food for you.
Lord of the great house in the city of the eight gods, celestial food, you are the beneficent soul among spirit souls.

Mighty One, who appeared in greatness at Abydos, your body was lying as Corpse under the Earth.
August Being, Isis recovered parts at every site and Temples were erected to worship the Just King murdered by evil and jealousy.
Now aided by divine wisdom, One of Many Names, you're the king who guides the land to prosperity, Ruler of Eternity, Eternal Master, Great God of Abydos.

AFRICAN NATIONALIST POETRY AND PROSE

You are very awful in Shashotep, Osiris, King of Gods.
Justified before the entire Ennead, a slaughtering was made for you in the great hall at Herwer.
Before you, the great mighty ones were in terror; these great ones rose from their mats.
Stablisher of truth throughout the two lands, perfect of power in every word, you are Lord to the end of the earth.
Lord of Kerer, with Nephthys, Thoth and Anubis as witnesses Isis performed the ceremony Revivification of Osiris.
Your son Horus at the Bar of Judgment was adjudged your rightful heir and successor.
He assumed the throne reigning as king of the two lands to fulfill the mission of his divine father, to Fill the Land with Excellent Laws.
Powerful leader of every god, you became Governor of Amentet to judge actions of men guided by Ma'at's laws, Ruler of the West.
You are a venerable God, Lord of the Great Dwelling in Sesennou, Lord of Tazoser.

God of all gods, most excellent glorified one; your head was buried at Abydos, your heart at Philae; and you established truth in Kemet/Egypt.
Ceremonies celebrate your birth, life, death, resurrection, and after life, as god who can invest his Body with All Forms as He Wishes.

FREDERICK MONDERSON

Throughout Egypt you were worshiped, Prince of Peace, first Cristos, wonderful spirit.
Men found salvation in your example and purpose for you lived as father, husband, king, betrayed, mutilated, died, revivified, resurrected as deity with power to maintain life indefinitely.
Kings and commoners, worshiped and praised your name, nature, spirit, soul, and divine body while the gods of the provinces are your forms, Primeval God Residing in Tattu, Soul of Ra.

Master of the Gods, Abydos, throne of your power, is the world's first pilgrimage site, for all seeking your immortality, serene one.
The Great Ennead praised you; the Lesser Ennead loved you, Everlasting King.
All realized there's no empty space on your back.
For millennia adherents imbibed and practiced the Osirian drama recreating your experiences.
Many chose burials near the staircase of the god, or they erected stelae or made pilgrimages for votive offerings as the last rites.

Your holy site immortalized by ten temples, span the duration of dynastic rule.
Still Seti's mortuary temple and Osireion at Abydos, birthplace of the sun is a wonderfully magnificent art and architectural testament praising you as God, Lord of the Length of Times in Abydos. This work of majesty recognized and saluted predecessor kings buried in the desert of his temple in your name.

AFRICAN NATIONALIST POETRY AND PROSE

Holy One of the White Wall you have twin souls, bodies and natures.
With the power to be born again you rise on the horizon.
Principles of Abundance in On, Creator of the World, the Heavenly Nile derives its water from you.
Soul of the Sun, the Gods Are Joyous at the arrival of Osiris.
The Earth lies upon your arms and its corners upon you even unto the Four Pillars of Heaven.
You stir yourself, the Earth trembles and the Nile comes forth from the sweat of your hands.
Because you rise and stand up, everything whereby man lives, trees and herbs, barley and wheat, is of divine origin, and comes from you.
Lord of the World, you made men and women to be born again.
Lord of the Seker Boat and the Neshmet boat, these vessels bore your beauty.

Governor of the two companies of gods, praised by your father Keb, beloved by your mother Nut, you established right throughout the two riverbanks.
Admirable in command, heir of Keb in kingship of the two lands, your father entrusted you to lead the two lands to good fortune.
Revered in Ehnas, mighty in Tenent with a great estate in Busiris, you appear on the throne of your

FREDERICK MONDERSON

father like Ra when he arises on the horizon to give light to those in darkness.
Lord of Eternity in Abydos, Lord of the Great Hall in Hermopolis, abundant in sustenance in Letopolis, the imperishable stars are under your authority.
The height of heaven and earth are open to you, praises are sung in the southern heaven and thanks given in the northern heaven.
Great Mighty One residing in Thinis, Lordship given in Heliopolis, future resurrection, Brother, many found fertile promise in your example.
In the resurrection and ascension men and gods shout for joy in the southern sky and adore you in the northern sky.
Thus, with hope of everlasting life, you have the Right to Command in the place of Double Justice, God of the Birth-house, your form is hidden in the temples.

Beneficent One, you are the mighty one of possessions in the shrine.
Good God martyred by malice and greed, resurrected, incorruptible, you judge the dead, Mysterious Soul.
Salvation of mankind rested within your bosom, for you possess power to unite bodies and souls.
Another gift of Africa to the world, born again and possessing knowledge, power, and mystery; the father sacrificed, the Black Madonna and Child forever forgiving, salvation is still attainable, Prince of Princes.

AFRICAN NATIONALIST POETRY AND PROSE

African Nationalist Poetry and Prose Photo. What promise as the juices percolate as taste buds wait in anticipation.

African Nationalist Poetry and Prose Photo. Close-up of the Master Drummer Shendo!

In this respect, Churchward states further: "... the first or Paleolithic man was the Pygmy, who was evolved in Central Africa at the source of the Nile, or Nile valley, and that from here all originated and were carried throughout the world, and that the most primitive phase of mythology is a mode of representing certain elemental powers by means of living types which were superhuman, like the natural phenomena. The foundations of mythology were laid in preanthropomorphic shapes of primitive representation. Thus, the typical giant, Apap, was an enormous water reptile. The typical genitrix and mother of life was a Water Cow, that represented the earth; the typical provider was a goose, etc. It was here, int eh Nile valley, that the dumb mythology became articulate. Egypt alone preserved the primitive gnosis and gave expression to the language of signs and symbols, and it was here that the first elemental powers were divinized, here that Totemism, Stellar, Lunar and Solar Mythology originated." Molefi Kete Asante. *Kemet, Afrocentricity and Knowledge.* (1990) 1992.

African Nationalist Poetry and Prose Photo. Getting the Drummers on!

AFRICAN NATIONALIST POETRY AND PROSE

African Nationalist Poetry and Prose Photo. Mr. Caldwell greets Erik Monderson, while a lady looks on.

African Nationalist Poetry and Prose Photo. Governor David Patterson was on hand at Keepers of the Dream Celebration.!

FREDERICK MONDERSON

African Nationalist Poetry and Prose Photo. Kings County, Brooklyn District Attorney Kenneth B. Thompson.

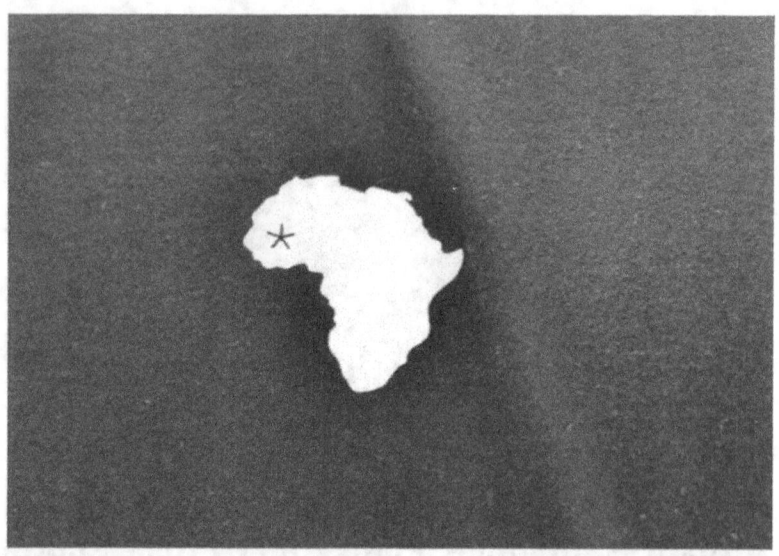

African Nationalist Poetry and Prose Photo. The West African Star.

AFRICAN NATIONALIST POETRY AND PROSE

"There are several elements in the mid of Africa that govern how humans behave with regard to reality: the practicality of wholism, the prevalence of poly-consciousness, the idea of inclusiveness, the unity of worlds, and the value of personal relationships. It is not trite for the African to say 'everything is everything.' And to the mind of the ancient Kemetic people this idea was thought to represent the whole universe as one. From beginning it was the oneness of everything that became the key with which the Egyptian mind unlocked the many secrets of the world. Thus, one's world, whether from the personal or the collective perspective, was based upon the actual quest to make the one world, to establish the interconnection of all things, to reconstruct the universe as it was in the beginning." Molefi Kete Asante. *The Egyptian Philosophers – Ancient African Voices from Imhotep to Akhenaten.* 2000.

23. BLACK HISTORY: CULTURE FOR LIBERATION
BY
DR. FRED MONDERSON

Increasingly across the spectrum of African-American discussion, religion but more especially history and culture are emphasized as potent tools of liberation whether of an intellectual or practical "Grass-roots" method. In this spirit, particularly during **Black History Month**, Egypt/Ancient Kemet should loom large in the scheme of things

FREDERICK MONDERSON

because of its significant legacy in the African evolution of ideas, methodology, achievements and scientific influence. This significance notwithstanding, we ought to be mindful of the transposition of ideas benefitting one group and their potential damage to another, particularly when the purported origination is based on a distorted perception and propagation.

Some years ago, on the bus to the Million Man March a tape depicted a young brother – articulate, sincere, revolutionary and committed – who kept repeating the cliché, "Tell Pharaoh to let my people go." The young speaker was certainly not aware "Pharaoh" was "one of our people." Herein then lies the need for solidarity in the methodology of liberation, where being versed in African history and culture as it relates to the Nile Valley experience: a history and its cultural legacy that is fundamental to African people's spiritual, psychological, intellectual and physical freedom must not be misplaced, displaced nor distorted or omitted from the putative record.

African Nationalist Poetry and Prose Photo. "Still a Man," on the 50th Anniversary March!

AFRICAN NATIONALIST POETRY AND PROSE

African Nationalist Poetry and Prose Photo. Chris Noble, son of **Gil Noble** of **Like It Is**, at **CEMOTAP** in one of its "Enlightening" sessions.

Therefore, and more so, after an intellectually and spiritually uplifting pilgrimage to the ancient "Holy Land' of Kemet, now Egypt, it is still appropriate to speak on behalf of the ancestors and elders on whose shoulders we stand today. To do so is to praise the wonderfully creative ancestral spirits from the banks of the Nile who engineered fundamentals disciplines of science, medicine, architecture, sculpture, painting, writing, navigation, astronomy, metallurgy, agriculture, philosophy and mathematics and moral and ethical systems of social value that shaped religious beliefs and practices. Such developments, as Ma'atian – espousing principles of equality,

FREDERICK MONDERSON

balance; order, propriety, goodness, truth, justice and righteousness undergirded their accomplishments and later influenced universal values. Today, our young must let such shining examples of faith and perseverance assist their paths to self-awareness, self-actualization and intellectual, cultural and spiritual empowerment.

Those ancestors artfully created conventions of wisdom, science and learning that benefitted all mankind and today must benefit their African-American progeny. For this to be meaningfully beneficial at this time, our young must enmesh themselves in study of ancient African history. Here, the development of African architecture imbued with divine essence instructs in worship and ritualization of the African gods providing the joys of festivals and frolics in praise of deity; skills of management of estates and wealth; knowledge of imperial wars, conquests and endowments; understanding tenets of observational and instrumental astronomy; experiencing the sweet harmony and joy of music and instruments; and appreciating the art of fabulously raised, incised and painted reliefs of art adorning their wonderful architectural accomplishments. Today, when we celebrate the fantastic developments unfolding in exploration of the heavens, we must remember that astronomy began in Central Africa, flowed down the Nile, crystallized in ancient Kemet and illuminated the

AFRICAN NATIONALIST POETRY AND PROSE

human consciousness of the vast divine and practical potential of the cosmos.

On any travel expedition designed to be educational, the crafters of the trip envision a general purpose as to what the outing hopes to accomplish. There are individual purposes for the many travelers. On my visit that past summer; some fathers brought their sons and grandsons. Nuclear families, singles and families complete with grandfathers and grandmothers intact were able to psychically and collectively experience the monuments and garner wisdom from their memories.

My principal and personal reason for going on that trip had been to take my sister Cherise on an experience I have so often enjoyed along the banks of the Nile at Aswan, Luxor and Cairo, where the ancestral heritage reigns supreme. Dr. ben-Jochannan's book *From Abu Simbel to Ghizeh* as guide included Abydos, "where it all began." In that journey we experienced the need for love of self, love of one's woman, and love for God. At the completion of the journey was reinforced love of self, love for one's neighbor, and love for one's country. This further empowered our love for the ancestors and enabled us more to appreciate the love for God.

FREDERICK MONDERSON

Except for those at Abydos, Luxor and the Ramesseum, Medinet Habu and Hatshepsut's temple at Deir el Bahari, New Kingdom structures, the other temples at Philae, Kalabsha, Kom Ombo, Edfu and Esna, were all constructed in the Graeco-Roman Period, twilight of the history of pharaonic Kemet, today's Egypt. More importantly, these later temples were built on much older foundations, chosen for their ancient sacredness. Equally significant, however, while erected under foreign Graeco-Roman domination, the builders nevertheless utilized ancient African ingenuity and techniques.

Quintessentially, the greater vision would be to imagine a "High Holy Day" with temples lit in their glorious splendor at the cardinal centers of religious practice and theological learning, viz., Ptah at Memphis, Ra at Heliopolis, Osiris at Abydos and Amun-Ra at Karnak and Luxor. Then add the slightly less illumined local centers buttressing those nucleuses of religious and spiritual expression here "Mother Africa" manifested quintessential cosmic influenced brilliance. Thus, how wonderful it is to envision the first great African nation at prayer! This cultural and spiritual realization is significant for enlightenment and inspiration for the young journeying into a new century and millennium and eternity.

AFRICAN NATIONALIST POETRY AND PROSE

African Nationalist Poetry and Prose Photo. Part of the Audience listening to Basir Mchawi, Chris Noble and Prof. James Blake at **CEMOTAP**.

As such then, one can picture the spiritual and divine powerhouse of Abydos with its splendid and magnificent depictions, wonderful collection of 3,000-year-old paintings, housed in a wonderful architectural structure where the power of Osiris in all his divine glory manifested amidst seven deities to whom the temple was dedicated. These, from right to left, are as follows: Horus, Isis, Osiris, Amun, Ra-Horakhti, Ptah and Seti. These are the members of the Osiris cycle, the three great gods of the Empire and the deified Seti I whose vision in construction now seems spiritually guided to create cosmic perfection in heaven on earth.

FREDERICK MONDERSON

What is significant about Abydos is its First and Second Dynasty Royal Tombs, and remains of an old fortress, as well as the strata of 10 successive levels of temples Petrie discovered at this holy place, dating back to 3200 B.C. If we therefore reconstruct the evolution and practice of this religiosity and spirituality, evidently the ancient temples evolved from leaves, mud and daub, then bricks, and finally into the brilliance and everlasting stone construction. Even more, these perishable materials could not tell us how long the ancestors were "making joyful sounds unto the Lord." That is, "having sweet communion with deity" and "crafting moral and ethical standards for their children." We all were children and our children will have children of their own someday, and thus they should be acquainted with this heritage to further the enlightenment, moral, spiritual, intellectual.

To further throw light on this phenomenon; in 1989, Dr. ben-Jochannan on one of his trips held a panel discussion among the traveling group. The members included a practicing minister, a former minister, a 12-year-old lad, an assertive sister and a young couple. As the discussion unfolded persons were asked to answer two simple questions: "What has coming to Egypt done for you?" and "Now that you have accumulated this knowledge, what are you going to do with it?"

AFRICAN NATIONALIST POETRY AND PROSE

The assertive sister on the panel during the 'question and answer' period asked the minister, a Reverend Doctor from Philadelphia, Pennsylvania. "How can you go back to your congregation and teach in your customary manner after what you have witnessed?" The astute minister simply responded: "I cannot teach my people there is no God! I can only teach them where God comes from!" In this writer's view, that was the most revolutionary, profound and sincere response one could have expressed given the situation. The Reverend must have realized, from the glorious heavens God first appeared to man in Africa. Albert Churchward believed this joyous expression began some 300,000 years.

African Nationalist Poetry and Prose Photo. Justice for Trayvon Martin means Justice for All.

FREDERICK MONDERSON

African Nationalist Poetry and Prose Photo. "Power-couple," NY City Councilwoman Inez Baron and husband, State Assemblyman Charles Baron at **CEMOTAP**.

To further understand African communion with deity, one needs to examine the ancient temples. In this respect, the essential elements of Kemetic temples built to manifest cosmic, heavenly perfection on earth, the principal requirement to encourage divinity's residence in his home, such august structures, generally built along the river's banks, included a quay where the royal boat would dock. This led to an "Avenue of Sphinxes" leading to the "Entrance Pylon." Among structures surviving at

AFRICAN NATIONALIST POETRY AND PROSE

Luxor Temple, built by Amenhotep III, one of two still standing Obelisks and two seated as well as one of four statues stand in front of the decorated Pylon. This entrance leads to an open "Peristyle Court" built by Rameses II and called the "Ramessean Front." Some courts had chapels, statues, an altar or two, kiosks, sphinxes and colonnades on both sides as one approached the temple's inner sanctum. Very often an old Nilometer was located nearby, an instrument used by the priests to measure the volume of the Nile River and to predict the level of agricultural taxation based on expected crop yield.

There can be an optional Second Pylon and the Hypostyle Hall with its varied arrangement of columns. A second smaller Hypostyle Hall led to the Sanctuary atop a gradual incline upwards as one approached the most sacred spot, the "Holy of Holies." In front of the Sanctuary along the central axis could be found stela, columns, sphinxes, kneeling or standing statues, obelisks and inscriptional depictions connected with the central worship. Some temples featured an assortment of buildings where a number of deities were in residence and supportive functions were performed. There was generally a Sacred Lake fed through some underground spring. In the Greco-Roman period, a Mammisi or "Birth House" was added. Temples developed self-sufficient industries as farming, trade,

FREDERICK MONDERSON

transportation and even art and architecture practices. There were also schools and "help centers" as well as gardens that provided flowers for daily ritual.

African Nationalist Poetry and Probe Photo. Discussion at the "Round Table" at **CEMOTAP** featuring Assemblyman Charles Baron (left), City Councilwoman Inez Baron, Basir Mchawi, with Prof. James Blake and Chris Noble in rear.

African Nationalist Poetry and Prose Photo. Drs. Rosalind and Leonard Jeffries, iconic intellectual warriors at **CEMOTAP**.

AFRICAN NATIONALIST POETRY AND PROSE

Therefore, understanding developments in religious theory and practice, accomplishments in astronomy, navigation, artistic and architectural constructions with their influence and fortitude, originality and visions of their creators allows both young and old to take pride in African genius as manifested in their multitude of works. Such awareness provides a significant beacon for knowledge of early African creativity as a powerful source of inspiration and strength.

African Nationalist Poetry and Prose Photo. Part of the audience listening to Chris Noble and Prof. James Blake.

FREDERICK MONDERSON

African Nationalist Poetry and Prose Photo. Chris Noble, prof. Blake and Basir Mchawi stand to greet the audience and shake their hands.

African Nationalist Poetry and Prose Photo. What a wonderful pair of activists, Sister Betty Dopson, Co-Chair of **CEMOTAP** and a member of the **December 12 Movement**, Mr. Clay.

AFRICAN NATIONALIST POETRY AND PROSE

"Just as contemporary physicists are trying to understand the nature of the universe, the ancient Kemetic people tried diligently to make sense out of their world, their universe and the universes. To them, as we have now come to understand, the universe was once a tiny ball so dense that it could not be penetrated by any light and it could never release the light that it contained. Physicists tell us that it was the Big Bang that started the universes. The ancient Kemetic people understood all of this in symbolic form. Thus, when Ra created the universe, it was Ra alone from whom everything flowed. Every living thing, all forms of creatures, and all humans descended from Ra's creation. Ra was to the ancient Kamites the dense ball out of which all things were created when the Big Bang happened. Whether in the form of the supreme deity Ptah or Atum, Ra was the supreme originator because without Ra noting that we know could have been possible. We owe even our lives to Ra's creation. The African believed that light itself was the creation of Ra." Molefi Kete Asante. *The Egyptian Philosophers – Ancient African Voices from Imhotep to Akhenaten.* 2000.

24. MA'AT VERSUS ISFIT IN PRESIDENTIAL POLITICS
By
Dr. Fred Monderson

History has shown any movement for the better is always first met with opposition and skepticism.

FREDERICK MONDERSON

Take the case of all great reformers, Osiris, Akhenaten, Buddha, Jesus, Joan of Arc, even George Washington with all his faults, not excluding Martin Luther King, Malcolm X and Medgar Evers. In that astute mountain of a man, Barack Obama, we see no difference as he has struggled to defend what is right, doing Ma'at even to his opponents while ignoring the stone throwers. Subscribing to the higher mission, President Obama realizes, as Maulana Karenga (1990: 32) says, "Creation, then, is constantly threatened by chaos, disorder or Isfet, and humans are morally compelled to share the responsibility with God of defending the boundaries of good, right and order, and expanding them. In this activity humans become like God." Perhaps the Mitch McConnells and even Donald Trump can learn a thing or two.

"The Ma'atian stress on moral social practice is rooted in the assumption that self-actualization of humans is best achieved in morally grounded relations with others." "The operative principle here is self-realization and grounding in moral relations with others. It is at this point that the ethic of care and responsibility or rather of love in the most human sense [merut] and service [wenut] are evident and required in Ma'at. To serve is to benefit not only others but also oneself."

Oh, what great wisdom the ancient possessed! For example, the Book of Ankhsheshonqi teaches "Service is righteous action towards and for God, humans and by extension, nature which in some

AFRICAN NATIONALIST POETRY AND PROSE

meaningful and moral way returns a reciprocal benefit." This moral responsibility to respect and protect the earth is what Karenga preached in his **Kwanza Message at Boys and Girls High School** in Brooklyn, New York, on December 27, 2011. Now, contrary to past deregulation, as per his mission, the president insists the Environmental Protection Agency must enforce strict regulation to play its part in saving the earth from becoming another Mars. Therefore, when Republican contenders tout "Abolish the EPA" they are acting as agents of **Isfet,** that is evil or chaos.

African Nationalist Poetry and Prose Photo. At the Microphone, Dr. Leonard Jeffries follows Dr. James McIntosh as he praises Prof. James Blake's new book, *God's Bad Boy*: *James Blake and the System*.

FREDERICK MONDERSON

This was a day in which Chris Noble's Birthday was celebrated at **CEMOTAP**.

African Nationalist Poetry and Prose Photo. Chloe Williams, who sang "Happy Birthday" to Chris Noble poses with Mr. Noble.

Again, Ankhsheshonqi cautions, "The only real good deed is the one done for one who needs it." Perhaps that proponent of ancient African deep thought foresaw and foretold of the conflict between the one and the ninety-nine percent. Within this same prophetic construct can be placed the "Millionaires Tax Cut" for those who do not need it; and to this we may add the Health Care Reform Act that benefits the fifty million Americans who need its protection. Can we thrown in the Lilly Ledbetter Act for women certainly need to earn the same as men? Last but not least, President Obama's insistence on and support for educational initiatives, upgrade of school facilities, repair of roads, ports, airports, rail lines and even high-speed rail service will not only improve

AFRICAN NATIONALIST POETRY AND PROSE

performance and infrastructure of the American landscape but also put Americans back to work, helping to improve their economic and social positions.

Now to contrast the "highly intellectual," "smartest guy in the room," "I'm going to be the nominee" arrogance of Newt Gingrich with the deep-thinking Barack Obama, the vision is like night and day and so too the thanklessness of a well-done job. Nevertheless, Ankhsheshonqi admonishes as Karenga has pointed out, "One should not be disappointed for not being recognized or thanked by everyone for whom one does good." Antedating the wisdom of the **Book of Ecclesiastes** which urges, as we all sometimes do, "Cast your bread upon the waters and after many days it will return to you;" Ankhsheshonqi admonishes, "If you do good by a hundred persons and just one of them acknowledges it, no part of it is lost." His optimism is reflected in the law of reciprocity in that, "Do a good deed and throw it in the water and when the water dries up, you will find it." Again, we see in the ancient Egyptian/African reservoir of deep thought wisdom many paraphrased modern wise sayings such as "It's better to give than to receive." In Ankhsheshonqi's original thought, "Sweeter is the water of one who has given than the wine of one who has received."

Today we recognize Republicans have borrowed Jesse Jackson's "Big Tent" idea that should shelter great diversity among its presidential candidates and supporters, but their tent has holes, many holes. This, however, is not the case for recently a young Black Republican on CNN decried the rhetoric of the recent **CPAP** convention's racism in modern dress, not considering the realities of 21st Century politics. Did Congressman Allen West from Florida hear the same message? After all, in addition to Jim Crow, Jr., Esquire, the Republican tent includes the "Black protester with guns;" his "praying for Obama's death" pastor; the "Koran burning Florida pastor" declaring his intention to run for the Presidency as a Republican; Ring-master Donald Trump with his magnetic attraction for clowns; illegal immigrant chasing Sheriff Arapaio; "Waterloo" DeMint; "You lie" Wilson; "Poisoning the well" Santorum; "Gangster government" Bachmann; "Corporations are people" Romney; "I'll be the nominee" Newt; "I can't remember which Department I will abolish" Perry; "Blacks are brainwashed for voting Democratic" Herman Cain; and hopefully, "Converted on the Road to Damascus" Ron and Rand Paul. All these jokers have been chosen to play a key role in effectuating the divine mission of Barack Obama. As such, they mirror the antithesis of Ma'at; or put in Christian historical parlance, they exhibit the "Petrine Syndrome" of denial, viz., Bachmann, Trump, Santorum; and "Judas Iscariot Syndrome," Cain, Allen West, "Black Protester with Guns," as well as Cornell West, Tavis Smiley and so many others. The participants on the Republican Band-

AFRICAN NATIONALIST POETRY AND PROSE

Wagon are many. In fact, they mirror "a ship of fools."

African Nationalist Poetry and Prose Photo. **CEMOTAP's** Treasurer is backed by another member as they prepare Chloe Williams to sing "Happy Birthday" to Chris Noble.

African Nationalist Poetry and Prose Photo. All Eyes are on Chloe Williams as she sings "Happy Birthday" to Chris Noble.

FREDERICK MONDERSON

African Nationalist Poetry and Prose Photo. One of the nearly two dozen **Olmec Heads** indicating Africans were in the New World before Columbus, though now resident on Troop Avenue in Brooklyn, NY.

AFRICAN NATIONALIST POETRY AND PROSE

African Nationalist Poetry and Prose Photo. Chloe Williams and Chris Noble pose for this photo after she sang "Happy Birthday" at **CEMOTAP**.

Now, as many of these players faded into oblivion and President Obama pursued his platform of better educational opportunities and practices, particularly with greater emphasis on the role of Community Colleges in retraining especially in the industrial arts; emphasizing the need for clean energy and a more vigorous enforcement of environmental use, paying greater attention to overhauling the nation's physical infrastructure and as the economy continues to improve, the American people came to see the wisdom of Obama's leadership and played their part in his re-election and in fulfilling his divine mission designed for their betterment.

FREDERICK MONDERSON

African Nationalist Poetry and Prose Photo. Dr. James McIntosh raises a glass in toast to Chris Noble on his Birthday as Charles and Inez Baron sit and look on.

African Nationalist Poetry and Prose Photo. Basir Mchawi and Veronica Phillips-Nickey at **CEMOTAP's** celebration of Chris Noble's Birthday.

AFRICAN NATIONALIST POETRY AND PROSE

African Nationalism Poetry and Prose Photo. Prof. James Blake, Queens Chairman of the **Million Man March** addresses the **CEMOTAP** audience.

"The United States Census Bureau is experimenting with an idea that could be disastrous for African-Americans. There will be a new classification on the census forms. If you're racially mixed, you can put down mixed. Now there are a whole lot of retreating blacks looking for their Dutch uncles and their Irish grandfathers. And there a whole lot of blacks of Indian descent related to Seminoles and related to everything except Africa. These 'mixes' can be used as a buffer. Then a lot of us will overlook something that we need to know our history in this country, about the role of certain mixed people in our history who are blacker than the backs in their actions." John Henrik Clarke. *Notes for an African World Revolution.* 1991.

FREDERICK MONDERSON

25. SPIRITUAL VALUES VERSUS SECULAR MATERIALISM
By
Dr. Fred Monderson

The Media has flashed information of various Anti-Obama groups such as Carl Rove's Super-Pac that has spent some $10m in Advertisement against President Obama with another $15m more waiting to be spent and Rickets of TD Bank fame donating another $10m in essentially the same cause. There is too much effort and rapidity to defeat President Obama and, in this money, becomes a primary God! After all, the motto of this nation is "One Nation under God, with liberty and justice for all." When oligarchic whites invest to gain profit from their investment, under the Judea-Christian religious and philosophic principle, the answer is privilege, profit and power. Since secular materialism buys the God, buys the government, the question becomes "is it one nation under god or under material mammoth?" Equally, one has to ask, 'What is the return and who gets it for such lucrative investments?"

Nevertheless, in the movie "Rocky" when confronted by the challenger who said, "I'm going to bust you up," Rocky said "Go for it!" These large sums spent to negatively paint Barack Obama will prove futile even though the forces arrayed against President Obama are wealthy, many primarily see his

AFRICAN NATIONALIST POETRY AND PROSE

race and this engenders powerful, unrelenting and formidable representation of materialism. Thus, despite his position, in those respects, President Obama become an underdog and America loves and underdog. It's been said one man can become a majority if he believes in himself and his truths are immutable. Thus, as this situation reflects his state of preparedness, honest integrity and bold vision, Mr. Obama will win the election going away! This is equally a view expressed by Bill Clinton on CNN's *Piers Morgan* on Thursday, May 31, 2012.

We believe the win is predictable because President Obama is collecting vast but small sums of American money to wage his campaign and this is being undergirded by his trump suit of "Spiritual Currency" with its potential miraculous effect. This secret weapon, enshrined and encapsulated in the Sunday morning prayers by the grandmothers, grandfathers, uncles, aunts, brothers and sisters and cousins across this land, invigorated by the good works of the ancestors who have seen and weighed in the balance the heart of the man and they have seen the illuminating beacon of his vision of the future. This is the idea and advantage Obama had and has over his adversaries and competitors. As such, if we follow some of the old aphorisms we're told, "Money is the root of all evil;" though Rev. Ike often proclaimed "The lack of money is the root of all evil!" Yet, in the movie **Green Berets** starring John Wayne and Raymond St. Jacques, when the soldiers tried to solicit assistance and offer protection to a nearby village of Mountainards, they promised "We'll give you money." The Chief asked "What is money?" Even these days, amidst much glaring Media fanfare Mr. Zuckerberg launched his **Face Book** IPO with shares set relatively high. Word has it, so many billion dollars were made and days after he was being raked over a bed of flaming coals for some form of stock impropriety. Thus, money is not always everything. For one thing, money can't buy health and it cannot thwart the will of the people determined and united in a cause they deem correct and inclusive.

Obama supporters should take heart, there is a "spiritual force" at work in Mr. Obama's campaign, an unseen power; the obstinate and arrogant cannot comprehend its prevalence, for it undergirds the divine mission of Mr. Obama. Interesting, he does not flaunt his spiritual values; he lets it permeate his being in doing god's work. He upholds the nation's and universal Christian philosophic admonitions to "love god, love yourself and love your neighbor." After all, the souls of the righteous are immortal and divine! Thus, in his humanity and social policy, Mr. Obama manifests the beatitudes Jesus admonished. These, according to Matthew 5: 3-10 are:

Blessed are the poor in spirit, for theirs is the kingdom of heaven

Blessed are the meek for they will inherit the earth.

AFRICAN NATIONALIST POETRY AND PROSE

Blessed are those who hunger and thirst for righteousness, for they will be filled

Blessed are the merciful, for they will be shown mercy

Blessed are the pure in heart for they will see God

Blessed are those who are persecuted because of righteousness, for theirs is the kingdom of heaven.

I could add, "Blessed are those who have no health insurance for they will have it under Health Care Reform." Thus, Mr. Obama adheres to the basic philosophic and moral tenets of this Christian nation. This the giddy multitude of anti-Obamaites could never envision nor comprehend!

African Nationalist Poetry and Prose Photo. LOVE!

FREDERICK MONDERSON

African Nationalist Poetry and Prose Photo. Tribute to the Ancestors – Images, 2019.

However, while I cannot equate Mr. Obama with Jesus, his philosophy of leveling the playing field, giving everyone a fair shot, everyone paying their fair share, even his concern for the millions with no health insurance is consistent with the aspirations inveighed in Matthew 5, which is also, the 'Meek shall inherit the earth....'

As he gives hope to the masses, the spirit of god is upon Barack Obama! He becomes the salt of the American earth! This light of the world is a beacon, a light of that shines from the City on a Hill making manifest the American mission as the last hope for humanity. Compare the President's compassionate concern with the secular materialism's privilege,

AFRICAN NATIONALIST POETRY AND PROSE

profit and power; we notice the nation has moved off its moral foundation; its moral compass, as Dr. Martin Luther King would say! This contradicts every spiritual value of one nation under god. His concern for the millions without health care, believing everybody is entitled to medical care forces us to ask, "Which stance or campaign worships secular materialism, which supports spiritual values?"

Therefore, as the forces of history teaches us, Christian belief holds Jesus and the Saints have amassed an enormous amount of good will through their good works, that is stored in a container in the Vatican which the Pope can draw upon to carry through his mission of mercy and salvation in the world. Equally, the African-American ancestors who have toiled unpaid in the fields of the institution of slavery, suffered the indignity of the emasculating experience of racism and been victims of racial discrimination and terror, created and experienced the joys of Negro Spirituals to ease their suffering while caring for the young, old and infirm, all the while still looking toward emancipation and salvation, looking for that "Sweet chariot to swing low." These are the people who, with faith in the future, could only bank "spiritual capital," "spiritual currency." Believe it or not, projecting their good works keeps America buoyed and "still standing" even though many are ignorant of the meaning and

FREDERICK MONDERSON

symbolism of this cosmic phenomenon or refuses to accept its possibilities. Nonetheless, their prayers, dreams, aspirations and expectations of these martyred visionaries, for all we know, foresaw the rise and elevation of Barack Obama. This spiritually long vision has also recognized the challenges to Mr. Obama as he sought to complete his mission and contribute to the elevation of their progeny through educational advancement, economic empowerment and political practicalities, also realized, that notwithstanding, "We shall overcome.". That is why these revered ancestors bequeathed the potency of a "spiritual currency bank" for Mr. Obama to draw on to contend and conquer the forces of materialism committed to derail his divine mission. Thus, the people's champion will prevail because through god "Spiritual capital" will win out against the financial prodigiousness of mammoth designed to thwart the will of destiny and the divine!

African Nationalist Poetry and Prose Photo. Tribute to the Ancestors – Images, 2019.

"Dr. Yosef ben-Jochannan made a mission of his life in looking at those corners and dimensions of his profession neglected by other writers, historians and

AFRICAN NATIONALIST POETRY AND PROSE

teachers. This small book, *The African Called Rameses 'The Great' II and The African Origin of 'Western Civilization,'* is no exception. In this book, he has looked at Rameses II of the 19th Dynasty in the manner that creates a need to re-assess this remarkable period in Nile-Valley Civilization. The pharaohs of the 19th Dynasty, especially Rameses II, restored Egypt's building-age and took it to the apex of its achievement as the best-known state of the ancient world. Dr. Ben also calls attention to certain debts that are owed to Nile-Valley Civilization by the nations that followed in its footsteps, awkwardly, without duplicating its achievement. In doing this, he is carrying on the high standard of creating research and scholarship set by his foundation works, *Black Man of the Nile and His Family*; *Africa: Mother of Western Civilization*; and *African Origins of the Major Western Religions.*" John Henrik Clarke. Foreword. Yosef A.A. ben-Jochannan. *The African Called Rameses* ("The Great") *II and the African Origin of 'Western Civilization'*" 1990.

African Nationalist Poetry and Prose Photo. Tribute to the Ancestors – Images, 2019.

FREDERICK MONDERSON

"'There a people now forgotten discovered while others were et barbarians, the elements of the arts and sciences. A race of men now rejected for their black skin and woolly hair, founded on the study of the laws of nature those civil and religious systems which still govern the universe.'" Yosef A.A. Ben-Jochannan. Quotes Count Constantin F. Volney in *Ruins of Empire. The African called Rameses ("The Great") II and the African Origin of 'Western Civilization,'* 1990.

26. Dr. YOSEF A. A. BEN-JOCHANNAN: A TRIBUTE
By
Dr. Fred Monderson

It is with great sorrow that I announce the death of my mentor, friend and world renown African historian, Egyptologist and humanitarian DR. YOSEF ANTONIO ALFREDO BEN-JOCHANNAN. At this time, AFRICAN PEOPLE HAVE LOST A CHAMPION OF GREAT MAGNITUDE, wisdom and intellectual fortitude. LET US WISH HIM A WONDERFUL RECEPTION INTO THE PANTHEON OF GREAT AFRICAN ANCESTORS who have never compromised in quest of the best for African people.

AFRICAN NATIONALIST POETRY AND PROSE

Among his many accomplishments, Dr. Ben has placed the Black Woman on the HIGHEST PEDESTAL to be admired and respected in the hope she will continue to do what no Black man can ever do!

DR. BEN HAS been a LIGHT and he has shown us the LIGHT!

LET US ALSO HOPE PEOPLE, YOUNG AND OLD, WILL CONTINUE TO READ HIS BOOKS AND FOREVER DRINK FROM THE FOUNT OF HIS ENLIGHTENMENT EFFORTS as Tour Guide, archaeologist and nationalist spokesman whose 97 years on earth have been a tremendously wonderful and enlightening experience. He possessed a vision that looked far into the future. His efforts HAVE KNOWN NO LIMITS in quest for the very best for AFRICAN PEOPLE! Again, his books should be introduced into the schools to let young people understand the man and forces at work against their best interests!

GOD BLESS DR. BEN-JOCHANNAN AND MAY HIS EFFORTS AND MEMORY CONTINUE TO BE AN INSPIRATION AND GUIDE TO US ALL!

Dr. Ben was an extraordinary man of many talents, but principally a man who held the African woman in

FREDERICK MONDERSON

the highest esteem. He taught us in the beginning was the African woman! Creation came out of the African woman! As the obelisk is a small pyramid on a tall base, this is the pedestal upon which Dr. ben-Jochannan placed the African woman. He honored the Black Woman who is the source of the Black Family! He taught us the Black Woman is a Goddess! He also led the light to the Nile Valley. He "took Egypt to challenge and destroy white supremacy!" It's like Marcus Garvey said on way to Atlanta Federal prison, "You may have caged the lion, but the cubs are running free out there," and thanks to Dr. Ben; intellectual cubs are challenging the distortions, omissions and putting Africa in its proper place in world civilization history given its accomplishments in Nubia and Egypt, Nile Valley cultures, that gave so much to the world.

The Twentieth Century has been blessed with great African and African-American writers and historians. These include Dr. W.E.B. Du Bois, Dr. Carter G. Woodson, Dr. Kwame Nkrumah, Dr. Ivan Van Sertima, J.A. Rogers, Cheikh Anta Diop and Dr. Leonard James, Emeritus Professor of **New York City Technical College** of the City University of New York, among others. This enormous collection of brain-power equally extends into the Twenty-First Century. However, none of these giants singularly surpass the literary production, commitment, tirelessness, and sincere dedication of Dr. Yosef Alfredo Antonio ben-Jochannan.

AFRICAN NATIONALIST POETRY AND PROSE

Outspoken visionary, iconic symbol and above his time; controversial and not afraid to take an iconoclastic and individual if a somewhat idiosyncratic point of view; Dr. Ben was always prepared to defend his position, irrespective. His friends and students, affectionately call this father, teacher, historian, friend and Egyptologist, "Doc Ben." In fact, back there in the early 1970s when even "Black folks" did not readily accept "Dr. Ben," ever wonder how he got his name? It was a young man named "Barney" and myself, Fred Monderson, who first started calling him not "Dr. Ben" but "Ben Jo" and the name stuck and finally when a fellow student Curtis Dunmoodie picked it up and said we must be more respectful, we began calling him "Dr. Ben" in defiance of those "feather bedders" who said "Dr. Ben has no PhD!"

African Nationalist Poetry and Prose Photo. Dr. Asante and beautiful ladies at **CEMOTAP'S** 31ST Anniversary Celebration.

FREDERICK MONDERSON

African Nationalist Poetry and Prose Photo. Reverends Jesse Jackson and Al Sharpton at a **Nation of Islam** function.

Ever on the "Front Line" of any battle, education or social, Jitu Weusi is always "Larger than Life."

Ever cried for Dr. Ben? This odious statement once made me cry at New York City (Community) Technical College. I hurriedly took the train to 125th Street to their second-floor office on Lennox Avenue across from the **Choc-Full-O-Nuts** Coffee Shop in Harlem, before Prof. George Simmonds calmed me down, showing me Dr. Ben's Doctorate in Anthropology on the wall. That is what some of the "false prophets" still do today in academia to him and others! And so, you ask them to match their literary production with their in-clandestine vituperativeness and they cannot! Period!

Here was a serious scholar, Dr. ben-Jochannan, who spent a lifetime researching, writing, and defending

AFRICAN NATIONALIST POETRY AND PROSE

the integrity and intellectual capabilities of African people worldwide. Dr. Ben pioneered in indigenous ancient African terminology. Imagine a European-American scholar discovered the bones of a fossilized African woman in Ethiopia and named her "Lucy" after an Englishman's song "Lucy with Diamonds," then playing on the radio. Dr. Ben said "No! Her name is Denk Nesh, not Lucy!"

In 1989, Doc Ben celebrated fifty years of visiting ancient Kemet, Ta-Merry (Egypt) and the Nile Valley cultures. This prolonged involvement has undergirded the basis of his researches, speeches, writings and educational tours. Equally, he began and for some time maintained archaeological digs on the Island of Elephantine and elsewhere. Alas, these have been discontinued.

This writer was happy to be a part of that epoch-making tour that marked Doc Ben's Fiftieth Anniversary visiting the ancient African "holy-land" and the next year for the **First Nubian Festival**. More importantly, I met "Doc Ben" in early 1972. This was right after the publication of his seminal "Trilogy" works, *African Origins of the "Major" Western Religions* (1970), *Africa: Mother of Western Civilization* (1971), and *Black Man of the Nile* (1972), later re-issued as *Black Man of the Nile and His Family*. The style of his writings, copious nature of referents employed to defend things African, and

FREDERICK MONDERSON

his Afrocentric pioneering approach has made "Doc. Ben," a very well-respected elder, and in his later years a sought-after speaking attraction, a man who "tells it like it is!"

Dr. ben-Jochannan has compiled an impressive thirty odd publications. He helped set the stage for a whole new approach in interpreting Africa's contributions to civilization and its legacy. He lit the fire of intellectual and cultural consciousness in Africans worldwide. The Diasporan style of dress with an Afrocentric flavor is also credited to him. Establishing connections between Africans in America, Africa, Asia and Europe are all attributed to Dr. ben-Jochannan, a man of vision, seer, and intellectual giant. Many of his books challenged the distortions of Europeans in writing, publishing and disseminating knowledge about the arts, sciences, religion, etc., of the ancient people today called Egyptians. Dr. Ben has rightly included omissions and corrected distortions systematically implanted and perpetrated by racist Western, European and American historiography that has falsified the historical past with a prejudiced interpretation against African people. Many of his books challenged the distortions of Europeans in writing, publishing and disseminating knowledge about the arts, sciences, religion, etc., regarding ancient Africa as represented in modern interpretation. Dr. Ben dared to expose the hypocrisy of western scholarship. He attacked the

AFRICAN NATIONALIST POETRY AND PROSE

foundational pillars upon which this false legacy rests. Naturally, he paid a price!

More than that "Bunny," Sister Viola Plummer keeps going against an American System she deems to be unconscionable, racist and oppressive.

African Nationalist Poetry and Prose Photo. Tribute to the Ancestors – Images, 2019.

Very early he also expressed the view some scholars are confused because they were taught from a wrong premise. In his own right, and as a result of his teachings, he had no choice but to produce, publish and distribute his works without the aid of major publishing firms. He was thus a pioneer in self-publishing, launching Alkebu-Lan Publishing Company and appealing and winning the support of

FREDERICK MONDERSON

many upcoming nationalists as "they purchased his books in first edition form!"

Initiating a new approach to history, the end result was an exposition and critical analysis of dynamic forces of Europe and Africa in struggle to claim heritage of the ancient and modern historical record. Dr. Ben addressed professionals, laymen, clergy, students and educators. He stressed vitality, resilience and creative expressions that shaped the modern African personality and worldview. Such an approach found ready ears among a people yearning for enlightening factual information about their illustrious African past in effort to free their minds from the devastating ramifications of slave trade and slavery; imperialism and colonialism; not to dismiss the many guises of Jim Crow, Sr. and Jr., joblessness, miseducation, police brutality, mass incarceration, and equally the "Willie Lynch Syndrome." As such, these young and old minds were enthused by the positive nature and potency of their cultural African heritage as "Ben" outlined it. He also took great pains to explain that there were lusterless pages in Africa's past. Nevertheless, his concern fueled their emerging aspirations. This outlook brought Dr. Ben the adulation and respect of a grateful people, he for long deserved. They understood and welcomed his contributions among the litany of great African-American literary artists, activists, scholars.

Dr. Ben's writings, lectures and educational tours over the years have stressed two essential themes.

AFRICAN NATIONALIST POETRY AND PROSE

The first is that the "emergence of civilization, viz., science, religion, government, architecture, agriculture, philosophy, and the arts, began in Africa." The mouth of these utterances became the conduit of today's Egypt and the Nile Valley. In his approach, Dr. Ben has shown how the structural foundations of western civilization developed from discoveries and scientific applications in this ancient African land. Lastly, he took great pains to show the writing and teaching of modern history has been distorted to elevate Europe and degrade Africa, which is clearly wrong and must be rectified. This fundamental view helped establish the need for African historical reconstruction and interpretation particularly as we navigate this new century and millennium.

The second of Dr. Ben's themes has been that "Africans worldwide should be proud of their ancestors' accomplishments. The arts and sciences that today govern the world are Africa's legacy. African-Americans should show great pride and dignity in their history and heritage." They must respect themselves and carry themselves with dignity and pride. Those who know can and should teach the young how to identify with Africa. In so doing, they must form study groups and visit Africa. Yet, they must also be aware of the machinations of cultural imperialism and cultural genocide constantly at work. Further, the young must immerse themselves

FREDERICK MONDERSON

in an African-centric perspective and research, write and teach others in turn. They must study the European or Romance languages, French, German, Greek, Latin, Coptic, African as well, Swahili, Arabic and Medu Netcher or Hieroglyphics. They must struggle to correct the recent distorted history of Africa's past. In this way, future leaders would help to better the lot of humanity and save the world from its impending moral, spiritual and scientific destruction. To accomplish these objectives, the good doctor has supplied a reservoir of information from his life's researches in the arsenal of published works he has created. Of course, these works must be read, ingested and digested and returned to time and again. This is important for as Dr. John Henrik Clarke once remarked, "People buy but never read Dr. Ben's books." Herein then is the dilemma.

African Nationalist Poetry and Prose Photo. David Dinkins, former Mayor of New York City and a well-known former boxer.

AFRICAN NATIONALIST POETRY AND PROSE

African Nationalist Poetry and Prose Photo. Tribute to the Ancestors – Images, 2019.

The author's major thesis of his *African Origins of the "Major" Western Religions* is that African religious practices were denigrated and called "fetishism" and "paganism." In fact, these early thought processes, he showed, are the fundamental bases of Judaism, Christianity and Islam. He argued that these ideas were first developed and nurtured in Central Africa among indigenous peoples and then migrated and extended throughout the Nile Valley. They found greatest fruition in Kemet (Egypt) and were preserved by the nature of its geography and its civilization advances. The early knowledge after oral teachings and local practices was first written down in such selections as the "Book of Gates," "Book of Knowing Ra," etc. These were part of the earlier "Pyramid Texts" (Old Kingdom); then "Coffin Texts" (Middle Kingdom); and the later *Book of the Dead or Book of Going Forth By Day* (New Kingdom); and the "Mysteries of Sais" (Egypt). The fortunes of geography enabled Africa's second cultural daughter, Kemet, to rise to greater prominence than did the eldest, Ethiopia, Dr. Ben

FREDERICK MONDERSON

explained! He stressed and still maintained to his last, despite all the "new evidence," that civilization began to the south of Egypt! However, despite modern falsification of history and the insistent propagation of such falsity, his thesis is as credible as ever.

Another of Dr. Ben's seminal works is Africa: Mother of Western Civilization. Its major thesis holds, the "fundamental laws, principles, philosophies, ideas, arts and crafts that educated the west, are indigenous to Africa through the Nile Valley cultural experience." For critical teachers who face this dilemma he has some advice. As such, he wrote: "The only credentials necessary in the experience of African history, otherwise misnomered 'the Black Experience' and 'Black Studies' are the documented proofs and the sources from whence they are taken."

For this reason, *Africa: Mother of Western Civilization* is an enormous compendium of facts, sources, illustrations, and analyses that challenge laymen and scholars alike. It suggests all educators and lay persons alike become involved in reclaiming the stolen heritage of Africa. This magnum opus opens new vistas for historical investigation and provides a wide array of references relating to the significance of Africa in world civilization.

Black Man of the Nile and His Family marks the third of the "trilogy of Dr. Ben's seminal works." This

AFRICAN NATIONALIST POETRY AND PROSE

particular source represents the maturity of his thoughts and presentations for it focuses on the role Black men and women have played in bequeathing science, religion, arts, metaphysics, agricultural method, boat building and Nile River navigation to the world through Africa's conduit in Egypt and Nubia. It also contains a number of objectives the author seeks to accomplish.

The first of these objectives is: "an attempt to create in young African, African-American (Black person), and all other African people, a sense of belonging in the great African heritage." It is, writes Dr. Ben "specifically directed to those who have criminally demasculinized, denuded, and otherwise denigrated the Africans of their CULTURAL, ECONOMIC, POLITICAL, SCIENTIFIC, SPIRITUAL, and all other forms of their heritage and human decency." To this we should add the intellectual heritage as represented in Egypt; that is, through "acquisition methods," and teaching, writing and representation of the artifactual evidence.

It also presents: "AFRICAN ORIGINS OF EUROPEAN CIVILIZATION" in a manner whereby, "scholars can find interesting use for it in their research; as much as the layman can for processing information."

FREDERICK MONDERSON

Dr. Ben views his role as gadfly presenting, "pertinent information needed in the African peoples' RE-IDENTIFICATION with their great ancestral heritage." Lastly, he continued, the "major desired accomplishment this volume seeks to achieve, is to provide anthropological evidence in the ancient heritage of the Africans" and their contributions all over the world.

Abu Simbel to Ghizeh: A Guide Book and Manual is in itself a useful piece of writing. But, there are other books.

In the acquisition of knowledge, Sir Francis Bacon (1561-1626) told us: "Some books are to be tasted, others to be swallowed, and some few to be chewed and digested." This much can be said of the trilogy of Dr. ben-Jochannan's works, *Black Man of the Nile and His Family*, *Africa: Mother of Western Civilization* and *The African Origins of the 'Major' Western Religions*. The others are equally interesting! Everyone must buy and read these books and pass them on to others particularly their sons and daughters.

Finally, as a student of his, and based on observations and analytic critique, this writer would like to add a 15-point summation of how we can view Dr. Yosef Alfredo Antonio ben-Jochannan's contribution as an unselfish and fearless elucidation of the historical record systematically distorted to elevate Europe and

AFRICAN NATIONALIST POETRY AND PROSE

denigrate Africa while wrecking psycho-social debasement of the African spirit and persona. Without question, whether through omission, distortion and even false presentation, the urban youth across America have most seriously been victimized in the systematic and alienated educational process they have been subjected to. As such, the potent cultural lifeline Dr. Yosef Alfredo Antonio ben-Jochannan has provided is today critical in rescuing these young people adrift in the academic and intellectual cosmos of these modern times going forward. The prescription therefore is as follows:

African Nationalist Poetry and Prose Photo. Councilman Al Vann and Jitu Weusi and a young activist they admire and support.

FREDERICK MONDERSON

African Nationalist Poetry and Prose Photo. Rev. Al Sharpton, Chairman of the **National Action Network** and Rev. Wyatt Tee. Walker, President of the Organization flank Activist Sonny "AB" Carson at the old **NAN** Headquarters 1941 Madison Avenue.

1. We must praise and show thankfulness for the man who, for more than half a century challenged the behemoth of western intellectual oppression of Africa and her offspring while enlightening many to the wonders of a creative African cultural heritage.

2. We must commend Dr. ben-Jochannan for the humanitarian work he did along the Nile River among the Nubians in Egypt and Sudan, viz., Aswan, Daboud, Wadi Halfa, Dongola Province and Fashoda.

3. We must recognize his call to action in combating the cultural genocide in the African-

AFRICAN NATIONALIST POETRY AND PROSE

American studies curriculum predating the Afrocentric insistence on multi-culturalism.

4. We should continue to emulate his style of critical analysis of contemporary developments, whether it was historical omissions in Alex Haley's Roots; misrepresentation in King Tut's exhibition that has taken place several times in America; taking to task T. Eric Peet's "The Problem with Akhenaton;" Criticism of Father Temple's *Bantu Philosophy*; challenge to another writer's description that Rameses II had "badly abscessed teeth," and so forth.

5. We can appreciate his identifying *"They all look Alike, All,"* thus linking African peoples across the globe who were victims of racial hatred and cultural aggression.

6. His early clarification of the differences between *The Black Nationalist Versus the Black Marxist* was very timely and inspiring and still is.

7. First to outline the *History of the Bible*, he challenged *The Black Clergy Without a Black Theology* and offered *A Black Bible for Black Spiritual and Religious Consciousness*.

8. We must acknowledge as a human he may have made some mistakes, miniscule, as they were outweighed by the foundational reservoir of ethical

and cultural Ma'at he implanted in the consciousness of African people worldwide.

9. His insistence that all African Americans visit the Nile Valley to imbibe in the cultural heritage and grow from the intellectual exposure, but more particularly their dress code and mannerism among the people must not be construed as the "arrogance of Ugly Americans" was and is still timely and insightful.

10. His outspoken nature, love for Marcus Garvey and his *Philosophy and Opinions of Marcus Garvey*, praise of Black Goddesses, critique of Academics who are "fifth columns" made him anathema to people with ill-intentions toward African people.

11. Dr. ben-Jochannan had little respect for people in high positions who never promoted the aspirations of their Black subordinates.

12. A staunch Pan-Africanist, he aspired to see accomplished sustained and measurable economic, political and educational empowerment for people of African heritage worldwide.

13. He said, "I took Egypt to show our people the proper way" and to challenge its misrepresentation, racism and religious bigotry.

14. He insisted we not just read books and do research on Ancient Egypt in Africa, but also form

AFRICAN NATIONALIST POETRY AND PROSE

study groups that debate and discuss these important issues raised by him as well as personally critique status quo's positions.

15. He asked us to standardize our learning and take responsibility for our own actions and history. He stated: "Until African (Black) people are willing, and do write their own experience, past, and present, we will continue being slaves, mentally, physically, and spiritually to Caucasian and Semitic racism and religious bigotry." This latter we must never allow to happen, for as Dr. John Henrik Clarke has admonished, "African people must write their own history."

Therefore, we must recognize that Dr. Yosef Alfredo Antonio ben-Jochannan has made a major contribution to African intellectual growth and consciousness. He created a cosmological vision over time that allowed us to see the light. His work has been seminal! In fact, he was our light! He taught us how to persevere to persevere! He asked that we establish and maintain a standard for our behavior, and don't fear, don't fear defeat, don't fear death!

FREDERICK MONDERSON

African Nationalist Poetry and Prose Photo. Movie personnel, Gordon Parks (left) his son (center) and Ossie Davis (right).

African Nationalist Poetry and Prose Photo. Dr. John Henrik Clarke and Sister Sybil Williams-Clarke and their escorts.

"Human intelligence normally strives to understand how all this came to be. Frequently, a demiurge, a creator, is imagined at the beginning of beginnings,

AFRICAN NATIONALIST POETRY AND PROSE

at the very origins of the universe. Creation, or the coming into being of the world, including all components of the universe, is supposed to be the work of that demiurge. This is a constant postulate in all the world's mythologies, save one. The exceptional vision comes from Egypt. Unlike all other mythologies, Egyptian mythology came up with the concept of a universe predating the present universe, a different universe that existed before the demiurge and all its creation. Here the mind, liberated from orthodox approaches to issues of genesis and origin, enters a realm with no questionable premises. What is posited is a kind of 'matter.' Yet it has no thematic form. It is absolute in its sovereignty, before it becomes involved, through the agency of the demiurge, in a process of becoming. The concept was of a sort of spatial medium antedating space and time, beyond time and space. All perceptible reality would, in future be projected from this originating 'medium' and within it. The result of that activity would be the generation of the universe as we know it now, the reality explored and exploited by human ingenuity." Theophile Obenga. *African Philosophy: The Pharaonic Period* 2780-330 B.C. 2004.

FREDERICK MONDERSON

"…original matter and the creatures shaped out of it through the creative agency of God were one and the same: original matter became diverse in the process of forming the cosmic Whole, thanks to God…. The ancient Egyptian view was quite contrary. Egyptian thinkers posited a state of matter before God and all his creation. Better still, God the artificer and creator himself emerged from this primal matter, itself un-created. The ancient Egyptians posited un-created reality before God the demiurge. Saint Augustine posited con-created matter, created by God at the same time as other creatures. Between the two conceptions, that of un-created matter is more materialistic than that of con-created matter." Theophile Obenga. *African Philosophy*: *The Pharaonic Period* 2780-330 B.C. 2004.

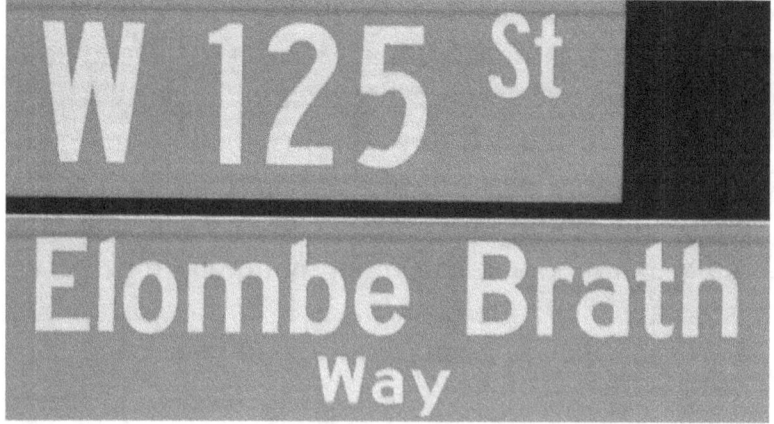

African Nationalist Poetry and Prose Photo. The "Little Giant" gets his well-deserved "Home Boy" Award.

AFRICAN NATIONALIST POETRY AND PROSE

27. DR. BEN, "OUR FATHER"
By
Dr. Fred Monderson

Dr. Ben is "Our Father," our intellectual father, who in travelling the road, first encountered then pointed out the pitfalls systematically arrayed against the African, as Marcus Garvey proclaimed, "Those at home and those abroad." The little man stood tall and illuminating, withstanding the intellectual, religious, educational and disguised economic assaults America and the West have perennially launched against African men of substance whose knees refuse to bend! Very early he grasped the significance of ancient Nile Valley civilization as advancing humanity's development within the context of state formation and the enlightenment of metaphysics as well as the African's origination, development, consolidation, expansion and spread of consciousness and knowledge enabling the world's people to advance religiously, culturally and scientifically.

Mirroring the actions of great black men challenging oppressive behemoths, viz., Hannibal and Rome; Shaka and the Boers; Nat Turner and American enslavement; Frederick Douglass as an abolitionist; Samori Toure halting the French advance in West Africa as part of the continent's nationalist assertion; Martin Delaney and Biblical distortion and the black

FREDERICK MONDERSON

man's place in early world history; Booker T. Washington and the exclusion of blacks from the industrial development of the nation; Menelik II repelling the Italians at the Battle of Adowa; W.E.B. DuBois and the significance of the struggle for Pan-Africanism; Marcus Garvey, the **UNIA** and the importance of black symbolism and motifs; Carter G. Woodson and the dangers of mis-education; Paul Robeson as a voice in the "wilderness;" Martin Luther King hewing "a stone of hope from a mountain of despair;" and Malcolm X as a grassroots visionary; Dr. Ben dazzled as a principal star in constellations of intellectual and moral giants who spoke truth to power.

In the spectacular journey of his life, Dr. Yosef Alfredo Antonio ben-Jochannan raised a loud and consistent voice against Western and American falsity, bigotry, distortion, omission and maligning of the African, his heritage, its legacy and the destiny of Africa's sons and daughters at home and abroad. He meticulously analyzed and challenged the writings of pseudo-scientific proponents and others as Father Placide Temples, M.W.D. Jeffries, Basil Davidson, Flinders Petrie, Wallis Budge and James Breasted, among others.

Possessing no pistols, canons or warships, Dr. ben-Jochannan went to war to recapture the African rightful place in the intellectual development of the human spirit. Encountering many obstacles, he still persevered despite the odds and opposition. Very

AFRICAN NATIONALIST POETRY AND PROSE

early he made the connection between the ancient African and the evolution of scientific study and religious practice, metaphysics and spiritualism. In intellectual analysis of Western holy books, he critiqued propagators of the "curse of the black man" syndrome, the stealing of the African's intellectual heritage falsely claiming to be its originator, then denying the victim access to the educational opportunities this knowledge promised. Conducting penetrating research, he discovered ancient commentators who were contemporary with Egyptians and other ancient Africans and who presented a different version of present history colored by the machinations of imperialism, racial discrimination and an indiscriminate propensity to propagate views of Western standards that purport the African to be inferior. He frowned upon the devastating and long-lasting psychological and social scarification of the slavery experience. He recognized ancient African man and cultures contributed more than is recognized today towards the development of the same Western standards of learning, religion, technology, architecture, science, and so much more. He railed against religious bigotry and surprisingly his efforts threatened the pillars of Western falsity that suppressed indigenous cultures in Asia, Africa and the Americas.

FREDERICK MONDERSON

African Nationalist Poetry and Prose Photo. Jesse Jackson and Dr. Roscoe Brown amidst other persons of significance.

As an anthropologist and archaeologist, he early discovered the conspiracy against ancient Egypt, recognized the mechanisms of the strategy of ancient artifacts acquisition and misrepresentation of such treasures in museum displays and other fields of publication. He took students to view Egyptian collections at museums and pointed out the positives and negatives in the displays. He also took students to his Harlem apartment showcasing his library to reinforce their realization of the existence of diverse and not easily disclosed sources of referents.

To counter the intellectual and cultural assault against the African personality, he began advocating, lecturing, teaching and writing and publishing correctives to standard negative portrayals. He initiated the concept of self-publishing because

AFRICAN NATIONALIST POETRY AND PROSE

established publishing houses recognized the dangers of his enlightening the people. Becoming tremendously pro-active, he began Tours of Egypt and encouraged others to so engage the yearning masses with the intent of unleashing intellectual uprisings that would educate and uplift Africans long denied the real advantages of constructive and systematic learning.

Contacting Dr. Leonard James, a longtime educator Emeritus of New York City Technical College of CUNY and admirer of Dr. Ben's courageous intellectual challenge, he reminded: "Dr. Ben is an unsung hero and a great African scholar who produced unbelievable scholarship." The strength of Dr. Ben's thrust was revealing the wide diversity of referents and encouraging young scholars to "Get the earliest materials and work from there." In Egypt, he always laid down the law, "Now that you've been to Egypt, seen what you have seen, what are you going to do with the knowledge?" He consistently advocated travel to Egypt to better grasp the industriousness of the ancient African and the lasting effect of his contributions. Dr. James continued, "Every modern African and African-American Egyptologist owes Dr. Ben a debt." Equally, and even further, "Each and every African and African-American educational program, owes Dr. Ben a debt."

FREDERICK MONDERSON

As time and toil took its toll, Dr. Ben faced and fought many health issues. Still he persevered. In his glorious march of fame, he "talk the talk" and "walk the walk" and "talk the walk" and "walk the talk!" He often boasted, "I took Egypt to combat racism and misrepresentation." This was particularly evident in Egypt where Dr. Ben's work among poor Egyptians and indigenous Nubians was tremendously significant. The construction of the Egyptian "High Dam," the "Damn Dam," displaced untold thousands of Nubians and submerged many Nubian temples, cemeteries and cultural history. In response, Dr. Ben adopted and worked with the village of Daboud, the operational center of the displaced Nubian villages. As such, through Dr. Ben's efforts, direction and generosity, Daboud became the nucleus of opposition to Nubian oppression.

Actually, as the story was told, on one 1980s tour going from Luxor to Aswan, the bus broke down on the outskirts of Daboud Village and as the Americans stood in the steaming desert sun, the villagers came to their assistance. Flabbergasted that "Nubian-Americans" would come to their land, they extended their meager hospitality, cherished at the time! Thenceforth, Dr. Ben would stop at the village, to great fanfare, each time he passed through. He encouraged brothers and sisters on tour to bring medicine, school supplies for the children, new clothing and other essentials. He helped build a school, a hospital and playground, worked with the Council and adopted and educated several students at

AFRICAN NATIONALIST POETRY AND PROSE

University level. Any donations collected at the village he would match twice over, give it to the Mayor who would then disperse the money and essentials to different villages. Dr. Ben's actions emboldened Nubian resistance sweltering under Egyptian yoke! Through bribery of travel agents his efforts were undermined. In no uncertain terms, he was told "Stop it!" Decades later Nubians, welcoming their "Nubian-American brothers and sisters" would ask "How is Dr. Ben?" "Is he still alive?" "How is he doing?"

An outstanding trait of Dr. ben-Jochannan has been his unselfishness and lavish praise and uplifting of Africans globally. Everywhere Dr. Ben traveled in Egypt he helped people. Every hotel his group stayed at in Cairo, Luxor and Aswan, people were rewarded. Housekeeping, food-service, gardeners, baggage-handlers, bus-drivers, musicians and gatekeepers at sites all got remuneration. Everyone benefitted. Each group received an envelope, no matter how small. He really distributed the wealth!

On the farcical 2003 trip, Dr. Ben was very sick. When I saw him in the Lobby of the Oberoi Hotel, and approached, I said a silent prayer for Dr. Ben! Then I thought, "Thank god he will die in his beloved Egypt!" Rushed home and thanks to the efforts of Dr. and Mrs. Lewis of Harlem, Dr. Ben was up and about and dancing within months. Subsequently, he was

FREDERICK MONDERSON

enstooled at National Action Network, in a chair no one sat in.

On June 5, 2011, the day Dr. Ben again (*Daily Challenge* March 1, 2000, Centerfold) recognized and endorsed my work, as a longstanding student of his, while having lunch at his favorite Harlem Restaurant, Dr. Ben said to me: "Monderson, can you take me back to Egypt one last time. I don't want to go to the sites, just to sit in the hotel lobby. The people will come to see me!" That is, the Oberoi Hotel Lobby at Aswan! Contacting his lawyer, he told me, "The Court will not permit me to allow Dr. Ben to travel."

Dr. Ben led an exceptional life. He expended great energy, time and resources in defending and upholding things African. He paid a price for his outspokenness! He was especially proud of and adored the African woman whom he placed on an obelisk pedestal. He was in the forefront of the "black is beautiful" movement; initiated wearing African clothing and insignia in America; greatly admired African heroes and heroines; he shined the light for all to see; and directed the focus of African intellectuals, encouraging their research on Egypt, Africa, as well as Africa's place in universal history. He pioneered use of indigenous names as Alkebu-Lan for Egypt and Denk Nesh for Lucy and frowned on such disgusting appellates as "Negro," "Nigger" and all such. He devoted his life to teaching African people to "Be proud of your color, culture and

AFRICAN NATIONALIST POETRY AND PROSE

history!" Dr. Ben has always been and will remain a "great light in the African pantheon of heroes" from Eternity to Eternity!

African Nationalist Poetry and Prose Photo. Myrlie Evers, wife of slain civil rights icon Medgar Evers (left) and Coretta (right) Scott King, wife of slain civil rights icon Dr. Martin Luther King (right).

FREDERICK MONDERSON

African Nationalist Poetry and Prose Photo.
Tribute to the Ancestors – Images, 2019.

AFRICAN NATIONALIST POETRY AND PROSE

"So, the topic of the anteriority of black civilization, championed by Cheikh Anta Diop (Pharaonic Egypt, Africa as the cradle of humanity, etc.), On the Heavens, On Meteorology, etc. These ancient sources consistently and unanimously emphasized Egypt's civilizing role in the Mediterranean. Western scholarship, however, no longer mentions these eyewitness accounts from the Phoenicians and the Greeks. The responses are obvious.... 'The most famous Hellenic scholars or philosophers crossed the sea in order to get initiated by (Egyptian) priests into new fields of knowledge.' ... The new science taught to Greek students (Orpheus, Homer, Solon, Plato, Thales of Miletus, Pythagoras, Oenopidus, Eudoxus and others) included geometry, astronomy, theology, philosophy, and an initiation into pure 'esoteric tradition' of pharaonic Egypt, the discipline of sacerdotal practice." Theophile Obenga. *African Philosophy: The Pharaonic Period* – 2780-330 B.C. 2004.

28. CELEBRATING DR. BEN-JOCHANNAN BY DR. FRED MONDERSON

How to tribute Dr. Yosef Alfred Antonio ben-Jochannan, "Dr. Ben," the giant; an icon, master teacher, scholar extraordinaire, nationalist and uncompromising gadfly in defense of Africa and her

FREDERICK MONDERSON

sons and daughters, is the challenge posed in this quest. Naturally, sugar, some spice and a little photographic nicety is a significant first step in the journey to celebrate the life and work of an individual not afraid to be a consistent iconoclast in extolling the meaning and significance of Egypt and the Nile Valley experience while challenging the distorted projection that falsely portray European origination of science, religion, art, architecture, culture, as the pillars that support human creativity and progress emerging from the mists of history to the illumination of high noon of man's philosophic, spiritual and moral journey. Just as the Sphinx of Ghizeh has outlasted time, Dr. Ben has remained a timeless sentinel extolling the great gift of Africans who fired the human imagination to create the dynamics of intellectual thought processes that advanced the pageantry of the human experience; he has criticized gross misrepresentation of the historical record and as a corrective, cultivated a cadre of young minds committed to the proper reconstruction and foundation of Egypt in African history placing it on a pedestal as he has also placed the Black woman for whom he has shown great respect, love and affection.

Dr. Ben-Jochannan brought the light of knowledge through his scholarship, lectures and encouraged trips to Egypt enabling Africans to see and experience glory on the ancient tabula rasa their forebears had created as the first cause of human enlightenment. Beyond intellectual exercises, Dr. Ben was a great humanitarian and philanthropist who

AFRICAN NATIONALIST POETRY AND PROSE

lived a long and exemplary life, and as a beacon and well-spring encouraged many to drink from his intellectual reservoir towards their own illumination. Unsung hero that he is, many African and African-American academic program and scholars owe him a huge debt enabling these cubs to create credible and defendable scholarship in the intellectual warfare unfolding over Egypt and its legacy. Whether in the writing of history, challenging mis-representation in Museum showcases and in the curriculum where young minds are constantly molded, the hand of Dr. Ben must be seen as a living memorial, a beacon, and his extraordinary scholarship must remain a fountain and guidepost, constantly showing the way and defining the parameters by which African people determine their future by creating revitalized generations of strong intellectual and moral warriors guided by the philosophic and spiritual principle of Ma'at.

From Abu Simbel to the Cairo Museum of Egyptian Antiquities, this Celebration of Dr. Ben-Jochannan seeks to cast some light on the path the old master has traveled, shown the way and guided untold numbers to take pride in the realization Africans can do anything others can and do it successfully because of the creativity Mother African has blest and endowed them with!

A long-standing student of Dr. Ben-Jochannan who traveled to Egypt with him on many occasions, Dr.

FREDERICK MONDERSON

Fred Monderson is an African Historian, Egyptologist and retired Educator who taught American History and Government in New York Public schools and can be reached at fredsegypt.com@fredsegypt.com. This book is published by SuMon Publishers, P.O Box 160586, Brooklyn, New York 11216.

MAKING DR. BEN'S DAY

On Thursday September 6, 2012 at 9:00 AM, I visited Dr. ben-Jochannan to show him the book, *Celebrating Dr. Ben-Jochannan: From Eternity to Eternity*, I wrote in his honor. Once Dr. Lewis gave me directions, I worked my way there from Brooklyn, thru Manhattan and into the Bronx. I found him sitting having coffee in the dining room. Once we began examining the book in color on my computer along with the black and white version of the book sitting on the desk, I was impressed with how sharp Dr. Ben's mind still is. He told me he will be 95 years old on December 31, 2012!

AFRICAN NATIONALIST POETRY AND PROSE

African Nationalist Poetry and Prose Photo. Judge Bruce "Cut 'em Loose Bruce" Wright and the iconic Jesse Jackson.

African Nationalist Poetry and Prose Photo. Black Power! David Dinkins, Haitian President Aristede, Jesse Jackson are flanked by Congressmen Charles Rangel and Major Owens.

"'I am the eternal. I am Ra who came out of Noun… I am the master of light. (Book of the Dead, Chapter 153B) …. Noun (Nounou), fluid, liquid ether; Ra rises from the Noun (Atoum or Ra, or Atoum-Ra, the ancient sun-god of the city of Heliopolis, plunged int eh primordial liquid with the potential existence of the gods). On the first day, Atoum, out of the Noun, brings forth the twin deities: God Shou and Goddess Tefnut, the first couple created. The air and humidity necessary to life had thus taken at the same time the temporal dimensions of the potential universe were given. 'Shou is eternal time and Tefnut infinite time' (The Sarcophagus Texts, 80 B1C). Shou is eternity and Tefnut immensity. Shou and Tefnut then gave birth to the spatial elements of the universe: Geb, God of the earth and Nut, Goddess of the sky. In Egyptian thought the earth is the male element, the sky the female; the sky being the fertile principle of the world by the fact that it conceals the life-giving the world by the fact that it conceals the life-giving light. Geb and Nut had four children: Osiris, symbol of the fertile powers of the soil, and Isis, the equilibrium of life; Seth, symbol of sterility and of unhappy upheavals, and Nephthys wo symbolizes protection." Theophile Obenga. *Ancient Egypt and Black Africa.* 1992.

29. CELEBRATION for "DR. BEN" - Part I
By
DR. FRED MONDERSON

When African people begin to count the stars in their heroic pantheon constellation, the large and small illumination emanating there from, Dr. Yosef Alfredo Antonio ben-Jochannan looms among the largest and most significant of these luminaries.

AFRICAN NATIONALIST POETRY AND PROSE

While many of these "stars" manifest in politics, war, nationalism, religion, education and civil rights activism, etc., Dr. Ben, as he is affectionately called, excelled in intellectualism, praise of African womanhood, cultural conscious raising, the challenging of western pillars of cultural genocide depicted in the form of historical distortion, omission of meaningful historical contributions of Africans, blacks, and the psychological damages resulting therefrom to their cultural heritage and futures. He pioneered in recognition of the significance of indigenous naming of themselves, their cultural attainment and the geographical locations in which their genius originated all the fundamentals of civilization, such as religion, architecture, writing, art, medicine, agriculture, science, river travel and transportation of large stone and economics, among other forms of intellectual creations. He challenged, at great peril, financial and stigmatic, the onslaught of so-called "EGYPTOLOGISTS, AUTHORITIES ON AFRICA, SEMITICISTS, HAMITICISTS, WHITE LIBERAL HISTORIANS, AFRICANISTS," and the like of them. Yet, "NUBIANS" were, supposedly, the only indigenous Ethiopians (Blacks) the "NEGROPHOBES" conceded were "N-E-G-R-O-E-S" whatever this disgusting and nauseating term meant to the 16th or 17th century Portuguese RACISTS that invented it; a term which some of the world's greatest "SEMITICISTS" and "CAUCASIANISTS" even breakdown to make the NUBIANS appear as

FREDERICK MONDERSON

"HAMITIC-TYPE CAUCASIANS, DARK-SKINNED CAUCASOIDS" and "NILOTIC HAMITES."

He frowned on the "SEMITIC NORTH AFRICA MYTH" and the equally ridiculous "CAUCASIAN NORTH AFRICA" which was "NEGRO-LESS." He severely criticized "EDUCATORS," "SCHOLARS," "AUTHORITIES ON AFRICA," characterizing them as all as very sick minds! He was particularly incensed over "DARK SKINNED HAMITIC EUROPEANS" and Seligman's Races of Africa's religious bigotry and Semitic racism as perpetuated by "AUTHORITIES," "LIBERAL HISTORIANS," "BLACK STUDIES PROFESSORS" who parrot racist and outmoded ideas of Africans, Africa and Egypt in the Nile Valley. Dr. Ben chose to "ignore the RACISTS actions and RELIGIOUS BIGOTRY of White and Black Jews, White and Black Christians, White or Black Muslims, in their bastardization and plagiarization of the history and heritage of our "MOTHER-CONTINENT" - Alkebu-lan. He spilled much ink on the Jewish myth of Noah's curse of Black people!

In *The Black Man's North and East Africa* (1971) by Yosef A.A. ben-Jochannan and George Simmonds, originally published by Alkebu-lan and now reprinted by Black Classics Press, the authors contend that there is much falsity and distortion in the manner in which the history of this particular region is presented in the guise of "academic scholarship" by

AFRICAN NATIONALIST POETRY AND PROSE

academicians, authorities and scholars, even men of the cloth as "Rabbi, Reverend, Minister, Priest, Imam." What is interesting about this groundbreaking critique of the presentation of African history beginning in the 1940s but published in the 1970s, the authors pull no punches but outline a scathing critique of academic falsity whose foundation is a complete distortion of the historical record whether preached particularly from the perspective of lay or religious history.

African Nationalist Poetry and Prose Photo. "Two Champions in One," Adam Clayton Powell Jr. and Judge Bruce Wright.

In this, *The Black Man's North and East Africa* is a wonderful tour de force challenge to western and American historical distortion and what the authors call religious bigotry and racial prejudice. They take to task, the manner in which Egypt and Nile Valley culture in general is presented to represent the indigenous creators of that magnificent civilization in Ancient Africa. They present a very cogent argument to show ancient writers, and they show a whole slew of them, viz., Herodotus, Aeschylus, Strabo, Eratosthenes, Homer in the Iliad and Odyssey, Philostratus, Statius, Philo, Eusebius, Manetho, Josephus, Diodorus, Lucretius, Poenuhis, Agatharclude, and even the Church Fathers of Christianity, such as Tertullian, St. Cyprian, St. Augustine, among others, who never used the term Negro, Semite nor Hamite to describe the people of ancient Egypt, Nubia, Kush, the Nile Valley. Equally, the name the people themselves and the ancients called the land, Africa, is a late Roman nomenclature rather than the names of Olympia. Hesperia, Oceania, Corpyle, Ortygia. The Greeks and Romans called it Africa and Libya and the Ethiopia called Africa Alkebu-lan.

In textual analysis, he states "Xenophanes was the first to use physical characteristics as a point of racial identification of the Ethiopians rather than color of skin. Of this point, I cannot subscribe; for, what was it but "PHYSICAL CHARACTERISTICS" when Herodotus wrote "... the Colchians, Ethiopians and Egyptians have the most wooly-hair of all mankind." He continued that, "Herodotus wrote of the 'BLACK FLATTEN-NOSED ETHIOPIANS I MET...' etc. Even Strabo 17.1.2 and 17. 1.5 cites Eratosthenes' works with regard to the Egyptians who fought

AFRICAN NATIONALIST POETRY AND PROSE

against Cambyses and his Persian invaders of Merowe being BLACK (Ethiopian); this he wrote about c. 525 B.C.E. Further verification came from other Greeks who fought with the Ethiopians at the battle of Xerxes."

Dr. Ben argues further: "It is written that 'Aeschylus was the first of the Greeks to place the Ethiopian" Kushites at a specific Geo-political "boundary in Africa." This may have been very much true; but Ionian merchants and mercenaries who served in the army of Psammetichus I (otherwise known as "Psamtik" biblically), somewhere between the years 663-609 B.C.E., also described the Ethiopians they met in Africa, Egypt in particular, with respect to their geo-political setting." He is concerned, contemporary with the Egyptians, these writers never used such terms as "Negro, Hamitic, Semitic," etc., to describe these ancient Africans and the authors show these are, and they criticize these, modern interpolations. In fact, the tone of the ancient commentators who used nothing but "Ethiopians" to describe the Africans, black people, contrasts remarkably well with the disparaging epithets moderns, fueled by racial hatred who distorted the evidence, omitted the facts and projected a description not found in the Egyptian, Greek or Roman lexicon. The racists invented disgusting terms as "Negro" not simply to disparage Africans and exclude them from Egypt, while misrepresenting even the religion the black man invented, claiming

FREDERICK MONDERSON

Judeo-Christian-Islamic origination and underscoring white, Caucasian, blond hair, blue eyed, superiority in all forms of human creation, whether religious, scientific or social. For the most part, modern teaching cast ancient Egypt in a Graeco-Roman mold, using Roman terms describing even Pre-Roman developments in the Nile Valley.

African Nationalist Poetry and Prose Photo. Queen Mother Moore "Holding Court" as she conducts an interview.

African Nationalist Poetry and Prose Photo. Brooklyn Activist Sonny Carson right) and Professor Patterson (light suit center) discuss images of "Bones" in the Brooklyn Navy Yard as part of the movement to repatriate his ancestor Samuel Carson "The Runaway" to Ghana, West Africa.

AFRICAN NATIONALIST POETRY AND PROSE

This little book is a powerful resource for its identification of classical writers who commented on Egypt, Ethiopia and Ethiopians as well as the modern writers whose listed books are key to creating the foundation of falsity permeating current academic teaching, historical writing, newspaper reporting and museum representation of a "Negro-less" or "white only Egypt" which is far from the truth. In this, Dr. Ben takes to task a whole army of wrong doing "authorities on Africa" such as M.D.W. Jeffries; Elsy Leuzinger - *The Art of Africa*; Basil Davidson - *Africa in History*; Donald Weidner; Hayes of the Met; James H. Breasted; Alan Gardiner; Bovill - *The Golden Trade of the Moors*; C.P. Groves - *The Planting of Christianity in Africa*; even Frank Snowden's *Blacks in Antiquity*, the authors mention Waddell's *Manetho*, the traveler and commentator Leo Africanus, G.M. James's *Stolen Legacy*; James Frazier's *Golden Bough*; J.H. Lewis - *The Biology of the Negro* (Chicago, 1941); Poesner's *Dictionary of Egyptian Civilization*, Count Volney's *Ruins of Empire* and Baron Vivan Denon commentary his and painting a graphic image of the Sphinx before its facial disfigurement.

Whether the proponents of a "white Egypt" are ignorant of the facts of history or knowingly misrepresent the record to proclaim white supremacy in religion and culture as they wage psychological and spiritual warfare against the black race, fearful that if the truth be told, the white race would be viewed as covetous, harmful and perpetrators of a gigantic fraud is the line of argument he "Ben" pursued.

Among the things Dr. Ben states, "Herodotus divided the Ethiopians into 'MACROBIANS, ASMACHIANS' and 'CAVE DWELLERS.' As far as he was concerned, obviously, all the Ethiopians (Egyptians, Nubians, Carthaginians, Garamantes, Ghanaians, Kushites, etc.), at least those he was aware of, were basically the same in physical characteristics (thick lips, broad noses, wooly hair) and color (black or 'burnt skin'). At no instance in his writings did he relate to any of them being SEMETIC or HAMITIC, nor even CAUCASIAN. He was equally certain that many of the Ethiopians could be found in goodly numbers in parts all over the Eastern countries (Arabia Felix – the Arabian Peninsula, Persia, India, etc.)."

The author writes, "Herodotus' anthropological descriptions of the Ethiopians (so-called "NEGROES") were not only verified by Aeschylus, who also delineated Ethiopia's geo-political boundaries; he also wrote about the Ethiopians of Kush beliefs and mythology."

The ancient writers, Dr. Ben holds, "made many references to the Africans' pigmentation, and of course made distinction in their remarks to the degree of BLACKNESS or variance of DARKNESS

AFRICAN NATIONALIST POETRY AND PROSE

between different national groupings of Ethiopians ("Negroes" or "BLACKS") on the continent of Africa (Alkebu-lan). This factor was best observed by Philostratus in his description of "MEMNON" not being as "... BLACK AS OTHER ETHIOPIANS;" indicating that the Greeks were quite observant of the variance in degree of BLACKNESS among the Ethiopians."

"As such, in Dr. Fred Monderson's 4th Annual Memorial Day Tribute to Dr. Ben, June 3 and June 10, 2012, at True South Bookstore 492 Nostrand Ave, between Halsey and Hancock Streets 3:00 – 6:00 PM, the venerable and well-liked educator, Egyptologist, historian, Anthropologist, nationalist, etc., was praised for his Avant Garde championing of "Black is Beautiful," pioneering the wearing the Dashiki when in the 1970s Blacks faced a cultural crisis and his audacious effort to "take Egypt" to educate and enlighten African people of their heritage and the forces arrayed against them where he said much about the man and his tremendous efforts He very early made it known how significant travel to Egypt really was and insisted his students and associates must continue this pilgrimage in order to view the monuments where he often told such visitors, "Now that you have come to Egypt, seen what you have seen, what are you going to do with the knowledge!" Thanks to his efforts, conscious raising groups as the Association for the Study of Classical African Civilization (**ASCAC**) was born and today continue

FREDERICK MONDERSON

his identification. Let us not forget, Dr. Ben placed the Black woman on a high pedestal in praise and appreciation for her tremendous contribution as mother, spouse, nurturer and educator. Part II will be held Sunday June 10, 2012 at 3:00 PM. See you then!"

African Nationalist Poetry and Prose Photo. Tribute to the Ancestors – Images, 2019.

African Nationalist Poetry and Prose Photo. Tribute to the Ancestors - Images, 2019.

AFRICAN NATIONALIST POETRY AND PROSE

"Now my heart turns this way and that, as I think what the people will say. Those who shall see my monuments in years to come, and who shall speak of what I have done." Queen Hatshepsut (c. 1500 B.C.)

30. POEM TO GODDESS ISIS BY DR. FRED MONDERSON

Hail O Isis, Black goddess of ancient Africans, from time immemorial you were destined to last forever. Your august presence was feared and respected among African gods, Lady of the Great House. Black female divinity, divine mother, among fellow luminaries you were equal in every respect. Champion of Osiris, Lady of the North-wind, Queen of the East, you reign in sublime and infinite, Mistress of the Pyramid. Daughter of Seb and sister and wife of Osiris, you embody the quintessential Black female.

Faithful and loving wife, devoted mother, great enchantress and fierce warrior, your name and attributes possess the power to heal, beneficent goddess, Lady of Words of Power. Men built the Lake of Isis and temples to worship you, Black Queen of the African divinities, Lady of Philae. Your symbols are a seat or throne, vulture headdress with horns, solar disk, plumes and uraeus.

FREDERICK MONDERSON

Mankind praises you, O great goddess Isis, giver of life; you are the Godmother, Sole Goddess of Egypt. You stood for equality of women and motherhood, you goddess of purity, healing and sexuality. Lady of Abundance, you support the union of men and women to create African families. Immortality is promised in your name, for as mistress of earth you espouse power of nature itself, Goddess of the Birth-house.

One of the four noble goddesses, when your beloved husband Osiris was slain by his Evil brother Seth, signs and sounds of sorrow and lamentations, proved you the highest type of faithful and loving wife. O Great Maati Goddess, your cries reached the famed Hall of African Judgement in the Heavens. Ra dispatched Thoth, Anubis and with your sister Nephthys, these deities offered succor to your sorrows and aspirations. Lady of Love, you are indeed a Lady of Joy and Gladness, divine one. The gods supported the search to locate your husband's dismembered body, and through magic you restored him to life. Such august actions inspired men to build temples praising your husband departed, hoping for life through you, beloved Isis.

These divinities, pillars and witnesses to the Revivification process, observed your creative feminine power. The depth of your sorrows, the sincerity of your pleadings, the purity of your spirit Great Lady, offer sufficient proof of your

AFRICAN NATIONALIST POETRY AND PROSE

faithfulness, 0 mourning Black Widow, you are woman and goddess! Thoth's power helped impregnate you with Horus, also resurrection of your husband, father, man, god. After restoring your husband to life, you raised the child, a quality that endeared you with the people.

Osiris rules the Underworld, Horus crowned King of Kemet, and you protect, care, feed and nourish these divinities. Power and sincerity in support of the Blackman is only a modicum of your majesty, Female Ra, Lady of the Solid Earth, 0 great queen, the first Black Madonna, heaven is satisfied with your work. After invigorating Africa, the Power and intent of your magic and persona saw the Mediterranean and western-world worship you, Great One. This in an age of great goodness and Blackness, Ethiopians the most noble, just and long lived of men. Pristine potency of your Blackness was honored, thou whose mouth is wise, you personify motherhood Goddess of Birth. Great Goddess Isis, Auset, Divine Mother, you must stand fast, lift your people and assist their forward progress.

Lady of Warmth and Fire, Maker of the New Year, today's challenges to Blackness are many.

Great Goddess of the Underworld, you are a mighty Earth Goddess, Maker of the Sunrise, Eye of Ra. Orgies and debauchery celebrate your festival, Female Horus, and Lady of Limitless Attributes,

FREDERICK MONDERSON

called 'The Great-Ka-of-Harakhte.' Goddess of the Harvest, Lady of Bread and Beer, you make cultivated fields and lands fertile. Support, rescue and vibrantly reconstitute the great Black family, man, woman, and child, 0 Lady Isis, Mistress of Heaven.

African Nationalist Poetry and Prose Photo. **CEMOTAP'S** Photographer and technician in a spiritually happy mood meets "Ancestor Tribute 2019 Ladies."

AFRICAN NATIONALIST POETRY AND PROSE

African Nationalist Poetry and Prose Photo. The Master drummer Shendo and assistants at work!

African Nationalist Poetry and Prose Photo. 50th Anniversary crowd gathered before the Lincoln Memorial in Washington, DC.

FREDERICK MONDERSON

African Nationalist Poetry and Prose Photo. This mural in Memorial to lost firefighters in Crown Heights is no longer visible but saved in this book.

African Nationalist Poetry and Prose Photo. Teaching the young one the importance of reading.

AFRICAN NATIONALIST POETRY AND PROSE

African Nationalist Poetry and Prose Photo. Honorable David Dinkins, former Mayor of New York City.

African Nationalist Poetry and Prose Photo. The **National Black Theater** in Harlem.

FREDERICK MONDERSON

African Nationalist Poetry and Prose Photo. The Message is clear: "Justice in the Courts, Justice at the Polls;" all behind the Red, Black and Green!

AFRICAN NATIONALIST POETRY AND PROSE

"As the Egyptians saw it, when God emerged from the Nun to create the universe and all things in it, including the various other appellations for the dimension and characteristics of the divine, this was the initiating of the First Occasion. This was not, though, the only thing that was to happen during the First Occasion. The divinities interacted with each other and in their relationships established patterns and behaviors that would constantly reappear in the mundane world. In the end, good will triumph over evil, although it might take a long time and many instances of conflict. As it was in the first Occasion, so it will be in ordinary time." Molefi Kete Asante. *The Egyptian Philosophers – Ancient African Voices from Imhotep to Akhenaten*, 2000.

31. HORUS: THE FALCON OF EDFU BY DR. FRED MONDERSON

Horus, Son of Osiris and Isis, Emerald Jewel in the Gold Sign, your history is marked with milestones. You inherited an illustrious tradition Divine Majesty, and sovereignty of the world was given you. As Horus the Elder, you were Horus of the Two Eyes. The Sun is the right eye and the left eye is the Moon. Horus Temple at Hierakonpolis was the place of worship of the Heru-Shemshu, 'Followers of Hours'

FREDERICK MONDERSON

- Panther of the South. Chief of the Nomes, Great Water God, you are God of the Northern and Southern Horizon, Prince of the Emerald Stone, Osiris.

Lord of Heaven, father murdered, mother grieved, the Nile Valley people adore you as the dutiful and loving son. Lawful Successor of Osiris, Gods Celestial and Gods Terrestrial serve you. He Osiris is yesterday, You Horus, grown up, is Today. Rising Sun, Horus Hawk, Symbol of Royalty, Successor to Ra, you Address your Father in Heaven.

African Nationalist Poetry and Prose Photo. "Mother Africa" in all her red and blackness.

AFRICAN NATIONALIST POETRY AND PROSE

Prince of Eternity, as the Guardian of Osiris' Coffin, and depicted with head of a hawk, triple crown, and body of a lion, you performed the ceremonies on your father's behalf. You became Superintendent of the Performance of Funeral Rites and Ceremonies. Such devoted efforts endeared dead men who hoped you would come to their assistance after death. Then, you introduced the Dead in the Hall of Judgement.

In that august place, the four Sons of Horus, Hapi, Tuamutef, Amset, Qubhsenuf, represent the Four Cardinal points. Later they have dominion over Four Pillars of the Sky, the Four Quarters of Heaven. These gods are the dead man's guides in the Sekhet-Aaru. Hapi and Tuamutef represent his two arms and Amset and Qebhsenuf his two legs, Diffuser of Light to the World, Chief of the Land.

God of the Ladder, heir to a long line of Horuses, you absorb attributes of all these Gods and exemplify gallantry, courage and Maat, characteristics of ancient African divinities.

From the Solar Mythology, through the prehistoric age, and into dynastic times, you were a Great God. Young and vigorous, you Horus the Child, Son of Hathor, to whom Isis gave birth, is a child on a lotus flower with forefinger to its lips. In this you represent Renewed Life, Life as Opposed to Death, Movement not Inactivity. Your biennial worship is mentioned

FREDERICK MONDERSON

in the Pyramid Texts, Lord of Mankind, whose Eye of Horus has Life Giving Qualities, God of Light, Red God.

Lord of the Double Horizon, through trickery and guile, out of jealousy, the evil Set-Typhon killed Osiris and Isis lamented. In sorrow and with magic, Light of the World, you were hidden in the Papyrus Swamps. Guarded by 7 scorpions, Tefen, Befen, Mestet, Mestetef, Patet, Thetet, and Matel, one stung you. Isis healed your aching body, Young Ear of Corn, Eradicator of Sins, Lord of the Heart, Sayer of Sayings.

New Sun Born Daily, at the trial of the Two Men in the Hall of African Judgement, Thoth, the God of Wisdom, God of Law, was your legal eagle. His expertise made you triumphant before the Whole Company of the Gods, and you were established by decree in the Chamber of Books.

As you overthrow Evil, Man of Great Strength, with face and back of a hawk, Double Crown with Feathers and serpent, metal Spear and metal chains, you earned the Title, Horus Avenger of his Father. With Crowns of Feathers, Lord and Giver of life, you are one of the Seven Great Spirits, Great One, Mighty One, Great Chief of the Hammer.

Mighty Bull, with seven heads as bull, ram, cat, crocodile, body of a man, ithyphallic, legs and hoof of a bull, wings of a bird, you are a serpent with knife

AFRICAN NATIONALIST POETRY AND PROSE

in his hands. Hapi protected the north and small viscera of the deceased; Tuamutef the east and heart and lungs; Amset the south and stomach and large intestines; Qebhsenuf, the west and lungs and gall bladder. The female counterparts of these gods were Nephthys, Neith, Isis and Selqet, O One who received Life from Osiris. Lord of Maat, Lord of Joy, you numbered your limbs; you upheld the Royal Standard and sat on the Gold Standard. At the end of your battle, you established the Temple of Horus at Edfu where festivals were held in your honor to celebrate your victory over the evil one, Seth.

Previously, from the City Center, visitors walked towards the North rear decorated Enclosure Wall then along the lengthy and profusely illustrated western enclosure wall. Today the entrance is from the east, towards the Entrance Pylon. In this approach, the visitor beholds the majestic splendor of an Egyptian/Kemetic Pylon, engraved with deities illustrated in the temple drama, where you were worshipped as avenger of your father and heir of a mighty tradition.

African Nationalist Poetry and Prose Photo. Purchasers at the "Papyrus Man's" tent, **IAAF** 2018.

FREDERICK MONDERSON

African Nationalist Poetry and Prose Photo. Art in its infinitesimal variety.

"After the cosmic order, comes the terrestrial order. One can also recognize the moral antinomy between good and evil. The Ennead is perfect: Atoum emerged of the Noun, Shu and Tefnut, Geb and Nut, Osiris and Isis, Seth and Nephthys, created by Atoum. Creation continues with that of humanity. The master of the universe created the four winds, the great flood, the inundation and each man resembling his neighbor (*The Sarcophagus Texts*, 1130). This system, elaborated with great care, accounts for the genesis and the origins of the essential components of the universe: (1) The initial principle, inexplicable: The Noun, foundation of the whole later universe. (2) Atoum-Ra, the demiurge, emerges from the Noun: creative, luminous intelligence, springs from raw, unorganized, primordial matter. (3) Advent of the cosmic order: Atoum-Ra creates Shou (air,

AFRICAN NATIONALIST POETRY AND PROSE

atmosphere) and Tefnut (humidity), the eternity and immensity of the Universe. (4) Advent of the terrestrial and celestial order: Geb, the earth; and Nut, the sky with the powerful sun. (5) Advent of human order: Osiris and Isis, Seth and Nephthys, Good and Evil, the balance of sterility, the fertilizing valley of the Nile and the arid desert." Theophile Obenga. Ancient Egypt and Black Africa. 1992.

African Nationalist Poetry and Prose Photo. Cherise Maloney of Brooklyn and Tony Mitchelson guests at **CEMOTAP'S** 31st Annual Celebration.

FREDERICK MONDERSON

32. CELEBRATION for DR BEN PART II. BY DR. FRED MONDERSON

Dr. Yosef ben-Jochannan's life has been one extraordinary experience of intellectual trail-blazing, daring cultural nationalism on a global scale, heavy in praise of African womanhood and in dynamic process as author, lecturer, publisher, architect, archaeologist, anthropologist, educator, historian and Egyptologist, among many others. Very few have done more extolling Africa in the forefront, lived as long and even many times challenged the angel of death, as the man lovingly called "Dr. Ben" by beloved fans and admirers worldwide. Ever wondered how Dr. Ben got his name? I made his acquaintance early in 1972 when a friend, Barney introduced me to this extraordinary individual through his classic *Africa: Mother of Western Civilization* at a time in the black consciousness movement when young people, even old people, were at a crossroad looking for leadership extolling nationalist sentiments, cultural patriotism, motifs, symbols, slogans and representing positive role models. That original, first edition copy was signed or autographed and "Given" to Fred Monderson by Dr. Ben-Jochannan. Since at first his name was puzzling to pronounce Barney and I began calling him "Ben Jo" in referring to his book Mother, and its message, imagery and bibliographic listing that

AFRICAN NATIONALIST POETRY AND PROSE

exposed his readership to a new world of reference material. After I enrolled at New York City Technical (then Community) College and met Curtis Dunmoodie, Curtis said we needed to show more respect and so we young students called him "Dr. Ben." By the time I moved to Hunter College in 1974 the name had stuck. So much so, when he came to sit in for Dr. Clarke in the Black and Puerto Rican Studies Department the fellow students began calling him Dr. Ben, on a grander scale. It should be known Dr. Ben was not-well-liked at first, both by the general public and in academia, particularly by black academics.

Having to defend his scholarship in challenge to Western and American distortion, omission, plagiarization and religious, cultural and historical racial bigotry in genocidal behavior towards Africa and Africans as well as the uncomfortable position he put black scholars in, many dismissed him, infinitesimally critiqued his work claiming "Dr. Ben has no PhD!" Well established publishers refused to consider his works. As such, he initiated Self-Publishing of his books, producing small amounts that young students and others bought as encouragement to enable him to continue the work. As a young student at NYCTC, an episode of "Dr. Ben has no Ph. D." made me cry. I ran to the A Train from school on Jay Street, rode to 125th Street and onto Lenox Ave where his office was located on the second floor, opposite to "Choc-Full-of-Nuts." There

FREDERICK MONDERSON

and then, Professor Simmonds consoled me showing Dr. Ben's Ph. D. in Anthropology displayed on the wall!

As an avid supporter of Dr. Ben, I purchased every book he wrote in first edition, traveled first with him to Egypt in the 1980s where he held the first and only "Panel Discussion" under the theme "What has coming to Egypt meant to you!" Subsequently he asked me, "Monderson, now that you have come to Egypt, seen what you have seen, what are you going to do with the knowledge?" Enthused by the subject of Egypt, motivated by the gifted scholar and in seeking advice as to the direction of my studies as a young student, Dr. Ben told me further, "Monderson, there are fifty nations in Africa, choose one and specialize in it. Be a specialist not a generalist on African." Then he later admonished, "In doing research on Egypt, get the oldest material you can find and work from there." In 1990, at a dinner in Dr. Ben's honor hosted by Dr. Lewis at Mini-Sink in Harlem, and given the opportunity to speak before the Elders, I said: "Dr. Ben, as your vision becomes cloudy and you're looking for someone to pass the baton to, look for Monderson for I'll be there!" On two occasions Dr. Ben recognized my work in letter form!

AFRICAN NATIONALIST POETRY AND PROSE

African Nationalist Poetry and Prose Photo. Dresses in all varieties at the International African Arts Festival.

African Nationalist Poetry and Prose Photo. More dresses in the Afrocentric mold at the International African Arts Festival.

FREDERICK MONDERSON

Years later, aged and infirm Dr. Ben, sitting in a Harlem restaurant Dr. Ben asked me, "Monderson, can you take me back to Egypt one last time? I don't want to see the sights; I just want to sit in the hotel lobby and the people will come to see me!" This is because of the good work Dr. Ben has done for the Nubians and truly Egyptian Africans in that country. Everywhere he went he dropped envelopes. From baggage handlers, bus drivers, cooks in the hotels, cleaners, gardeners, you name it, everyone got something! He did so much for those people; Dr. Ben was well-liked in Egypt. Even today in Egypt, People still ask "Is Dr. Ben still alive?" "How is he doing?" Contacting his lawyer, he told me, "The Court will not permit me to allow Dr. Ben to travel." As such then, I began to promote the Annual Memorial Day Tribute to Dr. Ben and here we are at the fourth one, hopefully there will be many others. While this was written earlier in 2018, I intend to hold the 11th **Memorial Day Tribute to Dr. Ben-Jochannan**. Equally, later in the Summer of 2018, I intend to deliver the **Third Dr. Ben-Jochannan Lecture at Karnak Temple**, Luxor Egypt.

In the co-authored *The Black Man's North and East Africa*, Dr. Ben and Professor George Simmonds, there is a final chapter entitled "Things done by Africa before Europe," where Dr. Ben lists accomplishments on which he elaborates.

AFRICAN NATIONALIST POETRY AND PROSE

Before we begin today's Part two of this tribute, I wish to reflect on an aspect from the book, discussed in last week's discussion. It goes as follows: "In this article the author will very briefly show some of the many 'Things' the continent of Africa has given to the world before the coming of Europe into history. It is taken from the writer's much more extensive work '**AFRICANS INFLUENCE ON EUROPEAN FEAR AND HISTORY**,'" presently being edited for publication. The larger work shows the reasons why **TRUE HISTORY** has been suppressed and kept from the peoples of the world. Because of the old myths and teachings that **AFRICA (Alkebu-lan) HAS NO HISTORY**" this article is written from a point to that perspective. The reader in this context, can then see many reasons for the terrible fear of African History being taught truthfully in a white (European)-oriented society or setting."

"In order to control the numerous former chattel slaves, it was (from a White-European perspective) - **AFRICA**; and make him psychologically ashamed of himself and the color of his skin. Such controls make blacks think that they ought to be grateful and thankful to the whites for discovering" (a term Europeans love to use whenever they first find out that something, someone, or some places existed of which they knew nothing) them in "backward Africa" and taking them to "stolen lands" in what is

FREDERICK MONDERSON

commonly referred to in history and other disciplines as the "New World" (the Americas – both North and South, and the Caribbean Islands.)"

THE BIRTH OF MAN OR MAN-LIKE CREATURES – Man-like creatures, fossil man, pithecanthropus, erectus, Sivanthropus, Zinjanthropus Boisie, are the oldest forms of the human species dating back millions of years old and only found in Africa.

THE STEP-PYRAMID – Created by Imhotep for Pharaoh Zoser of the Third Dynasty at Sakkara stands at the beginning of architectural history and attests to the ingenuity of ancient African science of building and organization, that early in time.

THE TRUE PYRAMIDS – The best examples are those at Ghizeh in terms of size, exquisite nature and preservation but they also represent the highest form of organization of manpower, quarrying and transportation of stone, building to predetermined architectural planning, with accompanying logistics including medical treatment for sick workers, nearby housing for the workers, ordinances for their meals and the coordination of construction over great distances of a colossal nature.

THE PYRAMID TEXTS - Sayings and scriptures that are now ascribed to famous Hebrew prophets and other personages as Job, Jeremiah and

AFRICAN NATIONALIST POETRY AND PROSE

King Solomon, had their origins in the Pyramid Texts.

THE COFFIN TEXTS – These grew out of the Old Kingdom Pyramid Texts in that now during the Middle Kingdom, the religious words of inspiration that accompanied the dead were placed on the inside and outside of coffins making such spiritual powers available to everyone who could afford it. These are ancient African thoughts and practices that were many millennia in oral existence before being literally codified and inscribed in the Pyramids of the Fifth and Sixth Dynasties of the Old Kingdom, 2600-2400 B.C.

African Nationalist Poetry and Prose Photo. Tribute to the Ancestors – Images, 2019.

FREDERICK MONDERSON

African Nationalist Poetry and Prose Photo. Cloths of all varieties for your liking.

THE BOOK OF THE DEAD – Represents a New Kingdom compilation of the Pyramid Texts with additional spells and incantations accompanied by colorful illustrations of the journey in the Afterlife and the obstacles encountered there.

THE WORLD'S EARLIEST NAVAL POWER – In a riverine country, the first thing one had to do was conquer the Nile. Even in the mythology the gods traveled by boat and in the Pyramid Age boats were actually interred in the Pyramid Complex for the king to journey to meet the gods. Found in 1954 and reconstructed, one is now housed at Ghizeh in the Boat Museum.

AFRICAN NATIONALIST POETRY AND PROSE

PLANNED PARENTHOOD – The Kahun Papyrus discovered by Flinders Petrie and dated to the 18th Dynasty discusses birth-control methods. This important development, like so many new features of pharaonic cultural practice have been attributed to the time of Queen Hatshepsut.

KINGS AND QUEENS IN EGYPT – Kings ruled Egypt in an orderly manner for more than three thousand years and they were often shown in surviving examples with their queens in a state of equality. This is evident throughout the 3000-year period of dynastic rule. Queen Merneith of the Old Kingdom, Mentuhotep II's mother Queen Aam, Queen Tetisheri of the 17th Dynasty and her daughter Queen Ahmes-Nefertari, ancestress of the 18th Dynasty, Queen Hatshepsut and Queen Tiy, wife of Amenhotep III, and Queen Nefertari II wife of Rameses II were all beautiful and fabled ladies.

BUILDING OF THE GREAT SPHINX OF GIZEH – Current evidence seems to indicate Khafre, builder of the Second Pyramid at Ghizeh did "repairs" to the Sphinx c. 2500 B.C. and that it is probably as old as 10,000 years based on water marks in the vicinity at a time when the area was not as dry as it is today.

FREDERICK MONDERSON

THE ONLY PERFECT GOVERNMENT RECORDED BY MAN – Rule by the gods who handed down their legacy to their son the Pharaoh but in time this dissipated.

THE ANKHS – Spiritual symbol of life often seen as an instrument of power accompanying the gods, when the gods imparted life to the pharaoh or when gods baptized the king before his entering the temple to conduct services.

SCOTTISH RITES – Secrets of the temple that migrated from Heliopolis and later the Grand Lodge at Luxor, built by Amenhotep and expanded by Rameses II.

TRADES: **"SON LIKE FATHER"** – Crafts and knowledge were handed down as family secrets.

THE EGYPTIAN ALPHABET – This is truly indigenous to the Nile Valley, evidence demonstrated in Upper Egypt. While Winkler wants to attribute this writing to Mesopotamia, evidence of the flora, fauna, geographical features are native to Upper Egypt and even Diop affirms the Egyptian origin of their writing. So too does Budge. Toby Wilkinson in *Origins of the Pharaohs* (2003) affirms these illustrations were "1000 years before Winkler's Mesopotamians."

AFRICAN NATIONALIST POETRY AND PROSE

THE EARLIEST KNOWN PAINTING - Not cave man scrawl but actual painting from the Old Kingdom.

COLLECTION OF TAXES – The first government to levy taxes on their citizens so that the work of government could progress as well as to replenish the royal treasury. Taxes were in the form of produced food, cattle, crafts, labor or precious instruments whether from citizens or as conquered booty and tribute.

NAMING OF THE GODS – Ra, Ptah, Osiris, Seth, Thoth, Amon-Ra, Montu, Khonsu, and many more who presided at the Judgment. There were national and local gods.

NAMING OF THE GODDESSES – Hathor, Isis, Mut, Ma'at, Selkis, Seshat, Neith, etc. These lady divinities were generally part of a triad of husband, wife and child, generally son. These divinities were also grouped in Enneads.

MAKING OF THE OBELISKS – A single piece of stone was quarried, transported and erected at site hundreds of miles away from place of origin. It is generally decorated before erection. Many were dispatched to European and American cities. The Washington Monument is an obelisk but constructed of steel and cut-up stone.

FREDERICK MONDERSON

DEVELOPMENT OF THE SCRIBES – Scribes were intellectuals of their day and all forms of recordings were the domain of these men of letters, whether letter writing, instruction, accompanying military expedition to record ordinances and events.

African Nationalist Poetry and Prose Photo. Tribute to the Ancestors – Images, 2019.

African Nationalist Poetry and Prose Photo. "Baba" and the "Shrine of the Ancestors."

AFRICAN NATIONALIST POETRY AND PROSE

CENTERS OF LEARNING – Heliopolis, Luxor, Abydos, Asuit, Sakkara. Generally, any place where temples were located acted as some form of center of learning with some being more important than others.

DEVELOPMENT OF THE NEGATIVE CONFESSIONS – This moral and ethical imperative guided the society and its citizens' behaviors. So much so, upon death at the Judgment before the Assayors, the deceased confessed to the things he did not do while on earth.

CREATION OF MANY RELIGIONS – Religion grew out of the need to explain local phenomena within the context of original thinking about this world and the next.

DEVELOPMENT OF BULLFIGHTING IN EGYPT – Bulls played an important part in the social as well as religious life of ancient Egypt.

INTRODUCTION OF THE WORLD'S EARLIEST KNOWN SOLAR CALENDAR – Depending on which scholar one reads the calendar was invented in 4241 B.C. as stated by Breasted, while Petrie gives 5701 and Maulana Karenga 6200.

FREDERICK MONDERSON

In stating his philosophy of the" Quintessential Nile Valley African Man" Dr. Ben elucidates in *The African Called Rameses ("The Great") II and the African Origin of "Western Civilization"* at a lecture he delivered on April 29, 1989 for The Third Eye, Inc., in conjunction with the **Rameses** (*The Great*) *II Exhibition* held in Dallas, Texas. This profusely illustrated 100-page book contains 97 illustrations and as part of a Table of Contents and Citations and acknowledgements he lists as follows: Illustrations, Glossary, Foreword by Dr. John H. Clarke, a Retrospection, all in Statistics, Greetings, Opening, Origins, Questions, Background, Direction, Family, Manhood, Leader, Symbol, Tragedy, Architecture, Myth, Image, Syncretism, Education, Literature, The Craft, Belief, Guardian, Justice, Conclusion, End Notes, Bibliography and Index.

Therefore, stating in a nutshell that he is "primarily a student and professor" of "Nile Valley and Great Lakes High-Culture of Africa with a major concentration on Ta-Meri," the Quintessential Nile Valley Black Man for Dr. Ben is embodied in Rameses II, "The great," who is a pharaoh, King, courageous leader, father, husband, conqueror, militarist, Imperial colonizer, architect, engineer and builder, patron of the arts and learning, peace maker, devotee of the gods, whose history and heritage is greatly distorted as taught today in and outside of Egypt.

AFRICAN NATIONALIST POETRY AND PROSE

Insisting that the continent of Alkebu-lan or Africa be "the first and most important land of call whenever African people decide to travel" he *admonished* "Let's always be prepared to meet the foe in full knowledge of Ta-Meri's High Culture before we visit, remembering always that among the Nubian population the truest seeds of the ancient Nile Valley African stock are to be found today in the 20th Century of the Common Era."

"I had a vision – and I saw white spirits and black spirits engaged in battle, and the sun was darkened – the thunder rolled in the heavens, and blood flowed in streams – and I heard a voice-saying, "Such is your luck, such you are called to see, and let it come rough or smooth, you must surely bear it." *The Confessions of Nat Turner*, the leader of the late insurrection in Southampton, Va. (1831)

African Nationalist Poetry and Prose Photo. *Black Star News* Publisher Milton Allimadi and one of the **CENTRAL PARK FIVE**, now **Exonerated**, young men.

FREDERICK MONDERSON

African Nationalist Poetry and Prose Photo. Congressman Major Owens and the great mathematician.

33. MAJOR OWENS: A Reflection
BY
DR. FRED MONDERSON

Reverend Clarence Norman, Sr., of First Baptist Church of Crown Heights in Brooklyn, began the beginning of the end of the service 'Celebration of Life for Hon. Major R. Owens,' with a familiar verse "It is well with my soul," and that, "Once again we stand on the shore and watch a ship sail" into the mist of the future. This time, however, those in attendance came "to celebrate the life, times and contributions of

AFRICAN NATIONALIST POETRY AND PROSE

Major Owens" and to "comfort his family." Telling the family, "God will take care of you," Rev. Norman called Major a "quiet, gentle person who was effective, dynamic and changed the life of so many." In fact, the Congressman was "a servant of god, who was called home, but he will always live" in the hearts, minds and motifs of the people.

African Nationalist Poetry and Prose Photo. Dr. Martin Luther King, Jr., "Civil Rights Champion."

FREDERICK MONDERSON

Not many people have had the indubitable distinction of having a US Congressman in their living room to discuss the dynamics of a local library, as I did. But then again, not only was Major Odell Owens a man of the people, but the only librarian ever elected to the US Congress! As a journalist I covered several Town Hall meetings Mr. Owens held at PS 167 on Eastern Parkway during the Giuliani years, in Major's efforts to create economic and political empowerment for his constituency. At an event regarding Panamanian politics and international peace, hosted by Dr. Wadalba Steward at the Eastern Parkway and Bedford Avenue venue, with Carlos Russell in attendance, Congressman Owens discussed the utility of the Congressional Black Caucus by saying, "People often question why we're there. It is not so much the legislation we sponsor, but those we block. So much frivolous legislation is introduced onto the floor of the US House of Congress, if we are not there to block such, it would be disastrous for black and poor people." Nevertheless, while Major was a tireless champion of Civil Rights and an advocate for funding of. Black Colleges, his singular legislative accomplishment was the Americans with Disabilities Act, of which beneficiaries Agnes Abraham, Peter Jones and Dorothy Williams-Pereira were there to say thank you and sing praises to a remarkable man.

AFRICAN NATIONALIST POETRY AND PROSE

African Nationalist Poetry and Prose Photo. Faces and more faces.

African Nationalist Poetry and Prose Photo. Wooden bowls, spoons and other amenities.

In his Prayer of Comfort, Reverend Daryl Bloodsaw said "Major Owens understood the power of words.

FREDERICK MONDERSON

He was a champion of education who bore the scars of battle of long campaigns against worthy opponents." An admirer of Rosa Parks, Martin Luther King, Jr., Mahatma Gandhi and Mother Theresa, and as an Adjunct Professor at Medgar Evers College, he inspired the youth. In fact, he wrote poems extolling the virtues of young people. His oldest brother, Ezekiel, Jr., described him, "On the floor of the House of Representatives he was 'the little man from Brooklyn,' this "Rapping Congressman," who "Was ready to put on his long white robes."

Dr. Rudy Crew, former Chancellor of the New York City Board of Education and now President of Medgar Evers College, spoke of the many people whose lives have been touched by this man. His story at Medgar was "one of truth, justice and honor." He said they met in 1995 when Rudy Crew was Chancellor of the New York City School System. Then they had a conversation about the Mayor! Major said, 'Son you're new, be careful. If you're grounded, you're all right. Stay strong.' "After all the hoopla and accolades, I was fired in 2000 and on my way out of town I met major who said, 'I read there's a problem. Don't worry. Time will come.'" He was "very gracious, very kind, very spiritual." His very "kindness, strength, character made sense to me." He reassured me, 'Don't worry son, you'll be alright.' In 2008, he became an Adjunct Professor at Medgar Evers College and was loved and revered by students and faculty. "He had so much pride in himself." In

AFRICAN NATIONALIST POETRY AND PROSE

July 2013 I became President of Medgar Evers College.

In an auditorium appearance he looked into the audience and saw a man who liked like his father. It was Major Owens. Then he looked into the faces of Major's children and said, "Your daddy looked just like my father. I felt so much better. It's Ok now. Not because I'm here but because he was here." Major told him, 'This is a good school. This is a good place. This is a good, earnest place. Just do right!' He later said, 'Stay strong, don't worry, I'm here. Do right!' Then Dr. Crew, turned to the Owens family and confessed, "We're better in our lives because your daddy did right."

African Nationalist Poetry and Prose Photo. "Baba" who maintains "the Shrine of the Ancestors" at the International African Arts Festival.

FREDERICK MONDERSON

African Nationalist Poetry and Prose Photo.
"His and Hers" among the artistic variety.

African Nationalist Poetry and Prose Photo.
In Africa, art is a cultural message.

Councilman Albert Vann, began by asking for a standing roll-call of those who came to pay tribute to Major, in which in a crowded church 6 Congressmen, 9 City Council persons, 9 State officials, 7 Citywide persons, the Brooklyn County Leader, 20 Clergy members and even Carl McCall, all stood up. They

AFRICAN NATIONALIST POETRY AND PROSE

came to commemorate the life and work of a former State Senator and Commissioner of Community Development Agency after serving as Bronxville Community Development Executive Director.

First, the Councilman admitted, "This is a humbling experience. Dying is a humbling experience. Honorable Major Owens, May peace be upon him!" The Councilman further explained, "Those who knew or knew of Major Owens respected him. He was an extraordinary, intelligent man who demanded respect and got respect." Second, Speaking of Major, he stated "He had an unbelievable work ethic. He had endless, boundless energy dedicated to seeking solutions of community problems. Multi-talented, he was a thinker, writer, community organizer." He was also a poet. Third, major Owens was a man of integrity who maintained a high standard of moral authority. Fourth, he chose to identify with the masses and empower the poor through economic and political empowerment initiatives, particularly through his anti-poverty programs. Fifth, Medgar Evers students were blessed to have Major Owens. The foundations of Medgar Evers were made stronger because of Major Owens." Finally, he admonished, "Take your seat dear brother, your job was well done."

Next, the Civil Rights Icon Congressman John Lewis, affirming, "You can tell a Morehouse man, but you can't tell him much," and insisting we "Never

FREDERICK MONDERSON

forget God is good," quoted the Roman philosopher and Senator Seneca, who said, "Nothing but nothing stops a good man doing what is good and honorable." He likened such to the efforts of Major Owens, who, like himself, served the nation and the world."

Finally, quoting **Acts** 13: 36 Reverend Norman believed Major Owens came or was born for a specific purpose. He said, "When a man has completed his work, god calls him home! Only the other day we announced the Congressman has passed. Immediately people began asking 'How did he die?' The Reverend iterated, "We should not ask how he died, but how he lived!" He was a dedicated servant of god. A man of the people. We're here to leave this world better than we found it. Ours must be a life of service, to be concerned about people." One aspect of this dedication is the founding of the Martin Luther King Commission emphasizing and encouraging young people to "Strive for Excellence."

Reverend Norman praised Major Owens as one "who stood up, he never forgot the poor. He believed, 'Education is a great equalizer.'" "He was a decent, kind, compassionate, honest, wise, respectful individual with a sharp mind." The Reverend confessed, "I feel more than lucky. I feel blessed to have Major Owens as a friend." The Congressman consistently insisted, 'to bring change people should be bold, be courageous, and find a way to make some noise. Don't get lost in a sea of despair.'

AFRICAN NATIONALIST POETRY AND PROSE

All were in agreement, this Congressional Warrior for Justice should, "Sleep, sleep well, take your seat. We'll see you in the morning. May God bless you? It is well with my soul."

"The great temptation in these difficult days of racial polarization and economic injustice is to make political arguments black and white and miss the moral imperative of wrong and right. Vanity asks, Is it popular?" Politics asks "Will it win?" Morality and conscience ask, "Is it right?"

African Nationalist Poetry and Prose Photo. Circles, squares and triangles in decorative art.

African Nationalist Poetry and Prose Photo. Yusuf Salaam, one of the "**CENTRAL PARK FIVE**," now **Exonerated**.

FREDERICK MONDERSON

African Nationalist Poetry and Prose Photo. A wooden lion behind the seat.

34. SENMUT'S PRAISE OF QUEEN HATSHEPSUT BY DR. FRED MONDERSON

Daughter of Amon-Ra, Hatshepsut, Ma'at-Ka-Ra, Her Majesty, Living forever, Queen of Egypt, Land under your Dominion. From the First Occurrence, Amon Lord of Thebes prophesied your birth and

AFRICAN NATIONALIST POETRY AND PROSE

promised you great power, Royal Dignity. The Great God decreed you exercise kingship. Consecrated to the Gods and purified with Water, in an epoch of ancient African glory, you challenged male supremacy to rule a kingdom and preside over a period of prosperity, art and architectural majesty, with Life, Stability and Health. Your accomplishments testify to boldness, god-like appearance, beauty and Black assertiveness. Given Life like Ra, Forever, Great in Oblations, 0, Majesty of your Father, the Maker of human beings, Maker of Truth.

Beloved, Khnemet-Amon Hatshepsut, with 12 Kas, you are more beautiful than anything. Boastful of kinship with Black-skinned Goddess Nefertari, your reign unfolded through divine inspiration and guidance. Made Wise by Amon's Excellent Spirit, Mistress of Offering, charm, beauty and intellectual daring symbolizes your integrity, and political astuteness, Horus Forever. 0 Daughter, mother, lover, builder, innovator, administrator and divinity, you celebrate many jubilees, for the heavens cover and the earth encircles you. Your father is Amen, fair of face, Beneficent Bull of the Company of Nine Gods. His names are many, countless, how many cannot be known for he is wide of stride. His form shines forth at the first Occasion and as the Great Cackler, he came into being at the First Occasion.

FREDERICK MONDERSON

Mighty in Strength, Obelisks and architectural marvels attest your desire to praise African gods who advanced your nation and inspired your people by their sincere blackness and clarity in Judgement. Today your image inspires many Black women to be the 'First Queen.' Glorious in Magic, how boastful is your Black ancestral heritage in Aahotep, Hetespheres, Tetisheri and particular Aahmes-Nefertari, later Queen Tiy and Nefertari, great king's wife. All the gods, Amon, Mut, Khonsu, Hathor, Thoth, Khnum, Anubis, Selkhet, Kheseti, Atum came to endow you with years. Divine Consort, His Majesty Herself, your Beauty the Spirits of Heliopolis fashioned. Your father Amon is the Lord of All, the first to exist. He came into existence in the beginning and none knew his mysterious nature. He shattered his egg himself.

Daughter of Ra, on the Throne of Electrum, you inspired architects to defy the ordinary and erect monuments praising your paternal and spiritual fathers. These noble gestures show love for great Africans, Thutmose and Amon, man and god. Such thinking reflects the great legacy you bestow on progeny who took on your history to gain strength, similarly meet challenges and raise notable African families. Support and inspire Black men, O Black Queen, as they chart the waters of new Horizons, into a new Millennium. Beautiful Lady, your father, President of his palace, is born early every day at dawn to rise in the Eastern Horizon and set in the Western Horizon as Lord of Truth. All knees spread

AFRICAN NATIONALIST POETRY AND PROSE

at his presence, all cattle frolic before his entrance, Perfect seizing his opportunity and none repel him.

0 Great Lady, Pure in Food Offerings, your Lineage is Divine. Amon visited your mother who slept in beauty of her palace. The God's Fragrance Woke Her, and in amorous encounter he conceived your divine birth. Meshkenet, goddess of births directed the midwives. She extended her arm before his majesty. Freshness in Years, Amon extended the Symbol of Life and Khnum Fashioned your Limbs. A brilliant mind envisioned such a concept, later to inspire Amenhotep III. His temple at Luxor and yours at Deir el Bahari, beautifully and graphically depict the experience of power manifesting in spirit through divine intervention, to create dynamics of social, artistic, philosophical and theological change furthering man's growth.

Golden Horus, Favorite of the Two Goddesses, Embraced by Amon, you are Powerful in the Two Lands. Horus Mighty in Ka your divine form flourish as your father, more eminent over nature than any God to whom praise is given in the Great House. It is his soul, men say, which is in heaven. His image is not spread out in Books. He is too mysterious that his glory should be revealed. He is too great so that men should ask questions concerning him. Too powerful that he should be known.

FREDERICK MONDERSON

Brilliant Emanation of Amon, your mortuary temple at Deir el Bahari with chapels to Anubis and Hathor erected by a humble architect Senmut, was inspired by love of a prototype and a beautiful Black lady. Love for God, incisive use of power and sincerity and integrity in Ma'at, echo creation in process, Life and Satisfaction. 0 Maiden, Beautiful and Blooming, Fresh in Years, you celebrate a glorious Past, which comes from Amon to appear on the throne of Horus, like Ra. You mirror the efforts of the Lord of Graciousness who is greatly beloved. He comes and sustains mankind. He sets in motion everything that is made. He works in the celestial water making to be the pleasantness of the light. He is Ra who is worshiped in the Apts.

Beautiful Black Pharaoh, King of Upper and Lower Kemet/Egypt, some see you as the first great woman of history. Your efforts portray great courage, wisdom and fortitude. With daring you styled yourself Chief Spouse of Amon, the Mighty One, the Lord of East and West, the Good Goddess, the Pious Lady, the Beautiful Falcon in her Risings, while your servants proclaim Her Majesty Himself. You rule like the one of many crowns in the house of the Ben-Ben stone. He is the God Ani, the Lord of the Ninth-day Festival. The Festival of the Sixth-day and the Tenat Festival are kept for him. He is king, Life, Health, Strength to Him, as to you, Beautiful Maiden. Your father is fair of face when he comes from God's land.

AFRICAN NATIONALIST POETRY AND PROSE

Mistress of the Two Lands, Divine in Diadems, the Electrum of Kings, you Give All Life and satisfaction. All Stability, All Joy of Heart, Favorite of the Two Goddesses, you advocate your Truth. The inspiration Amon provided to secure Obelisks at Karnak mirrors your efforts linking Deir el Bahari to Valley of Kings by tunnel manifesting theological and metaphysical creativity. All while the Heavens Labor for you respecting the Greatness of the Fame of your Father Amon. He is Beautiful Governor crowned with the White Crown, Lord of Light, Creator of Splendor. He gives his hand to him that loved him. The Flame destroys his enemies. He hears the cry of him that is oppressed and gracious to him that appeals to him. He delivers the timid man from the man of violence and regards the poor man, considering his misery, all traits you espouse.

Direct passage from mortuary temple to tomb utilizes a brilliant Old Kingdom conception. Architectural nicety in proportion, lines linking columns in the shadow of cliffs with powerful reflection at evening time convey the awe, majesty and reverence, intellect, Wisdom and Hidden-ness of the Inexplicable Nature of Amon, worshiped here, Everlasting. Amon gave you Lands Which the Sun Encompass and Established Your Great Name Like the Heavens that you may Be Given Life. Only he is Amon and Ra and Ptah, together three. Father of Fathers, and Mother of Mothers, he is the Bull for the Four Maidens. The Mighty One of mysterious birth,

FREDERICK MONDERSON

he created his own beauty. The Divine God who came into being of himself, of mysterious forms and gleaming shape, he is the wondrous God with many forms.

0 Revered Amon, Lord of Heaven, Lord of Earth, Lord of the Two Lands, looking at your Sanctuary in Ipit Isut, with great praise, radiates light in inspirational fortitude, we beseech thee, continue to inspire Africa's sons and daughters and support their efforts to help humanity. All this, in the same manner Ma'at-Ka-Ra, Hatshepsut, worshiped you in splendor and in true religion, with art, joy and festivity. Bestow that divine inspiration, wisdom, fortitude and humility that Black men and women will continue your task of saving the children, blessing the elders and invigorating our leaders to prevail in sincerity, fortitude and love.

African Nationalist Poetry and Prose Photo. Congresswoman Yvette Clarke, Yusuf Salaam, Gary Byrd and Milton Allimadi are joined by two other ladies at *Black Star News* Award Ceremonies.

AFRICAN NATIONALIST POETRY AND PROSE

African Nationalist Poetry and Prose Photo. How creative can one be in decorating benches?

35. BOB LAW'S TRIBUTE TO NELSON MANDELA BY DR. FRED MONDERSON

The incomparable Bob Law of "Night Talk" fame sponsored another of his tremendously informative Forums at historic Church of God in Christ on Kingston Avenue in Brooklyn, December 17, 2013, 7:00 – 10:00 pm, this time in tribute to Nelson Mandela. After Bob Law had laid the foundation for

FREDERICK MONDERSON

comprehensive understanding of this recent phenomenon of Mandela's passing. Dr. Leonard Jeffries provided a scintillating analysis and then synthesis for some 100 persons who braved the inclement weather to see beyond the outward appearance of global, even South African, tribute to the fallen leader, icon and freedom fighter. Both Mr. Law and Dr. Jeffries were painstakingly meticulous in turning on its head much of the Mandela tribute from world leaders and Western media by focusing not on the man as a mountain, but as a "tree" in a forest of freedom fighters.

This point was lucidly elucidated in "Mandela and the Unfinished Freedom Struggle" Daily Challenge, 12/17/13, p. 5, where Ron Daniels wrote, "Mandela was the 'tallest tree' in a forest that included many movements and stellar leaders, e.g., the Pan African Congress, Black Consciousness Movement, Mass Democratic Movement, Steve Biko, Bishop Desmond Tutu, Allan Boesak, Cyril Ramaphosa, Albertina and Walter Sisulu and Oliver Tambo to mention a few. This is an important note because there is a tendency to cast successful movements as the result of the acts of a solitary heroic figure." We should also include the Afrikaner cleric Byers Naude. Many attributes as demonstrated loyalty to his tribal heritage, his education and profession as a lawyer, his activism and daring; and his role as student, husband and family man. These scholars who conceptualize so readily and well, were quick to point out the cliché, he went from "Prisoner to President" and his

AFRICAN NATIONALIST POETRY AND PROSE

steadfast "commitment to reconciliation;" does not tell the full story that he was forced into armed struggle; convicted and while in prison those 27 years became a symbol, an icon; yet, the struggle continued to be waged by others on the outside suffering at the hands of the oppressive and repressive regime that banned, tortured and killed many.

It's universally recognized, the Afrikaners who perpetrated the racist, evil system of apartheid, did not suddenly have an epiphany and decided to free Nelson Mandela. Like Ian Smith of Rhodesia, they hoped to rule for another 1000 years, though in 1000 days, power was wrestled from Smith by "the boys in the bush." In the case of South Africa, it was the insistence, commitment and unrelenting struggle of the women, the young people, the African National Congress cadre and the global mobilization for divestment to rid the world of the evil system that apartheid represented, despite President Reagan and Chester Crocker's policy of "constructive engagement" that contributed to Mandela's and South Africa's freedom struggle. This is what forced the half-hearted offer by President Pieter Botha's offer to free or release Mandela in 1988. Such release, however, was dictated only if he would renounce violence! Clearly, if Mr. Mandela did accept an early release under such conditions it would have undermined everything he stood for, what he spent those many years incarcerated to achieve, and he would have lost the respect of the South African

FREDERICK MONDERSON

people whom he represented as well as the people of the world who stood with him, represented and pressured change agents demanding his release.

It has been acknowledged; globally Africans see the world differently because of their shared and victimized racist imperial and colonial experience. That is why Mr. Law wanted his audience to begin to understand the continuity of that experience. That is why he insisted "We not let others tell the story," for when they do it's with a twist that actually distorts the experience. The "Prison to President" cliché is thus not correct! First of all, he did not commit a crime; yet, as a man of principle, he was willing to forgive all the wickedness of the apartheid regime and this demonstrated his humanity was of a higher standard than theirs.

Though he was called a terrorist, he was actually a freedom fighter who became President! Prison was only a step on the way! In the horrendous experience, there was a long history of struggle against the murderous, vicious racist expropriators of the very best African land confining Africans to "black spots," then removing them into balkanized and barren reserves called "Bantustans" that were supposed independent nations, yet dependent on South Africa, of course, with the whites in control, politically and economically. This behavior and much more forced the African National Congress to pick up the gun. These African people of that nation were actually pressed into the armed struggle amidst the

AFRICAN NATIONALIST POETRY AND PROSE

hopelessness and dehumanization instituted through fear and intimidation and use of stooges such as the Inkatha Movement of Chief Buthelezi. That is why Mr. Mandela insists Xhosa, Sotho, Zulus, all Africans, are one people suffering under the same oppressive system. The racists fermented a blood bath between the Africans before they could fight the white man! Yet, Mr. Mandela would say, "Let us forgive these wicked people who have oppressed us for so long!" Importantly, nobody went behind his back-seeking vengeance! No one sought to assassinate or injure those who perpetrated the system. Much more significant, because Mr. Mandela refused to compromise his principles, his was liberation in a real sense! This demonstrated the tremendous patience of the African people while these so-called "superior white folks" were stealing their land and its riches. Showing magnanimity, in his uncompromising stance, he denounced violence from both black and white elements. This is because Mr. Mandela understood the potency of violence and its impact on the people and nation in its policy, infrastructure and view of the world.

Naturally, most people never really or fully understood Mr. Mandela or his strategy. It can be assumed Mr. Mandela went to prison an angry man after his trial but he was still a proud man! Observe his walk into prison! He probably never expected to be freed one day. In that "Long Walk," he experienced much and had the time to reflect, think and strategize. He said he matured! He knew he represented the people; he had them on his side. He also studied his enemy. He learned Afrikaans, the language of the oppressor, so he better understood their history and culture and this was important in his negotiations to end apartheid.

In reflecting, Madiba probably thought "We may be able to kill some whites but Africans would suffer more in any bloodbath." They knew he was coming and expected riotous behavior, so they stockpiled their armaments. They strategized and erected their forts and barriers, their "Alamos" to create their "Amritsars." Madiba outfoxed the devils! He said no recrimination! "Africans, let us forgive the white citizens of our nation." Thus, their arms were useless, ineffective, their barriers yet showed their thinking and bunker mentality! As Sun Tzu advised, "Win the battle before taking the field!" To recall, even more, Nkrumah had said, "Seek ye first the political kingdom." In the South African system, whites-controlled economics and politics. Mandela realized he could not dislodge them from economic control. By virtue of the Black majority and to keep democracy alive he chose the democratic way to political power. Ron Daniels said it best. Mandela theorized through political power the African people will whittle away at the preponderance of white economic dominance. One African lady explained why she loved Mandela in part; Soweto had no electricity, the night belonged to whites! Now they have electricity and she a fridge and TV. The muddy

AFRICAN NATIONALIST POETRY AND PROSE

roads are now paved. These were government efforts initiated by Mandela. Unrelenting political effort over time will economically empower Africans much further!

Much more significantly, Mr. Mandela's humanity pulled the mask off the white racists and he exposed their true selves. He was well versed in his historical responsibility, coming as he did from a community with a royal duty to the people of his land. That is why we must seek to fully understand in putting him in proper perspective. The Western and American media does not tell or focus on Mr. Mandela's and the ANC's true role in the total liberation of African people and the struggles of pushing back colonialism as well as the significance of true elimination of the immoral system of apartheid. In reality, it's who he forgave rather than what he forgave them for is really the issue and this forces another look at the Afrikaner Boers, South Africa and Mr. Mandela.

In one of the features run in the media recently about an Afrikaner Museum, a young woman visiting boasted of her need to know her history! It is clear the museum would not recount the brutality, the killing, the African humiliation, the wrongs, so that is why the Africans must know and tell their story to get a more balanced view for historical recounting. Mandela's insistence on the Truth and Reconciliation Commission was a masterful stroke! In the many confessions it gave the "monsters" a chance to reveal

FREDERICK MONDERSON

their mechanism of control for the world to realize how right they were that apartheid must go!

Changing pace, in a musical interlude Craig Crawford played a beautiful jazz rendition of a tribute and he followed this up with another really great song. Also, Xavier Bost sang two wonderful pieces, "Shattered but not Broken" and "A Hero Lies in You." Bob Law then praised the musicians and audience for being "Credoso Africans" who were "strong and resilient." He even tied this personality trait to the tenacity of braving the weather to attend the event, insisting more such forums are planned.

African Nationalist Poetry and Probe Photo. Still more creative wooden seat backs.

AFRICAN NATIONALIST POETRY AND PROSE

Not discounting that Mr. Mandela was a good man; they however, pointed out, but he was not unique as a freedom fighter! Mr. Law expressed, "We came from a long line of freedom fighters who fought courageously in liberation struggles." This is why he insisted, "It is important that we claim our own history." At that point he mentioned African leaders of Mr. Mandela's stature such as Ghana's Kwame Nkrumah, Guinea's Sekou Toure, and Congo's Patrice Lumumba who liberated their country and gave their all in its cause. These leaders were uncompromising liberation fighters. Of course, Mr. Michel of Mozambique must also be numbered in this lot. At this point Mr. law waxed philosophical by telling the audience, "When you celebrate Mr. Mandela, you celebrate yourself; you celebrate the African liberation struggle." He spoke of "something on the inside that is so strong, Holy Spirit, Holy Ghost," that cannot be touched or conquered that contributed to his and successes. Then he reflected on an old African liberation saying, "The higher they build the barriers, the taller you will rise." Even further, "To celebrate Mr. Mandela, let every leader be a Mandela" who refused to hate, was uncompromising, principled, and a man of great integrity. Despite his circumstances, he continued to fight which showed his character. He fought for what was right and would not compromise. This is what his enemies had to recognize. He fought against poverty, against inhumanity of man to man. He recognized gay rights and praised education.

FREDERICK MONDERSON

Bob Law insisted, we must guard against "People who will come to confuse us, who will betray us." Because Mr. Mandela would not compromise, would not back down, Mr. Law quoted biblical wisdom to reflect his strong, principled personality, for "No weapon formed against me will prosper." Even more philosophical and spiritual, he offered, "You think you are doing it on your own," but divinely guided forces are at play in guiding your every move! To explain where Mr. Mandela got his strength poses a profound proposition; for Mr. Law quotes Isaiah the prophet who wrote, "They that wait on the Lord shall renew their strength, they shall mount up with wings of eagles; they shall run and not be weary; they shall walk and not faint." This strength, this life in commitment to struggle, is a reminder of how great as a people the audience really is! This again is why we must not let them separate Madiba Mandela from the continuity of the history of his people.

African Nationalist Poetry and Prose Photo. Two distinguished attendees at *Black Star News* Awards.

AFRICAN NATIONALIST POETRY AND PROSE

African Nationalist Poetry and Prose Photo. Nelson Mazikela Mandela, African nationalist, freedom fighter and world figure who lived and died for the right to vote and be a man of substance and worth.

FREDERICK MONDERSON

Bob Law used analogies to get his point across. He asked the audience to Google two interviews between Malcolm X and Mike Wallace and Farrakhan and Wallace on "The Hate that Hate Produced." He veered off to speak on the disrespect Blacks receive, especially when shopping at high-end stores such as Barney's. He spoke of the young lady at Barney's who "Was not arrested for shoplifting but for spending too much" when she bought the "$2500.00 Ladies bag!" He also talked about new and upcoming ventures of the church in addressing the suffering of families, families of loved ones in prisons. People never really understand the hurt they put their families through when they commit a crime and go to prison. The family, the mothers, brothers and sisters, sons and daughters, also do the time on the outside. This suffering is what the church will now address.

Next it was Leonard Jeffries' turn, late as he always is! Jokingly Mr. Law referred to the keynote speaker as "The Late Dr. Jeffries." Pulling no punches, he focused not just on Nelson Mandela but the movement of African Liberation. While the focus today is on Mr. Mandela, Dr. Jeffries insisted, for 27 years he was only a symbol! At the funeral Winnie and Graca demonstrated the strength of the black woman. These women were the wind that powered their husband's sails!

There were many similarities in the struggles of the **ANC** (1910) and the **NAACP** (1912) who sought to

AFRICAN NATIONALIST POETRY AND PROSE

restore African humanity in a world of white rapaciousness. In South Africa it was the **African National Congress**, **The Pan-African Congress**, **The Student Movement** that gave us Steve Biko and of course the church, in close association with the **World Council of Churches** under the leadership of Dr. Philip Potter in which Dr. Jeffries and Professor Scobie, in Geneva, were lending assistance to coordinate activities in the South African struggle. From this vantage position he realized and stated emphatically, "The most devastating destruction of the Black man was in South Africa."

In that horrific experience was the 1962 Sharpsville massacre and the June 16, 1976 student uprising in Soweto that demonstrated the viciousness of the white minority regime. However, efforts to brainwash the students in demands that they learn Afrikaans was "more than a bridge too far," it was a tremendous miscalculation! The Africans suffered but the move failed!

First, in laying out his presentation, Dr. Leonard Jeffries reminded the audience, the Boers comprised Dutch, German and French elements from Europe mingled with Britons. With the discovery of the gold and diamond wealth of South Africa in late 19th Century, his "3 Rs," were not reading, 'riting and 'rithmetic, but Rothschild, Rhodes and Rockefeller who conglomerated to exploit the riches. A secret society called the Broderbund of some 20,000, men swore to maintain power no matter what. This is what Mandela challenged!

Thus, "If there is a place for Reparations it is South Africa." The Boers fostered unity among Europeans and divisions among Africans. They used the Zulu Mpande to kill his brother Shaka. The same way they "encouraged" Chief Buthelezi of ferment violence among Africans. This created a universal moral crisis. In their grab, that minority took 85 percent of the land. However, despite Mandela's victory, "We won the battle but they won the war" by remaining in control of the nation's economics.

Dr. Jeffries shed light on Afrikaner examination of the role of the church in the struggle. They studied Archbishop Tutu's many speeches, dissecting the many times he mentioned the ANC. They realized they were fighting the church on the inside and the freedom fighters on the outside. They entrapped and neutralized Rev. Boesak rendering him ineffective as a voice in liberation theology.

Dr. Jeffries explained further, "Politics is what you do to control your economics." His synthesis depicted a triangle compromising economics, politics and culture, the mind values, he called it. Importantly, he pointed out, the 1948 election victory of the Nationalist Party "set in motion the dehumanization process of Africans." This resulted

AFRICAN NATIONALIST POETRY AND PROSE

in "The African people suffering from a shattered consciousness and a fractured identity." Again, emphasizing the need to organize economics, politics and culture, and the role of women – Winnie Mandela; children – Steve Biko; church – Archbishop Desmond Tutu and Rev Allan Boesak, Dr. Jeffries insisted, "To serve the people, the curriculum of inclusion is not sufficient, we need a curriculum of liberation."

African Nationalist Poetry and Prose Photo. Wow. Twins and their cousins.

FREDERICK MONDERSON

African Nationalist Poetry and Prose Photo. Beautiful.

"I am somebody. I may be poor, but I am – Somebody! I may be on welfare, but I am – Somebody! I may be uneducated, but I am – Somebody! I may be in jail, but I am – Somebody! I am – Somebody! I must be, I'm God's child. I must be – respected and protected. I am black and I am beautiful! I am – Somebody! Soul Power!" Jesse Jackson. *Operation Breadbask*et Rally 1966. Jesse Jackson (Robert E. Jakoubek, 1991).

AFRICAN NATIONALIST POETRY AND PROSE

36. KWANZAA AT CEMOTAP
BY
DR. FRED MONDERSON

In a packed house full of gifts on December 28, 2013, Dr. James McIntosh and Sister Betty Dobson, Co-Chairs of **CEMOTAP** welcomed young and old citizens to celebrate this year's Kwanzaa Festival which was tremendously interactive with the young people performing African Dances to the beat of the young drummer Naim Blake. The adults and elders sat attentively, clapped their hands, applauded and enjoyed themselves. Everyone recited the Nguzu Saba, 7 Principles of Kwanza.

1. **Umoja** - Unity

2. **Kuji Chakagulia** - Self Determination

3. **Ujima** - Collective Work and Responsibility

4. **Ujamaa** - Cooperative Economics

5. **Nia** - Purpose

6. **Koomba** - Creativity

7. **Imani** - Faith

FREDERICK MONDERSON

Not only did the full-house joyfully recite the Principles, but they also did vigorous Harambes after the 7th Principle. How apropos, in this storehouse of intellectual fortitude and a reservoir of cultural and historical motifs, a prominently displayed Class Magazine of 1989 Black History Month Cover featured a photograph and lead article entitled"

Sister Ilene Edwards did a display and short talk explaining the meaning and significance of Adinkra Symbols. She pointed out, much of the "Iron Works" concepts we see fronting and decorating the entrance to buildings are actually imitations of African Adinkra Symbols.

Because the Keynote Speaker Prof. James Blake was running late, Dr. McIntosh decided to feed the attendees as we waited. In a specially choreographed exercise Dr. McIntosh was able to fit the entire audience in the dining hall where a wonderful and delicious meal of some 10-courses of food including sweet potato, potato salad, chili, egg parmesan, shrimp, cabbage, chicken, macaroni shells, Mac and Cheese, Mac and vegetable with tuna, topped with juice, pound-cake and a still wider assortment of desert satisfied the "sweet tooth." With stomachs filled we sat back to enjoy Dr. Blake's Kwanzaa Message.

Prof. Blake's Theme centered on the "Million Man March," a topic not much talked about these days,

AFRICAN NATIONALIST POETRY AND PROSE

said the Chairman of the **Million Man Coordinating Committee of Queens** and currently a Professor at the Borough of Manhattan Community College. Beginning with the Muslim greeting of "Salaam Wali Kom" "Salaam," he asked if everyone ate and then focused on the third principle of the Nguzu Saba, celebrated this Saturday, Ujima which is "Collective Work and Responsibility."

Emphasizing "We're in this together," Prof. Blake insisted, "We must build and maintain and keep our committee together. If we don't, no one else will!" Further, "We must make our sisters and brothers' problems our own and work to make them better. We have to solve each other's problems and take inventories of what we have accomplished." Insisting that media negatively portrays and does not serve our people, Prof. Blake said we must do "self-criticisms" and will realize, "We have achieved a lot in our community. We must celebrate our accomplishments." Then he gave a partial listing of things accomplished while emphasizing their impact and why we must work together in the same fashion.

1. The "**Million Man March**" was "The greatest assemblage of Black men in the world. The numbers varied but there were more than one, maybe two, million men who gathered in Washington, DC on October 16, 1995. These men were a group. A

group has purpose, aims and goals. It is like a contract, an agreement."

2. We must not focus on differences; we must only focus on what unites us. We must realize; liberation is not something you will get easy. Collective Work and Responsibility was crucial on the March. We have to always be aware of individuals who want to destroy or to betray the collective effort! We came home from the March with goals in mind.

3. We agreed to keep the local Organizing Committee together and plan a series of activities to benefit our community. We created the Historic Black College Tour and took 500 youths to **Historic Black Colleges**. They visited Howard University, Fisk, Morgan State, Tennessee, Spellman, North Carolina Central, Virginia State and Morehouse College. Some mothers praised our efforts saying, "When my child came home, he or she said I want to go to this or that college. Several have already graduated."

4. We organized the first "Father and Son March" on Merrick Boulevard and into Roy Wilkins Park. We created a chant:

"What do we want?"

"Fathers!"

AFRICAN NATIONALIST POETRY AND PROSE

"How do we want them?"

"Strong!"

African Nationalist Poetry and Prose Photo. "Stars and Stripes" of a different persuasion.

African Nationalist Poetry and Prose Photo. All the carved wooden seats.

This "Father and Son March was peaceful!" Rosa Parks was our Grand Marshal! She came out just to be with us!

FREDERICK MONDERSON

5.   We created an "Annual Youth Day" with committees divided into Youth, Social Justice and Economic Development, etc.

6.   The legendary lawyer Johnny Cochran came to speak to our young people. Here at **CEMOTAP** we engaged in Collective Work and Responsibility. It is amazing what we can do when we work together. We must 'Look for the good and praise it.'"

7.   Dr. Blake further informed, they "Created a VIP Youth Committee." Between 1999 and today they prepared young people and secured 8,000 jobs. The Committee has some terrific sisters such as Zynga and Rosa. Sister Henrique is a jewel who sits on the Board. There are 50 parents in the group. Sister Erica did all the hotel arrangements for the Black College Tour." He continued further, "They are building prisons faster than they are building schools or colleges. Today prisons are a profit-making enterprise and the statistics are frightening. The people in prison look a lot like us."

With that, it was time to share out the gifts and the young people lined up. Everyone was to take a gift and return to the end of the line and repeat this until all the gifts were gone. Some young people got as many as four or five gifts and so they really had a happy Kwanza!

AFRICAN NATIONALIST POETRY AND PROSE

37. POEM TO THOTH BY DR. FRED MONDERSON

O Divine Thoth, how revered is thy name and being, three times great, Trismegistus, majesty! Rising with Ra in primeval times and Prime Minister of Horus, you are Intelligence of the Gods. Chief administrator in the African Hall of Judgement, Lord of the Books, Prince of Laws, you are the Heart of Ra. The infallibility of your instrumentation and integrity you give the process, determine the faith of millions who enter. God of Wisdom, their spiritual destiny held in balance in your Ma'atian Psychostasia, Lord of Heliopolis, Patron Divinity of the Learned. Thoth, as ibis, you were on Narmer's Palette together with Hathor, the Lady of Heaven.

You Lord of Hermopolis, who combines with four pairs of gods, are Self-created, Self-produced. Shrines were constructed at Hermopolis, place of the 'high ground', at Abydos and elsewhere. Strength of Gods, you possess Life, Stability, Sovereignty and Dominion, Moon in Heaven, Bull among the Stars, Leader of the Gods, Lordly Ibis you took the place of Horus in the Titulary of Khufu, Letter Writer of the Nine Gods, as Governor of Mankind, you are Lord of Kindliness. In the Horus/Seth conflict, with words of power you created a cow's head for Isis.

FREDERICK MONDERSON

When Osiris fell victim to the plot of Seth, Isis and Nephthys lamented the loss of their beloved. This protestation of sorrow and anguish reached Ra's ears in Heaven. As father of the gods, Ra dispatched you Thoth and your companion Anubis, to make Osiris True of Voice. O One of Red Jasper and Quartz, you became emissaries of comfort, intelligence and security providing Isis with magical formulas. Your Knowledge of Divine speech gave confidence to Isis, and this brought victory to her quest. Thus, Thoth, strong deliverer, Scribe of Truth, together with Nephthys and Anubis, you bear witness to the revivification of Osiris, Lord of Goodliness.

When Horus staked his claim in the Imperial Court of the Divinities, Master of Laws you defended him. Lordly Ibis, your legal mind vindicated his right to Mount the Throne of Egypt.

Unquestionably your departed companion Osiris lauded your legalism on his behalf. Victorious Horus, his mother Isis and aunt Nephthys were equally pleased with your actions, Scribe of the Gods, who sails in his divine boat, and stands among the Lords of Truth, Vicar of Ra.
Your attributes are impressive, Lord of Divine Words. You gained mastery over your own heart and opened your mouth to bestow life, embracer of heaven. As Divine Patron of Writing, the arts, astronomy, and science your origination heralded these gifts of Africa to the world. Back in ages when Black men and women were founts of creativity and

AFRICAN NATIONALIST POETRY AND PROSE

wisdom, your intellect Thoth and the Quintessence of Maat, your counterpart, were great African contributions.

Thoth, as an African divinity of brilliance and integrity, you are Master of Physical and Moral Law. Your knowledge and power calculated the heavens and the earth, keeping them in equilibrium. Moon God, symbol of the Equinoxes, your compatriots, the Gods, respect your judgement without question. For in that august weighing of the hearts of men in the Great Balance, 0 Lord of Divine Words Your findings determine instant death or Life and Eternal Existence, because you speak truth and are accustomed to Justice. Lord of Khnumu, you record in writing deeds and actions of Gods and men, so continue to Open Your Eye to Give Life.

Thoth you symbolize the grace and majesty of the Ibis, and clear-sightedness of the baboon. Your scales of Balance represent order in every situation, God of Equilibrium, Lord of Maat.

You transcribe and interpret the thoughts and aspirations of eternal African spirits who breathe life into creation, 0 Lord of Heaven, Great Deliverer and Creator of Everlastingness, You illuminate the Earth with your Beauty. Great Dom Palm sixty cubits in height, Sweet Well for one that thirst in the Wilderness, you give prosperity and advancement to

FREDERICK MONDERSON

mankind who worship you, Patron Divinity of the Learned, who stood in place of Ra.

How interesting these Black immortals have destined the talents and intellect of the God Thoth.

Lord of Knowledge and understanding who Possess Power Greater than Osiris and Ra, empower us to cultivate the development of arts, sciences, intellectual growth, ethical and moral advancement. This way we can save humanity, within the philosophical construct of the fatherhood of god and the brotherhood of man, as African creation had so destined it.

African Nationalist Poetry and Prose Photo. Tribute to the Ancestors – Image, 2019.

AFRICAN NATIONALIST POETRY AND PROSE

African Nationalist Poetry and Prose Photo. From the **Black Lady Theater**. "Black man which one are you?"

African Nationalist Poetry and Prose Photo. Tribute to the Ancestors – Image, 2019.

FREDERICK MONDERSON

African Nationalist Poetry and Prose Photo. Angela Davis, revolutionary, Professor and woman of distinction.

AFRICAN NATIONALIST POETRY AND PROSE

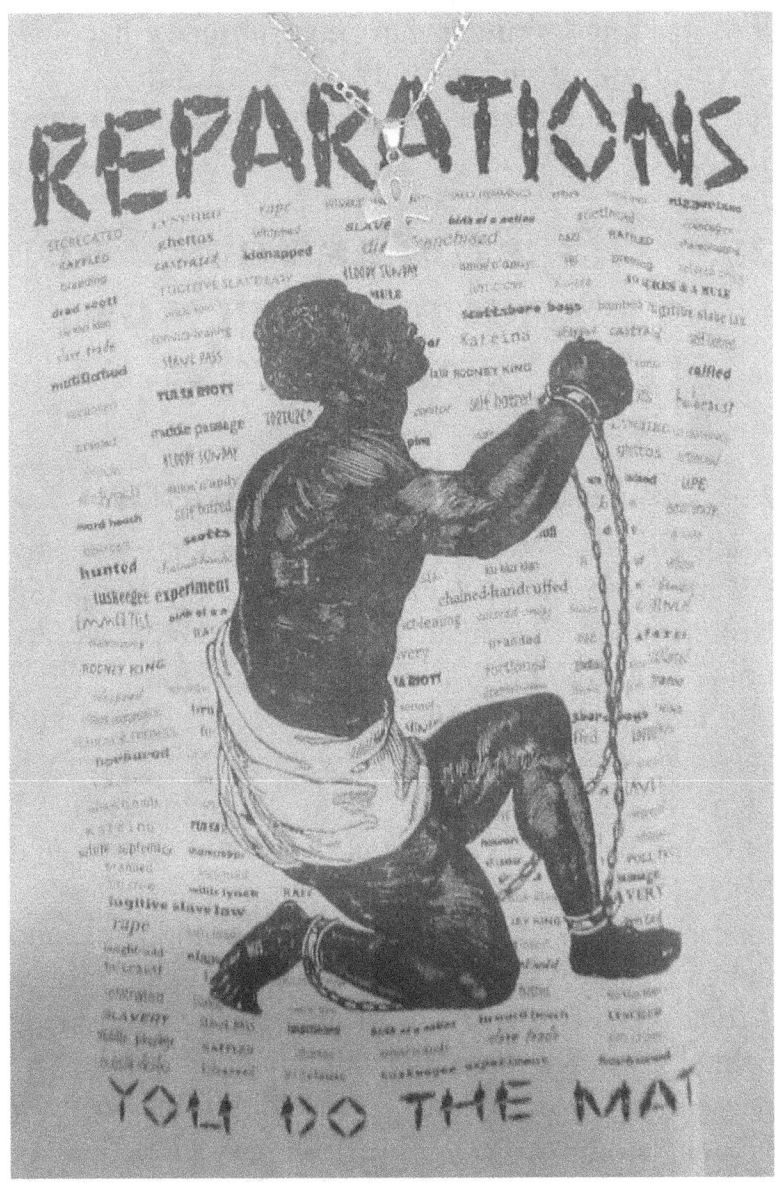

African Nationalism Poetry and Prose Photo.
You do the math!

FREDERICK MONDERSON

"If I can conceive it and believe it, I can achieve it. It's not my aptitude but my attitude that will determine my altitude – with a little intestinal fortitude!" Jesse Jackson. *Ebony* Magazine, August 1988.

38. SHARPTON AND BENJAMIN CRUMP'S "MARCH ON WASHINGTON" BY DR. FRED MONDERSON

Joining the Reverend at the rally and in an Academy Award presentation, legal eagle Attorney Benjamin Crump eloquently made the case of "Why we are going to March on Washington!" Mr. Crump first of all thanked and congratulated Rev. Al Sharpton for "always answering the bell, whether the camera is there or not, he is there when it is not popular." Praising his fellow lawyers Jonathan Moore and Michael Hardy for their stalwart role in quest of justice, he praised "Young people who stood up!" and indicated the National Bar Association, the largest African-American organization of lawyers, stands behind Rev. Sharpton and this movement. Then he recognized "Eric Garner inspired and galvanized young people who crafted their own slogans," which the marchers chanted: "Hands Up, Don't Shoot" and "I Can't Breathe;" "Black Lives Matter," "I am Michael Brown" and "Justice for Michael Brown!"

AFRICAN NATIONALIST POETRY AND PROSE

Next Mr. Crump explained his "Theory of the case!" because "the system needs to be indicted!" He insisted, "The system is what breaks our hearts." He decried the "closeness in time" of the killings of Eric Garner, Michael Brown, Tamir Rice and pointed to the symbolism and seemingly inherent conflict of interest, "Even Stevie Wonder could see," when a local Prosecutor must investigate a local police officer. Calling Ferguson "a fraud" he advised, "We must be specific. It's about chess not checkers!"

He then proposed a precedence by which he questioned Ferguson! That is, for 30 years the Prosecutor has been presenting cases to the Grand Jury. All of a sudden, he changed his strategy!

Mr. Crump insisted the audience see what he termed "attempts to demonize young Black men" because as he pointed out, "Police officers are hired to protect and serve the community," but what you get is "Police protection for police and Police enforcement for Black victims." Searching for precedence he stated, "In 1982 the Supreme Court ruled, 'not to allow a suspect to testify!'" In such manner, for 30 years the Ferguson District Attorney presented to the Grand Jury but did not allow any suspects to testify. "All of a sudden he wants to be fair," and in presenting to the Grand Jury, allows the suspect, Darren Wilson, to testify. He therefore asked, "Had he not been fair for 30 years?" His view of "police demonizing young Black men" is seen, first, where

FREDERICK MONDERSON

Officer Wilson compared his encounter with Michael Brown as "Hulk Hogan to a 5-year old." Then he pointed out how they use the terms "Supporters for Officer Wilson" but "Protesters for Michael Brown and Eric Garner!" Then again, three seconds after the police arrived, he shot Tamir Reid, yet he claims he told him to put down the gun three times. With Eric Garner they tried to play up he was arrested previously and that he was selling "loose cigarettes" which he was not doing at that time.

Vowing "Due Process" for Michael Brown, Eric Garner and Tamir Rice, Mr. Crump quoted former Supreme Court Justice Thurgood Marshall that "the Constitution guarantees the same equal rights to a Black, uneducated, poor, mother who gives birth in Mississippi to an affluent, educated, wealthy, white mother born anywhere in the United States. That is what being born in this country means."

Rev. Sharpton reminded all the **National Action Network** will provide free buses at different locations across the five boroughs but those interested must sign up for a seat. Go to **National Action Network**.Net or call and add your name. Buses December 13, 2014, to rendezvous at Pennsylvania Avenue and 13th Street.

AFRICAN NATIONALIST POETRY AND PROSE

"We believe in the freedom of Africa for the Negro people of the world, and by the principle of Europe for the Europeans and Asia for the Asiatics, we also demand Africa for the Africans at home and abroad." Marcus Garvey. *Bill of Rights* – 1920.

39. BLACK INFLUENCE ON THE SUPREME COURT BY DR. FRED MONDERSON

No ethnic group has had more of an impact on the United States Supreme Court than African-Americans for the Court has ruled against Black interest and has even had to reverse itself, before making its most significant rulings in favor of Blacks. However, huge as this influence has been, it has been excluded from the general narrative of history. Nonetheless, this influence has been exerted through the significance of the United States Constitution, enacted legislated acts in federal statues and the working of the Supreme Court itself. Thus, we must follow its most important cases and even measure how Blacks have wielded their influence whether as subjects, attorneys before the bar, or as in the extraordinary work of Jurist Thurgood Marshall who rose from the law ranks to be one of the most influential voices on the bench. Now, the African-American President Barack Obama has appointed two women to the Court. In the history of the Republic, Presidents Washington, Jackson, Lincoln, Grant, Harrison, Taft, Harding, Franklin Roosevelt, Truman, Eisenhower and Nixon have appointed four or more members of the Court. A prevailing belief has been, in the event of his being re-elected, President Obama would have the opportunity to impact the Court even more with one, possibly two additional appointments and join this exclusive group of presidents. This latter reality was especially troubling for many people who were disposed to see him defeated in the 2012 election. As such, this election proved truly historic to determine whether the nation moved forward or return to its tattered conservative past.

Nevertheless, President Obama was re-elected and with the passing of Justice Scalia, the President's opportunity materialized. In this he nominated Justice Merrick Garland who was, however, never given any consideration of a hearing or a vote by the "axe-grinding" Senate Majority Leader Mitch McConnell who had failed to "make Barack Obama a one-term President." McConnell played a delaying and waiting game until after the 2016 election giving President-Elect and now President, Donald Trump the opportunity to appoint his own man, Justice Gorsuch.

Thus, to understand the Black influence and how it has shaped the Constitution, and how such status has been shaped by the Constitution, especially through

AFRICAN NATIONALIST POETRY AND PROSE

the Court, one has to even antedate the Supreme Court creation and initial sitting under Chief Justice John Marshall; for the **"Three Fifths Clause"** or **Compromise of 1787**, impacting the Constitution was about politics. This Compromise has had to do with apportioning enslaved Africans to win Southern representation initially in the political and tax dispensation to create the new National instrument of government. Make no mistake; after the **1808 Outlawing of the Slave Trade** by the United States, the **Compromise of 1820** helped define the condition and status of Blacks in this nation.

Nonetheless, even with the later **Compromise of 1850** the Court remained silent on the condition of Blacks as chattel, meaning property. However, within less than a decade the Court could no longer hide behind the fait accompli of silence and was forced to show its true colors in the 1857 case of **Dred Scott v. Sanford**. However, while the Supreme Court ruled on a wide array of issues affecting Blacks, they were generally a result of lower court ruling affecting segregated education, segregation on transportation facilities and other forms of accommodation and ultimately on citizenship. After Dred Scott, while there were others of a lesser import, the 1896 *Plessey v. Ferguson* case affirming "separate but equal," the culmination of

FREDERICK MONDERSON

"Jim Crow," is another milestone in landmark Supreme Court rulings. Again, while the **"Grandfather Clause"** reversal in 1915 is also of minor import among others whittling away at the second-class Black condition, cases such as **Smith v. Albright** outlawing the "white primary" in 1944, and the more landmark 1954 **Brown v. Board of Education of Topeka, Kansas** affirming "segregation is illegal" represented the next and most significant Black impact on the Court. After that, Thurgood Marshall, the man who led that fight would ultimately wield untold influence on the Court and at his death praised for his efforts, even by his adversaries on the bench. To his efforts we could add the various Civil Rights and Voting Rights Acts passed to strengthen previous legislation and to protect Black gains that also benefitted other Americans.

Historically speaking, the **"Three-Fifths Compromise"** of 1787 was instrumental in moving forward with acceptance of the Constitution. However, as Chief Justice Roger Taney later pointed out in the Dred Scott decision of 1857, Africans then enslaved were not considered American citizens! In fact, they were not considered as fully human at the time of the formation of the Constitution, but only subsequently elevated to "Three-fifths" of persons. Equally, that year of 1787, The Compromise also outlawed the importation of slaves after 1808 but this practice continued unabated surreptitiously through

AFRICAN NATIONALIST POETRY AND PROSE

the "Internal Slave Trade" until the Civil War of 1860. Initially, to get their way, the South played hardball supporting significant legislation to enforce the system because their economy depended on slavery. This is made clear by Mary Frances Berry (1971: 7) who pointed out: "The Fugitive Slave Clause was scarcely noticed by northern delegates to the ratifying conventions, but in the South, it was used as a definitive selling point. James Madison particularly emphasized its usefulness in Virginia, as did some of the Federalists in the North Carolina convention. These debates lend credence to the view that the southern states would not have ratified the Constitution without the proslavery compromises." The Compromise required two thirds of the Senate to approve treaties and prohibited the national government from taxing exports or interfering with the slave trade until 1808, the year after the *British in 1807 outlawed* their involvement in the trade.

In the *American Political Dictionary* (1989: 29-30) Plano and Greenberg make reference to the significance of this agreement. They state, Southern delegates, "feared that northern majorities might cut off the slave trade and discriminate against the profitable cotton trade.... It was believed that a sufficient number of slaves would be available by 1808, although illegal slave trade continued until the Civil War of 1860. The treaty and foreign commerce provisions continued to influence the making of American foreign policy." To this we may also add

FREDERICK MONDERSON

the "Internal Slave Trade" enabling tremendously depraved practices on Southern "Slave Farms." Yet, the Supreme Court chose not to be "activist" in this respect and in its silence upheld the institution of slavery that denied Africans any rights which in turn supported the falsely construed de-facto sub-human status of Blacks. To be sure, in a *Brief Review of United States History and Government* (2001: 94) Briggs and Peters write: "Until the Civil War, the Constitution had recognized and protected slavery in three ways: The Three-Fifths Compromise, the provision that Congress could not end the importing of slaves before 1808, and the fugitive slave clause. These compromises had been made in order to encourage southern states to ratify the Constitution. With the expansion of American territory in the West, controversy brewed over whether these new territories should allow slavery or not."

African Nationalist Poetry and Prose Photo. Part of the **Million Man March** 20th Anniversary in 2015.

AFRICAN NATIONALIST POETRY AND PROSE

African Nationalist Poetry and Prose Photo. Another colorful "Mother Africa" version.

FREDERICK MONDERSON

African Nationalist Poetry and Prose Photo. You probably know this Brother!

After the Louisiana Purchase by Thomas Jefferson c. 1800, the status of the states, free and slave, became a Sectional issue regarding division of the new territory. The North wanted more Free States; the

AFRICAN NATIONALIST POETRY AND PROSE

South wanted more Slave States. To settle this matter, Irving L. Gordon's *American Studies* (1984: 106-107) points out: "The North and South agreed to the Missouri Compromise of 1820 admitting Maine as a free state and Missouri as a slave state and prohibiting slavery in most of the Louisiana Territory." Thus, Sectional balance was maintained. To recall, after the killing of Michael Brown, an activist in St. Louis remarked "Racism is in the DNA of this state."

The Industrial Revolution in America was spurred by Eli Whitney's **Cotton Gin** of 1793 among other inventions that ultimately saw Cotton become king on the backs of free Black labor. And, in 1815 at the end of the War of 1812, Internal Improvements opened the way. As labor demands of the agrarian South expanded within plantation culture of tobacco, rice, sugarcane, and cotton, *Encyclopedia Britannica's The U.S. Government: How and Why It Works* (1978: 210) explained: "By 1850 there were 3,204,000 slaves in the area, and it has been estimated that 1,815,000 were connected with the cultivation of cotton. Perhaps this is why the Court cast a blind eye to abolition and reform until the Compromise of 1850 tried to settle the significant issue of expanding states." Three key provisions were agreed to in this measure, and these include:

"California entered the Union as a free state.

FREDERICK MONDERSON

The **Fugitive Slave Law** required that escaped slaves be returned to their owners, providing Slave Catchers with unchecked power.

Through a vote, people living there would determine whether a territory in the Mexican Cession chose to be slave or free."

Again, Mary Frances Berry's *Black Resistance, White Law* (1971:7) explained: "The Fugitive Slave Clause and the commitment of the national government to protect slavery, but not interfere with it, were indispensable parts of the Constitution. However, this Band-Aid solution as part of denial of black rights was short lived in the abolitionist and reform era, forcing the 1957 *Dred Scott v. Sandford* landmark decision which clearly defined the status of the African in America."

According to the evidence, Dred Scott was an enslaved African whose master took him into a Free State in 1834 and back into a Slave State. Upon his return in 1846, Mr. Scott sued for his freedom on grounds of having set foot on free soil; he therefore claimed he was entitled to be free. In 1857, Chief Justice Roger Taney (1836-1864) ruled in this historic case. In *American Historical Documents*, Edited and with an Introduction by Harold C. Syrett (New York: 1965, 250), we are informed: "The Court considered the following points: whether Scott was a citizen of Missouri (if he was not, he could not sue in a federal court); whether residence in a free area gave

AFRICAN NATIONALIST POETRY AND PROSE

Scott his freedom following his return to Missouri; and whether the Missouri Compromise (under the terms of which slavery was prohibited in the Wisconsin territory) was constitutional."

In answer, Bonnie-Anne Briggs and Catherine Fish Petersen in *Brief Review in United States History and Government* (2001: 95-96) have argued: "The ruling held that no African-Americans, slave or free, were citizens, and therefore, they were not entitled to constitutional protection. The ruling also held that the Missouri Compromise was unconstitutional because Congress could not deprive people of their right to property - slaves - by banning slavery in any territory." Still, we know of Lincoln's "House divided" speech and its subsequent implications resulting in the Civil War.

Soon, however, despite Taney's decision on Dred Scott, a few years later, John S. Rock of Massachusetts was the first Black invited to practice at the Supreme Court under the new Chief Justice Salmon P. Chase (1864-1873). Entering the bar and wearing 'Buck Wheat,' to plead his case he stood defiantly, as Page Smith in *The Constitution: A Documentary and Narrative History* (1978: 440) stated, "[I]n the monarchial power of recognized American manhood and American Citizenship, within the bar of the Court which had solemnly pronounced that Black men have no rights which white men were bound to respect.... By Jupiter the sight was grand!" Even further, Smith (1978: 441) continued: "The Court in the case of *Ex parte Milligan* ruled that Lincoln had acted unconstitutionally when he ordered military courts in places where civil courts were functioning." Lincoln saw this action as necessary, notwithstanding Chief Justice Chase's contention: "The Constitution of the United States is a law for rulers and people, equally in war and peace, and covers with the shield of its protection all classes of men, at all times, and under all circumstances."

African Nationalist Poetry and Prose Photo. Ms. Jermaine-Berger at **NAN's 2018 Convention** in Manhattan.

AFRICAN NATIONALIST POETRY AND PROSE

African Nationalist Poetry and Prose Photo. Dr. Molefi Asante of Temple University's Afrocentric Institute.

African Nationalist Poetry and Prose Photo. A Message from "Slave One" by Judge Phillips.

FREDERICK MONDERSON

African Nationalist Photo and Prose Photo. Jackie Robinson, Baseball legend.

This was a powerful statement for the Civil War settled two questions as *Encyclopedia Britannica* (1978: 215) states: "First, it killed the idea of state sovereignty and the right of secession. Second, it ended the institution of slavery." It did, however,

AFRICAN NATIONALIST POETRY AND PROSE

little to change the agrarian basis of the South's economy and essentially the condition of the newly freedman who was promised but did not get the 40-acres and a mule; since slavery was an economic system of slave ownership and racial control. Still, *Britannica* (1978: 215) continued: [T]he institution of slavery was replaced by three others. The economic system of sharecropping, the political system of one-party politics, and the social system of segregation supported both by law and by custom." Clearly then, despite the Civil War 13th, 14th, and 15th **Amendments**, Reconstruction was betrayed and white southern backlash gave birth to "Jim Crow" and white primaries. Aided by **Black Codes**, this new state of affairs began to curb the newly secured rights of African-Americans. As part of the grand strategy to gain political power in the South, while some whites sought legal means, some conservative southerners employed terror groups as the Ku Klux Klan, Red Shirts and Knights of the White Camelia to intimidate and terrorize Blacks from going to the polls and retard all forms of social and economic progress. Now having successfully wrestled political control in returning to power, southern legislators-imposed poll taxes and literacy tests on the Freedmen and used the "Grandfather Clause" to empower poor whites who could not pass the literary tests, but also deny Blacks to vote because their "grandfathers" did nor could not vote. In Joanne Grant's *Black Protest: History, Documents* and *Analyses – 1691 to the*

FREDERICK MONDERSON

Present (Fawcett Publications, 1968: 389-391) the author discusses the impact of the Southern Backlash in the form of voter discrimination, citing the "Grandfather Clause," "White Primary" and the "racially exclusive pre-primary party caucus," as emphasized as part of Roy Wilkins, Executive Director of the **National Association for the Advancement of Colored People** address to Congress regarding the 1965 **Voting Rights Act**. She states: "Yet, it is clear that the legal technicalities, the slow pace of court decisions and in some cases complete judicial hostility have combined to restrict participation of voters in national, state and local elections." Mr. Wilkins explained the position of the **Leadership Conference on Civil Right** urged Congress to strengthen a bill introduced by Congressman Celler that does not go far enough in addressing the question of voter intimidation and suppression. As such then, "Jim Crow" laws created segregation of African-Americans and whites in schools, parks, public buildings and on public transportation.

As early as 1849, 5-year old Sarah C. Roberts sued the City of Boston to secure a quality education. She was represented by Charles Sumner and Robert Morris, a black attorney. By 1871 Sumner, sought to correct the loss by introducing legislation that created the 1875 *Civil Rights Act*. By 1883, the Supreme Court found the 1875 Act unconstitutional by stating, the "Thirteenth Amendment abolished slavery but

AFRICAN NATIONALIST POETRY AND PROSE

did not prohibit discrimination and that the Fourteenth Amendment prohibited discrimination by government but not by individuals."

The African-American historian Max Logan labeled this period, 1870-1920 the "Nadir" or low point, in the African-American experience because of the mood of the country fueled by "Jim Crow" practices. Thus, prevailing conditions of "**Jim Crow**" forced the historic ruling in *Plessey v. Ferguson* in 1896 upholding a Louisiana law requiring separate railway carriages for Blacks and Whites. The Court upheld "Jim Crow" by ruling in favor of "equal but separate" or "separate but equal" facilities, which in fact, was actually "separate and unequal." Such a ruling contradicted both the 13th and 14th **Amendments** to the constitution. Plano and Greenberg (1989: 296) pointed out: "Under this doctrine, a wide pattern of segregation developed in schools, transportation, recreation and housing." As such, the ruling encouraged the highest forms of social depravity visited upon Blacks until the conscience of the Supreme Court really began to stir. First it outlawed the "Grandfather Clause" in 1915 and several minor racist rulings until the 1940s when even the armed forces became desegregated.

FREDERICK MONDERSON

In the 1954 *Brown v. Board of Education of Topeka, Kansas* the Supreme Court under Chief Justice Earl Warren delivering the opinion, ruled "separate but equal" inherently unequal and therefore unconstitutional. In *United States History and Government*, Paul Stich, Susan Pingel and John Farrell (1989: 241) recognized the roles of the Truman and Eisenhower administrations in facilitating integration despite southern senators' use of the "filibuster" to stymie legislation. However, the Supreme Court was not hamstrung by these tactics. They write: "After World War II, in a series of civil cases brought by the *National Association for the Advancement of Colored People* (**NAACP**), the Court began applying Amendment's 'equal protection of the laws' phrases against various state segregation laws. In 1954, the Court issued its decision in *Brown v. the Board of Education of Topeka, Kansas*, which reversed the doctrine of 'separate but equal' put forth in the 1896 *Plessey* case." At the time of Brown, racially segregated schools were the norm in nearly 20 states, particularly Kansas, South Carolina, Virginia and Delaware which, bound together in challenge became a sort of class action suit.

In Kansas it was *Brown…*; South Carolina, *Briggs v. Elliott*; Virginia *Davis v. County School Board*; and Delaware, *Gebhart v. Belton*; In *Brown*, after its ruling, the Court used a procedure called 'orbiter dictum' to 'speak beyond' the Topeka situation and announced that racial segregation of schools was

AFRICAN NATIONALIST POETRY AND PROSE

inherently wrong and must cease throughout the nation." This they moved expeditiously to correct! Naturally, there was tremendous opposition to desegregation and thus we entered the Civil Rights Era. That galvanizing of the people, taking to the streets, organizing across religious, civic and social streams of consciousness is what brought about the successes of social and political changes that resulted.

This was underscored by the simple reality, in many such states, for every one dollar spent on Black education, ten dollars was invested in a white child's education. This was the embarrassment that needed to be changed.

Often times the work of a single person is overlooked but that of Thurgood Marshall, first as a lawyer challenging the Court, and then as jurist influencing the Court's direction is unparalleled among American men of law. This enormous capability is best reflected in the laudatory commentary by the trustees of Howard University after Marshall, ten years out of law school, successfully argued *Smith v. Allwright* overthrowing the "white primary" in 1944. According to Michael Davis and Hunter R. Clark in *Thurgood Marshall: Warrior at the Bar, Rebel on the Bench* (1994: 11) the University's citation read: "You are winning significant and enduring victories for a disadvantaged people. Your increasing labors are opening the way for the achievement of an even

FREDERICK MONDERSON

greater measure of justice and equality under the law. Your star still rises, and though it is not yet at its zenith the brilliance of your accomplishments and the value of your service to your fellow man already marked you as an advocate, a legal scholar and humanitarian of the highest magnitude."

African Nationalist Poetry and Prose Photo. Dr. Lenora Fulani asking a question at **NAN's 2018 Convention**.

African Nationalist Poetry and Prose Photo. **NAMES....**

AFRICAN NATIONALIST POETRY AND PROSE

African Nationalist Poetry and Prose Photo. Councilman Charles Baron alongside Carmen and Emma Merneith-Mitta.

FREDERICK MONDERSON

African Nationalist Poetry and Prose Photo. Harriet Tubman "Revolutionary" and Ptah, "God of Artisans" and creator of the heavens in Egypt.

AFRICAN NATIONALIST POETRY AND PROSE

Eulogy at his death summed up the work and influence of this extraordinary man of law. Davis and Clarke (1994: 385) additionally noted: "[I]nscribed above the front entrance to the Supreme Court building are the words 'Equal justice under law.' Surely no one individual did more to make these words a reality than Thurgood Marshall. Thus, with the all-inclusive phrase 'no one,' Rehnquist ranked Marshall alongside Washington, Jefferson, and Lincoln. This statement was from the same man who, as a law clerk some thirty years earlier, had urged that Plessey's separate-but-equal doctrine be upheld." William T. Coleman, former transportation secretary who also worked on Brown, observed, "History will ultimately record that Mr. Justice Marshall gave the cloth and linen to the work that Lincoln's death left undone." Equally, Vernon E. Jordan of the **National Urban League** and advisor to President Clinton said Marshall's mission, according to Davis and Clarke (1994: 388) had been "to cleanse our tattered Constitution and our besmirched legal system of the filth of oppressive racism and to restore to all Americans a Constitution and a legal system newly alive to the requirement of justice."

Clarence Thomas replaced Thurgood Marshall as the only Black on the bench. However, his policies and writings were utterly opposed to those of Marshall. Explaining, Davis and Clarke (1994: 376) write, in 1990 President Bush No. 41 appointed Thomas to the U.S. Court of Appeals and in 1992 he was appointed to the Supreme Court. "At first, Thomas's nomination appeared to be a shrewd political move on the part of the president. By making effective, if cynical use of the skin color of a nominee opposed to racial preferences, Bush threatened the Democratic coalition of liberals, women's groups, and blacks. Liberal feminists were aligned against Thomas because of his conservatism and outspoken opposition to abortion. At the same time these groups risked antagonizing blacks whose paramount goal was to have an African-American succeed Marshall. The white liberal leadership of the Democratic party knew that by opposing Thomas, they also risked further alienating white middle-class voters - the so-called Reagan Democrats - who regarded racial preferences as reverse discrimination." Even further, Davis and Clarke (1994: 378) continued: "During the 1991-92 term, his first as an associate justice, Thomas demonstrated himself to be exactly what his conservative proponents had hoped and his liberal opponents had dreaded. Most often, he aligned himself with the Court's two most conservative members, Rehnquist and Scalia. He has voted to restrict constitutional protection accorded prison inmates; he has called for softening the wall that has traditionally separated church and state; and, dissenting from the Court's ruling in *Planned Parenthood of Southeastern Pennsylvania v. Casey*, decided on June 29, 1992, he has called for *Roe v. Wade* to be overturned outright." Still, Justice Thomas characterized Thurgood Marshall as "a great lawyer, a great jurist and a great man."

AFRICAN NATIONALIST POETRY AND PROSE

Nevertheless, so much has transpired once the Court assumed an "activist" posture recognizing and safeguarding the rights of African-Americans. Given the vote, educational and other social and economic opportunities, and flexing newly won political, even economic, power, Blacks began making strides in electing representatives and finally became an election force owing to the backing of the Court. Now, an African-American President has made his impact to move this historic legal institution even further in recognizing and securing a more just future for all America's people, first in appointing two females and the expectation of a third nominee. Without question, however, rights gained by Blacks have benefitted all segments of the American populace whether Black or White, Jew, Gentile, Catholic, Protestant, Asian and Latino, Gays and Lesbians, handicapped and especially women and the work of the Supreme Court has been instrumentally prodded by Black influence, far, far beyond what Chief Justice Roger Taney ever hoped for in his *Dred Scott v. Sanford* decision in 1857, a century before *Brown v. Board of Education of Topeka, Kansas* on May 17, 1954.

Looking for wisdom from the great ones, we note, Frederick Douglass very early affirmed, "Power concedes nothing without a struggle. It never did and it never will." As such, and to understand Black influence on the Supreme Court, one has to view this

FREDERICK MONDERSON

from a litany of evolving situations or circumstances and a number of resulting landmark legal rulings. Much of this extends for a hundred-year period ending in the 1954 landmark *Brown v. Board of Education of Topeka*, Kansas, ruling.

1. *"Three-Fifths" Compromise* - 1787 - Five Blacks to count as three Whites. This concession encouraged Southern support for the new Constitution.

2. Eli Whitney's *"Cotton Gin"* - 1793 - a machine to separate the seed from the cotton. This encouraged greater production requiring more hands to produce and process the cotton, thereby creating an even greater demand for slave labor.

3. *Outlawing the Slave Trade in 1808* - Submitted in 1787 it took effect some 20-years later in 1808. The British outlawed their involvement in the Trade in 1807. Still, Americans sought to maintain a sufficient number of enslaved persons to supply the Southern work-force demands.

4. *Missouri Compromise - 1820* - Apportioning the lands of the Louisiana Purchase of 1800 under Jefferson. It sought to maintain an equal number of slave and free states.

5. *Crandall Quaker School* - 1831 Ms. Crandall created a school to teach black and white girls. When parents objected, she fired all the white girls and

AFRICAN NATIONALIST POETRY AND PROSE

recruited only black girls. Many had to come from out of state, so they passed a law only in-state girls could attend. Then she was forced to close the school and leave the state.

6. *Sarah C. Roberts* - 1849 - A 5-year old girl who sued the City of Boston to get a quality education.

7. *Compromise of 1850* - "California entered the Union as a free state.

The **Fugitive Slave Law** required that escaped slaves be returned to their owners, providing Slave Catchers with unchecked power.

Through a vote, people living there would determine whether a territory in the Mexican Cession chose to be slave or free."

8. *Dred Scott v. Sanford* - 1857 - Blacks were not citizens and could not sue in a court of law. "Blacks had no rights which a white person was bound to respect." Thus, we have in the Lincoln-Douglas Debates, Abraham Lincoln declaring, "A House Divided - slave and free - cannot stand."

FREDERICK MONDERSON

African Nationalist Poetry and Prose Photo. Rev. Herbert Daughtry (right) and a young admirer.

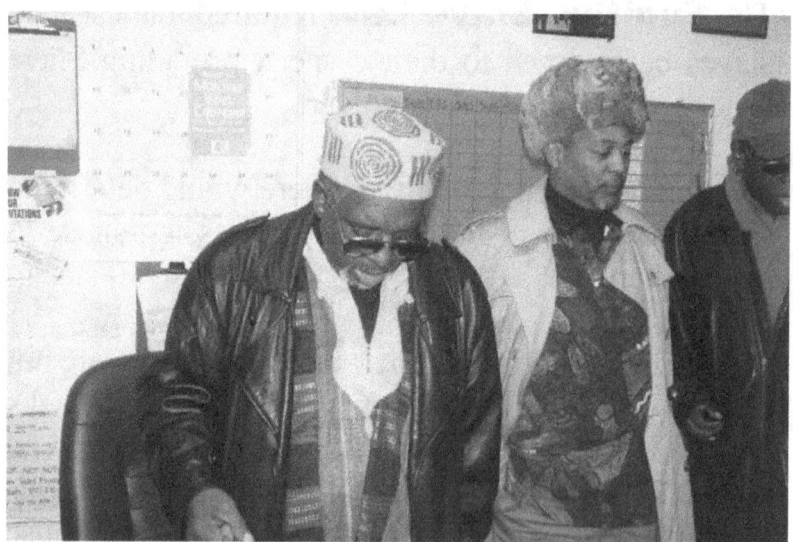

African Nationalist Poetry and Prose Photo. Sonny Carson, his "Chief of Staff" Atiem Ferguson and son Lumumba Carson at Akbar's funeral in Brooklyn.

AFRICAN NATIONALIST POETRY AND PROSE

African Nationalist Poetry and Prose Photo. Malcolm X, icon, nationalist and "Shining Black Prince."

FREDERICK MONDERSON

African Nationalist Poetry and Prose Photo. Sister Dr. Betty Shabazz - educator, nationalist, humanitarian and wife of Malcolm X, now among the revered ancestors, and buried alongside her husband.

9. *Civil War Amendments* - **There were essentially three, Radical Republicans, the Party** of Lincoln promoted and passed while

AFRICAN NATIONALIST POETRY AND PROSE

in control of Congress. They granted the newly Freedman some protections but only to the extent that the Federal Government backed the Supreme Court in upholding these rights. By 1877, the efforts of **Reconstruction** of the nation following the War, were severely curtailed by all forms of machinations when Rutherford B. Hayes succeeded Ulysses S. Grant as President. Many viewed this as vigorous federal retreat from enforcement and federal government betrayal of the Freedman, never giving him his 40-acres and a mule and then cast a blind-eye to the Southern terrorism and lynching of that age. *The New York Times* newspaper, some two years ago, published a report of 3950 documented lynchings in Southern states between 1870-1950. Equally, a CBS program reported on "100-unsolved Civil Rights murders" the FBI is aware of.

13th - 1863 - Freedom
14th - 1865 - Citizenship
15th - 1868 - Right to vote

10. Charles Sumner's *Civil Rights Act* in 1871, was ratified in 1875 and declared unconstitutional in 1883. Only government not private discrimination was protected. Mr. Sumner was attacked on the floor of the House of Representative for his courageous stance in support of Black causes. No wonder such ilks as Joe Wilson of South Carolina could disrespect the president in that very chamber.

FREDERICK MONDERSON

11. *Plessy V. Ferguson* - 1896 - Separate but equal - Enshrined separate railroad cars for black and white riders. This idea and practice extended into other areas.

12. *"Grandfather Clause"* 1915 - Overturned - This was a backdoor way of giving uneducated whites the right to vote who could not pass literacy tests blacks were subjected to.

13. *Smith v. Allwright* 1944 - Overturned "White Primary" - Which held only whites could hold political office.

15. *Sweatt v. Painter* 1950 Sought law school admission to the University of Texas and won the right to attend, because the practice of hastily setting up law schools to keep blacks out of white schools was unconstitutional. The same was done in 1948 in *Sipuel v. Board of Regents of the University of Oklahoma*, insisting Blacks must be admitted to white universities, particularly when their course of study was not available in black schools. Equally, in 1950 the Court also ruled in *McLaurin v. Oklahoma State Regents*, that the school had discriminated by setting up a separate Black cafeteria and seating arrangements for students. Thus, these three cases especially set the stage for the final confrontation in Brown v. Board.

16. *Brown v. Board of Education* - 1954 - "Separate but Equal" was ruled unconstitutional and

AFRICAN NATIONALIST POETRY AND PROSE

across the nation, and ultimately began the outlawing segregation in all social settings.

17. *Gantt v. The Clemson Agricultural College of South Carolina 1963.*

18. *The Civil Rights Act* - 1964 ended all forms of discrimination in social and educational practice. However, being on the books did not mean others had to comply.

19. *The Voting Rights Act* - 1965 - Extended the right to vote to all African-American citizens, natural or naturalized citizens. This voting privilege naturally benefitted anyone who became a citizen from whatever place of origin. However, designed specifically for African-Americans as a result of the Civil Rights upheaval, it contained a voting-rights provision that had to be renewed every 25-year period to prevent it being weakened. However, as late as this age, we know Republicans have used all manner of machinations to purge blacks from the voting rolls because they primarily vote Democratic, having bolted the Party of Lincoln and voted for FD Roosevelt and the New Deal in 1932. Let us not forget, Malcolm X identified the "Dixie-crats" as ill-concerned about Black causes as they were primarily members of the forces of 19th Century terrorism.

FREDERICK MONDERSON

African Nationalist Poetry and Prose Photo. Dr. Marc Lamont Hill at **NAN's 2018 Convention**, "Keepers of the Dream," In New York City

"There are more criminals out of jail than in jail, the only difference is that the majority of those who are out, are such skillful criminals that they know how to keep themselves out." Marcus Garvey. *Speech at Carnegie Hall, New York* August 1, 1924.

40. POEM TO GODDESS HATHOR
BY
DR. FRED MONDERSON

Beloved Hathor, Good Goddess of the West, you are the Oldest Known Goddess of Egypt.
As cosmic deity, your existence heralds the beginning of time, offering pleasure, beauty, and motherhood. Mistress of Myrrh, you supported Narmer in his quest of Unifying the crowns of the south and north. There, he inscribed your name on

AFRICAN NATIONALIST POETRY AND PROSE

his commemorative stela, for you symbolize truth and goodness. As symbol, you are the Alpha and Omega, Mother of Light, First Act of Creation, Lady of Rejoicing, Mighty Among Mankind. Even more, you are a beneficent goddess of maternal and family love, of beauty, of light and joy. You are the fairy godmother who is present at childbirth.

Old, then Middle and New Kingdom Pharaohs rushed to offer you praise, Chieftainess of Thebes. They built temples to praise and espouse your holy name, Black-skinned daughter of Goddess Nut, the unknown; Budge places your origin in the Sudan. Throughout dynastic times your name and symbols, whether horns, disk or plumes, ruled supreme as Egyptians, Nubian, Greeks, and Romans, extol you Patron Goddess of Singers, Dancers, Wine, and Love. Millennia apart, they sanctify the symbolism of your existence, Great Power of Nature Perpetually Conceiving, Creating, and Bringing Forth. You are the best in woman as wife, mother and daughter; with Innumerable Names, your Sanctuary is the 'Place of Drunkenness', a 'Place with Pleasant Life', Sun goddess.

The existence of your sacred abode at Dendera in worship of Seven Hathors, spans many millennia. Here, you are the principal in the trinity of Hathor, Horus, and Horsmataui. Your great triumphs mirror New Kingdom achievements at Thebes where testaments of glory abound. Goddess of the Western

FREDERICK MONDERSON

Necropolis at Thebes, you play a prominent part in the welfare of the dead. You emerge from the nearby hills over the Valley of the Kings, Valley of the Queens, Valley of the Nobles and Valley of the Artisans. Hatshepsut immortalized you in a shrine at Deir el Bahari, and the arrangement of eleven columns in her colonnades herald your symbolism, Queen of the Underworld, Lady of Diospolis Parva, the Cow Goddess.

Hathor Goddess of Beautiful Women, other writers place your origin in inner Africa at Somalia-land. Early you were in the company of African Gods, being Ra's principal female counterpart, goddess of the cow. He sent you to decimate those who laughed and made mockery of the most high. Slayer of Mankind, you drank beer to a drunken stupor. Realizing the severity of his decision, God the Father recanted with a rouse to halt your destruction. He stopped the slaughter you so relished in order to correct the anger of his judgement. Restoring you to normalcy in order to save mankind, you became the Eye of Ra, Lady of Music, Lady of the Cow, who issues forth from the western hills.

The Nubian Desert with its hostile environment is a place that tempered your fiery spirit.
Divine Hathor, as Goddess of the West, Mistress of Amentet, you wear horns with solar disk, vulture tiara, uraeus with five uraei on top, and plumes, even a sun with horns are some of your attributes. You are guardian of the Realm of Silence providing spiritual

AFRICAN NATIONALIST POETRY AND PROSE

and celestial food to its inhabitants. They enter to pay homage to your beneficence, magnanimity, solemnity, and eternal nature, O Daughter of Ra, Cow Goddess, fair goddess from the Land of Punt.

Worshipers fashioned a temple column in your honor Lady of Heaven and Mistress of the Gods. They raise and rattle a sistrum in your praise, Lady of the Southern Sycamore and Palm Trees.
Pharaohs bow down to your majesty, Goddess of Joy and Happiness, Mistress of Song, 'Lady of Leaping,' and Mistress of Wreathing Garlands. Nobles prided themselves as having conducted the "Voyage of Hathor.'

Patron deity of life and light, Goddess of Beauty; your eyes are the sun and moon, Mother of her Father, Daughter of her Son. Hathor you represent all Great Goddesses of Egypt, you are Thoth's Counterpart, Assistant Chronographer and Chronologist. August praise of your power, divinity and everlasting nature, Lady of the West, you have no equal. As a Goddess of the Africans, your Blackness is illuminating, symbolizing a rich and glorious past.

FREDERICK MONDERSON

African Nationalist Poetry and Prose Photo. Luis and Erik and a Distinguished Doctor at **CEMOTAP**.

African Nationalist Poetry and Prose Photo. Erik Monderson joins Dr. James McIntosh at the Microphone.

AFRICAN NATIONALIST POETRY AND PROSE

"When one goes in search of the Obama persona or policies that created such enormous amount of bitterness one inevitably discovers race. Although Obama's political ideology was contrary to that of the Republicans, they challenged him on both personal and policy grounds but the coalescence seemed to always be around the issue of his race. While it was true in some instances that the assaults on him were personal when it came to race most of the attacks against him appeared to have something to do with the symbolic nature of his presidency, not even the substantive policies which he championed. If the attacks came on the policies it was because they were seen as favoring the poor and often blacks. Increasingly blacks liked Obama from the very beginning but there was a general belief that his election could bring out the worst in white people. During Obama's final years in office the assaults on him were often directed toward the generalized black community as some whites felt that they had lost the country and had to win or take the country back from blacks at all costs. In fact, the mass murderer, Dylan Roof, who killed nine African Americans in a Charleston AME Church in 2015, claimed that blacks 'rape our women and have taken over our country.' This was clearly misguided because Obama did not produce the fear and trepidation that the young while Charleston killer felt although Obama's election and presidency many have created a sense of powerlessness in some whites." Molefi Kete Asante. *Lynching Barack Obama.* 2016.

41. THE LEGACY OF MICHAEL JACKSON BY DR. FRED MONDERSON

History has always shown "Good triumphs over evil" and the goodness Michael Jackson exhibited over more than four decades as an entertainer, humanitarian, philanthropist and businessman, and father, son, inventor and human being in general manner so pleasing to the almighty, is what posterity will remember of a man, many times victimized in unproven allegations.

African Nationalist Poetry and Prose Photo. Dr. King and President Barack Obama, "Dreamer and the Dream."

AFRICAN NATIONALIST POETRY AND PROSE

African Nationalist Poetry and Prose Photo. The Revolutionaries – Malcolm X, Marcus Garvey, Huey Newton and Steve Biko who says - "You can jail a **Revolutionary** but you can't Jail the **Revolution**."

At the Apollo Tribute, Tuesday, June 30, 2009, Rev. Al Sharpton commanded the audience to "tell our stories and to talk about Michael's legacy. He was not a freak; he was an innovator ... he was an

FREDERICK MONDERSON

extraordinary entertainer and we love him with extraordinary love." Herb Boyd in the *Amsterdam News* (July 2 - July 8, 2009) informed how "love for Michael is universal, and there is no better testament to his power and influence as an artist and entertainer than the millions around the globe who were shocked by his sudden death as they were awed by his incomparable talent."

Checked early, the work of the wolves, vultures, vampires and zombies who fed at his lucrative trough will be forgotten in time. Along with their architects, they will either be consigned to footnotes in history or overshadowed by the sheer bulk of the positive contribution of a mega star of towering fame, not unlike a comet, that only passes this way "once in a very long time."

First, Michael Jackson will be remembered for his enormous body of work, particularly the earliest and freshest of his productions that exhibited great magnitude, vision, simplicity and charged fun-filled emotions. His lyrics, style and grace appealed to many people across race, culture and religion where parents, white, black, brown and yellow, felt comfortable with their children listening to and imitating young black boys in their living rooms. The **Jackson 5** recorded 14 albums with Motown Records, and Michael also did 4 solo albums with the company. Yet, these early creations simply set the stage for the maturing genius of an emerging solo artist with extraordinary talent, who, in teaming up

AFRICAN NATIONALIST POETRY AND PROSE

with music impresario Quincy Jones, produced even more mega hits following his departure from Motown.

African Nationalist Poetry and Prose Photo. Jitu Weusi and some of the early ancestor giants.

FREDERICK MONDERSON

African Nationalist Poetry and Prose Photo. Musicians entrancing Commodore Barry Park are about to pour a **Libation** for the fair's success. Notice Manuel in Roots Revisited t-shirt in the rear coming into the Park.

African Nationalist Poetry and Prose Photo. A female statue with pendulous breasts and long hair.

AFRICAN NATIONALIST POETRY AND PROSE

African Nationalist Poetry and Prose Photo. Drums and other articles.

One commentator wrote, in "Don't Stop" ('Til you get enough) - the music riveted attention: Jackson' imperial achievement 'Thriller.' The first single 'Billie Jean' began with a uniquely undulating bass line that Jackson topped with a frenzy of curt breaths and huffy exhales. The interplay between Jackson' Jim Farber's "A Wacko yes, but also a genius in many ways," in *Daily News* Friday, June 26, 2009, p. 4, referred to Michael and Quincy's "Off the Wall" production as, "a work that gave their mix of funk, soul, jazz and pop a universal stamp. From the opening track - (Don't Stop) His falsetto had both vulnerability and confidence and the music ruled the dance floor." Then he writes about "Jackson's

FREDERICK MONDERSON

inventive vocals and the forceful music entranced pop fans in every country around the world."

His creative genius, coupled with energetic performances full of life and exhibiting incomparable dance moves enabled "Off the Wall" and "Thriller" and their videos to break down the segregated walls of MTV and, importantly, aiding the music station's solvency. It also opened the door for African American performers to be aired on MTV's popular cable TV network. Michael won 8 Grammys for "Thriller," the most by a single artist. The album boasted 7 No. 1 hit singles. It sold more than 100 million copies worldwide. After its 1982 release, it stayed 37 weeks on the charts as No. 1. "Off the Wall" had sold more than 20 million albums worldwide after its 1979 release. Michael's efforts revitalized economic aspects of the music industry in devastating musical brilliance.

Year after year, Michael Jackson wrote and produced award winning music that sold millions of records and he continued to fill venues when on tour and in concerts. Excitement and anticipation awaited his every performance and this was no doubt the case with his last scheduled set of appearances. Randy Tarraborelli, who wrote a biography about Michael Jackson informed: "The primary reason for the concerts wasn't so much that he wanted to generate money, as much as it was that he wanted to perform for the kids. They had never seen him perform before."

AFRICAN NATIONALIST POETRY AND PROSE

Naya Arinde of the New York *Amsterdam News* (July 2-July 8, 2009) described him as a "man who changed the music game with his singing; dancing; writing and producing." Michael also vocally protested racism in the music industry. Michael Jackson had a down-to-earth quality about him. In June 2002, Michael asked the National Action Network audience "What's more important than giving people a sense of escapism?" "What would life be without a song, joy, laughter and music?"

Selling more than 750 million albums, plus untold numbers of singles, of which 13 were No. 1 as a solo artist, the winning of 13 Grammy Awards, 8 for "Thriller" and awarded 2, a never before and since accomplished, introductions into the Rock and Roll Hall of fame; one as a member of the Jackson 5 and one as a solo artist, Michael has had a very distinguished creative career. These distinctions established Michael Jackson as an unparalleled and extraordinary entertainer possessing talent seemingly inspired by divine guidance. Again, Michael's soft-spoken nature seemed spiritually and mystically divine and his humanitarian nature underscored that godly connection destined to do good for those in need.

As an interesting article by Edna Gunderson in **USA TODAY** (July 2, 2009) entitled "The King of Pop

FREDERICK MONDERSON

reigns over Music Charts," graphically chronicles initial purchasing reactions to the passing of Michael Jackson, because of his melodious sweet harmonic and joyful expression in his songs and videos; their sales are sure to set trends for generations and generations of love and respect for the man and his music.

His message was clear, just like Michael! Even more important, and this should be a reminder to all, while Michael Jackson' legacy is assured it is also not tarnished, thanks to the efforts of Rev. Al Sharpton and others who would not let the media wolves devour the lifeless body and image of "our golden boy." Sharpton's message at the Apollo Memorial was unequivocal: "We love and will defend our heroes." That is, from the destructive machinations of the vultures, vampires and unsavory characters who not only sully people's character and image but grow rich in the process.

Even more significant, Michael's legacy is also evident in his good works, his humanitarianism, and his charitable work through contributions and physically visiting the "trenches of maladies." Michael has been praised, beyond his creative and artistic genius, as being a "take no prisoners showman and entertainer;" but also as a shrewd businessman and one who shared his bread. He was also a master at give back! This generosity certainly went a long way in "netting" his enemies' "swoop down" in his most vulnerable moments!

AFRICAN NATIONALIST POETRY AND PROSE

African Nationalist Photo and Prose Photo. Another image of the boat and passengers atop a two headed animal.

African Nationalist Photo and Prose Photo. A wide array of sculptural pieces.

FREDERICK MONDERSON

African Nationalist Poetry and Prose Photo. Tribute to the Ancestors – Image, 2019.

Because of the symbolism of Michael Jackson and the Jackson 5 in the early years of their careers; in aftermath of the Civil Rights Movement, Black newspapers particularly *Ebony*, *Esquire*, *Jet*, and many others including *Peoples Weekly*, *Time*, *TV Guide*, *Glamour*, *Ladies Home Journal*, *Life*, *Newsweek*, *Vogue*, *Publishers Weekly*, and other magazines, radio and early TV programs carried the image, spread the word and this helped raise people's consciousness to their goodness, creativity and otherwise. This local exposure helped stamp his enormous imprint on black and white culture. Such groundswell response is what encouraged Michael Jackson to begin his low-key give back that later mushroomed into **Guinness Book of World Records** recognition of his charitable giving. Michael underwrote projects, he visited the sick, and

AFRICAN NATIONALIST POETRY AND PROSE

he fed the poor, all this at home and abroad. He "helped cancer-stricken children, burn victims, terminally ill children, and those with illnesses as AIDS and juvenile diabetes." He worked for social justice! He visited and assisted the less fortunate in Africa and when he finally realized the gravity of poverty in Africa, he formed the Heal the World Foundation. Then he produced, wrote and performed, with Lionel Richie, "We Are the World" and "Heal the World" and played his part in "Live Aid."

In as much as one's legacy is also shaped by what that individual leaves behind and since Michael Jackson left much of his work, the revenues gained there from will continue to support his charitable works. Michael's mother, Katherine, and family members of like mind including his children, will most definitely seek to see his charitable gift-giving continue. Possibly, they will support other ventures in his name; so, decades later, when a poor person wherever, at some auspicious or inauspicious occasion benefits from a meal, a coat, footwear, school supplies, a clinic, etc., they will always remember to say **GOD BLESS MICHAEL JACKSON** because he deserved it.

Whenever **THE WIZ** is performed, his version will be remembered!

FREDERICK MONDERSON

African Nationalist Poetry and Prose Photo. Intricate and detailed features of art.

African Nationalist Poetry and Prose Photo. Part of the throngs who attended the 20th Anniversary of the **Million Man March** in 2015.

AFRICAN NATIONALIST POETRY AND PROSE

African Nationalist Poetry and Prose Photo. The **ANKH**, Egyptian symbol of life, in Brooklyn.

FREDERICK MONDERSON

African Nationalist Poetry and Prose Photo.
The message is clear.

African Nationalist Poetry and Prose Photo.
Tribute to the Ancestors – Image, 2019.

AFRICAN NATIONALIST POETRY AND PROSE

African Nationalist Poetry and Prose Photo. Tribute to the Ancestors – Image, 2019.

"If I knew I was gonna live this long, I'd have taken better care of myself.' Eubie Blake. *Observer*. London (February 13, 1983). "Saying of the Week."

42. "UNROLLING THE MUMMY OF RAMESES THE GREAT."

[From a translation (in *Sunday School Times* of Aug. 14, 1886) of Prof. Maspero's Official Report.]

The mummy (No. 5,233) [discovered in 1881 in the tomb of the priest-kings at Dayr-el-Bahari] first taken out from its glass ease is that of Rameses II., Sesostris [the first Pharaoh of the oppression, according to the view of many eminent scholars], as testified by the official entries bearing date the sixth and sixteenth years of the reign of the high-priest Her-Hor Se-Amen, and the high-priest Pinotem I written in black ink upon the lid of the wooden mummy-case, and the further entry of the sixteenth year of the high-priest Pinotem I, written upon the outer winding-sheet of

FREDERICK MONDERSON

the mummy, over the region of the breast. The presence of this last inscription having been verified by His Highness the khedive, and by the illustrious personages there assembled, the first wrapping was removed, and there were successively discovered a band of stuff (sic) twenty centimeters in width rolled round the body; then a second winding-sheet, sewn up and kept in place by narrow bands placed at some distance apart; then two thicknesses of small bandages; and then a piece of fine linen reaching from the head to the feet. A figure representing the Goddess Nut, one meter in length, is drawn upon this piece of linen, in red and white, as prescribed by the ritual. The profile of the goddess is unmistakably designed after the pure and delicate profile of Seti I, as he is known to us in the bas-relief sculptures of Thebes and Abydos. Under this amulet there was found another bandage; then a layer of pieces of linen folded in squares and spotted with the bituminous matter used by the embalmers. This last covering removed; Rameses IL appeared. The head is long, and small in proportion to the body. The top of the skull is quite bare.

On the temples there are a few sparse hairs, but at the poll the hair is quite thick, forming smooth, straight locks about five centimeters in length. White at the time of death, they have been dyed a light yellow by the spices used in embalmment. The forehead is low and narrow; the brow-ridge prominent; the eyebrows are thick and white; the eyes are small and close together; the nose is long, thin, hooked like the noses

AFRICAN NATIONALIST POETRY AND PROSE

of the Bourbons, and slightly crushed at the tip by the pressure of the bandages. The temples are sunken; the cheek-bones very prominent; the ears round, standing far out from the head, and pierced like those of a woman for the wearing of earrings. The jaw-bone is massive and strong; the chin very prominent; the mouth small but thick lipped, and full of some kind of black paste. This paste being partly cut away with the scissors, disclosed some much worn and very brittle teeth, which, moreover, are white and well preserved. The moustache and beard are thin. They seem to have been kept shaven during life but were probably allowed to grow during the king's last illness; or they may have grown after death. The hairs are white, like those of the head and eyebrows, but are harsh and bristly, and from two to three millimeters in length. **The skin is of earthy brown splotched with black.** Finally, it may be said that the face of the mummy gives a fair idea of the face of the living king. The expression is unintellectual, perhaps slightly animal; but even under the somewhat grotesque disguise of mummification, there is plainly to be seen an air of sovereign majesty, of resolve, and of pride. The rest of the body is as well preserved as the head; but in consequence of the reduction of the tissues its external aspect is less life-like. The neck is no thicker than the vertebral column. The chest is broad; the shoulders are square; the arms are crossed upon the breast; the hands are small and dyed with henna; and

FREDERICK MONDERSON

the wound in the left side through which the embalmers extracted the viscera, is large and open. The legs and thighs are fleshless; the feet are long, slender, somewhat flat-soled, and dyed, like the hands, with henna. The corpse is that of an old man, but of a vigorous and robust old man. We know, indeed, that Rameses II. reigned for sixty-seven years, and that he must have been nearly one hundred years old when he died.

African Nationalist Poetry and Prose Photo. Brother Minister Hafeez Mohammed and **CEMOTAP's** resident artist.

AFRICAN NATIONALIST POETRY AND PROSE

African Nationalist Poetry and Prose Photo. Another example of a wide diversity of colorful African art.

African Nationalist Poetry and Prose. Saucy, Sauce.

FREDERICK MONDERSON

African Nationalist Poetry and Prose Photo. Tribute to the Ancestors – Image, 2019.

African Nationalist Poetry and Prose Photo. The **Ankh**, Egyptian "symbol of life."

AFRICAN NATIONALIST POETRY AND PROSE

43. **LIFE IN DEATH: MEDGAR EVERS BY DR. FRED MONDERSON**

Riding along Bedford Avenue in Brooklyn, New York, and viewing the mural gracing Medgar Evers College that read "Courage," "Strength," "Fortitude" an interesting thought crossed my mind. This individual, Medgar Evers is very much alive even though he is now a revered ancestor. Murdered for standing on principle, as a pillar of the Civil Rights struggle who fearlessly challenged the racial hatred and terrorism of his era, Medgar Evers refused to go quietly in the night. Because of his courage, tenacity, inspiration and the symbolism he represented, the founders who envisioned the significance of Malcolm-King resurrected this fearless leader and armed him, not with the deadly projectile that similarly ended his life and a selfless career of working for the betterment of others, but with an even more significant device. That is, the mechanism of freedom of the mind, designed to encourage creativity, create model-citizens, and so engage in a perpetual state of grace through symbolism of freeing the shackled-mind of his people to become an influence and symbolism for the wider world. Alas, what more fitting form of employment for this "light" than to be a torch bearer of intellectual inspiration and fortitude, especially in times of challenge and as Dr. King pointed to controversy. After all, Victor Hugo

FREDERICK MONDERSON

held, "Beneath the tred of mighty armies, the pen is mightier than the sword" and "there is nothing mightier than an idea whose time has come."

People sometimes do stupid things that initially seem right though wrong, wherein the "arc of the Moral Universe," in working its profound magic transforms such behaviors into a wonderful creative expression forcing purveyors of evil wishing to recall the crass deed but to no avail. It is as if in the sorrow of the experience Mr. Evers' family and community were sold lemon in which they creatively produced an elixir of lemonade that has quenched the thirst of ignorance and so for forty years; more than a generation, the symbolism and significance of Medgar Evers is encouraging, directing and infusing untold numbers of young people with a tenacity to elevate themselves and make a constructive mark on society through effective direction of the mind. Such is no greater gift the ancestors hoped for and welcome.

Malcolm X spoke of finding himself in prison but this is late; however, better late than never. What is significant; first, Black Stalin the Calypsonian monarch sang, "The more Africans they gun down, the more Africans keep coming." In that horrifying experience of their ever continuing struggles, African people in America were forced to craft constructive and effective strategies to combat the depraved and intolerable conditions they were subjected to through Slave Trade and Slavery; the

AFRICAN NATIONALIST POETRY AND PROSE

terrorist misfortunes throughout the Nadir, 1880-1930, in which Jim Crow, Ku Klux Klan activities, Sharecrop peonage, all in face of national government abandonment of its citizens to which we may add, "More than 100 unsolved civil right murders" and "3900 lynchings in southern states from 1870 to 1950," were essentially and factually perpetrated by white men professing Christian principles and values. Yet, today the "Oppressor" says, "Get back" but we say, "No, fight back." In such a courageous stance, reinforced in ancestral wisdom through moral fortitude and philosophical support, the true nature of this psychological and spiritual soul-force actively crafted a methodology to combat the symbolism of fear and intimidation in the wanton killing of Black leaders. Realizing "sometimes no one cares" and the need to do for self, African-Americans endured the sorrow and responded in an unexpectedly and unbelievable manner to create something positive out of each such tragedy.

African Nationalist Poetry and Prose Photo. Tribute to the Ancestors – Image, 2019.

FREDERICK MONDERSON

African Nationalist Poetry and Prose Photo. A gathering of distinguished Elders in Guyana.

African Nationalist Poetry and Prose Photo. Dr. Johnson making a Presentation at **CEMOTAP**.

AFRICAN NATIONALIST POETRY AND PROSE

African Nationalist Poetry and Prose Photo. Stones of different varieties.

African Nationalist Poetry and Prose Photo. Baskets.

FREDERICK MONDERSON

African Nationalist Poetry and Prose Photo. Minister Hafeez Mohammed and Drs. Johnson and Wright field questions after their Presentations at **CEMOTAP**.

The killing of the "Mother Emanuel 9" in South Carolina is a powerful example of hurt, grief, sadness, but the power of such forgiveness is a true example their tragic circumstances combatted the "ball and chain" burden of hate as the victims' families quickly jettisoned that burdensome guilt of hating the killer Dylan Roof. The world realized, he in turn has to live with not simply the folly of his actions; the mere crassness of his deed; but the fear, being in prison which has its principled rules, one day he may meet an untimely death, perhaps long before his state sponsored execution. The thought is so remindful of Jeffrey Dahmer, the young man who killed and ate several Black victims and he was stoned to death on a labor rock pile in prison. This is perhaps the most inhuman way in which to die as the

AFRICAN NATIONALIST POETRY AND PROSE

body is repeatedly wracked in the violent force of stone striking flesh repeatedly, again and again. The thing about memorials is they pay tribute to sometimes fallen heroes cut short in the execution of their destiny or simply good people as those who did good things to benefit humanity and expired as their time on earth had ended. Remembering the good they had done later their names were resurrected to grace structures, streets, even sailing vessels or the symbolism they stood for will continue to inspire others in all walks of life. Fortunately, the tragedies and life experiences of Africans in America is replete with those glorious souls, revered ancestors, whose lives are still meaningfully benefitting not simple a single race but humanity in general. The question then becomes, where and when do we begin, in fact, continue to recognize and praise these individuals, even movements for the many ways, they benefited the human spirit.

Strange, an idea, a single phrase, never gets the recognition it deserves certainly by the people it is actually aimed at, even though it has taken flight, even across oceans, to become tools of liberation for people across the globe seeking justice and to redress grievances. Rather than beginning with the work of individuals, a focus on key terms set the stage for better understanding of how ideas can galvanize people, become movements, challenge oppression and become effective change agents.

FREDERICK MONDERSON

In looking at the challenging, yet glorious history of African-Americans, take for example Gabriel Prosser's statement after his revolt was betrayed proved even more profound in that he spoke truth to power saying, "What is all this farce of a trial, I know you intend to shed my blood. I have only one life to give for the salvation and liberation of my people. It is no different than what George Washington would have said if he was captured by the British. So, take me to the gallows and quickly end my life in cause of liberation of my people." The times and circumstances may be different, but in Officer Wilson killing of Michael Brown and his rationalization it was "Hulk Hogan against a five-year old" an idea soon forgotten because of its silly and perverted nature. Here we have a police officer, trained, equipped, been on the force for some time; yet, he refers to himself and perhaps thinks "as a five-year-old." Are we to believe his version of events, even that he is "a five-year-old?" Nevertheless, and in response, the galvanized young people's more creative expressions, "Hands up, Don't Shoot;" "Black Lives Matter;" "I am Michael Brown" were words of sentiments of power; if you will, "Ptahhotep 'Wisdom at the millstone.'" These shibboleths went viral globally, mobilizing demonstrations of young people in sympathy with this tragedy and wanting a world where people aspire to more equality in their expressions, treatment more just to echo Rodney King's pliant, "Can we all get along?"

AFRICAN NATIONALIST POETRY AND PROSE

The interesting thing about ideas as expressions, while some galvanized and sustain themselves, others issue an echo and streak across the heavens into oblivion. In 1941, A Philip Randolph, long in the field of Civil Rights activism and deploring the plight of African-Americans who had essentially voted democratic for the New Deal. In apprising the President of ongoing lynching, discrimination and lack of job opportunities for Blacks in AFL and in the War Industries, threatened to "March on Washington" if something was not done to address the problem of jobs and quality and equality of treatment. President Roosevelt listened attentively at the dinner, passed out cigars and told Mr. Randolph, "Go out there (in the streets) and make me do it."

But first, Marcus Garvey's "Look for me in the whirlwind," and "You have caged the lion, but the cubs are running free out there." Even more important, the Red, Black and Green fluttering in wind and sunlight wherever especially at the African-American parade in Harlem is a reminder the old lion is not really caged. Much more significant, however, in Minister Louis Farrakhan calling for the "Million Man March" on October 16, 1995, to see that same iconic **Red, Black and Green** flying proudly on the Capital Building alongside the Red, White and Blue, was truly a day of significance in more ways than one. Still and just as significant, that "Go out here" and "March on Washington" is a stark reminder there will be opposition to "Business as usual."

FREDERICK MONDERSON

African Nationalist Poetry and Prose Photo. "Baba" spiritual elder who heads-up the "Shrine of the Ancestors."

African Nationalist Poetry and Prose Photo. Marcus Garvey, the legendary nationalist and Pan-Africanist, hero through the ages here and abroad.

AFRICAN NATIONALIST POETRY AND PROSE

Dr. King and the "Big Six" marched in 1963 and announced the possibilities of a "Dream." In 2013, Reverend Al Sharpton, Dr. King's son, Martin Jr., Jesse Jackson, Marc Moral and thousands including Erik and Dad, returned to Washington to commemorate this historic event. And today, every 4th of April weekend when Al Sharpton and the **National Action Network** hosted their "Keeping the Dream Alive" Congress, this is a reminder the "dream" is not yet achieved but countless numbers are in the field fighting to attain such. Importantly, however, Sharpton's efforts is not simply about meeting for discussion and forcing formulated policies but equally activist marches against Giuliani's brutal polices, expressing outrage against the tragedy of Sean Bell, the murderous death of Eric Garner, against the authorities handling events surrounding Michael Brown's killing, that of Travon Martin, Dorismond, Eleanor Bumpers and Amadou Diallo were all attempts to arouse the nation's and the world's conscience seek to invoke legislative action to address wrong-doing and inequity but also to put the oppressor on notice, there's a price to pay, particularly through the economic boycott mechanism, not to forget the ballot box. While Malcolm put it forcefully, the ballot or the bullet, Minister Louis Farrakhan more rightly stated, "Justice or Else."

FREDERICK MONDERSON

African Nationalist Poetry and Prose Photo. Icons Dr. Jack Felder (now an ancestor, left) and Dr. Leonard Jeffries (right) still speaking truths about African history and culture.

African Nationalist Poetry and Prose Photo. The power and intricacy of African sculpture as represented in these two images is breathtaking.

AFRICAN NATIONALIST POETRY AND PROSE

> SHOTOKAN, JUDO JIU JITSU, AIKIDO, KOREANS WITH TAE KWAN DO, HAPKIDO. EUROPE; WRESTLING, BOXING AND OTHERS. SLAVE DESCENDANTS OF THE UNITED STATES HAVE SEARCHED FOR A SYSTEM OF PHYSICAL POWER, WITH A TWO LEGGED ANATOMY AS HUMAN, THE HAND OF FATE DEALT THE FIERCE LOOKING GORILLA OF BODY STRENGTH AND THE GNAT, OF NO PHYSICAL EFFORT, BUT TO SURVIVE ON MENTALITY ALONE. TOGETHER AFRICAN SLAVE DESCENDANTS, HAVE DEVELOPED THE GO-RILLA GNAT SYSTEM OF DIVERSE MOVEMENTS IN SCIENTIFIC DEFENSIVE FIGHTING.
>
> THE CONSUMMATE POWER OF BLACK MANS SELF DEFENSE AND SELF DEFENSE. THIS SYSTEM ALLOWS AN OPPONENT ONE MISTAKEN MOVEMENT (WHAT HE SAYS, WHAT HE DOES). THEN IT IMMOBILIZE HIS FIGHTING INSTRUMENTS BY BREAKING HIS ARMS AND LEGS AND CLAWING HIS EYES OUT. THEN SYSTEMATICALLY DESTROYING HIS ANATOMY. A SYSTEM WITH: CIRCULAR MOVEMENTS OF DEATH WITH FATALITY-1 THROUGH 24
> "MASTER TECHNIQUES TO KILL."

African Nationalist Poetry and Prose Photo. Self-defense techniques.

African Nationalist Poetry and Prose Photo. Dr. Jack Felder and Dr. Leonard Jeffries are joined by a bookseller from Harlem.

Powerfully, when Herman Ferguson insisted on Malcolm X's birthday, vendors on 125th Street in Harlem close for a set number of hours to honor the slain icon, there was some resistance but the potency

FREDERICK MONDERSON

of the idea was full of message that took root. Equally too, when the nationalist Sonny Carson chose to re-inter his great-uncle "The Runaway," Samuel Carson to Ghana, West Africa, opening the "Door of Return" and creating a site of pilgrimage for African-Americans seeking their "roots" anywhere in Africa, not only was this memorial a long time in coming as point of departure waiting for this symbol; this man, this time, we recognized that, the idea, the symbolism, the movement of "Life in Death" had "gone international."

Just as the Negro Activist anthem "We shall overcome," even as uttered in the US Congress by President Linden Johnson following the death of John Kennedy and on eve of passage of the 1964 **Civil Rights Act** and the 1965 **Voting Rights Act**, it has been replaced today by "No Justice, No Peace." This has a similarly galvanizing theme becoming an international shibboleth for people seeking justice and equity in redress of grievances. This coming of age of activist mantras has been recognized, from the suffering, trials and tribulations of the struggles of African-Americans. Rightly then, this strategy has and continues to better the lot of humanity.

However, in all these efforts and circumstances let us not forget, Frederick Douglass' profound question, "What does the Fourth of July mean to a slave?" and that "Power concedes nothing without a struggle, it never did and it never will." Such profound thoughts

AFRICAN NATIONALIST POETRY AND PROSE

were contemporary with another historic ancestor, Harriet Tubman the Underground Railroad Conductor who insisted, she never ran her train off the tracks, but boldly reminded her charges, "I would rather see you dead, than a slave." Even she recognized, "I could have saved more, if they only realized they were slaves." However, and even more significant, she insisted, "I must live free or die!"

Of equal significance, Marcus Garvey's "Africa for the Africans, those at home and those abroad." His admonition was matched by W.E.B. DuBois' efforts as the "Father of Pan-Africanism," who recognized the 20th Century as the "Century of Race" or "color line. In that era of heightened Africanist activism, Booker T. Washington laid it down, "Pan-Africanism is the destiny of African people." And following, Kwame Nkrumah issued his insightful insistence, "Seek ye first the political kingdom and everything else will be added."

On the other side of the world in Guyana, President David Granger's recently declared, "No one can tell us who our heroes must be nor where we celebrate our historic moments." Meanwhile, back home, Maulana Karenga the founder of **KWANZAA** enquired, asked, "Can you put something positive on Facebook?" In a challenge, however, Anthony Browder, more practically insisted, "Get off Facebook and put your face in a book!"

FREDERICK MONDERSON

All this notwithstanding; the most potent idea to have been issued from the creative arsenal of the African-American experience has been the "Million Man Movement" and for this we have to thank Minister Louis Farrakhan and the **Nation of Islam**. The potency of this idea is not simply the message in the initial shibboleth but the frequency and multi-faceted nature of the tree morphing into a forest of activism, positive organizing ad organizational building as the strategy unfolds in recurring "Million anniversaries." Imagine, millions of Black men, Black woman, and people of like minds convening on the grounds of the nation's capital, in recurring and proximate anniversaries to be recognized, speak truth to power and demand justice. Then, rejuvenated in the coordinated spirit of activism to return, home and organize, educate our people and build on the momentum the Washington message delivered, perhaps President Johnson echoing the chorus "We shall overcome" reminds all concerned, Dr. King had been to the "Mountaintop" and rightfully exclaimed, "I may not get there with you, but I want you to know, we as a people will get to the promised land," for "Mine eyes have seen the glory of the coming of the Lord." His Truth Marches On!

AFRICAN NATIONALIST POETRY AND PROSE

African Nationalist Poetry and Prose Photo. Kashida Maloney and her daughter Chloe and friends at the International African Arts Festival.

African Nationalist Poetry and Prose Photo. Dr. Jack Felder and Dr. Leonard Jeffries are joined by an adoring fan who sat at their feet.

FREDERICK MONDERSON

"The Egyptians gave the world a concept of value, Maat, which was a consciously pursued objective of human agency. One may speak of Greek, Jewish, Chines, or Indian civilizations but none of these cultures seem to have a Maat-like concept. While we know that the Greek Homer was the first eloquent voice of the Greeks, Moses of the Jews advanced the Ten Commandments, the Chinese Confucius laid down the wisdom teachings, and the Hindu thinkers sought Dharma, none of these groups could pattern themselves after the Egyptian Maatian ethics. Indeed, Egypt belongs to Africa." Molefi Kete Asante. *The Afrocentric Manifesto*. 2007.

44.   "SOUTHERN SHERIFFS"
BY
DR. FRED MONDERSON

Whether it was Rod Steiger or Archie Bunker who played Sheriff Gillespie as the lawman in the movie **In the Heat of the Night**, the Black detective had to enlighten him about the intricacies and perspectives of coming to correct conclusions regarding police work. This time, two contemporary sheriffs from South Carolina and Georgia are in the news not simply for exceptional performance of their jobs but equally for statements that many consider controversial with other implications. There is another sheriff from Arizona, who also came under scrutiny because of statements and the degree with which he executed his responsibilities as they relate

AFRICAN NATIONALIST POETRY AND PROSE

to immigration and whether person are legal residents or not. However, this latter official is not the focus of this essay; his case has been known, scrutinized and settled, sort of.

The South Carolina Sheriff recently questioned President Obama ordering the American flag lowered in honor of the passing of Nelson Mandela, one of the great leaders of the 20th Century. It is interesting, at the memorial Service in South Africa in which President Obama and First Lady Michelle Obama represented this nation, he was accompanied by an American star power delegation including former Presidents Jimmy Carter, William "Bill" Clinton, and George W. Bush. First Ladies Rosalind, Hillary and Laura, respectively accompanied their husband. Chelsea Clinton was also in attendance.

Nearly 100 world leaders, active and retired, came to pay their respect to a man whose life was like no other; a unique figure in history; who inspired the world through political and personal forgiveness and thus effectuated the power of unification in a land torn apart by the crimes of apartheid standing on the precipice of a destructive race war. In anticipation of this gathering and the solemn nature of the occasion, the president's actions were prudent policy.

The other Sheriff from Valdosta, Georgia pronounced the death of a very athletically active teen-ager, Kendrick Johnson ("KJ") as a tragic

FREDERICK MONDERSON

accident claiming the young man climbed into an enormous rolled up floor mat in the gymnasium of his school. There, searching for his shoe, he ostensibly suffocated. An autopsy was performed and the family notified about the cause of death. Not satisfied with "the official version," for nearly a year, six days per week, the family staged a demonstration outside a local courthouse, bringing attention to the case and demanding more satisfactory answers. Finally, attention focused on their plight and a new interest ensued in efforts to get to the bottom of things.

Listening to the Steve Harvey **Morning Show** in New York on December 10, 2013, an attorney for the family; a Mr. Benjamin Crump who was the Trayvon Martin family attorney in that tragedy; informed on some troubling developments in the case. Mr. Crump explained the gymnasium area was under video coverage and in several angles the view was crystal clear where Mr. Johnson was clearly identified taking part in gym activities. However, the video covering that part of the gym where the potential "foul play" may have happened, where Mr. Johnson supposedly climbed into the rolled-up mat to retrieve his sneakers, that part of the film is very cloudy, essentially unidentifiable, useless. More important, however, when the family insisted on a more detailed report on the examination of the body, it turned out there was traces of blood, whose ownership the attorney did not specify. Additionally, examination of the exhumed body revealed the internal organs of Mr. Johnson were missing and his insides was stuffed

AFRICAN NATIONALIST POETRY AND PROSE

with newspapers. Even more important, Mr. Johnson's nails at the fingertips were all cut deep as if to remove all traces, potentially, of blood ostensibly indicating perhaps there was a struggle, he scratched someone and blood remained. Cutting off the fingertips was designed to get rid of potential DNA evidenced.

Now, we know in the case of suspicious death, and not from natural causes, law-enforcement conducts extensive investigations to determine the cause or death. In the case of this very healthy teenager who played baseball, football and basketball, it stands to reason he did not die of natural causes! Given that law enforcement investigates and the now coming to light revelations regarding Mr. Johnson's end, it challenges the Sheriff's firm declaration as to the cause of death. It raises a question why he never became suspicious given the now revealed facts of the case; thus, one would wonder whether he is willing to stake his career on his official cause of death declaration? Is there a cover-up? Was the Sheriff ever suspicious of events? In this day and age, how could he believe the family would accept that coca mammy story? How did he determine the kid crawled up into the folded-up mat? Again, given that law enforcement investigates, did the Sheriff put two and two together to arrive at 300? Does this sloppiness call into question other "causes of death" officials report of his office? All this force us to wonder about the behaviors of "Southern Sheriffs"

FREDERICK MONDERSON

and others whose behaviors can certainly use some scrutiny.

Well, in terms of the South Carolina Sheriff who questioned the President of the United States' decision to fly the Stars and stripes at half-mast, did he know the US has done so since 1957 for world leaders? Does this "porgy" trying to swim in "whale waters" realize such pronouncements are above his "pay grade?" Given such, is his pronouncement that the flag should only be flown at half-mast for Americans is actually an anti-Obama statement. Also given South Carolina's history as home of the virulent anti-Obamaite Senator DeMint; uncensored "You lie" Congressman Joe Wilson; and as Jessie Jackson exclaimed a few years ago, "South Carolina has 36 state prisons and 1 state college." In a stretch of the imagination, the Sheriff could easily fit in this "cabal."

These associations, notwithstanding, the Sheriff is so wrong! The United States lowered the flag for Winston Churchill, Pope Paul II and several other deserving world leaders. The interesting this is, President Obama is a very intelligent visionary whose every action, decision has been questioned, challenged, some say even sabotaged by persons acting in a "treasonous" manner and all a part of the President is a Black man; and, despite the virulent opposition designed to make his administration a failure. After all, Republican Senator Mitch McConnell expressly stated his goal "to make Barack

AFRICAN NATIONALIST POETRY AND PROSE

Obama a one term President." However, unable to prevent the President's re-election in 2012, Mr. McConnell never renounced his goal and *The New York Times* of October 6, 2013 expressly maintained and named individuals who met and planned to sabotage the President's every legislative and otherwise action on behalf of the American people! While this occurred after the 2012 election, every reason suggests the plot was effected after the 2008 election and all the principal players remained involved and named in the latest revelation.

Fast forward to the sorrowful passing of the South African leader and statesman and recognizing the personal strength of Mr. Mandela; as his health began to decline, President Obama instituted plans for a high-level American delegation to attend the funeral. This show of American Presidential star power consistent with lowering the flag was not simply above the South Carolina Sheriff's intellectual comprehension and pay grade, but as a stroke of genius he put America on the right side of history recognizing and tributing what he called Mr. Mandela, "The last great liberator of the 20th Century."

Here was a man who "earned his place in history through struggle." After the enormous suffering of South Africans for much of the 20th Century, Mr. Mandela's trials and tribulations; his lengthy prison incarceration, until global activism in its many ramifications forced the racist South African government to free this long serving prisoner. Upon his release, he held no recriminations against the whites, urged his people to peacefully accept the transfer of power and exercise the long-sought after franchise.

To set the record straight, he established a Truth and Reconciliation Commission under Bishop Desmond Tutu and the Afrikaner Reverend Byers Naude, long a critic of Apartheid.

When all is said and done, Mr. Obama has always provided excellent leadership. Despite the enormous efforts expended to sabotage his presidency, Mr. Obama always lead in the best interest of the American people and nation. History has always been the best judge of leaders and their tenure and as it has judged Mr. Mandela, so too it will judge Mr. Obama as well as the Southern Sheriffs, those mentioned here and others whose performance will ultimately become public record.

> IN ANCIENT TIMES MANS IN-
> HUMANITY TO MAN, CAUSED DIFFERENT
> GROUPS AND TRIBES TO BAN TOGETHER
> IN THEIR DEFENSE. THEY WERE WITHOUT
> PHYSICAL WEAPONS. CONSEQUENTLY
> THEY DEVELOPED THEIR GIVEN ANATOMY
> INTO A FIGHTING TOOL, WITH SYMBOLS
> OF DIFFERENT ANIMALS AND FOWLS.
> EVERY RACE ON EARTH DEVELOPED SUCH
> TOOLS. CHINA WITH SYSTEMS OF KUNG FU,
> 157 STYLES EMERGING THEREFROM;
> JAPAN WITH SYSTEM OF KARATE, NEW,

African Nationalist Poetry and Prose Photo. Self Defense techniques (2).

AFRICAN NATIONALIST POETRY AND PROSE

African Nationalist Poetry and Prose Photo. Some members of the "Monderson clan" as they join the Author at his "Books for Sale" table at the International African Arts Festival.

African Nationalist Poetry and Prose Photo. T-Shirt says – "Free Mumia."

FREDERICK MONDERSON

African National Poetry and Prose Photo. Wow. Horus in all his Red, Black and Green glory!

45. MORE THAN TEN IMPORTANT SUPREME COURT DECISIONS IN BLACK HISTORY FROM DRED SCOTT TO AFFIRMATIVE ACTION

The U.S. Supreme Court

Related Links

Milestones in Supreme Court History
Timeline: Civil Rights
Timeline: Affirmative Action
Timeline: African American History
The History of Affirmative Action
The History of Black History

AFRICAN NATIONALIST POETRY AND PROSE

Quiz: African-American History (for Kids)
500 Notable African-American Biographies
African-American Quotations
Justice Overdue: Civil Rights Cases Reopened
Dred Scott v. Sandford (1857)

Decreed a slave was his master's property and African Americans were not citizens; struck down the Missouri Compromise as unconstitutional.

Civil Rights Cases (1883)

A number of cases are addressed under this Supreme court decision. Decided that the Civil Rights Act of 1875 (the last federal civil rights legislation until the Civil Rights Act of 1957) was unconstitutional. Allowed private sector segregation.

Plessy v. Ferguson (1896)

The Court stated that segregation was *legal* and constitutional as long as "facilities were equal" — the famous "separate but equal" segregation policy.

Powell v. Alabama (1932)

The Supreme Court overturned the "Scottsboro Boys'" convictions and guaranteed counsel in state and federal courts.

FREDERICK MONDERSON

African Nationalist Poetry and Prose Photo. More art in its colorful and intricate details.

Shelley v. Kraemer (1948)

The justices ruled that a court may not constitutionally enforce a "restrictive covenant" which prevents people of certain race from *owning or occupying property.*

Brown v. Board of Education of Topeka, Kansas (1954) - Reversed *Plessy v. Ferguson* "separate but equal" ruling. "[S]egregation [in public education] is a denial of the equal protection of the laws."

Heart of Atlanta Motel, Inc. v. United States (1964)

This case challenged the constitutionality of the **Civil Rights Act of 1964**. The court ruled that the motel had no right "to select its guests as it sees fit, free from governmental regulation."

Loving v. Virginia (1967)

AFRICAN NATIONALIST POETRY AND PROSE

This decision ruled that the prohibition on interracial marriage was unconstitutional. Sixteen states that still banned interracial marriage at the time were forced to revise their laws.

Regents of the University of California v. Bakke (1978)

The decision stated that affirmative action was unfair if it led to reverse discrimination.

Grutter v. Bollinger (2003)

The decision upheld affirmative action's constitutionality in education, as long it employed a "highly individualized, holistic review of each applicant's file" and did not consider race as a factor in a "mechanical way."

> HELLO! - It's nice to see you. Welcome to our home. "Slave One" PLEASE, IN YOUR SPEECHES OR CONVERSATIONS HERE, NEVER INDULGE IN ANY RACE HATING REMARKS AGAINST: Other Groups, Colors, Religions or Races. Remember, the real God made mankind: White, Black, Brown and other colors. If you hate a person because of his color or race, you must hate God!... "THEN, WHO THE HELL ARE YOU!" Our theater, "Slave One", represents UNDERSTANDING of RESPECT and LOVE, for ALL of GOD'S HUMANITY! Please feel at home here in our theater. We know who you are. We love you all the Best to you. COME AGAIN PLEASE. God Bless You.

African Nationalist Poetry and Prose Photo. **Slave Theater's** Welcome invitation.

FREDERICK MONDERSON

African Nationalist Poetry and Prose Photo. Dr. James McIntosh, Co-Chair of **CEMOTAP** at the podium addressing his audience at another of his highly informative forums.

46. STATEMENT OF PURPOSE BY DR. FRED MONDERSON

The strategy utilized in these reading selections is designed to develop critical problem-solving tools of analysis in the young scholar to further develop intellectual autonomy. In this approach focused primarily within an African-American centered cultural framework, the student is encouraged to

AFRICAN NATIONALIST POETRY AND PROSE

focus on and tap into all forms of literary, grammatical tools to enhance the reading process but more particularly to emphasize and learn from the wide and varied significant accomplishments of the African-American experience. Students in general and African-Americans in particular need to be familiar with contributions African people worldwide have made to the pageantry of humanity's progress, certainly over the last 10,000 years. As such, then, and in order to cultivate the methodology and framework of mind inherent in intellectual autonomy, the student must first identify and develop the basic building blocks of literacy paramount in the standard language of the culture.

In this:

Grammar, punctuation, spelling, dictionary usage, writing skills and much more will be emphasized and enhanced.

Types of sentences, main idea, cause and effect, comparison and contrast, types of questions, sequencing, use of analogy, paragraph identification, and building, transition of ideas, cultural themes and application engaged in historical method. Various forms of method will be emphasized and students encouraged to apply these important tools writing skills in focused assignments.

FREDERICK MONDERSON

Throughout the reading process emphasis will be placed on vocabulary identification and development, use of analogy as a tool in critical, comparative analysis, and the identification of historical distortion and selective, even purposeful omission to bring into focus counterbalancing the former, all in an effort to correct and emphasize historical misconceptions.

The structure of the selections, emphasizing not simply vocabulary definitions, syllabication, parts of speech, cultural vocabulary, catch-phrases, as well as questions on the subject matter will encourage writing on the various aspects of the material presented. In addition, to answer to specific questions, student sill be encouraged to comment in oral and discussion mode and in writing form, "What do you think of the new information?" "How has it shaped your view of the past?"

Use of vocabulary to strengthen reading and writing, spelling, and a whole host of tools such as synonyms, antonyms, forms of nouns and verbs, adjectives and adverbs, punctuation, whether commas and periods; semicolon and colon; apostrophe, hyphen, capitalization, prefixes and suffixes; but most particularly recognition of the 8-parts of speech, viz., nouns, pronouns, verbs, adjectives, adverbs, conjunctions, propositions, interjections.

AFRICAN NATIONALIST POETRY AND PROSE

African Nationalist Poetry and Prose Photo. Basir Mchawi and a friend at the International African Arts Festival.

Even finding parts of speech such as verbs, nouns, subject, object, subject-very agreement, clauses and phrases, even the use of quotation marks, italics, parentheses and brackets will be components will be asked to further investigate to strengthen their reasoning skills to enhance the desired intellectual autonomy outcome.

African Nationalist Poetry and Prose Photo. Tribute to the Ancestors – Image, 2019.

FREDERICK MONDERSON

47. CAN WE TRUST REPUBLICANS?
BY
DR. FRED MONDERSON

"Our want of trust justifies the deceit of others." La Rochefoucauld!

In a recently concluded New Hampshire Republican presidential debate, the contenders certainly looked impressive on paper, as the pundits debated who did well. While the candidates made their case as to whom, a year from today, will be their party's standard bearer, one weak link in their chain may have been evident from an answer given to a question by the Moderator John King. Mr. King asked Congressman Ron Paul, one of the eight hopefuls, "Can you think of one good thing President Obama has done for the economy?" Either Ron Paul did not want to appear a lover of President Obama, soft among his colleagues, or he is a downright liar or does not remember well; perhaps this malady comes with age.

Some years ago, President Number 43, George Bush, was asked "Can you think of one bad thing you have done in your Presidency?" The President thought long and hard, racking his brains for an iota, then he replied in the negative. "I cannot remember anything I have done wrong in my Presidency." Not that "Mission was Accomplished;" or even one day

AFRICAN NATIONALIST POETRY AND PROSE

choosing the wrong tie or cuff links with the right shirt can be considered. It's generally believed, Mr. Bush is a piece of work! The same line of reasoning characterized Congressman Paul, both in question and answer. This makes him so "Bushesque!" But, does this mean if elected President, despite what he says, there will be no more wars; foreclosures will not rise; unemployment rates will not quadruple; Wall Street will not tank; and the world will not again have a negative view of the United States?

Since history tends to repeat itself, maybe Barack Obama will comeback, again rescue the nation from its economic ditch and Sarah Palin, "Joe the Plumber," Senator DeMint, even Joe Wilson will ask for an encore! Even more important, perhaps, Donald Trump will insist on prolonging the "Birthers" issue.

Congressman Ron Paul could have responded, if he remembered, after thinking for a while; the December 2010 bill he voted for, where the wealthy Republican base got a hefty tax break, could have been a good thing for the economy. But it was not; it was simply a "money grab for the Republican base," the rich, that is! To Mr. King's question and holding the President's feet over the fire; to get that concession in the Bill which Republicans voted overwhelmingly for was either good for the economy or Republican would appear hypocrites voting adamantly for a measure that did not help the nation's economic situation but only benefitted the "One Percent."

Equally, the "Debt Ceiling Debate," where Republicans held the President and the American people hostage, is another example of Mr. Obama making concessions and taking heat for appearing bipartisan in a seemingly hopeless situation. In many respects, after Speaker John Boehner had disrespected President Obama by not returning his phone calls and had been in contact with the Media, he was ultimately able to boast "We've gotten 98 percent of what we wanted." Right after the negotiations, Senator Mitch McConnell of publicly stated "I intend to make Barack Obama a one term President" fame, gave his now famous thumbs-up, a veiled communicated boast "I got that Nigger" in the White House! and won for my base in congruence with Speaker Boehner's boast of besting the President. As these events unfolded, it would be naïve for anyone to believe what may seem disparate elements of the Republican Party and its associates, that they do not coordinate various avenues of their strategy in attacks on President Obama.

For example, a number of early Ads against the President have been not simply negative but also false. Americans for Prosperity financed by David H. and Charles G. Koch have been behind criticism of the President because of his support for a tax increase on those making high incomes. Equally, the Conservative Advocacy group Crossroads of Carl

AFRICAN NATIONALIST POETRY AND PROSE

Rove recently spent some $2.6 million in a negative Ad charging "President Obama, it's time to attack problems, not people." This is because he had been speaking out about Republican behavior towards him. No one in recent memory has been more attacked, ad hominem and performance wise, than Mr. Obama. Yet, Republicans want "blood out of their stone!" Thus, without a doubt, every "victory" of the Republicans against President Obama is also a victory over the American people. It's like the one percent and more against the ninety nine percent and less. We know who is winning!

Let us remember, on his assumption of the Presidency Mr. Obama, as the nation's Chief Executive, inherited an America losing more than 500,000 jobs per month. The Housing Industry experienced severe hemorrhage with new construction at a standstill and foreclosures on the rise. The Auto Industry experienced severe challenges from foreign competitors whose autos promised greater performance, better fuel efficiency and labor costs that were below American standards. As a result, the industry needed significant government assistance to avoid bankruptcy. In rescuing the Auto Industry, Mr. Obama not just saved many jobs of an industry America pioneered but he insisted on reorganization, better efficiency in performance, management and operation. This resulted in these companies becoming much more productive and competitive. In this, they have not simply held their own of market share but have also been increasing sales, particularly due to Japan's nuclear troubles.

With the fall of AIG and Bears Stearns, the nation's financial and economic sectors were greatly in need of regulation, reform and resuscitation. So much so, the government bailout Mr. Obama's advisors recommended, not simply rescued the banking industry and Wall Street financial sectors but allowed them to be put on a firmer footing. For example, by the time of Mr. Obama's first day in office, the DOW industrial numbers had plummeted somewhere between 6500-7000! Today it stands at approximately 11,500! This particular rescue was so significant; Wall Street, to the consternation of many, began issuing tremendous bonuses to its traders. Since the CEOs and traders were making big bonuses and corporations were also reporting gains, then industry, investors of these firms, corporations, and such entities were benefitting. For example, if we were to possibly accept the Republican Romney's contention that "Corporations are people too;" then Barack Obama benefitted the economy by way of enabling Corporations and the American investors to be profitable. Thus, in this way, through his initial policies of bailout, coupled with financial and economic reform and regulation; unquestionably, President Obama brought the American economy back from the precipice of collapse with even greater global impact.

AFRICAN NATIONALIST POETRY AND PROSE

African Nationalist Poetry and Prose Photo. Minister Hafeez Mohammed and Drs. Johnson and Tyrene Wright at another of **CEMOTAP'S** enlightening Presentations.

African Nationalist Poetry and Prose Photo. The "Bones of Samuel Carson" on way to "Open the Door of Return" in Ghana, West Africa.

FREDERICK MONDERSON

African Nationalist Poetry and Prose Photo.
Art in its many forms

African Nationalist Poetry and Prose Photo.
More baskets.

AFRICAN NATIONALIST POETRY AND PROSE

African Nationalist Poetry and Prose Photo. Inside the "Shrine of the Ancestors" at the Internationalist African Arts Festival.

Seems **Psalms** 2: 12 - had Barack Obama's efforts in mind in the saying: "Blessed are all they that put their trust in him!"

However, one has to wonder if people like Mitch McConnell, John Boehner, Senator DeMint and others who often parrot the "I like the President" party line; if they had "truly shown the man love from day one," the American economy and social situation would have been far better today.

Without question, every commentator at home and abroad has recognized and given the President credit

FREDERICK MONDERSON

for bringing the nation's economy back from the brink of economic collapse. Now, for the Republicans; either they were "out to lunch," grabbing "98 percent" for their special interest base, and the likes of Ron Paul, either have "clouded vision," bad memory or are downright liars if they cannot think of any one thing good that Mr. Obama has done for the economy! Then again, the "Party of No" could never say Yes!

That same "Party of No" whose affiliates as the "Tea Party Movement," militias and other right-wing groups hammered Barack Obama on way to and in the White House; and together with their allies in Congress littered the path of Mr. Obama creating a minefield to sabotage his every legislative initiative. Still, he persevered in passing Lilly Ledbetter Equal Pay Law, Health Care Reform, Credit Card Reform, Student Loan Aid Reform, and a slew of social programs to benefit broad segments of the American populace.

Recognizing that along every journey an imprint is made, Republicans and their allies have said some of the darnest things about Mr. Obama. We know "Joe the Plumber" called Mr. Obama a "socialist" which stuck. Significantly, this became a campaign issue and in the debate between John McCain and candidate Obama, Joe's name was mentioned more than twenty times. Still Obama persevered! Today, Governor Rick Perry released an Ad parroting this ancient line of socialism. Next Sarah Palin charged

AFRICAN NATIONALIST POETRY AND PROSE

"Obama is not like us" and "we must take our country back." Among her other nonsensical mis-statements, Ms. Palin also said, "I can see Russia from my front porch." However, many commentators expressed even this statement was incorrect.

Senator Mitch McConnell, Republican Minority leader, seemed to have let slip an intent now called the "McConnell Mandate" of his commitment to make Barack Obama a "one term President." What is significant about this statement, with his "McConnell's Mandate," the Senator may have honed this strategy with any number of individuals and groups of like minds with the same objective to thwart and stop Obama! While this was a "day one" strategy, it could have also been a contingency plan from the time he announced his candidacy for the Presidency.

When the President proposed his Health Care Reform Agenda, this legislative action generated a great deal of animosity among Republicans whose efforts on the street painted the President in the most malicious manner imaginable through characterization that appeared honestly, racist! In Congress South Carolina's Senator DeMint exhorted, "If we could derail Obama's Health Care Reform Agenda, this would be his Waterloo!" Then he added more malicious fuel saying he likes the President but that Mr. Obama gives "false numbers." Chirping in, Billy Crystal admonished, "Go for the kill!" Birds of a

FREDERICK MONDERSON

feather, when the President addressed a Joint House of Congress to some given data, Carolina Congressman Joe Wilson retorted disrespectfully "You lie!"

Seems like not only are the Republicans not to be trusted but they are also tremendously disrespectful of the Presidency and this latter is especially so because of President Obama's race. One scholar likes to say, "Blacks may be crazy, but they are not dumb." Blacks are observing all these developments particularly how these people are treating their hero, a man of high integrity and unquestioned patriotism, all because he is Black!

African Nationalist Poetry and Prose Photo. Two Muslim Sisters join Dr. Wright at her **CEMOTAP** Presentation.

AFRICAN NATIONALIST POETRY AND PROSE

Even though the economy got better but not great, the attacks against Obama continued unabated. That is, while the nation is not losing 500,000 jobs per month it is only adding low 100,000 jobs. Still, the Republican wealthy base that got tax cuts for the last 10 years have not helped in creating jobs but everyone blames the President who must contend with Republicans at war with him. Are we to believe the Republicans are terrorists? Imagine, noble men and a woman attacking each other to be first to challenge an even greater noble! Yet, these Republican presidential debate attacks make seriously false statements that have exposed a sinister side of these contenders as they wade into Mr. Obama. Earlier Speaker Boehner remarked "I like the President," still he remains committed to the "McConnell Mandate." On the other hand, Megan McCain, daughter of John McCain opined, "I like the President and am praying for him to succeed." Meanwhile, from the bottom of the pile, Rick Santorum has charged, "President Obama is dividing the country." Whereas, President Obama was attacked before he got to the White House, while he resides there and perhaps even after he leaves! A more sinister charge of Rick Santorum is that President Obama has "poisoned the well!" Can honest men, in this modern world, accuse the President of the United States, of using "poison" against the nation he took an oath to defend and administer even as he has spent the last three years eliminating some of its most feared enemies, has

FREDERICK MONDERSON

rescued its economic slide and improved its image abroad! This is a serious charge! However, either the former Senator does not understand the potency of his language or such language is truly reflective of the nature of the man. Maybe Republican voters truly understand this issue more than any other and that is why Mr. Santorum gets low marks.

"The man that hath no music in himself,
Nor is not mov'd with concord of sweet sounds,
Is fit for treasons, stratagems, and spoils;
The motions of his spirit are dull as night,
And his affectations hard as Erebus

Let no such man be trusted" says Shakespeare in *The Merchant of Venice* V, i, 83

Former Speaker Newt Gingrich has been described as highly intellectual, yet, unintentionally he has betrayed the true nature of the opposition to President Obama in the statement, "The day after Obama's defeat jobs will return to America!" A good question is whether this statement is accidental or a design?

AFRICAN NATIONALIST POETRY AND PROSE

African Nationalist Poetry and Prose Photo. Muslim Sisters embrace Dr. Johnson at her **CEMOTAP** Presentation.

African Nationalist Poetry and Prose Photo. The Logo of the International African Arts Festival.

FREDERICK MONDERSON

African Nationalist Poetry and Prose Photo. Luis, Erismell and Erik at the International African Arts Festival.

African National Poetry and Prose Photo. Baba (right) and fellows with a view inside the "Ancestor Shrine" at the International African Arts Festival.

AFRICAN NATIONALIST POETRY AND PROSE

African Nationalist Poetry and Prose Photo. Dr. James McIntosh and Sister Betty Dopson, Co-Chairs of **CEMOTAP** at the Mike with young Erik Monderson at the 31st Annual Celebration.

African Nationalist Poetry and Prose Photo. Tribute to the Ancestors – Image, 2019.

FREDERICK MONDERSON

African Nationalist Poetry and Prose Photo. A side assortment of carved sculptures emanating from West Africa at the International African Arts Festival.

Even Governor Rick Perry of Texas made a charge that President Obama is elitist being raised in a "privileged" background. From a man who has

AFRICAN NATIONALIST POETRY AND PROSE

enjoyed both parents accusing a person with no parents, such talk is more than ingenuous. Former Massachusetts Governor Mitt Romney recently released an Ad criticizing the President, deemed to be based on falsity; but Michele Bachman takes the cake. Imagine, Congresswoman Michele Bachmann accused President Obama of "running a gangster government in Washington, DC." In the heart of a nation of laws, with such great power and oversight it should be criminal to utter that the leader is a "gangster." That he heads a "gangster government." Imagine Vice President Joe Biden, who spent more than three decades in service to the nation, would countenance to serving second to a "gangster" which makes him a "gangster" also!

"They that put their trust in him shall understand the truth." The **Wisdom of Solomon** 3: 9

Now this cursory sketch is just a fraction of insidious Republican behavior towards President Obama. Republicans seems to be playing to win by whatever means necessary, even if false and disrespectful claims are made in process. As President Obama has said, "Republicans drove the car into a ditch and now they want the keys again." But, the American people can see through this deception and will deny them leadership of the country because, perhaps, Republicans cannot be trusted with the true welfare of the nation; that is, well-being of all of the American people!

FREDERICK MONDERSON

African Nationalist Poetry and Prose Photo. Part of the audience listening to Dr. Johnson and Dr. Wright at another **CEMOTAP** Presentation.

"I don't care whether you're driving a hybrid or an SUV. If you're headed for a cliff, you have to change direction. That's what the American people called for in November, and that's what we intend to deliver." Barack Obama

48. ORIGINAL BOYS WEARING HOODS BY DR. FRED MONDERSON

Make no mistake the "Original Boys Wearing Hoods" were members of the Ku Klux Klan and many have argued they metamorphosed into elements of the "Tea Party Movement's"

AFRICAN NATIONALIST POETRY AND PROSE

conservatism as a new assertion of the Klan, born of a hatred that never seems to end! Much of this is evidenced in the manner they attacked the First African-American President Barack Obama. Suppressed by the federal government's use of marshals and troops authorized under the Force Acts of 1870 and 1871, the Klan's terrorism was halted during Reconstruction though it was replaced by Jim Crowism and similar sinister strategies in alliance with the southern white power structure who influenced poor whites through the notion of white supremacy against political action by the newly freed African-American. However, by 1915, the year the "Grandfather Clause" was repealed, the Klan rose again to fight, as Unger states, "for native born, white, gentile Americans" against Negroes, Jews, Catholics and foreigners. By the end of World War I, Klan members were incensed by black soldiers returning from Europe, as Lerone Bennett, Jr. says in *Confrontation: Black and White* (1966: 121) because Blacks had been "killing white men and sleeping with white women." In the post-war years they gained attention by distributing literature and selling Klan paraphernalia; so much so, membership increased to more than five million members in the 1920s. But, as Unger (1971: 120) writes, "By 1927, however, the Klan had begun to overreach itself and its excesses of violence and vigilante tactics, as well as the corrupt and immoral behavior of some of its leaders, repelled many Americans. By the end of the decade, it had declined leaving behind an ugly legacy of hatred and violence endorsed in the name of one hundred percent Americanism."

Nevertheless, this terror group continued to function somewhat openly, somewhat under cover though somewhat checked by strategies of black assertiveness and many believe the election of Barack Obama galvanized that brotherhood of sinister behavior; only at this later time the hoods were replaced by casuals and business suits, still in the name of conservatism. However, while the Civil War Amendments were designed to free and empower the ex-slave, southern conservatism engaged a number of devious strategies to regain power and limit black new-found effectiveness. In one instance, Irwin Unger's *American History* II: *Reconstruction to Present*, New York: Monarch Press (1971: 7) ties southern Conservatives to the Ku Klux Klan in the following statement: "Some of these Southern Conservatives were happy to use the regular political process to achieve their ends. Others were willing to use violence and intimidation against Scalawags, Carpetbaggers, and Negroes. The more violent conservatives organized groups like the Ku Klux Klan, a secret society founded in 1866 to help 'redeem' the South from Radicals, black and white. The Klan was most active between 1868 and 1870 when its members, dressed in white sheets and hoods, threatened, beat and even killed supporters of the Radical state governments."

AFRICAN NATIONALIST POETRY AND PROSE

This was generally in response to events of 1867 in which, as Lerone Bennett in *Before the Mayflower* (1964) (1978: 196) writes: "During the summer and fall of 1867, the Negro masses were stirred by an unparalleled ferment of political activity. Negroes flocked to huge open-air meetings, registered and organized political groups. Leaders emerged from the masses and demanded political and civil equality. The white South was stunned. It was believed at first that 'Sambo' would fall flat on his face. But the freedmen disappointed their late masters: They demonstrated a real genius for what one writer called 'the lower political arts.'" Explaining Klan origins and intent, Bennett continued further (1978: 196-197) that the first national meeting of the Klan occurred in April 1867, Room 10 at the Maxwell House in Nashville where in attendance were: "Confederate generals, colonels, substantial men of church and state, from Georgia, from Alabama, from all over. The leader: Nathan Bedford Forest, the strong man of the Fort Pillow Massacre. The plan: reduce Negroes to political impotence. How? By the boldest and most ruthless political operation in American history. By stealth and murder, by economic intimidation and political assassination, by whippings and maimings, cuttings and shootings, by the knife, by the rope, by the whip. By the political use of terror, by the braining of the baby in its mother's arms, the slaying of the husband at his wife's feet, the raping of the wife before the husband's eyes. By fear. Soon the South was

FREDERICK MONDERSON

honeycombed with secret organizations: The Knights of the White Camelia, the Red Shirts, the White League, Mother's Little Helpers and the Baseball Club of the First Baptist Church."

In a somewhat prejudiced analysis attempting to explain the above dynamics, William Dunning of the "Dunning School" at Columbia University, according to Norman Hodges's *Black History*, New York: Monarch Press (1974: 113) theorized an interpretation on influential events in the South following the Civil War, of which the last of five states how: "driven to desperation by misrule, the long suffering Southerners formed vigilante groups like the Ku Klux Klan to rescue the region from the carpetbagger regime." Hodges (1974: 113) continued his insight by stating further: "Morison has summed up the imagery of the Dunning interpretation in these words: 'The accepted fable represents Reconstruction as the ruthless attempt of Northern politicians to subject the white South, starving and helpless, to an abominable rule by ex-slaves … and from which it was rescued by white-hooded knights on horseback who put the Negro 'back where he belonged.'" However, in *The Afro-American in United States History* (1972: 211-212) Da Silva, Finkelstein and Loshin remind us in this new advantage "the men who gained power in Southern local and state governments could do much as they pleased. The power of the Federal government was not used to protect rights. That left each town, county

AFRICAN NATIONALIST POETRY AND PROSE

or state its own master. The KKK and groups like it could attack a black person without fear of real punishment. The men who owned newspapers in the south began to work with the political leaders and KKK groups. They filled the minds with Jim Crow ideas. Terror silenced all men, white and black, who could not agree with them. They forced all of the south to accept Jim Crow." In this, "White men in the south built a wall between themselves and all blacks. They did this by laws and customs that pushed black people lower and lower. Rich and poor whites worked together to make this wall higher and higher. Rich men did it so they could keep their wealth and power. Poor whites did it to feel better than someone – in his case the Afro-American." Today we ask, 'Is that where we're heading' as we listen to the rhetoric of the conservative right wing?

Thus, as "forward to the Past" Newt Gingrich and "Poison the well" Rick Santorum vie to be considered the most conservative one has to wonder if this is where they want to take the Negro and the nation? After all, and we must never forget, as Hodges (1974: 117) writes: "The historical record strongly supports the view that the former rebel White South was unrepentant and vengeful in its treatment of Blacks during the two years of home rule that followed in the wake of war (1865-1867). A Black doctor, Daniel Norton, of Williamsburg, Virginia, described the situation to a Congressional Subcommittee, in 1866 [where he states]: '… the spirit of the whites against

FREDERICK MONDERSON

the blacks is much worse than it was before the war …" In addition, he declared Klan behavior was such that blacks 'would be in danger of being hunted and killed.' In many respects, a century and a half later this attitude has continued though the law has more vigorously prosecuted such practitioners.

If we explore this some more, we recognize it's a fact, "Newspapers tell the story of a nation" and that "One picture can tell a thousand words" but equally one movie can graphically implant images in the mind that, on the one hand, paints a picture of events but also send a message of past issues or a reminder to others of returning to behaviors of the past. Take for example, the movie **Ten Commandments**, perhaps the most shown of all produced films; about ancient Egypt but purportedly shot in Arizona and seen thousands of times around the world; it is a great distortion yet considered "gospel" in the minds of many. Additionally, Dr. Yosef ben-Jochannan always railed about social upheaval events in this nation that preceded the return showing of **Gone with the Wind**, while the book The Clansman by Thomas Dixon is another example of a moving tale, depicted in the movie Birth of a Nation portraying Klan misdeeds. In *Race*: *The History of An Idea in America* (1963) (1968: 339-340) Thomas F. Gossett writes Birth of a Nation's "version of history is frankly and crudely racist. The last half of the movie deals with the horrors of carpetbagger and Negro rule in South Carolina during the Reconstruction. Negroes are shown wildly reveling at elections,

AFRICAN NATIONALIST POETRY AND PROSE

voting with both hands, and keeping the white man from the polls by force. As members of the state legislature, Negroes sit with their hats on and their bare feet on the desks as they drink liquor from flasks and pass an intermarriage law. The leading white Radical Reconstructionist in the North is shown with his Negro mistress. In the climax of the film, a renegade Negro pursues a young white girl through the woods. In order to avoid rape, she leaps to her death from a high rock. Her brother leads a mob to lynch the Negro and then organize a unit of the Ku Klux Klan to regain control of society by white men. He breaks up a crowd of rioting Negroes just in time to save another white girl from forced marriage with the mulatto lieutenant-governor. The film was one of the great box-office successes of all time; millions of Americans flocked to see it and to absorb its 'message'"

African Nationalist Poetry and Prose Photo. Brother Minister Hafeez Mohammed and members of his entourage at **CEMOTAP**.

FREDERICK MONDERSON

African Nationalist Poetry and Prose Photo.
Ben Jealous at **NAN's 2018 Convention**.

African Nationalist Poetry and Prose Photo.
Sure, you're right, sign!

AFRICAN NATIONALIST POETRY AND PROSE

African Nationalist Poetry and Prose Photo.
Rasta holding Ankh.

FREDERICK MONDERSON

Even Gene Hackman's movie **Mississippi Burning** painted a grim reality of events that is a powerful reminder of behaviors still not extricated from the history or current practicing mindset of some in this nation.

Recently, within the last week, the movie **Oh Brother, Where Art Thou** was shown on a local channel. While the general theme said one thing, thousands of words of a photograph and one million of a movie enabled people with vision to see the subliminal messages extrapolated from imaged realities past and present.

One particular scene in **Oh Brother**, while it never got to that horrifying scene of a "hung and burning black man" as in **The Great Debaters**, or as in **The Black Book** showing "a roasting black man" surrounded by jeering white men, the movie scene depicts the Ku Klux Klan in full panoply, battledress, white uniforms, in measured formation in white headgear as the "Original Boys Wearing Hoods." While a seeming glimpse of a colorful spectacle, the scene is actually a microcosm of longstanding practice of terrorism against the African enslaved in America, dehumanized and debased in a system practicing lynchings, tar and feathers, intimidation, denial of human and civil rights, Blacks discriminated against at the ballot box and even killed. So much so, commentators have labeled the

AFRICAN NATIONALIST POETRY AND PROSE

decades following the Civil War that destroyed the system perpetuating the "Crime against humanity" within the Institution of Slavery as the "Classic Age of American domestic terrorism." This is because institutions of men on horsebacks and in hoods, particularly in collaboration with the white southern elite spewed carnage against black men, women and children in this nation as they sought to instill and reinforce a false notion of white supremacy. What was not apparent at the time, contrary to some of America's greatest theorists, the African or Negro in America was never inferior mentally but got inferior treatment in a land that boasted of freedom and equality.

Another interesting thing about **Oh Brother**, it reinforced the view of Ku Klux Klan as an organized and regimented racist system. However, like all organisms in nature, these do not terminate themselves but evolve in strategy, tactics, make-up, all forcefully albeit, designed to perpetuate their founding philosophy. In this manner they attract new converts to their way of thinking despite new generations' attempts to distance themselves from that disdainful past.

The **CBS** public affairs program **60 Minutes** ran an episode of the **FBI** investigating one of more than one hundred unsolved Civil Rights murder cases in Mississippi and elsewhere in the South. The subject

FREDERICK MONDERSON

of one case in particular was still alive but no one was talking except the victim's family members. The FBI's lead detective did say, in the climate of the time anyone who wanted to run for any office had to be a member or espouse the philosophy of the hooded terrorist groups as the KKK, Knights of the White Camellia, White Citizens Council and so on. None of these groups truly disbanded, revoked their philosophy or left their area of operation. They may have gone underground, changed their tactics and their attire from hoods to business suits, studied the law to more effectively get around it and been elected to government as conservatives serving as clogs in the system or patronage mills for people of similar minds, yet still continuing to recruit members. Thus, thinking people must wonder, particularly when presidential candidates, seeking to unseat President Obama tell how conservative they are, one has to wonder, is there a connection with past terrorism?

African Nationalist Poetry and Prose Photo. Sure, **BLACK LIVES MATTER**!

AFRICAN NATIONALIST POETRY AND PROSE

"The final responsibility of African history is the responsibility of scholars of African descent." John Henrik Clarke. *Address to the Regional Conference on Afro American History.* University of Detroit. (May 11-13, 1967), "A New Approach to African history."

49. POEM TO IMHOTEP BY DR. FRED MONDERSON

O Divine Imhotep, you are the greatest of the great Africans, man of wisdom, seer.
Your name, deeds and attributes span millennia,
Adjudged the world's first multi-genius
Your intellectual gifts to the world are manifold.
You are famed as High Priest, architect, administrator, astronomer, and mathematician.
Nevertheless, your contributions to helping the living and dying are most revered.

As a physician your healing powers remain unparalleled. As poet, you remind mankind, 'Eat, Drink, Be Merry, for Tomorrow You Die.'
As architect your lasting contribution,
The step-Pyramid constructed at Sakkara for Pharaoh Zoser
From the Third Dynasty to Today, this monument remains erect.

FREDERICK MONDERSON

For five millennia that architectural masterpiece withstood the ravages of time

Acting as prototype for Black African achievements. It is a testimony to your stature and those mountains of Black innovations from that age of intellectual awakening of the world.
Some believe your 'Eat, Drink, Be Merry, Tomorrow you Die' a classic admonition of the ages.
Such profound philosophical realization, early establish your reputation as thinker.

As physician at the court of your esteemed monarch, you defined the parameters of the healing discipline. Still, not considered the 'father of medicine,' is a boon, for Divinity is more your station. You deserve credit for a profession, the healing art and propagation of life, so essential to humanity's future. Throughout the land of ancient Kemet temples erected proclaim your healing prowess at Karnak, Deir el Bahari, and Edfu. Equally, at Dendera, Kom Ombo, Philae, your name resounds in great reverence. Inscriptions speak of your kinship with Memphite Ptah, Black African Pygmy God of the Artisans. You are the third in the Memphite Triad, Son of Ptah, creative.

In these troubled times, your accomplishments and exploits are cherished ideals to emulate.
For millennia you undergirded the African art of healing, then praised by the Greeks as Aesculapius, their 'God of Medicine.'

AFRICAN NATIONALIST POETRY AND PROSE

You stand as symbol of Blacks entering the medical profession who must marvel
For eons a Black African has been guardian to their cherished quest, a vocation indeed noble.
All in all, Imhotep, as symbol you manifest the great intellectual, scientific and moral gifts of Africans to advance the cause of humanity.

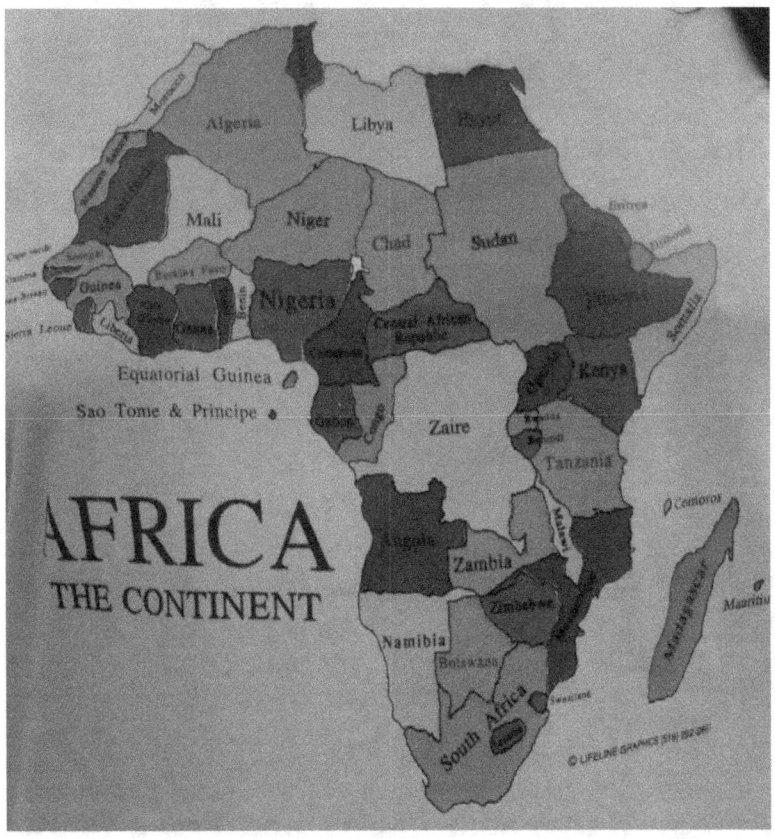

African Nationalist Poetry and Prose Photo. "**Mother Africa**" in full and colorful regalia.

FREDERICK MONDERSON

African Nationalist Poetry and Prose Photo. Members of a **Panel at NAN's 2018 Convention.**

African Nationalist Poetry and Prose Photo. Need I say more about African art!

AFRICAN NATIONALIST POETRY AND PROSE

50. VOTING RIGHTS AND REDISTRICTING BY DR. FRED MONDERSON

Attorney General Eric Holder gave an interesting speech on Tuesday December 13, 2011 at the Lyndon B. Johnson library in which he took on the issue of redistricting that has been causing some concern across the South as the nation gears up for the 2012 national elections. President Johnson, who signed the 1965 **Voting Rights Act** would have been proud of Mr. Holder whose Justice Department promises to move aggressively in reviewing, according to *The New York Times* Wednesday December 14, 2011 in which Charlie Savage's "Holder signals Tough Review of State Laws on Voting Rights" "Voting laws that civil rights advocates say will dampen minority participation in next year's election. Pulling no punches and promising to use the full weight of his department to ensure that new electoral laws are not discriminatory, the Attorney General held protecting ballot access for all eligible voters "must be viewed not only as a legal issue but as a moral imperative." Thereupon he called on all Americans to urge their "political parties to resist the temptation to suppress certain votes in the hope of attaining electoral success and, instead achieve success by appealing to more voters."

FREDERICK MONDERSON

For some time now, attention has been focusing on voting rights as it has been affected through redistricting which occurs every ten years after the census count. The argument has been made that the dominant political party in state legislatures tends to redraw the lines in a manner that benefits that party's incumbent members and the new candidates they intend to field. This method of manipulating the political boundaries has been called gerrymandering after an original theorist called Jerry. Apparently, such an individual had been assigned to draw up a particular voting district and he skewed the configuration to such an extent, one observer remarked the new district lines looked very much like a salamander. The author then responded, "This is not a salamander, it is a gerrymander!" The name stuck and so any attempt to carve unusual district voting lines that include certain groups or exclude or hinder others, is considered "Gerrymandering." However, while this "pre-carving" may not be considered illegal, it certainly is unethical and immoral in that it seeks to diffuse, limit or diminish the voting strength of one or more groups to aid or advance the cause of another to give that group an edge at upcoming elections.

Gerrymandering is not the only way in which the voting strength and ipso facto voting power of different, albeit minority groups are targeted as part of a general strategy of disfranchisement. In various regions of the country people convicted of a felony

AFRICAN NATIONALIST POETRY AND PROSE

are deprived of their voting rights. Some have argued in several southern states the criminal justice system is used as a mechanism to disfranchise minorities who disproportionately comprise prison populations. In this, the argument has been made that misdemeanor criminal behavior is oftentimes elevated to felony standard and as such these individuals are removed from the voting rolls. Advocates for these dispossessed persons have argued once a person has paid the debt to society then all of these natural and civil as well as political rights should be reinstated.

Another method used to purge the voting rolls is to insist people who have not voted in recent elections be deemed ineligible. However, while this may create a gray area, nefarious individuals with a party agenda often take the initiative and remove persons in unscrupulous move. This form of behavior is a throwback to the past civil war era when southern voting and polling individuals went to great lengths to deny and invalidate the intent of the 13th, 14th and 15th Amendments that followed the conflict. To recall, southern polling officials required of freedmen that they take literacy tests, show proof of property qualification, evidence of paid poll taxes and they even invented a "grandfather clause" which held, if one's grandfather had voted, then regardless of one's literacy, intellectual or other qualifying factors they were entitled to vote. Naturally, Blacks who had been enslaved and denied the ballot previously were

FREDERICK MONDERSON

automatically disqualified. For more than four decades the "Grandfather clause" held sway and helped and hurt voters until it was declared unconstitutional by the Supreme Court in 1915. Matching these "legal machinations" of voting denial, threats and intimidation in face of a national government turning a deaf ear, black voting rights had been effectively nullified and a manipulated "White Primary" further alienated those who were hardy enough to attempt to exercise the franchise.

There is evidence of white men with guns at polling stations and this was designed to intimidate black voters. The secret nature of the ballot was betrayed and an individual's voting preference was reported to his employer the next day almost certainly to get him fired from a hard-won job. In addition, signs indicating polling sites were often turned around sending voters in the wrong direction to be often waylaid by highwaymen as all part of the conspiracy to nullify black and other minorities' votes. These sinister deeds do not exhaust efforts to block legitimate black ballot expression. What is interesting, as later as the 2008 national election Republicans engaged in similar dishonest practices such as insisting on "Day One" Republicans vote and on "Day Two" Democrats vote. This was designed to confuse persons not really astute about the process. People were informed if they had outstanding warrants or parking tickets the police would be there to arrest them if they tried to vote. People's jobs were threatened if they tried to vote and a whole lot more

AFRICAN NATIONALIST POETRY AND PROSE

strategies were used to dissuade would-be voters who tended to vote democratic. In addition to the above, disqualification methods may be mentioned "mental incompetents, election law violator and vagrants."

While the 13th Amendment freed the slaves, the 14th gave citizenship to persons born in the United States and the 15th Amendment, adopted in 1870, forbade any state from denying persons the right to vote because of race, color, or previous condition of servitude. Jack C. Plano and Milton Greenberg in *The American Political Dictionary* (1962) (1989: 71) summed up the significance of the Fifteenth Amendment. To explain this, they wrote: "Although the Fifteenth Amendment does not give anyone an absolute right to vote, it does prohibit any discrimination because of race or color. Not until recent years have blacks made significant advances in realizing the goals established by the amendment. In 1960, for example, the Supreme Court ruled that the racial gerrymandering of Tuskegee, Alabama, so as to exclude all Black voters from city elections violated the Fifteenth Amendment (*Gomillion v. Lightfoot*, 364 U.S. 339). The **Civil Rights Acts** of 1957, 1960, 1964 and the **Voting Rights Act** of 1965, 1970, and 1975 war passed by Congress and the Twenty-Fourth Amendment prohibiting poll taxes was adopted to aid backs in overcoming the various devices used by some southern states to frustrate the purposes of the Fifteenth Amendment."

FREDERICK MONDERSON

It may well be that history has repeated itself as gerrymandering is being driven in the rush to redistrict in the several states and as such Attorney General Eric Holder's intervention is not only timely but necessary.

We recognize time is up for the process of redrawing political boundaries based on the newest census data is due to determine how recourses and representation in local school board, city council, county commission and state legislatures. However, what led to the Attorney general's intervention is the manner several state legislatures under Republican control seem to rush to target black areas that potentially vote democratic.

"I can make a firm pledge, under my plan, no family making less than $250,000 a year will see any form of tax increase. Not your income tax, not your payroll tax, not your capital gains taxes, not any of your taxes." Barack Obama

"We have a huge opportunity, at this moment, to bring manufacturing back. But we have to seize it. Tonight, my message to business leaders is simple: Ask yourselves what you can do to bring jobs back to your country and your country will do everything we can to help you succeed." Barack Obama, State of the Union Address, January 2012

AFRICAN NATIONALIST POETRY AND PROSE

"My only concern was to get home after a hard day's work." Rosa Parks (Commenting on why she refused to leave a "white only" seat on a bus December 17, 1978)

51. LAWMAKERS IN HOODIES
BY
DR. FRED MONDERSON

Taking the law into their own hands, several lawmakers have made a clear and unmistakable statement by wearing a "Hoodie" on the floor of their legislature. First, the **New York Post** of Tuesday March 27, 2012 featured a photograph of New York State Senators Kevin Parker, Bill Perkins and Eric Adams wearing Hoodies "in Albany yesterday in tribute to Trayvon" which said "The demonstration of minorities by policies was born here in New York City!" Now, Congressman Bobby Rush (D. Illinois) has been removed from the U.S. House of Representatives chamber for wearing a "Hoodie" on the floor of that legislative body while giving a speech on Trayvon Martin, the young man shot to death by Neighborhood-Watch Volunteer George Zimmerman. The significance of such social protest within a legislative body seems designed to call attention for government to more closely view this case, examine existing laws that actually undercut citizens' rights and equality by even more serious

FREDERICK MONDERSON

undercurrents taking Black-Americans more seriously.

Every American takes pride in their ethnic heritage and so does the African American. When Barack Obama declared his candidacy for the Presidency of the United States, having declared his ethnicity, African Americans took great pride in seeing a Black man with a black wife and two lovely daughters representing the best of an American family. They turned out in droves to vote for Mr. Obama for President to be part of the historic moment when the nation would elect its first African to the nation's highest office. After all, we have experienced the first Black Governor, senator, Congressman, Police Captain, Corrections Officer, General, Admiral, Cabinet member and so much more. Therefore, many argued, the nation was ready for a Black President, Commander-In-Chief and a Black First Lady and a Black First Family. Many people hailed this as the beginning of a "post-racial America." However, subsequent events proved this was wishful thinking because of the many "fifth wheels to the coach" and the numerous individuals setting backfires that did nothing but agonize the soul of this nation.

Many people argued the birth of the "Tea Party Movement" was an outgrowth of the Ku Klux Klan with the same racist outlook as they evolved from white hoods to business suits. As they caricatured the President, observers noticed the racial animosity in the attacks. Yet, Mr. Obama, smart as he is and more

AFRICAN NATIONALIST POETRY AND PROSE

American than most of the critics of his birthright and patriotism dismissed those roasting simply as "youthful temper tantrums." However, others saw a more sinister side to it. African Americans complained, "Look at how they are treating the President, our hero!" The "Tea Party" attacked the president! They questioned his birthright, his religion, his patriotism, his leadership skills, his right to be Commander-In-Chief, his sincerity, his numbers and his judgment. No one said anything to challenge this venomous behavior from in and outside of government. Race baiters accused the President of going to change the constitutional right to bear arms and in response they stocked up on armaments in preparation for a race war they thought would come but didn't.

When Mr. Obama set about tackling the many challenges facing the American nation such as profuse job loss, home foreclosures, Wall Street in rapid retreat, the auto industry failing miserably, deterioration of social and physical infrastructure, education in decline, while two wars waged in Iraq and Afghanistan, Al Qaeda terrorists threatening, Somali Pirates abducting on the high seas and the world angry at the image of America, he got no cooperation from Republicans. Despite the trumping of every conceivable anti-Obama sentiment the President was proved successful in tackling nearly ninety percent of those listed maladies despite "I got that Nigger" thumbs up Senator Mitch McConnell's

FREDERICK MONDERSON

mandate to make Mr. Obama "a one term president;" Jim DeMint wanted to create his "Waterloo;" and every Republican in total opposition to the president and his policies.

African Nationalist Poetry and Prose Photo. Dr. Jack Felder, now an ancestor (left) and Dr. Leonard Jeffries (right) iconic champions of African people and culture.

African Nationalist Poetry and Prose Photo. Erik and Luis hanging out at the "**Papyrus Man's**" display while Cherise works the tent.

AFRICAN NATIONALIST POETRY AND PROSE

"I know my country has not perfected itself. At times, we've struggled to keep the promise of liberty and equality for all of our people. We've made our share of mistakes, and there are times when our actions around the world have not lived up to our best intentions." Barack Obama

52. POEM OR ODE TO QUEEN TIY BY DR. FRED MONDERSON

Queen-Tiy, you came at a time, end of the XVIIIth Dynasty, during the golden age of the New Kingdom. Nonetheless, your name has meaning, linking you with great predecessors. Wife of Amenhotep III and mother of Amenhotep IV, Akhenaton,
Some credit you with being behind the Aton intellectual revolution.
Your son so zealously espoused in his new creation of religious worship, artistic expression and scientific possibilities.
0 Beautiful Queen of Kemet/Egypt/Ta-Meri, we admire your august persona.

Your husband, that magnificent Monarch, built you a palace called Malcata
And besides a Sacred Lake for you to sail at times when festivals are celebrated.

FREDERICK MONDERSON

With him you stood in equality sharing power and majesty, while inspiring your beloved in affairs of state. We know, all such Black rulers of magnanimity advanced the role of their women. An inferno of Black African charm, beauty, intellect, astuteness, wisdom is always a motivating factor.

Your portrait in the Berlin Museum depicts your Nubian features. Your time was an age when Black women were astute, strong, powerful. The artists of your era captured the grace, beauty, and dynamism you radiated. Such portrayals underscore the power and influence you wielded. You continue the tradition of African women of power and substance, who presided over the affairs of state and worshiped ancestral gods for whom were built magnificent temples to praise their religiosity and omniscience.

Those structures are considered architectural masterpieces embodying theological, theosophical and metaphysical philosophy of African ancestors. Millennia later these structures still evoke the great achievements and symbolism of Africa's golden age. They tell of a time when powerful Black men and women ruled their nation. When intellectual activities, science, medicine and the arts, were pursuits of wise and noble monarchs. Here espoused the gods' gift to humanity and these early Africans their conduits of creativity in Ma'at.

Queen-Tiy, your name, portrait, image and persona are like magnetic beacons of pride and joy.

AFRICAN NATIONALIST POETRY AND PROSE

Reaching across millennia you inspire Black men and women who meet and vanquish modem challenges. Remembering you, Tiy, Queen of Egypt/Kemet, ruled a wonderfully creative ancient African culture that bequeathed much art, science, religion, and theosophy, metaphysics and joy to the world.

May your name and magnanimity, 0 Beautiful African Queen remind Black men, women the world over, Egypt or Kemet is African, a Brilliant legacy to claim and defend.

African Nationalist Poetry and Prose Photo. A wide assortment of sculptures at the International African Arts Festival.

FREDERICK MONDERSON

African Nationalist Poetry and Prose Photo. Tribute to the Ancestors – Image, 2019.

53. BARACK OBAMA AND THE POWER OF SYMBOLISM BY DR. FRED MONDERSON

Imagine a Black student standing among graduates at Notre Dame University's Commencement, watching President Barack Obama receive a resounding applause as he walked to stand on the platform, then to the podium to give his Address. The significance of the President's visit, that of being a black President of the United States, the audacity of accepting the invitation despite all the controversy surrounding the choice of speaker, to be present at that historic moment in time, witnessing a prestigious academic institution giving an honorary degree to a constitutional scholar and the prospect of a Commencement Address that praises young graduates to engage the world and constructively build the future in the interest of humanity is phenomenal. However, the symbolism of being a part of all this is a powerful stimulus and motivator

AFRICAN NATIONALIST POETRY AND PROSE

to a young mind setting out on a constructive path of who knows where into the future, and as such, this is an experience that comes once in a lifetime.

From the vantage point of being among the graduates, that young black student would experience any number of emotional, philosophical and spiritual reverberating highs to last a lifetime. As to the true meaning of a day as this; when a black person would be awarded a college degree as an alumnus of the President and also be privileged to witness the President of the United States give the address that begins the new journey of the rest of his life, is truly an unforgettable experience. The significance of the day is even more meaningful for the student because of the historic nature of the 2009 Commencement. For here is a Catholic University, celebrating 163 years dating back to 1846, a time when it was illegal for enslaved Africans in America to learn to read, much more be able to attend such an institution, to graduate and to see the President of the United States, an African American, receive an honorary degree and have the honor of addressing its 2900 graduates, of which that student is a member.

There was much press coverage and controversy in the days leading up to Sunday, May 17, and numerous questions as to why a Catholic University, guided by strict religious principles, particularly strongly anti-abortion, would not only invite to speak but also bestow an honorary **Doctor of Norris**

FREDERICK MONDERSON

Causa degree on someone, the President of the United States, who strongly believed in a woman's right to choose, as upheld by *Roe v. Wade*. Yet, in the aftermath of the pre-graduation publicity, protests, and arrests and even heckling drowned out by a rousing "Yes we can," President Obama had chosen to speak, and delivered his message, because in his view, many of those who were in attendance welcomed his appearance.

Father John Jenkins, President of Notre Dame University, in introducing President Obama, recounted a litany of accomplishments; while not spanning a great number of years, contradicted Arizona State University's contention that Obama had not achieved sufficient; which reflected the human side and simplicity of the man despite the powerful nature of his office he now held.

In his Introduction, Father Jenkins identified a sign on the East Bay of Notre Dame's Basilica that reads God, Country and Notre Dame. In his message, he recognized the President's trait of appealing to reason and his efforts to dialogue based on ethical principles, healing not being hateful, and engaging in responsible and respectful dialogue. He is endowed with tremendous human reason and emboldened to serve mankind, seek god and serve humanity, which is consistent with the mission of Notre Dame. His is a human reason, tempered by faith seeking common good in life. Notre dame is a primary and privileged place for dialogue between gospel and culture. The

AFRICAN NATIONALIST POETRY AND PROSE

President listens carefully and speaks honestly. For that, a great deal of attention surrounded his visit to Notre Dame. He is one who does not stop talking with those who differ with him, and this is a quality the American people admired whey they elected him. For that, his appeal transcends race and he is a healer, Father Jenkins concluded.

African Nationalist Poetry and Prose Photo. Dr. Anthony Browder joins other attendees at the **International Decade of People of African Ancestry** Conference in Guyana, 2018.

FREDERICK MONDERSON

African Nationalist Poetry and Prose Photo. Former President Barack Hussein Obama depicted in a Street Art mural, in Brooklyn, New York City.

Before issuing the first among the eight honorary degrees on Sunday, Father Jenkins praised President Obama for his "enormous potential to impact the

AFRICAN NATIONALIST POETRY AND PROSE

world for others." This ability culminated his rise from being the child of a single mother whose family was on food stamps, yet, he engaged in a struggle for a quality education. He chose to serve the people of Chicago as a Community Organizer and worked alongside a diverse group of people. Significantly, from "relative obscurity" Obama triumphed in a political world; demonstrated a tremendous ability to build consensus and bring world leaders and opposing side together, which demonstrates his desire to ease hateful divisions among mankind. Even more important, Father Jenkins pointed out, President Obama, while realizing all the controversy awaiting him at Notre Dame, did not decline the invitation but chose to come and give his address. For this, it was not so much that the University in South Bend, Indiana was honoring President Obama but that Dr. Obama, a constitutional scholar in his own right, was honoring the University by coming to speak at that glorious occasion of its commencement.

For his part, President Obama, like so many great orators, punctuated his presentation with anecdotes of humor; began by being "honored to be here," "grateful to be part of your graduation" and reminded the audience, "Honorary Degrees are hard to come by;" in that he is "one for two," referring to his denial by Arizona State University. Recognizing his motivation to speak has "not been without controversy," he insisted no one should "shy away from things that are uncomfortable." He informed

FREDERICK MONDERSON

the graduates, they have "come of age at a time of great challenge in the world," but they were "privileged and have a responsibility to be constructively meaningful." He faulted the "global economic crisis caused by greed and short term thinking that was rewarded over hard work." Yet he admonished his audience, "We must find a way to live as one human family." This way, we must strive for "greater cooperation and great understanding among many people."

Quoting Dr. Martin Luther King, the President reminded those in attendance, "our fate is tied up in a single garment of destiny" and that "no one person or religion can meet world challenges alone." Therefore, "we must work together for humanity," even though "finding common ground is not easy." Continuing, he pointed out, "We too often seek advantage over others" and "bringing together people of goodwill can be difficult." Yet, he asked, "How do we work through these conflicts?" He insisted, we "remain firm in our principles without demonizing others on the other size" or making "caricatures" of them.

When he ventured into the abortion debate, he spoke of a doctor who wrote him insisting he use, "fair minded words" to find the "possibility of common ground." Rightly pointing out, "Abortion is a heart-wrenching decision for a woman." Therefore, he offered alternatives of reducing abortion, and the need to help that mother carry her child to full term.

AFRICAN NATIONALIST POETRY AND PROSE

He suggested that adoption be made easier; that there be "support for women who give birth and honor the conscience of those who disagree with our views."
]
Recognizing that everyone is entitled to passion and conviction in their beliefs, President Obama insisted opposing views on abortion may be "irreconcilable" but we ought not to mock people to "caricature." He praised Notre dame as a "lighthouse" that stands at the "crossroads" of religion, culture and love. Then he praised the graduates for the "maturity and commendable responsibility" they demonstrated in their approach to the issue of abortion and the controversy surrounding his coming to the university. Showing his respect for Catholic beliefs, he confessed how Cardinal Bernadine of Chicago and the Catholic Church helped him learn cooperation and understanding, and the importance of "finding common ground." He quoted Cardinal Bernadine who taught "you can't get on teaching the gospel until you touch hearts and minds." Then he told the graduates "you will be drawn to public service or to be an active citizen. You will be called to restore a free market that is also fair. You must stand as a lighthouse. Remember, you can also be a cross-road." He insisted the graduates "have confidence in the values with which you've been raised;" and that they "hold firm to your faith and allow it to guide you on your journey."

FREDERICK MONDERSON

President Obama called on everyone in attendance to live by the "Golden Rule," to "Love One Another as you have others love you." He then issued a "call to love; call to serve. Call to share this law of love on your brief sojourn here on this planet." Praising Father Hessberg who President Eisenhower appointed to the Civil Rights Commission in 1957 to work on behalf of humanity and who also walked with Dr. Martin Luther King, Barack Obama believed those in attendance should "make the tradition of love a part of life." He reminded them "community service breaks down walls, fosters cooperation." Ending his speech, he reminded all, "life is never easy" and that "somehow we are all fishermen," expressing the view of Jesus when he admonished St. Peter to propagate the faith and be the rock on which the Church was built.

Father Jenkins, who described the President as someone who never stops talking with anyone who disagrees with him, also informed Mr. Obama, "you bring honor to this University by being our commencement speaker. You also felt honored at the crossroad and lighthouse. We thank you."

To be part of that tremendous experience, to bear witness to such history is an extraordinary motivator for that young black graduate and many students across the nation who can gain inspiration from the symbolism that President Obama represents.

AFRICAN NATIONALIST POETRY AND PROSE

African Nationalist Poetry and Prose Photo. A wide selection of human and animal masks.

African Nationalist Poetry and Prose Photo. Masks and other forms of sculptures.

FREDERICK MONDERSON

African Nationalist Poetry and Prose Photo. Again, more of a variety of sculptures.

54. OBAMA: "FAITH IN FACE OF DOUBT"
BY
DR. FRED MONDERSON

President Barack Obama is a man of unbounded faith in America in face of doubt demonstrated by the many who contend for his job, those who hate and malign him and those waiting in the wings to return the nation to bygone days when its image was tarnished and its capacity severely tested. But, again, Mr. Obama's religious conviction and his unmatched faith in the goodness the nation is capable of will not allow him to surrender in face of the untold numbers marshaled against him and his vision for his beloved nation. As **Corinthians** 5: 7 holds, "He walks by

AFRICAN NATIONALIST POETRY AND PROSE

faith, not by sight" and so he came "fresh and full of faith" knowing that as Moliere 1622-1673 noted, "Doubts are more cruel than the worst of truth" and that is why the nation must be rescued. That is why, in some people's view, the struggle, particularly from a political power perspective as waged in Washington is a contest between good and evil and Mr. Obama stands firmly on the side of good for evil has had its day but its agents are busy at work. As such, Obama believes as Franklin Delano Roosevelt has informed "the only limit to our realization of tomorrow will be our doubts of today. Let us move on with strong and active faith."

As for example, strip away all the spurious claims Republicans and their allies have made and continue to make against President Obama and the only credible deduction left is the color or race of the man. These factors aside, the intellect of Mr. Obama is also an issue of contention because he has to "stay ahead of the pack" in terms of demonstrating fortitude, defending himself against the unrelenting attacks on his character, actions even his family and still initiate policies indicative of superb leadership that characterize the position he holds as Head of State, Commander-In-Chief of American forces and leader of the Western Alliance confronting challenges of a military, economic, foreign policy and terrorist nature. Then against there is the political challenge Mr. Obama faces waged by Republicans and their allies whether conservatives or other radical elements who find issue with a Black President! Notwithstanding, the "black magic" of **Black Women Praying** (BWP) for his success that serves as halo or a "Staff of faith to walk upon;" the love of his family; and the man's unbounded religious faith all keep propelling Mr. Obama into the future he envisioned. Yet, he has realized "the dream" is still far from being accomplished and only unrelenting perseverance, commitment and hard work of keeping his "Eyes on the Prize" will save this nation and bring about the equality of legality and opportunity that will encourage the creativity to keep America competitive rather than allow "the little people to overcome Gulliver."

All this can be accomplished only through unflinching "Faith in Face of Doubt" as the President sketched in his prayer meeting with Christian ministers during this "Holy Week" preceding the climax of the Christian experience that promises so much to human religious beliefs as this nation does to the future of the social welfare of humanity. Nevertheless, in his address to the Christian ministers at that Prayer Breakfast during this "Holy Week," Mr. Obama reiterated his Christian conviction and even posited the view suffering was a natural redemptive elixir. He even saw goodness in the suffering of Jesus and tried to equate such with attacks on his person and character. More important, he emphasized his faith in the meaning and significance of the American creed particularly in view of the doubt and animosity directed to and at

AFRICAN NATIONALIST POETRY AND PROSE

him by a wide range of negativists who, as "people of little faith" question his patriotism, intellect and vision because of his race!

A number of spurious challenges directed against Mr. Obama can be seen particularly from a religious perspective for in deconstructing the contradiction it becomes very apparent. A recent book reports Mr. Obama complained Fox News has perpetuated a falsity that he is a Muslim though he has insisted he is in fact a Christian. On Easter Sunday, April 8, 2012, Mr. Obama was photographed walking with his wife Michelle, and daughters Sasha and Malia accompanied by Secret Service personnel on his way to church across the street from the White House. A credible argument for the myth of his Muslim faith is fueled by his Kenyan father's Muslim background and after his death Barack's mother's marriage and sojourn in Indonesia. We hear so much of "conversion" and even "born again" yet one in five Americans have consumed the falsity Mr. Obama is a Muslim. Other than his reception of and interaction with Muslim world leaders, besides his visit to his father's homeland, perhaps the closest Mr. Obama has come to Muslims was when he delivered two important speeches to the Muslim World in Turkey and Cairo. Still, these were masterpieces of foreign policy steeped in superb oration because as a tactician Mr. Obama realized strategically it was in the best interest of the nation to make such deliveries.

FREDERICK MONDERSON

African National Poetry and Prose Photo. The great South African anti-Apartheid fighter Nelson Mandela, depicted in Street Art Mural.

African National Poetry and Prose Photo. The Author in the fake Oval Office Photo, Wash. DC.

AFRICAN NATIONALIST POETRY AND PROSE

African Nationalist Poetry and Prose Photo. Cherise Maloney of Brooklyn, New York, at the International African Arts Festival, July 4, 2017.

The conundrum in this situation is confounded in Mr. Obama's position as an adult having declared he is a Blackman, African American and a practicing Christian. In the remarkable confrontation with the radical African American preacher Jeremiah Wright it was reported Mr. Obama had attended his church for 20 years. Now, this lengthy attendance certainly challenges the contention that he is Muslim for it seems unreal that he could attend a church publicly

FREDERICK MONDERSON

for so long yet, privately practice Muslim tenets. Equally, feeding this false claim of being Muslim, Mr. Obama visited his paternal homeland Kenya, where elders enthused by the visit of a sitting US Senator with roots to their country dressed him in the traditional garb to show their appreciation, anoint him with their blessings and declare to the world his ancestral connection as shown in photograph. The then "Tea Party" and other miscreants who challenged his candidacy and Presidency extracted much mileage from the event. The reception and fanfare Mr. Obama received was not unusual. Any successful American with foreign roots returning to his or her ancestral homeland generally receive this same type of treatment but therefore, in the concoction against Mr. Obama, those who wanted to malign or criticize him used the photograph along with other elements of their pernicious arsenal with great effect.

To understand the dynamics of the above doubt in challenge to his faith, one has to view the experience in three parts, viz., (1) the decade preceding Mr. Obama's election; (2) the events of his Presidency; and (3) Mr. Obama's faith grounded in his view of the future of an America in which he has a vested family interest and as a constitutional scholar he must be mindful of how history will treat his legacy.

George Walker Bush was elected President under questionable circumstances in 2000. The false confidence of the nation created in the prize of

AFRICAN NATIONALIST POETRY AND PROSE

victory and the "big payback to the Republican base" emboldened enemies as Al Qaeda to set in motion and accomplish the events of 9/11 with resulting mortality at the World Trade Center. Equally, the involvement in two wars in Afghanistan and Iraq and on the domestic front the severe economic problems; Wall Street mismanagement; prolific hemorrhaging of jobs losing some 500,000-800,000 per month; melt down of the housing market in home value and foreclosures; the significance of the auto industry loss of market share; and deterioration of the social infrastructure as well as the negative perception elements of the nation and the world had cultivated about America. In that Chaotic climate, one of the worst recessions since the great depression that brought the nation to the cusp of a failed state, together with an assertive and effective campaign enabled Mr. Obama to win the Democratic primary and ultimately the Presidency. After all, British Prime Minister Benjamin Disraeli in his March 17, 1845 Speech on Agricultural Interests reminded all, "A conservative government is an organized hypocrisy." And no one wanted to return there!

Mr. Obama's tenacious faith in the need to rescue his nation coupled with his vision of a bright future and assisted by the prayers and well-wishing of so many, set sail his administrative ship of state. Mr. Obama's brilliant team of economic, environmental and infrastructure experts put in place plans that halted the decline, removed the "car from the ditch" and

FREDERICK MONDERSON

repaired and set it in motion. He even began to change national and international views of the nation. Just then, conservative Republicanism happened by and his sailing vessel was hit by an iceberg of targeted racial doubt fed by a Republican "Party of No" whose stated mission was to do everything in its power to see the first Black President of the United States fail in his mission to rescue his nation from the ditch its previous guardians had driven it into. Yet, because of his faith, religious and secular, he ignored the criticisms of the "doubting Thomas's" and persevered in his objective quest of providing for all Americans not just the wealthy few who could bankroll the election of men with conservative interests. Still, in this Mr. Obama could have said to such individuals as Rudolf Raspe (1737-1794) in *Travels of Baron Munchhausen* (1785) reminded, "If any of the company entertains a doubt of my veracity, I shall only say to such, I pity their want of faith."

However, let us also not forget, in his First Inaugural Address on March 4, 1801, Thomas Jefferson spoke of "Equal and exact justice to all men, of whatever state or persuasion, religious or political; peace, commerce, and honest friendship with all nations, entangling alliances with none …. Freedom of religion; freedom of the press, and freedom of persons under the protection of the habeas corpus, and trial by juries impartially selected. These principles form the bright constellation which has gone before and guided our steps through an age of revolution and reformation. The wisdom of our sages

AFRICAN NATIONALIST POETRY AND PROSE

and the blood of our heroes have been devoted to their attainment. They should be the creed of our political faith, the text of civil instruction, the touchstone by which we try the services of those we trust; and should we wander from them in moments in error or alarm, let us hasten to retrace our steps and to regain the road which alone leads to peace, liberty and safety." Still, it seems the Republicans have crossed the Rubicon and cannot walk back their behavior.

Thus, Mr. Obama continues to be driven by his faith and as fate has it, many of his policies have begun to bear fruit; whether it is stock market gains, new housing starts, gradual but steady increases in job creation, extrication from foreign wars, greater market share of the automobile industry, insistence on greater efforts to improve education and more experimentation to produce clean and renewable energy resources. All this is because President Obama has not succumbed to the pounding assaults and consistent non-cooperation as he maintained a "strong faith in face of doubt!" Nevertheless, however things turn out, in the end Barack Obama can boast as the **Second Epistle of Paul to Apostle Timothy** 1: 7 "I have fought a good fight, I have finished my course, I have kept the faith."

FREDERICK MONDERSON

African Nationalist Poetry and Prose Photo.
Human and animal sculptures.

African Nationalist Poetry and Prose Photo.
Tribute to the Ancestors – Images, 2019.

AFRICAN NATIONALIST POETRY AND PROSE

African Nationalist Poetry and Prose Photo. Art in its many forms and guises.

55. YOU CAN DO MORE
QUEEN AAHMES-NEFERTARI
BY
DR. FRED MONDERSON

O great Black goddess of the Nile River culture, gift of ancient Africa to the world, as ancestress of the XVIIIth Dynasty, a time of great marvels,
Your progeny deified your legendary courage, beauty, compassion and inspiration.
In time your name became an amazing potion for healing, helping and identification, thus attesting to the universality and magical potency of you as symbol.

FREDERICK MONDERSON

When Hatshepsut asserted and exercised that astute political power of African womanhood, in a world dominated by males, she thwarted her critics and challengers affirming her affinity with the revered Nefertari, ancestress of the XVIIIth Dynasty.

You Nefertari who married Ahmose, founder of the New Empire Cannot be compared with Nefertiti (Thadukhippa's daughter), wife of Amenhotep IV.
Though Nefertari, your namesake, whose portrait rests in the Valley of the Queens, married Rameses II of the XIXth Dynasty and he built a temple to her at Abu Simbel; you Nefertari, sister and wife of Ahmose, mother of Amenhotep I, who was similarly deified, as a legendary and beautiful queen are incomparable, with mere mortals.

Daughter of Sekenenra and Tetisheri, sister of Kamose and grandmother of Thutmose I the courage and rich bold blackness of your heritage is evident. Your family courageously expelled the dreaded Hyksos, "who ruled in ignorance of Ra" as they set in motion one of the greatest intellectually, morally, spiritually and artistically productive periods of Africa's greatness, never again matched in cultural achievement. Today you continue to inspire people, particularly Black women and men, the world over.

The powerful New Kingdom monarchs and their progeny of beloved Ta-meri, KMT, Egypt, who issued forth from your sacred loins, left indelible impressions on the nations of the world. They

AFRICAN NATIONALIST POETRY AND PROSE

glorified African deities, these Black men and women of intellect, courage, and piety.

Equally, Ma'atian ethics undergirded their scholars, scientists, priests, artisans and architects, as they built majestic places of reverence and truly amazing houses or temples for eternal worship all helped crystallize and found great glory in African theology, spirituality, and metaphysics.

Today the world relishes the culture your inspiration helped to bestow. Temples, tombs, feats of navigation, quarrying, transportation, and erection of stone are some accomplishment. Then, the art and architectural wonders of such holy places as Karnak and Luxor, the sacred Valley of the Kings and the wonderful "mansions of millions of years" that adorn the great city of Thebes, are all testaments to the great majesty of a Black African queen. Your posterity ruled the world, then bequeathed the light of wisdom that shined so beautifully to advance the lot of humankind.

African Nationalist Poetry and Prose Photo. Tribute to the Ancestors – Images, 2019.

FREDERICK MONDERSON

African Nationalist Poetry and Prose Photo. Curtis Jackson, aka, "Fifty-cent" rapper, author and actor.

O great Nefertari, wife who stood in equality with your beloved husband Ahmose, Your portrait in the British museum, draped in earliest Red, White and Blue tri-color, is truly an inspiring and enlightening joy to behold; for you embody the rich fullness of African male-female complementarity principle; now therefore, it's time to wear Red, Black, and Green. This makes your name and your beauty forever inspirational, timeless and legendary. And now resurrected, it will continue to motivate and propel Africa's sons and daughters forward.

AFRICAN NATIONALIST POETRY AND PROSE

African Nationalist Poetry and Prose Photo. An ancient Egyptian admonition **MAN KNOW THYSELF** is about inner reflection and resulting strength.

"There are not many males, black or white, who wish to get involved with a woman who's committed to her own development." Eleanor Holmes Norton – *The Black Family and Feminism* – (The First MS Reader – Francine Klagsbrun, ed. 1972)

56. OBAMA AND THE SUPREME COURT BY DR. FRED MONDERSON

Quite frankly, because President Obama is a straight shooter, any measure of his that Republicans oppose is good for America! Let us not forget, a recent Newsweek magazine cover story "Why are Obama's Critics So Dumb" summed up the flaw in

FREDERICK MONDERSON

Republicans' methodology and any challenge to President Obama's statement regarding the Supreme Court's review of his Health Care Reform legislation, amidst unimaginable rancorous discussion is in keeping with their consistent obnoxious behavior. So much so, Republican Senator Grassley of Ohio said, President Obama, as an ex "constitutional professor" was "stupid." It is a stretch to say a scholar, particularly of the United States Constitution is "stupid." Perhaps "stupid" Grassley did not understand the comment and intent, for after all, if you're on the fourth floor speaking it can be difficult for someone in the basement to grasp fully your meaning on an issue. That is, the issue of Health Care Reform, its meaning and means are unprecedented, the President's considered opinion is in itself equally unprecedented and the Supreme Court's role in this particular issue is also in itself unprecedented. But first, let us look at some of the facts that have led to President Obama's statement.

In order to balance the distribution of power in the national government, "founding fathers" created three branches of government that is Legislature, Executive and Judicial in what is considered "Separation of Powers. In this unique concept, created when it was, the Legislature, meaning both Houses, makes the laws; the Executive signs and executes the laws; and the Judicial Branch acts as a sort of people's referee to see the laws are fair and do not infringe on the rights of the people guaranteed by the Constitution. Fact is, government's grab for power has been a source of contention from the beginning and that is why this system was created. Nevertheless, the first to extend its reach or powers was the Judicial Branch.

The Judiciary was created under the Judicial Branch of government and John Marshall presided as the first Chief Justice. The first real constitutional test in that fiery age in the long way forward, came in the form of the case of *Marbury v. Madison* which has remained a significant constitutional benchmark. The issue, as Irving L. Gordon in *American Studies* ((1975) (1984: 222) puts it reads: "William Marbury, a Federalist, was appointed justice of the peace for Washington, D.C. by outgoing President John Adams in 1801, but was denied his official papers, or commission, by James Madison, the incoming Democratic-Republican Secretary of State. In accordance with the *Judiciary Act of 1789*, Marbury went directly to the Supreme Court for an order, called a *writ of mandamus*, to compel Madison to deliver the commission." In the competing political drama of the nation this case threatened the stability of the young republic and only the wisdom of Mr. Marshall was able to navigate through the minefield the issue presented.

In the Chief Justice's decision of the case, Gordon (1984: 222) writes, "Speaking for a unanimous Court, Marshall declared that, although Madison was wrong in withholding the commission, the Court could not grant Marbury the requested writ. Marshall explained that the section of the 1789 Judiciary Act expanding the Supreme Court's original jurisdiction to include the issuing of writs of mandamus violated the Constitution. Marshall reasoned that (1) the Constitution is the supreme law of the land, (2) the Supreme Court is the final interpreter of the Constitution, and therefore (3) the Supreme Court may declare unconstitutional and inoperative any law contrary to the Constitution. Acting boldly and confidently, Marshall thus established the precedent of judicial review." Even more, Jack C. Plano and Milton Greenberg in *The American Political Dictionary* 8th Edition (1989: 259) further explained the significance of the decision: "Few cases have had the impact upon American governmental development as has *Marbury v. Madison*, in which Chief Justice Marshall struck down a decisive blow for judicial supremacy. The case was essentially a political controversy between the defeated Federalist Party and the incoming Jeffersonian party over last-minute Federalist Party appointments to the federal courts. Marshall used the occasion to write a strong, logical defense of the role of the judiciary under the separation of powers doctrine, which is generally assumed to reflect the views of the framers of the Constitution. Although the Constitution fails to mention judicial review, the American people have accepted its exercise by the courts as an integral part of the American constitutional system. In 1974, in rejecting President Richard M. Nixon's claim that the separation of powers doctrine precluded judicial

AFRICAN NATIONALIST POETRY AND PROSE

review of his claim of executive privilege, the Supreme Court relied heavily on the statement from Marbury v. Madison that 'it is emphatically the province and duty of the judicial department to say what the law is'" (*United States v. Nixon*, 418 U.S. 683). Of course, Nixon's case was about an individual's behavior shielded by the pejorative of Executive Privilege while Health Care Reform is a medical-economic issue about the whole nation proposed from a grassroots groundswell.

African Nationalist Poetry and Prose Photo. Mr. Wallis known as "Biggie Smalls" famous rapper.

Plano and Greenberg (1984: 259) states further, "A portrait of the *Judiciary Act* of 1789 was declared unconstitutional in the famous case of *Marbury v. Madison*, 1 Branch 137 (1803), because in it, the Congress had unconstitutionally added to the original jurisdiction of the Supreme Court. Changes of significance include the Act of 1891, which ended 'circuit riding' by Supreme Court justices and established the courts of appeals, the **Act of 1925**, which gave the Supreme Court discretionary authority to issue writs of certiorari, and the Act of 1988, which gave the Supreme Court virtually complete control over its docket by eliminating most mandatory review requirements. In 1982, Congress established the Court of Appeals for the Federal circuit, the first court of appeals to have specialized subject matter jurisdiction from all over the nation on specified matters of business, international trade, and civil service." Notwithstanding the expanded powers of the Constitution, Health Care Reform is in a different category, to be explained later, which allows the constitutional scholar to declare the Court's actions unprecedented.

Additionally, a Bill is a law that emanates in the House. Plano and Greenberg (1984: 114) describes a Bill as a proposed law in which: "members of the House officially 'introduce' bills by dropping them into a 'hopper;' in the Senate, bills are introduced by verbal announcement. All bills introduced during a two-year congressional term are designated 'HR' and 'S' in the Senate, with consecutive numbers assigned in the order in which they are introduced in each chamber. After introduction, bills are sent to a standing committee where, typically, they receive their most thorough airing and consideration. Committees and subcommittees often revise bills in a process called a 'markup session' in which the bill is approved or revised on a section-by-section basis.

AFRICAN NATIONALIST POETRY AND PROSE

On occasion, the committee will completely rewrite a bill during a markup session, with the new version called a 'clean bill.' Each bill must have three readings in each house, be approved by a majority vote in each house, and, normally, be signed by the President to become law. A bill passed in one house is called an 'engrossed bill' and the final authoritative copy of a bill passed by both houses and signed by their president offices is called an 'engrossed bill.' Public bills deal with matters of general concern and may become public laws. Private bills are concerned with individual matters and become private laws if approved."

Now, having reviewed **Judicial Review** and how a Bill become law, we turn to Mr. Obama's Health Care Reform issue and the reason why he took that position. In the case of Mr. Obama, here we have a private citizen who decides to run for President. He formulates an idea of Health Care Reform and makes this a Plank of his campaign. He campaigns on this issue in which the electorate votes to elect him President which means they support his Health Care Reform proposal by a majority. As such, with a majority in Congress he introduces his Health Care Reform measure and it was approved. As President, he signs the historic measure into law. Now, with Republicans marshaled against him, a judicial challenge against Health Care Reform is mounted and the measure makes its way to the Supreme Court. Mr. Obama's statement that it's

FREDERICK MONDERSON

unprecedented that the Court would overturn his legislation is simply because it is not like a Bill that originates in the House and voted into law after deliberation. There is a big difference in the two types of measures and as such, the Supreme Court, as in the case of *Marbury v. Madison* will do well to reinforce its right to judicial review but maintain that the president was right in creating the law and in his statement. Let us not forget, as a principal item in his campaign the people were told of Health Care Reform and in essence, in electing him President voted to approve the measure. After all, as a constitutional scholar he must have a basis for thinking this particular measure creates the particular unprecedented nature that prohibits overturn. It is a pity Mr. Obama's critics cannot see past the race of the man and see the brilliance that keeps him light years ahead of the clowns arrayed against him in their circus costumes.

African Nationalist Poetry and Prose Photo. Dr. Obery Henry at **NAN's 2018 Convention**.

AFRICAN NATIONALIST POETRY AND PROSE

57. POEM TO GODDESS NEPHTHYS
BY
DR. FRED MONDERSON

Nephthys, African Goddess, faithful sister of Isis who stands behind Osiris in the Judgement Hall, You never share the spotlight. You never get the praise you deserve, opposite of Isis.

You're the hardest working woman in the Divinity business, Sister of the God, Eye of Ra, Lady of Heaven. As a pillar of support, you are quintessential, Mistress of the Gods, Lady of Life.

You are numbered in the great Heliopolis Company of Gods and equally fashioned the body of the gods.

Resolute companion, Lady of the Body of the Gods, Isis represents regeneration, you corruption, she light, you darkness, she birth, growth, development and vigor, you death, decay, diminution and immobility, yet you assist in the Risings of the sun god. In the Pyramid Texts, King Unas sat on your thighs. You espouse magnanimity of African womanhood, 0 Creative Goddess, mighty one of words of power. One of the two Merti Goddesses, Nephthys you constantly labor yet your efforts are unnoticed. You are the essential twin in the Alpha and Omega, one of the two Maati Goddesses. With horns, disk and symbol, Black woman, goddess, you labor with diligence, sincerity, and resoluteness.

FREDERICK MONDERSON

In the fratricidal conflict among those early African gods, you supported your sister, Isis.
Her husband Osiris was murdered by your husband, his brother, yet you prepare Osiris' bed and swath the mummy. Manifold literature, Book of Respirations, Lamentations of Isis and Nephthys, Festival Songs of Isis and Nephthys, Litanies of Seker, extol your attributes and virtues.
Double twins, born of the God Ra, you symbolized good and bad, night and day, illumination and darkness. Your coming was a joyous event, 0 possessor of magical power, female counterpart of Ithyphallic Amsu. The astronomers intercalated your manifestation and with Horus or Khnum, you were born on the fifth day, so extending the calendar from the quintessential 360 to 365 days.

Nephthys, daughter of Seb and Nut, when Isis languished in her sorrows, you advised the goddess to lament to Ra, in his boat of millions of years. In lamentations, travail and challenges you both traversed the land of ancient Kemet, saddened but full of hope. Without your support Isis could not manifest her miracles, for you helped Osiris to rise. You were the generator that powered Isis's illumination. The Book of the Dead mentions Isis on the left and you kneel on the right of the Tet of Osiris at Abydos.

The conception of Horus and resurrection of Osiris are yours equally to celebrate, One Crowned King of

AFRICAN NATIONALIST POETRY AND PROSE

Egypt, the other Overlord of the Underworld. None of these brothers could claim their rightful place, sister of the god, had you not fulfilled your destiny Black Goddess, Essential to Ma'at, Lady of the House. Destined to redeem reconstitute, and reclaim the Blackman, essential to a constructive African Family.

Virgin priestesses personify you, sister of the god, creative goddess who lives within An. In December, your feast is celebrated at Abydos, Protector of Osiris. Born in the house of the sistrum Mistress of the Two Lands, One of your favorite pastimes is listening to wonderful tambourine music.

African Nationalist Poetry and Prose Photo. A street dedicated to the great freedom fighter Harriet Ross Tubman.

58. "THE AMERICA WE KNOW!" BY DR. FRED MONDERSON

Appearing on **John King's America** on CNN, May 22, 2012, Reince Priebus spoke of defeating President Obama and "returning to the America we know and love." While the Chairman of the Republican National Committee may be speaking to a particular segment of the American electorate, thinking Blacks certainly query his meaning and see more than the average person does. These days, key words or code words have replaced the more blatant, some say racist, Republican rallying cry. Whether it is Sarah Palin's "He's not like us;" Joe the Plumber's "Sounds like socialism to me;" "We must stop Obama," this will be his "Waterloo" Senator DeMint (R. SC); "I intend to make Barack Obama a one term President" Mitch McConnell (R. Kentucky); are only some of the blatant and code words used to disparage in efforts to derail the President's agenda. But what has Mr. Obama done other than earn the position of being the first Black President, having succeeded forty-three white Presidents of the Republic who in turn succeeded President Henson, a Black man who headed the nation under the Articles of Confederation and whose blessings and spirit may have been instrumental guiding the successes of the new nation under the Constitution. Most Americans, black and white, are unaware of Mr. Henson's role in shepherding the newly independent nation.

While astute Blacks may understand Republican code words, people in general may not reasonably decipher Reince Priebus' "The America we know!" Depending on where you stand or sit, the America we know may be different from the narrow Republican view and the historical America molded in the caldron of its experiences. That is, an America for

AFRICAN NATIONALIST POETRY AND PROSE

centuries enslaved people like Michele Obama's ancestors in an institution of slavery considered "a crime against humanity;" exterminated native Americans as settlers traversed the length and breadth of the nation; fought a Civil War to defend a way of life grounded in an oppressive system; and in terrorism's origins, denied the humanity of black men through Dred Scott v. Sandford and instituted "Separate but equal," really, "Separate and unequal;" created fugitive slave laws, the Ku Klux Klan, "Jim Crow" and the "Grandfather Clause," pure mechanisms of terror. While the Supreme Court and other institutions of law and order remained silent in face of untold lynchings, segregation, incarceration and emasculation of Black men in particular; the society allowing Black unemployment to soar, mis-education to fester and health and nutrition maladies to remain rampant while still recruiting Blacks and other minorities to defend the "American way of life" as we know it, at home and abroad.

Unmistakably, had it not been for men of great conscience as William Lloyd Garrison, John Brown, Sumner, John Kennedy, Lyndon Johnson, Teddy Kennedy aiding the efforts of true Americans as Frederick Douglass, Mary McLeod-Bethune, A. Philip Randolph, Martin Luther King, Malcolm X, Randall Robinson and Colin Powell, we would not be in a position where Barack Obama could be free to be elected, would rescue America from the abyss of two concurrent wars, escalating unemployment,

FREDERICK MONDERSON

skyrocketing home foreclosures, bank and investment firm failures, crumbling social infrastructure, escalating medical costs and a whole lot more, while the wealth of the top one percent, the "Republican base," increased tremendously at the expense of the ninety-nine percent. That is, as rich Americans got richer in good and bad times, the ranks of the poor, homeless, those without medical care, etc., escalated.

African Nationalist Poetry and Prose Photo. Marcus Garvey Boulevard in Brooklyn, New York.

African Nationalist Poetry and Prose Photo. Wooden tables and basins.

AFRICAN NATIONALIST POETRY AND PROSE

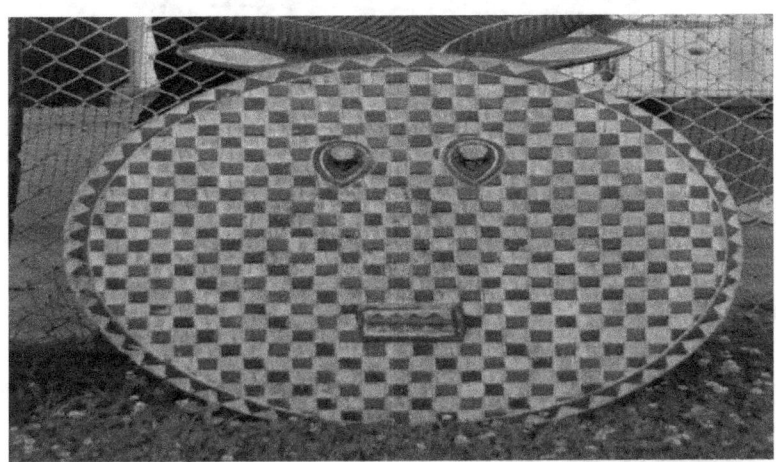

African Nationalist Poetry and Prose Photo. What a beautiful piece with extraordinary alignment of the horizontal and diagonal patterns.

African Nationalist Poetry and Prose Photo. Brooklyn District Attorney Ken Thompson with iconic Congressman John Lewis, attending Major Owen's funeral in Brooklyn.

FREDERICK MONDERSON

African Nationalist Poetry and Prose Photo. Wow.

That "America we know" was clearly enunciated during the challenges of the Republican presidential primary under the banner of conservatism where people like Newt Gingrich wanted to take the nation into that storied past as he and Rick Santorum vied to be more conservative. In that contest, these straw men rather than set the nation afire were themselves burnt because even using the Hubble Telescope they failed to observe the brilliance of Barack Obama who rescued the nation's economy despite his every step, act, his leadership feat was sabotaged by the "Party of No" guided by "Mitch McConnell's Mandate." Mr. Obama brought equality and dignity to the value of women labor by passing "Lilly Ledbetter." He alleviated the stigma against gays by renouncing "Don't ask, Don't tell" and rightly affirming the right of gays to be married, what the **NAACP** called a

AFRICAN NATIONALIST POETRY AND PROSE

"civil rights issue." Mr. Obama changed the world's view of America, got bin Laden, ended the war in Iraq conflict and negotiated an Afghanistan exit strategy. With some luck and due diligence, terrorist plots have been foiled; the nation has enjoyed some 26 months of consistent job growth in the private sector, foreclosures have slowed, housing sales and starts are on the rise, Wall Street is booming so much, they're giving out big bonuses and the wealthy "Republican base" is still getting richer. Still, the ingrates want to crucify Mr. Obama forgoing all that he has done to return the nation to normalcy and pointed in the right direction. Former Vice President Chaney's "new normal" is the rescue of the nation from the economic and fiscal abyss and all the trappings Republicans bequeathed Mr. Obama as he continues to innovate creative strategies to meet the unending challenges.

However, thinking Americans do not want to return the nation to the arrogance we know and despite the millions being spent by Carl Rove's group and other Super PACs, the President will be reelected because his vision is of the future not the past. Perhaps people of Mr. Priebus' hue, familiar with, perhaps linked to that tremendous and turbulent experience may be even beneficiaries want to hold back the dawning new era. Mr. Obama is working to make America a better place free of inconsiderate and obnoxious Neanderthal bigotry choosing to live in America's

FREDERICK MONDERSON

tattered past than coming forth to experience the light of the new and prosperous high noon!

African Nationalist Poetry and Prose Photo. An important intersection where Futon Street meets Utica Avenue or Malcolm X Boulevard at Harriet Ross Tubman Avenue.

African Nationalist Poetry and Prose Photo. The school named for Malcolm X on Malcolm X Boulevard in Brooklyn, New York.

AFRICAN NATIONALIST POETRY AND PROSE

59. POEM TO GOD MIN BY DR. FRED MONDERSON

Amsu/Min, Lord of the Highlands in the august Primeval Mountain, as the fertility god, Personification of the Power of Generation, you are the salt of the earth. Great God, you were from the beginning and will be till the end, Heir of Osiris in his Two Lands, whose Triad is Min, Peshpu and Kent, Lady of Heaven. Creator of Brilliant Rays, Thunderbolt, your face is Beautiful and you receive the Atef Crown, beloved of the South and North, Prince of All the Gods.

Divine Shadow, Bull of your mother, Ithyphallic, Pharaohs acknowledges your strength, virility and exuberance as attributes to admire and emulate. Male Principle, God who cause the Earth to be Fertile, your strength is in the Kings' limbs, and rulers offer wine before you Min, Excellent God, Lord of Joy. Lord of the Ureret Crown, your Tiara is one of Beauty. Beautiful Prince who rises like the Sun, Lord of Radiant Light your White Crown is Lofty, Lord of the Amesu and Makes scepters, Disk and Whip.

August God, the tool of your fertility, erect phallus, emerges from your navel not scrotum. In this you recognize this important organ in the propagation of mankind. Chief of Heaven, Kings relish in being

FREDERICK MONDERSON

Beloved of the Lord of Coptos, Lovely like Min, Him of the Two Lofty Feathers.
Min, Horus the Victorious, you are a Member of the Great Body of the Ennead. Amun's ascendance in the Middle and New Kingdoms gave you equal billing with that Great God.

Your potency, Horus in Spirit, is revered and celebrated in the Apts, Karnak and Luxor, where lives Amon Mighty in Wealth, Great in Love. Amsu, the Risen Horus, or Head, is the Chief of the Gods. Sole God with erect Phallus, in the Mythology, you cause the Earth to be fertile. In the Eschatology, your erection is typical of the Resurrection or re-erection of the mortal in Spirit.

Lord of Eternity, the Temple at Coptos with three gigantic limestone statues painted Black, is the main shrine of your worship, and your Shadow put on the Temple Door. The potency of your majesty cause gods to incorporate your being, Min of Koptos, City with immunities, which are in Upper Egypt. In the House of Min, where is celebrated the Feast of the Going Forth of Min, there are Gardens with every Pleasant Tree and Lettuce, an aphrodisiac, and other Vegetables for Divine Worship of the God of Agriculture. This protected Domain of Min, the King exempted for the Length of Eternity. Joyously, Peasants dance in thankfulness to God Min to celebrate the First Fruits of the Harvest. You are the Mighty One in the Thrice Bent Position.

AFRICAN NATIONALIST POETRY AND PROSE

Maker of Everlastingness, Creator of the Gods, God of the Lifted Hands, you support not hold the whip, in the right hand. Min, as a God of nature you are feared in Nubia and offer special protection to travelers in the Desert, the Divine Land. Friend of the Deceased, with Crook in hand, you Shepherd the Flock of Ra beyond the Grave. O Risen Horus, Grand Master, with your help, the Deceased Received the Amsu Staff, a Protective Power, to roam the Heavens.

Lord of Panopolis, you Create of the Pure Costly Stone of the Hammamat Mountains, Partner of Mut. Head of the Troglodytes, Mighty in Fear, imperialist Kings assume your Likeness in the Year of Terror. Governor of the Apts, Lord of the United Crown of the South and North, God of the Reproductive Power of Nature, your Flame makes your Enemies to fall and your eyes overthrow the Sebau fiends. Master of Terror, Avenger of your Father, you Silence Violent Set.

African Nationalist Poetry and Prose Photo. Tribute to the Ancestors – Images, 2019.

FREDERICK MONDERSON

African Nationalist Poetry and Prose Photo. Nas, the Rapper.

60. CONSPIRACY AGAINST BARACK OBAMA? BY DR. FRED MONDERSON

Now that most of the dust has settled after nearly four years, as President it's time to ask whether there is a conspiracy against the Presidency of Barack Hussein Obama, the first African American to hold the office of President. When, as we approach the next general election and President Obama is attacked for his record as the Executive President of the United States, it is appropriate that we evaluate the people, events and sayings seemingly waged against Mr.

AFRICAN NATIONALIST POETRY AND PROSE

Obama by Republicans, allies, supporters and donors. We can also question whether race has anything to do with it. However, when all is said and done, the putative record depicts a super abundance of negatively pernicious behavior directed against Mr. Obama at a time when he has full-fledged devoted tremendous intellectual, moral and spiritual leadership to combat the enormous economic, financial and social quagmire he inherited in a nation at war while having equally to contend with pernicious Americans practically at war with him. Given the situation he inherited, the effort he expended to address such and nevertheless, have had to contend with such animus directed towards him, one has to conclude, all things being equal, racist behaviors undergirded the attacks on Mr. Obama's integrity, nativity, patriotism, judgment, even leadership skills. So, reasonable people can only conclude Mr. Obama's racial heritage, African American, is at the root of his many problems despite claims, party politics, to the contrary. This is problematic because many people felt his election signaled a post-racial America was underway. Nevertheless, remaining tremendously optimistic and even more strategically astute, Mr. Obama chose to dismiss such action attributing all such behaviors as "Good ole boys" being "Good ole boys!"

There is hard campaigning and then there is hard campaigning but from the inception Barack Obama's very humanity was challenged, fueled particularly by

FREDERICK MONDERSON

right wing media. In the Presidential Primary against Hillary Clinton, his experience and leadership skills were an issue as to what he would do "when the Three AM call came in." He weathered that storm! Having overcome that hurdle as the first African American nominated by a major party, Mr. Obama turned to face his Republican challenger, John McCain. Just then, the "Birther" issue surfaced giving rise, perhaps by whomsoever initiated the "Tea Party Movement," to an unrelenting denial of his nativity and resultant patriotism and right to the Office of President. In their nascent stage, then Senator Barack Obama was caricatured in the most ridiculous fashion; who could forget the "Witch Doctor" and "Hitler" associations as well as the hanging effigy. At their rallies some supporters, whipped up by Sarah Palin's "He's not like us," "Cross hairs" invective, elements within shouted "Kill the Nigger!" No Republican of substance disavowed this! As the "Birther" propaganda fermented people would inject such questions in a racial tone. In one incident, during the presidential campaign, McCain was man enough to extol a female member of an audience, "No madam, he is a citizen, we only have differences on the issues." Nevertheless, as President Obama would later confess, Fox News was behind the "Birther" viral. The "Birther Mama" ran with it. Michele Bachmann took it up conveniently then dropped the issue before Donald Trump embraced "Birtherism" and been running with it ever since. In view of the power of American law and enforcement mechanisms, at the last round of Trump's "Birther

AFRICAN NATIONALIST POETRY AND PROSE

malady" Wolf Blitzer though he was being ridiculous and another commentator thought him a "jackass!"

Given America's racist past, many believed the election of Barack Obama would herald a new post-Racial America but old ideas die hard. Threats against the new President's life increased, rising beyond what George Bush or any other president faced. One "Christian Hypocrite" I mean pastor, began praying for the President's death! How do you square this with a beneficent god or are we now subscribing to radical terrorist posturing? One of his young "stool parishioners" earned the title "black protester with guns" as he came out to greet the President to show his right to bear arms. We know the President is not losing sleep over the Reverend and his praying parishioner. Question is, 'Are they still praying, every day, once a week?' Are they getting tired? Have they looked like jackasses?

The "circus criers" notwithstanding, Republicans running blocks of every legislative move the President initiated forces one to question their motivation and who gave them their marching orders. Not content with waging ad hominem war on Mr. Obama, every legislative action he initiated, Republicans said no to this, no to that. His most significant measures, viz., Lilly Ledbetter, Health Care Reform, Repeal of Don't Ask, Don't Tell, Credit Card Reform, the TARP Funds, Stimulus Package, etc., were all successes when the Democrats

FREDERICK MONDERSON

held a majority in Congress. When that fragile majority dissipated, they held him at a standstill. Yet still, as Republicans full-court press of negativity escalated, they eroded the edges by don'ting everything they could. Whilst, unbeknown to everyone a field of young Tea Party Republicans did a "Faust" and sold the American people a package of goods, got lucky and ended up in control of Congress.

African Nationalist Poetry and Prose Photo. Baskets.

AFRICAN NATIONALIST POETRY AND PROSE

African Nationalist Poetry and Prose Photo. Tribute to the Ancestors – Image, 2019.

The little men of tunnel vision form, viz., Republican leadership in and out of Congress especially the Tea Party cabal in the House and right-wing commentators and talk show hosts, choose to put politics before the economy. They refused to acknowledge the gravity of the nation's economic plight that Mr. Obama inherited, but simple mindedly choose to focus all their attention and effort to make his tenure a failure. Rather than put their shoulder to the wheel to move the coach they have sought to remove the wheel. In a jet age, their pedestrian understanding of the impact of Europe's debt and China's slowing economy on the American system signaled they could not comprehend ore refused to recognize the sincerity of the President's efforts to clean the stables inundated with Republican manure.

FREDERICK MONDERSON

So much so, they dismissed the positive 4.3 million jobs created during his administration when upon his assumption of leadership, the nation was losing some 500,000 to 800,000 jobs per month.

Adding injury to insult, among the things the Republican controlled House refused is to pass the President's jobs bill now in congress and Equally downplay the Auto Industry rescue that saved more than one million jobs, his economic renewal effort and the infrastructure refurbish program, his program of tax cuts for small businesses, tax cuts for businesses that hire Veterans, as well as increases in exports of American made products. All this Republicans have done to deny Obama "a win" in his vision for the country. They're doing a "Nero fiddling while Rome is burning syndrome!" Blindsided by the need and effort to "make Obama a one term President" Republicans have demonstrated insensitivity to the American people's economic plight of unemployment, home distress, etc., while proffering worn out policies and promises of tax cuts for the wealthy which do not produce jobs as history has shown.

AFRICAN NATIONALIST POETRY AND PROSE

African Nationalist Poetry and Prose Photo. Nova Felder, son of Dr. Jack Felder, and kids at the International African Arts Festival, 2018.

61. POEM TO GOD SETH BY DR. FRED MONDERSON

Seth, most mighty one, you were a pre-Osirian drama good being. First Stellar God, author of astronomy, first born of Chavvah, you were ruler of the Primal Pole Star and first of the Star Gods. Nonetheless, Despicable God your role is essential to counterbalance the harmony manifesting in the world. Son of Nut and Seb, in the birth of quadruplets

FREDERICK MONDERSON

your siblings were Osiris, Isis, and Nephthys. While Osiris married Isis, you married Nephthys and she bore you a son, Anubis. Mighty One of two-fold strength, personification of the powers of darkness and of evil and of forces of water that resist light and order, your kingdom in the northern sky is a place of darkness, cold, mist and rain.

Great God and Lord of Heaven, for the duration of Nile Valley cultural experience, you opposed goodness and truth. You were combatant of Horus the Elder, being the cause of clouds, mist, rain, thunder and lightning, hurricanes and storms, earthquakes and eclipses. As an opponent of Ra, threatening his daily risings on the eastern horizon, with your fiends, you personify sin and evil. Still, Ra rises with burning and destroying heat of the sun and darts and heat of the light. You were a combatant of Osiris, paralyzed his left hand and then you slew Osiris. Abominable to that god, Horus, his son, avenged his father. Deity of the first Egyptian Nome, whose domain is in the south, the red crown was given to you Seth, the Egyptians Satan, builder of the mound and believed buried in one of the pyramids.

King of Darkness, anthropomorphic type of evil, you were drowned by Horus in the inundation. Prince of darkness, sower of tears, thorns and thistles, redheaded Egyptian Judas, you have the power to assume the form of detested animals. Chief of the Tesheru deities, gods of the desert, in their distaste of your persona, people kill your animals and establish

AFRICAN NATIONALIST POETRY AND PROSE

a calendar of the wounding of Seth. The black boar of darkness pierced the Eye of Horus. Whether a serpent or giant hippopotamus, you were chained and wounded and imprisoned by Horus. Dragon of Drought, You are the enemy who is wounded and guarded but not dead, Apep.

Brother of Horus, God of the South, Seth, despite the negative image you personify, you were a friend and helper of the dead, who longed from Amenta for the ladder of Seth. You also gave a ladder to Osiris and in your favorable relationships, when Osiris stood up, he is Horus, when he sits down, he is Seth. You were a god who gave service to the underworld. Seth, you were a twin god with Heru-ur. He is god of the Sky, by day, you god of the sky, by night. Indispensable attribute, you were the two powers of nature. As light and darkness, day and night, life and death, good and evil, he is above, you below. The deceased was believed to conquer Seth as Osiris had done and prayed that Thoth would loosen the bandages you placed over his mouth.

Not to be outdone, first-born son of Apt, in the XVIIIth Dynasty you instructed Thutmose III on the use of the bow. In reconciliation with Horus, you both pour libation on Seti I and perform his coronation ceremony, giver of life, strength and health. Horus purifies and Seth strengthens, Seth purifies and Horus strengthens. For loadstone is the 'bone of Horus', and iron the 'bone of Seth.' You both place the double crown of the north and south on the head of Rameses II. Seti II, Merpentan were the last kings of this dynasty to recognize and worship you as a benevolent spirit.

Antagonist of the beloved hero Osiris, the primal pair of Egyptian mythology, you despised his every accomplishment and envied the majesty of his rule. While your companions watched you concocted schemes, murdered Osiris, and deprived him of his legitimate birthright. The kingship of Egypt, a prize of great honor and reverence was at stake when you made your move on him. In the greater scheme of things, your role was destined to oppose goodness, honor and orderly rule of law, one body with two heads. God of the downward motion of the sun, its southerly direction, its destructive heat of summer, Seth you let loose the storm clouds and the thunder of the horizon of heaven.

God whose disposition is hostile to man, when Osiris was away preaching and civilizing communities, you hatched a plan as final solution to the problems of your birthright. At a banquet with dignitaries in attendance you captured the Good God. Your trickery encased him in a coffin then tossed in the Nile. With Thoth, Anubis and Nephthys, Isis found the body and performed the revivification of Osiris. In short lived triumph you seized the throne. In a stroke of luck, you found the body, hacked it into 13 pieces and scattered them throughout the land. The god's penis you threw into the Nile to be eaten by the

AFRICAN NATIONALIST POETRY AND PROSE

catfish. Isis in mournful sorrow searched the land, found the scattered pieces and buried them, head at Abydos and heart at Philae.

The divine godparents hid and raised the young Horus to manhood. Seth, with Thoth as his legal eagle, Horus contested your right to the throne of Egypt. In the Hall of the Gods his case was adjudged rightful in the eyes of the gods. He declared the rightful heir of Osiris, Horus girded himself for the earthly battle to claim his birthright. You fought as men and as bears. Demolishing his opponent and his hordes, Horus captured his detestable uncle. Isis took pity on you Seth, loosened your bonds, and set you free. This fight affected the destinies of the gods. It attached the moral idea of victory of good over evil.

African Nationalist Poetry and Prose Photo. Guyana's President David Granger and Dr. Fred Monderson stand before the nation's Symbol.

FREDERICK MONDERSON

African Nationalist Poetry and Prose Photo.
Jay Zee, Rap Mogul.

62. NO TO THAT "NO-BEL" PRIZE!
BY
DR. FRED MONDERSON

In times past the Noble Prize meant something! Sure, it meant a recognition of exceptional performance or function in a particular area of expertise. Concomitantly, the behavior exhibited must represent high moral standards of conduct befitting a "Noble" recipient. The great Blacks who received the Noble Peace and other Prize, Albert John Luthuli, Ralph Bunche, Martin Luther King, Anwar el Sadat, and Barack Obama, Sir William Arthur Lewis, Archbishop Desmond Tutu, Wole Soyinka, Derek

AFRICAN NATIONALIST POETRY AND PROSE

Walcott, Toni Morrison, Nelson Mandela, Kofi Annan, Wangari Maathai, Barack Obama, Ellen Johnson Sirleaf, Leymah Gbowee, and Tawakel Karman were awarded the prestigious award for peace, in science, literature, whatever, but all were "civilized." That is, they demonstrated and functioned at the highest level of social acceptance, intellectual fortitude and possessed elegance of mind and nobility of spirit, such behaviors undergird the prestigious nature of the achievement, as expected by the global community for such behavior. Conversely, the Warlords, Winston Churchill, Joseph Stalin, Delano Roosevelt and Dwight Eisenhower, who saw the great war to its end, even possessing noble character equally demonstrating exceptional work habits; still, these individuals never received the Noble Peace Prize for ending that great conflict. That is because "Noble means Noble" despite the work one puts in contingent upon behaviors the recipient exhibit before and after the recognition. Lying is not a positive trait nor is egotistical behavior, even trampling on the rule of law in exercising high elected office designed to represent all, not some individuals of a community or nation.

Today, questionable characters vigorously seek this prestigious Noble award that praises exceptional accomplishment. However, this globally respected achievement comes with the expectation its awardees are people of high moral character and ethical behavior in their actions. Banter now being

FREDERICK MONDERSON

propagated insists, Donald J. Trump should be awarded the "Noble Prize for Peace" along the Korean Peninsula. In objection, one may argue, his "baggage," is "greater than Kareen in 'Coming to America'" which not only disqualifies this insidious individual but sullies global perception as to awarding this "high hanging fruit" to one so undeserving. Equally, Mr. Trump's overall thoughts, actions, behaviors also color global perception of America for the world is watching and wondering, what's going on in these United States of America.

Sure, the current debate regarding nuclear weaponry on the Korean Peninsula is significant yet raises profound questions as to who should get a Noble Prize for any breakthrough. In this respect, what must be considered is the character of the individuals who are to receive such; whether any of the parties are actually pushing the award for personal reasons; and how, truly significant this breakthrough will really be, how much time it will take to be complete all of which depends on a number of factors beyond potential cessation of hostilities. President Jimmy Carter was awarded the Peace Prize for bringing Anwar Sadat and Menachem Begin to Camp David where they hammered out a Peace Treaty between Israel and Egypt. This agreement has held for more than 40 years because the parties vowed to make the agreement work. Naturally and sadly, Sadat paid with his life for taking the bold step in breaking with Arab intransigence towards Israel.

AFRICAN NATIONALIST POETRY AND PROSE

Now, after Donald Trump's supporters have given him "a Mulligan," should there be "several Mulligans?" Clearly, the question is, 'how many Mulligans will it take to erase the stains and odious offense of this hypocritical behavior emanating from deep in a questionable mentality?' According to the award-willing journalist Carl Bernstein, we are forced to admit "Trump is president of his base and not all Americans." He calls this relationship, "a cult of is base." Equally significant, not only does Mr. trump not apologize when he makes mistakes or lies, he never accepts correction and so many have placed him, as hugely egotistical, in an alternative universe. Realistically, the man's behavior and personality disqualify him from being a Noble awardee.

to affirm that view, if we assess how Trump has dealt with former President Barack Obama, we can begin with the "5-year Birther charade" of falsity that elevated Trump politically. The man is seen as uncomfortable with his victory, and his administration's hostile propaganda tirade and actions that are designed to effectively undo every constructive accomplishment Mr. Obama achieved on behalf of the American people; and such behavior is appalling, to say the least. He Trump has "Nit Picked" NAFTA, the IRAN-Nuclear Deal, the PARIS Climate Change Agreement, the Pacific Partnership, the Cuba Agreement and especially the long overdue reforms the Obama Administration

FREDERICK MONDERSON

instituted in Criminal Justice practices. To these we could include Mr. Trump's unending insistence that "Barack Obama wire-tapped Trump Tower" during the 2016 election; and more recently, again, seeming falsely claiming the "Obama Administration planted an FBI spy in the Trump campaign." These claims have been debunked through **FACT-CHECK**, especially by Mr. Trump's personally appointed heads of the FBI, CIA and NIS. His unending conspiracy theories span the "deep-state" and "spy-gate" claims, insertion into the NFL unfolding practices and accusations against ABC News, the Washington Post, even Amazon are not only personal but represents the works of a sinister ubiquitous mind. NFL, ABC, Amazon, "deep-state," and "spy-gate," and more. Now Trey Gowdy, a high-ranking Republican representative who led the Benghazi investigation against Hillary Clinton has publicly debunked the "spy-gate" falsity similarly as heads of intelligence agencies have done.

The Cretans have long held, "All Cretans are liars." Whether Mr. Trump is a Cretan is debatable but he is certainly a LIAR, with 3401 [today 10,976] lies to his credit and counting. Beside him dictating a description of health to his doctor and more especially wants to be privy to the investigation about himself helps shed some light into the mind of "the man who wants to be Noble." Let us not forget, Mr. Trump and is propagandists are doing everything to discredit the Muller Probe into Russian interference in the 2016 Election and so his actions are designed

AFRICAN NATIONALIST POETRY AND PROSE

to trample upon the rule of law. As General Michael Hayden, former CIA and NSA Chief earlier explained, alluding to Donald Trump's seeming hatred for former President Obama, Trump, "sees himself not as his predecessor" is putting it mildly diplomatic. Later and regarding Trump's "Memorial Day Tweet," the General continued, "Presidents often put people behind them such as EMS, Fire, Police, the Clergy, etc. In this case, the President placed the **FALLEN** behind him." This meant Memorial Day was not about those who served and gave their lives for this country, but for a Commander-in-Chief businessman who, as a young man sought and got several military deferrals for such ridiculous ailments as "Bone spurs." Americans cannot forget, Trump evaded serving in the military; neither his sons or son-in-law served but today they are "riding in military style." McCain served and bled; Bo Biden served and died; even Trump's Chief-of-Staff General John Kelly's son served and died. Today the evaders are setting military policy and calling out persons. Trump also disrespected the wife of the soldier who died in Niger, during his watch as Commander-In-Chief.

Trump never served, he never showed any evidence of patriotism, other than evasive actions and crafted words. Yet, if memory serves correctly, the Supreme Court ruled "flag-burning" was "constitutionally protected speech." However, in Trump's sordid world, "taking a knee is unpatriotic" and he has referred to those who do as "Sons of Bitches." Inserting his personal views into the sports arena is part of his disregard for people's feelings, refusal to acknowledge the purpose of such protests and his "unrelenting assault on the rule of law." The undermining of law enforcement and intelligence institutions all create the belief he is above the law. When we assess such behaviors, it is equally fair to assume, the "King of Lies and Bankruptcy" must have trampled upon many in his rise to becoming a real estate mogul and as Jeb Bush pointed out, "Trump is insulting his way to the presidency." Let's not forget Obama's profound question, "What if we were wrong" in electing Donald J. Trump president? Highlighting that same vein, Trump's mantra to "Make America Great Again" has, as some have pointed out, in fact resulted in "Make America Hate Again." Pundits have also opined, putting "America first" really results in placing "America alone." Evidence therefore seems to show, the climate emanating from the Trump White House manifested in behaviors such as "Roseanne's;" "Charlottesville;" calling NFL players who 'take a knee' "sons of bitches;" his unrelenting "birther falsity;" demeaning Mexicans, women, judges, the disabled, and a whole lot more are certainly not "Noble behaviors.". Mr. Trump has so far been silent on 4600 Puerto Rican deaths from Hurricane Maria, even though these are American citizens. Call it character flaw or what, this intractable individual even demeans those who work for him such as Jeff Sessions and Rosenberg. Assessing all such behaviors, Max Boot believes,

AFRICAN NATIONALIST POETRY AND PROSE

"Trump is normalizing racism," but more important, "he disagrees and demeans the opposition." Imagine him saying, "Nancy Pelosi loves MS-13."

In analogy, after former president Obama came upon the American economy badly wounded by the roadside, he stemmed the bleeding, bind the wounds and began treatment as a corrective measure. Along came Donald Trump. He removed the bandages, lacerated or opened the wounds, rolled back much and took credit when not deserved. In all this, President Trump created and encouraged a climate of racism, hatred and disrespect towards his predecessor Barack Obama and this evil intent has never let up. In furthering his shameful and destructive character flaw, as Frank Bruni of The New York Times put it, "Trump changed from borderline to full racist." In pedaling and promoting racism and bigotry from his high office, the end result as Republican strategist Ana Navarro put it, "Bigots now proclaim: 'Yea, I'm a bigot, The President does it.'"

Michael D'Antonio who wrote the book on Trump feels, "he lacks the intelligence and creativity to be president. He does not take the responsibility of the office seriously. He is more interested in his own economic and egotistical aggrandizement. He has opened the door to the worse in us. Such behaviors demean and lowers our standards." That means American standards and standings are lowered in the global mindset of nations and peoples who will judge

FREDERICK MONDERSON

the current Noble award issuance and recipient, as they stand in amazing wonder how, "the White House has fallen down." According to Jeff Flake, "The good news is we have reached rock-bottom." The million-dollar question is whether it is in "the shithole!"

Therefore, in the broad sweep of his behavior, many have argued, Mr. Trump has surrendered the moral high ground. But, perhaps, he never stood on such high ground. Philosophically speaking, a man's life in his later years is a clear indication of the challenging, perhaps destructive climb demonstrated in his rise to the top. While an old adage holds, "Cream rises to the top," so do does "garbage after the flood."

Still, we are left to believe the Noble Committee can and will be able to smell the "stink of garbage," human and moral, and respect and prize their award more than anyone who receives it.

African Nationalist Poetry and Prose Photo. Tribute to the Ancestors – Image, 2019.

AFRICAN NATIONALIST POETRY AND PROSE

African Nationalist Poetry and Prose Photo. The South African anti-Apartheid fighter Nelson Mandela.

63. A CONSEQUENTIAL ELECTION BY DR. FRED MONDERSON

The African-American "Shining Prince" Malcolm X, often held, "History is a good teacher." Today, as we seek to determine what is meant by a "Consequential Election," there are a number of landmark instances along the historical continuum that serve as good examples of this important occurrence. The time periods in which these elections occur, the resulting social, civic even economic consequences that result,

FREDERICK MONDERSON

always serve as barometers of future political and election action. As such, and to further help understand elections, we look to the U.S. Census which happens every 10 years and is the basis upon which "redistricting" of Election Districts is done. Generally, the party in government, more often than not, redraw district lines that favor them in the next and hopefully subsequent elections. Oftentimes they go too far and such actions are termed "gerrymandering." When challenged in the courts, their actions are oftentimes deemed illegal since their skewing of the political landscape is generally designed to suppress the voting strength of a particular group who may vote against the interest of the party in power.

Because elections are a state responsibility, that party with a legislative majority generally seeks to legislate any number of measures that "cleanse the voting rolls" which in fact is disfranchisement. Recently pushed by Republicans, this has been in the form of requiring state issued identification which slows the registration process when offices are closed, sparse or placed at a distance making it a challenge to get there. Some voter registration offices are even closed, reducing the number of such places in which voter services are facilitated, thereby reducing the number of registered voters. Felony prisoners are often stripped of their right to vote, generally even after they have paid their debt to society. When calamities such as hurricanes, floods, even fires destroy record keeping centers, this sets back the

AFRICAN NATIONALIST POETRY AND PROSE

identification process and hinders registration and therefore affects the right to vote. Registrars sometimes make demands for identification of Seniors and the poor which is often difficult to provide. As such, if persons are not vigilant, upgrade and frequently maintain their voting record, they can be easily purged from the voting rolls. Then there are the natural, run-of-the-mill errors, which happens at the Board of Election, whether human or mechanical. These can include mis-filing of names of persons registered, broken machines, otherwise missing or defective registration, and let's not forget, more negative campaigning directed against opponents and all other possible means hopefuls can concoct to get elected. Very often, caught up on the throes of being elected or getting re-elected, politicians or representatives "low key" addressing citizens' concerns and together with election day shenanigans which impacts turnout, these go a long way in determining the consequential nature of an election and final vote tally. Thus, the end result of not being active and vigilantly involved results in what former President Barack Obama expressed regarding the 2016 election, "What if we were wrong," about the projected outcome.

The Constitution requires federal officers face the voters every two years. That is to say; first, they are 435 Representative Districts across the country creating that number of House of Representative members. This number is calculated and demarcated

FREDERICK MONDERSON

based on population size occupying each district. These House of Representative members essentially serve for a two-year period and in this category are, therefore, up for re-election. The Senate is representative of the 50 states with two senators each who serve for a period of 6 years per term. Because of the great responsibility of this deliberative body; more so than the House of Representative which is essentially a "money" or "finance" institution as part of its legislative function; only one third of the Senate faces the electorate every two years. For example, in case of the upcoming 2018 Mid-Term Election, all 435 House of Representative members are up for re-election but only 33 Senators of a regular term and 2 special elections slots for the full six-year term are on the ballot. However, because of contemporary and prevailing societal conditions in the "Age of Trump," this mid-term becomes Consequential; and in 2 years, 2020, the same situation applies but with even more dramatic impact. The Office of the President, however, is the principal office up for reelection in 2020 and every four years. Oftentimes persons run on the President's "Slate" and this is called "coat-tail effect." Given the current situation, the 2020 election takes on more meaning.

AFRICAN NATIONALIST POETRY AND PROSE

African Nationalist Poetry and Prose Photo. Dr. James McIntosh, Co-Chair of **CEMOTAP** as he listens to Dr. Johnson and Dr. Wright Presentations.

African Nationalist Poetry and Prose Photo. Brother John at **CEMOTAP**.

FREDERICK MONDERSON

African Nationalist Poetry and Prose Photo.
"End Mass Incarceration and the New Jim Crow."

African Nationalist Poetry and Prose Photo.
More of the throngs at the 20th **MMM** Anniversary.

AFRICAN NATIONALIST POETRY AND PROSE

African Nationalist Poetry and Prose Photo. The iconic Malcolm X.

Back in time, Adam Clayton Powell gave a remarkable speech in Harlem, New York, in which he asked, as entitled, "What's in your hand?" There he highlighted Jesus' "two nails on the cross" and the

FREDERICK MONDERSON

significance of the 1965 Voting Rights Act, which in fact reinforced the 1868 - 15th Amendment to the Constitution giving the vote, essentially, to males born in the U.S. Significantly, these two legislative accomplishments empowered African-Americans through the right to vote. However, nefarious individuals especially, often choose to nullify that entitlement or are generally happy when Blacks refuse to exercise the inherent power such political gains represent. Malcolm X, on the other hand, insightfully recognized how evenly divided or politically balanced Republicans and Democrats were, and so emphasized the importance of the Black vote which could help determine, "Who goes to the White House and who goes to the dog house." A modern example of this phenomenon was the "Judge Roy Moore for Senate" fiasco in which the race was "close" until; unexpectedly, Blacks threw their weight, their vote, behind the Judge's opponent, and this force of will determined the result.

Even more significant, given African-Americans have fought unending for America's defense and traveled a long and arduous road to win the vote, register to vote, and struggled to exercise the privilege of the vote; we must, therefore, never lose sight of voting significance. In South Africa people spent hours and hours standing in line to cast the ballot for the first time in the most consequential election of their time brought about by global pressures against Apartheid and Nelson Mandela's

AFRICAN NATIONALIST POETRY AND PROSE

26-years in prison standing on the principle of the sanctity of one man, one vote.

Perhaps elements of the population in these United States do not understand the inherent power of the vote; how the vote influences the nation's economic, political and moral-social landscape and the true meaning of a consequential election. On the other hand, people with a true sense of history and an understanding of the African-American experience and how difficult it has been to ascend to the mountain-top Barack Obama represented, are involved to the political hilt. Sadly, however, within a mere 18-months gains Mr. Obama struggled to achieve as the nation's first twice-elected African-American President, much have been revoked by Donald Trump; others that "still stand" are threatened and strictures are being put in place that will impact, control and determine the nation's path for the "next 40-years." While the cat is away, the mouse will play to win! Nevertheless, traps and glue sticks can keep that mouse in check.

As an example, of the inherent hatred of the Blackman, what else, since he "footballs" Mr. Obama every day, the following are some significant Obama accomplishments Donald Trump has reversed.

1. DACA – Deferred Action for Childhood Arrivals - 2012

FREDERICK MONDERSON

2. Transfer of surplus Military equipment to local police – 2015
3. Normalizing Relations with Cuba – 2014
4. The Paris Climate Agreement
5. Offshore and Artic Oil Drilling – 2016
6. Net Neutrality – 2015
7. The Clean Water Rule
8. Caps on Greenhouse Gas Emissions at Power Plants
9. Scope of National Monuments
10. Bathroom Protections for Transgender Students
11. NAFTA North America Free Trade Agreement
12. Trans-Pacific Partnership.

Given Donald Trump's unending invoking of the "Cool Ruler's" name, one has to wonder whether it is, "P, Q, R. S, or T" envy.

Nevertheless, torrential outpouring of voting strength can send a clear and convincing message not simply to Mr. Trump but to Republicans and Democrats as well. "Respect the Black vote!" This way, Black respected input can help shape the future direction of the nation. Again, we must never relinquish the significance of the vote.

In January of 2016, Rep. James Clyburn (D. SC) pointed to the consequential nature of the upcoming presidential election. Throughout that year, President Obama strenuously and vigorously expressed such in

AFRICAN NATIONALIST POETRY AND PROSE

campaigning for Hillary Clinton. With all her "imperfections" Blacks would have had influence with Hillary! Instead, many followed Sean Combs, "Puff Daddy," "Puffy," "P. Diddy," "Diddy," a confused young man, who insisted Blacks "Hold the Vote." Instead we get Paris Dennard, Mark Burns, Kanye West, Ben Carson, the Heritage Foundation poster image, all of whom earned their "30 pieces of chitlins," Malcolm X called it "guts." To these we also recognize Black guards for Mr. Trump, Black waiters, Black men with mops, no Black millionaires, but significant roll backs of Criminal Justice reforms, designed to be more equitable in sentencing, time served and re-entry efforts designed to reduce recidivism. Noticeable is the private prison industry undergoing a tremendous resurgence and Black and Brown people overwhelmingly their tenants behind the profit motive surge.

African Nationalist Poetry and Prose Photo. More of the Attendees at the 20th Million Man March Anniversary.

FREDERICK MONDERSON

African Nationalist Poetry and Prose Photo. Biggie!

Nonetheless and much more significant, many still do not realize, the transformation of America Donald Trump is effectuating can practically be viewed especially from the judicial appointments he has put in place. The Internet is reporting, "as of July 10, 2018, the United States Senate has confirmed 43 Article III judges nominated by President Trump, including 1 Associate Justice of the Supreme Court of the United States, 22 Judges for the United States Courts of Appeals, 20 Judges for the United States District Courts, and 0 Judges for the United States

AFRICAN NATIONALIST POETRY AND PROSE

Court of International Trade.[2] There are currently 91 nominations to Article III courts awaiting Senate action, including 1 for the Supreme Court, 12 for the Courts of Appeals, 76 for the District Courts, and 2 for the Court of International Trade.[3] There are currently [1 vacancy] on the Supreme Court, 14 vacancies on the U.S. Courts of Appeals, 129 vacancies on the U.S. District Courts, 2 vacancies on the U.S. Court of International Trade,[3] and 31 announced federal judicial vacancies that will occur before the end of Trump's first term (1 for the Supreme Court, 7 for the Courts of Appeals, and 22 for District Courts).[4] Trump has not made any recess appointments to the federal courts."

As we look to the future, African people must never forget African people's blood, sacrifice and tears soaked and fertilized this American land; and they must also realize, "there are no permanent enemies only permanent interests." Our ancestors were oftentimes worked to death, unpaid and penniless under cruel and inhumane conditions; our men, women and children were brutalized, disrespected, killed and abused, as we faced racism, discrimination and terrorism responsible for nearly 4000 lynchings from 1870-1950. There's been no accounting for this tragedy and none held accountable as the government turned a blind eye toward our plight. Still, like Mother Emanuel Saints, we forgive the "dirty, Rotten Scoundrels."

FREDERICK MONDERSON

While African-Americans have fought in every war America was a part of, from Crispus Attucks to World Wars One and Two with Dorian Miller "our Hero," then "Pork Chop Hill" in Korea, Vietnam and even Afghanistan and Iraq. Now the theater is Africa to extinguish the "bogey man" threatening America; yet, the most potent and viable weapon we have is the vote. While Malcolm X pointed to the "Ballot or Bullet" option, we recognize across today's political landscape the former is more potently effective if we use it wisely and consistently. Without question, we must hold both Democrats and Republican accountable. However, in this we must force Republicans to respect and contend with the Black vote while keeping Democrats' feet to the fire. Clearly, as Republicans continue to ignore Mr. Trump's nearly 4000 lies, falsity and other pernicious shortcomings, ignore the supposed illegitimacy of his election caused by Russian meddling in this sacred American institution practice and as they process and band together to protect him in seeking to discredit the Muller investigation, Black issues are not even on the "back burner." Thus, we must take a stand for our children and grand-children, against the oppressor and to save this great Republic which voted Barack Obama the Greatest American President of our lifetime.

Therefore, we must play a more active role in unfolding circumstances and not be passive bystanders. As such then, if the Black vote turns out enmasse to Spearhead an effective coalition with the

AFRICAN NATIONALIST POETRY AND PROSE

#Metoo Movement, Black Lives Matter, disrespected Latino voters, women across the spectrum, youth affected by gun violence and good and decent people, this combined effort can upset the Mid-term Election, hold Donald Trump in check, then send him packing in 2020.

64.　　ODE TO KWAME TURE (STOKELY CARMICHAEL) BY DR. FRED MONDERSON

O great Black mountain of a man
Your name will forever echo
Among the great heroes

FREDERICK MONDERSON

In the Black Pantheon.

When white power was evident
You sounded the bell demanding Black Power
How fortunate you are to pass
Within the bosom of beloved Mother Africa.

You were a child of the Fifties
A warrior of the Sixties
More than anything, a Pan-African nationalist in the Seventies
A statesman of the Eighties and
A revered and respected elder in the Nineties.

Your indomitable spirit created
An unquenchable fire to see
Africa's sons and daughters free
Your ideas brought us to the end of this century
Now, the new Millennium will bear
The fruits of your earned victory.

In the clarion call
You helped all to see
Whether economic, politic, culture or history
There's no turning back now
The demands for Black Power
Will set us all Free.

O great and noble warrior,
Now go take your rightful place among revered ancestors
Whose efforts have been similarly Noble

AFRICAN NATIONALIST POETRY AND PROSE

Good Brother, your place is assured
You fought the good fight
Now join your namesakes
Kwame Nkrumah and Sekou Ture.

How easy it is to see
Marcus, Malcolm, Martin
Elijah, Robeson, DuBois
Fannie Lou, Mary Bethune
Sojourner and Harriet.

All standing at the stairway
Of your ascent into Africa's paradise
Marvin, Duke and Gillespie
Singing and playing sweet music
Welcoming you into their Blessed Company.

African Nationalist Poetry and Prose Photo.
Various sculptures.

FREDERICK MONDERSON

65. THE RISING TIDE OF COLOR BY DR. FRED MONDERSON

When Lothrop B. Stoddard wrote his Rising Tide of Color there was more than a racial and negative component to the message he conveyed. Recently, when Prince Harry married Megan Markle, Reverend Al Sharpton in prophetic fashion pronounced the "end of white supremacy" though American practitioners were not paying attention. Dr. Leonard James, a scholar possessing a profound global vision and understanding emphasized, in his Methodological Plan of Historical Evolution, that internal and external factors and the significance of antecedent and precipitate causes project states and individuals along the continuing pageantry of human experience. Nevertheless, persons with keen insights recognize individuals who seek to "hold back the dawn" even "stop the sun from rising" relative to the social and intellectual, even political ascendency of Africans, whether at home or abroad recognize how such methods operate.

Evident from four years ago in Brazil, Africans were well-represented among the various teams of the FIFA World Cup soccer matches in that country. Though the African nations' teams were eliminated early in the contest, still Africans were very well-represented among winning European teams

AFRICAN NATIONALIST POETRY AND PROSE

especially England, France and Germany. Four years later in Russia, 2018, the dominance of Africans on these same teams again reinforces Rev. Sharpton's contention regarding the "end of white supremacy" and those not listening or observing should really take note.

France, as the 2018 World Cup winner against Croatia, is the perfect and underscored example of this contention, that in a way highlights the immigrant connection which not simply brings diversity but enrichment of the culture in question. The African players on the French team, Paul Pogba, Ngolo Kante, Kylean Mbappe, Nzonzi, Matuidi, Mendy, Umtiti and others were fantastic in carrying France to be world champions. Mbappe especially at 19 years old, has "forever etched his name in the history books." Much more important, however, that France would win is sweet, rich and ripe in its manifestation for a nation that has suffered so much from terrorism over the last two years and that immigrants or sons of immigrants would help in this way is even more joyful. In that vein, the current negative projected view of immigrants flies in the face of Donald Trump who sadly paints those "wretched" fleeing persecution with a broad, filthy brush. In another and historical context, as Germany pounded French manhood in World War I, French President Georges Clemenceau dispatched the French Deputy Blaise Diagne to recruit soldiers in French West-Africa. He Diagne returned with

FREDERICK MONDERSON

100,000 recruits that helped save the day for France. The world gathered at Versailles, France, to discuss terms of the Peace Treaty ending the war. In America, the African-American scholar Dr. W.E.B. DuBois, dubbed the "Father of Pan-Africanism," in view of the condition of Africa and Africans across the world, decided to call the "First Pan-African Congress." This idea was anathema to America and colonial nations and venue for the Conference was nor easily forthcoming.

However, DuBois' "Hole-card" was Blaise Diagne whose efforts were significant on behalf of France. When the French Deputy approached him, Clemenceau, perhaps to the chagrin of America and Britain, Clemenceau agreed, saying "Have the conference, but keep it low-key." The Congress did meet, followed by several others in America and elsewhere culminating in the Fifth Pan-African Congress in Manchester, England after World War II in 1945. Because of the significance of this Congress empowering Africans with marching orders to return and struggle to decolonize the continent. The success of this effort materialized in Ghana becoming Independent 12 years later on March 6, 1957. In a way, such actions can be considered an early Rising Tide of Color, for it motivated many who subsequently led Africa, from Nkrumah to Mandela, to rid the continent of the scourge of colonialism and racism.

AFRICAN NATIONALIST POETRY AND PROSE

Much more significant, adding the many players of African ancestry across the spectrum of sports underscores not just exhibition of talent; but, again, the erosion of "white supremacy" on a massive scale. In a way, we are reminded of young Tiger Woods winning the Masters Golf Championship and "Old Fogies" complaining "The Black guy is beating us at our own game."

Interesting that on the eve of the Trump/Putin Summit, after France won the World Cup, the Russian President was there to present the trophy and ribboned medals and shook the hands of members of both teams. The French President Macron not simply shook the hands of his winning team but kissed, on both cheeks each player especially the Black players while winning teams in America refuse to visit the White House to meet with President Trump. Another example of the current extreme aberration; Donald Trump, despite his millions, rose to political prominence by promoting the "Birther" controversy falsity and though achieving the highest office in the land; he yet descended to the lowest level by "footballing" the Obama name. In so doing, Mr. Trump has sought to overturn every legislative accomplishment Mr. Obama valiantly secured despite the Republican "Party of No" obstructionism and systematic efforts "to deny the Black guy a win." Nonetheless, and given that words matter, as Michelle Obama appropriately extolled, "When they go low, we go high!"

FREDERICK MONDERSON

It's been said, "While Rome burned, Nero fiddled." Similarly, and sad, not a Republican nor any member of Mr. Trump's "base," seems have an inkling of the injustice in his totally disgusting behaviors. As revealed, while Mr. Trump insulted and demeaned the German President, in comparison, hundreds of thousands of German citizens had turned out to give Mr. Obama the "rock star" treatment. England seemed a carbon copy of Germany and while "Mighty Michelle" floored the British and the Queen, Melania could not save the tarnished "Trump baby" who was told, "Go home," you are "Below par! Resist!"

What's alarmingly troublesome, the "base" which regards Donald Trump as "the best thing since sliced bread" does not realize or choose to see or believe the world thinks of their hero as a "zero." They certainly don't hear Lt. col. Ralph Peters call Mr. Trump's actions, a "disgrace" a "betrayal of the country and its national interest." John McCain called it "shameful." Others held "Russia hit the lottery with Trump" and such terms as "despicable," "shameful," "tragic mistake," "treasonous," "high crimes and misdemeanors," "unbecoming," and "Trump has no shame," representing a "defining moment of the Trump Presidency." Still, President Obama is too decent a person to laugh at Mr. Trump. Thomas Friedman, who thought "The Chinese believed Mr. Trump a chump," and given "Rocket Man" "played Trump," Friedman believed it "unbecoming" and

AFRICAN NATIONALIST POETRY AND PROSE

that, in his many actions, Trump "destroys the norms and institutions of this country." Even Michael Anton, a strong Trump supporter took a stand and said, "I can't defend Trump today." Meanwhile, in his ongoing efforts, as Trump goes "low" on Obama, the former President stays "high" with a 53 percent approval rating at the end of his service and is regarded as the most well-liked of contemporary Presidents. While Republicans raised hullabaloo about a supposed "lie" Mr. Obama made regarding the Affordable Care Act, they have been silent about Mr. Trump's "4000 lies." Are Republicans public servants or legislative cultists? While Mr. Obama consistently flashed that captivating smile, Mr. Trump perennially smirks perhaps anticipating history's treatment of his odious behavior.

The most potent asset a Black public servant has is his integrity and while Mr. Obama demonstrated nobility of sprit and possessed a terrific work ethic of honesty and integrity, despite the avalanche of negativity directed towards him, there were no scandals associated with his administration. Mr. Trump's tenure, eighteen months in, has been inundated with turnovers, nepotism and scandal. Now, who's the better man? Obama, by a longshot. Added to this, tom Ridge believed Mr. Trump's behavior, particularly after his disgusting criticism, denigration, humiliation of America's greatest leaders, Britain and Germany, and Now in Helsinki his actions are "beyond disappointment." So, "after a bad day for America" in retrospect "the Black guy finally gets a win" for his civility, intellect, noble spirit and being the complete opposite to is successor in the Office of the President.

African Nationalist Poetry and Prose Photo. Dr. Jamal Watson and Kirsten Foy at **NAN's 2018 Convention**.

African Nationalism Poetry and Prose Photo. Malcolm X and Martin Luther King, Jr., what a pair!

AFRICAN NATIONALIST POETRY AND PROSE

African Nationalist Poetry and Prose Photo. Jitu Weusi, "Founding Father" and extraordinary educator and nationalist.

African Nationalist Poetry and Prose Photo. Some of the ancestors who have helped pave the way for us to be "Still Standing."

FREDERICK MONDERSON

African Nationalist Poetry and Prose Photo. Minister Hafeez Mohammed greets Sister Richadena Theodore at **CEMOTAP**.

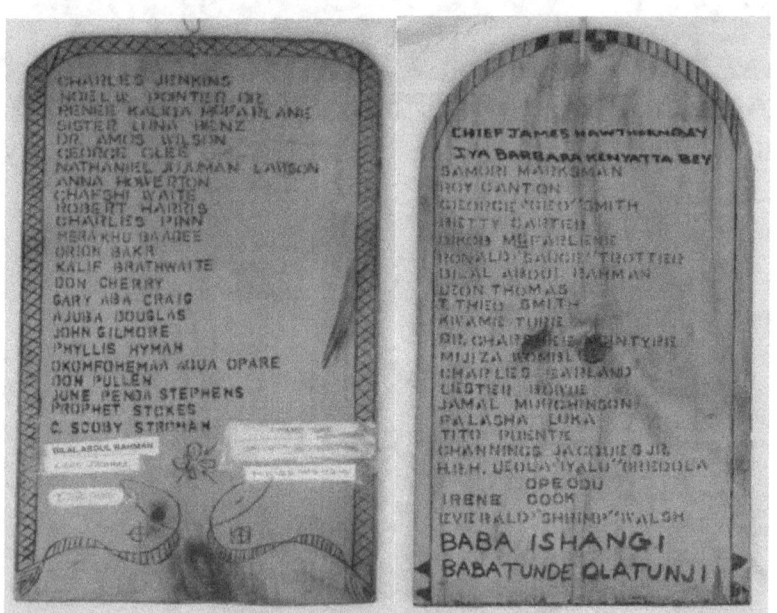

African Nationalist Poetry and Prose Photo. More Stelas with names of glorious ancestors.

AFRICAN NATIONALIST POETRY AND PROSE

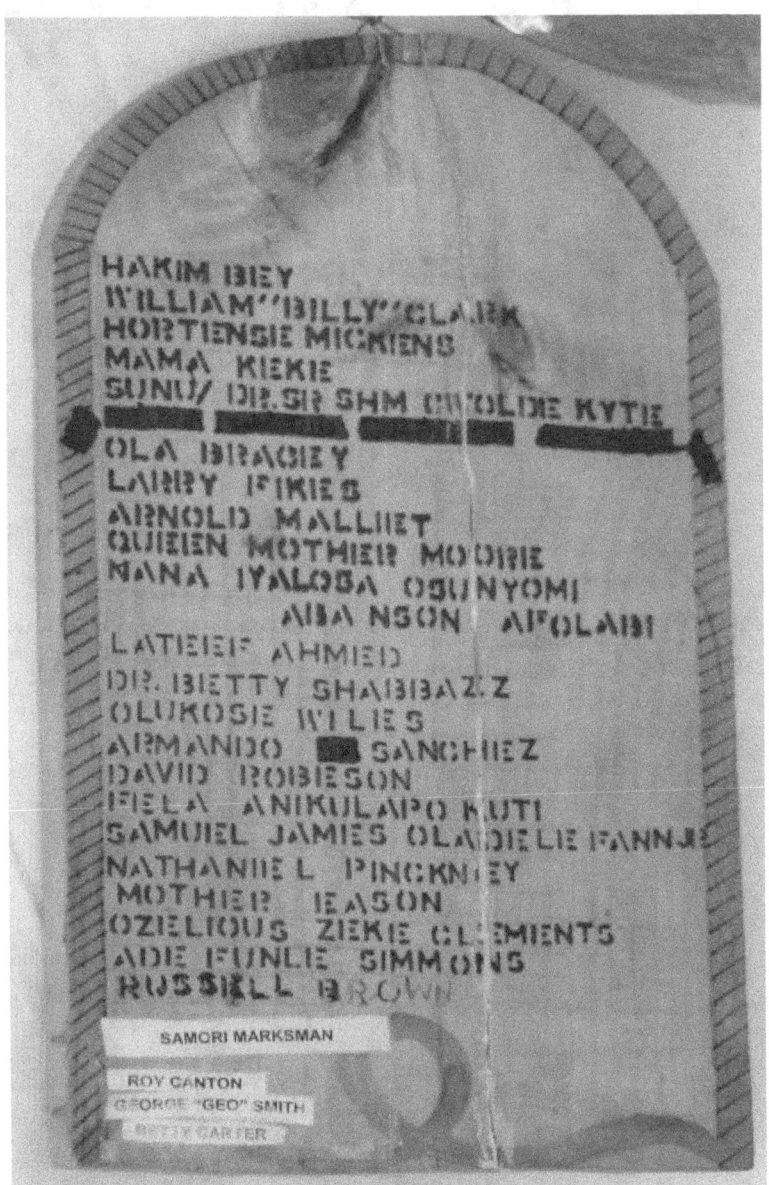

African Nationalist Poetry and Prose Photo.
Even more Steles with names of the Ancestors.

FREDERICK MONDERSON

African Nationalist Poetry and Prose Photo.
Still more names of Ancestors.

African Nationalist Poetry and Prose Photo.
Dr. Adelaide Sanford at her magnificent best.

AFRICAN NATIONALIST POETRY AND PROSE

African Nationalist Poetry and Prose Photo. Even more steles with names of worthy Ancestors.

African Nationalist Poetry and Prose Photo. Dr. James McIntosh and Sister betty Dopson, Co-Chairs of **CEMOTAP**, with Erik Monderson at the Podium.

FREDERICK MONDERSON

African Nationalist Poetry and Prose Photo.
Jay-Zee, Rapper and musical mogul.

AFRICAN NATIONALIST POETRY AND PROSE

African Nationalist Poetry and Prose Photo. Mos Def, Rapper.

FREDERICK MONDERSON

African Nationalist Poetry and Prose Photo.
Ray Charles, Blind Genius and musical legend.

African Nationalist Poetry and Prose Photo.
Still more of the throngs of people at the Million Man March 20th Anniversary.

AFRICAN NATIONALIST POETRY AND PROSE

African Nationalist Poetry and Prose Photo. Michael Jordan, Basketball legend.

66. ABOUT THAT 96 PERCENT BY DR. FRED MONDERSON

During the time Donald Trump was waging his campaign in the 2016 Presidential Election, even after he had exposed his racist underbelly in the "Birther falsity;" expressed his "proclivity for

FREDERICK MONDERSON

grabbing women by the genitals;" accused Mexicans of being rapists; mocked a disabled reporter; accused an American born federal judge of Mexican heritage of potential bias in a case he was presiding in; had unflattering things to say about Megyn Kelly and Rosie O'Donnell; Mr. Trump had the unmitigated gall and temerity to proclaim, by the next, 2020, election 96 percent of African-Americans would vote for him. Evidence seems to indicate Donald Trump is so contaminated from his disgusting description of African nations, there he relishes in a false sense of clarity and fragrance, others see odiousness and disgust.

While President Trump may boast of having the greatest memory, he yet has lapses in remembering things such as the "Stormy Daniels" debacle despite being smacked on the bottom with her **TIME** magazine. Naturally Mr. Trump forgot "in ancient times," he and his dad were sued by the Federal Government for racist practices in their real estate dealings. When the "Central Park Jogger's" unfortunate incident broke, Donald Trump practically "lynched" the "Central Park Five" by taking out a full-page AD in *The New York Times* newspaper. Strange, at that time and for convenience, *The Times* was not "fake news." There he insisted on all manner of horrible resolutions such as "They should be executed" and "Bring Back the Death Penalty, Bring Back Our police." Yet, after their lengthy years in prison and being declared innocent, New York City offered a settlement for wrongful

AFRICAN NATIONALIST POETRY AND PROSE

imprisonment. Mr. Trump objected to the payment in compensation.

Not only is Donald Trump labeled a bigot, liar and racist, an "idiot," "professional liar," but those in his camp, 99 percent of Republicans, including Kelly-Ann Conway, Sarah Huckabee Sanders, and the untold numbers who "enable him," rationalize his behavior, defend his actions in words and deeds, even believe his untruths are not really what they actually are. Given he has told his supporters, "Don't believe what you see. Don't believe what you hear. Don't believe what you read. This is not what is happening." Does this mean Trump's supporters are blind, deaf and dumb who "See no evil, hear no evil, speak no evil" against him. Can they be painted with the same filthy and disgusting brush he deserves? Strange that many have criticized Sarah Huckabee Sanders for enabling, even lying, for President Trump and while her father, Rev. Huckabee criticizes so many but won't say a word regarding his daughter's daily misleading at the White House briefing. They both are included in Hillary's "basket of deplorables."

While people of goodwill strive to correct the nation's misdirection, the President continues to move the nation off the page. This pseudo-leader; clocked at 4720 lies and misstatements in 18 months in office, some half-a-dozen per day, has no remorse about his truthlessness because he never apologizes

FREDERICK MONDERSON

and if he ever does as with "Birther" it is generally not genuine. Sadly, the "moral majority" and others who supports and enables the Trump aberration have not only lost the moral high ground in religious, political and ethical discussions, but as history will acknowledge, they are mired yet and falsely, relishing in the cesspool that has infested the White House. With the exception of Fox News, all commentators are agreed the behemothic Trump administration is a "culture of corruption." Unfortunately, that misogynous leader, having been "played like a fiddle" by North Korea's Kim Jung Un; considered a "chump" by China; laughed at by Vladimir Putin as Ohio governor John Kasich has demonstrated in a tweet, and because he is supported by a few blacks, viz., Carson, Dennard, West, Darrell Scott, and, oh yes, that "Blacks for Trump" individual who acts clownish and is probably very underpaid. Notwithstanding, Mr. Trump foolishly stated and still believes, "96 percent of African-Americans" are ill-informed enough and don't care about si record but will flock to the polls to vote for an "equal opportunity abuser." Oh well, time will tell.

Now, gauging the ante-bellum mentality of many in the Trump's base whose ancestors helped encourage the reality of the **3/5 Compromise**; cultivated and managed slave farms in an institution of degradation, destitution and death; that gave support and strength to the reality of the Dred Scott Decision; relished in Jim Crow practices and benefitted from the "Grandfather Clause;" perpetuated share crop

AFRICAN NATIONALIST POETRY AND PROSE

peonage that essentially created economic enslavement; participated in KKK and Knights of the White Camelia intimidation, terrorism and death that resulted in some 3,973 lynchings from 1870 to 1950; many of those benefitted from the "White Primary" and Southern disfranchisement of Blacks aided through literacy tests, poll taxes and denial of the secret ballot. These and similar machinations as that of the "Bull Connors" and his cohorts unrestricted functioning brutality in an age of more than 100-unsolved Civil Rights murders; thinking individuals expect Mr. Trump will be proven wrong in his expectation of Black support.

The putative record indicates there have been 43 white men as President and once Barack Obama, an African-American, secured the democratic nomination then elected to the Office, Donald Trump and associated ilks unfolded and perennially perpetuated their "Birther" falsity seeking to delegitimize the man and his presidency. Thus, there resulted many fronts of assault on the integrity of Mr. Obama and his administration; yet he persevered because people of goodwill, black and white, prayed for him and showered good vibes on his efforts. This tremendous spiritual support strengthened his resolve and helped bring about his divine mission of rescuing a ship of state adrift, yet many fails to acknowledge this effort particularly because a Black President brought it about.

FREDERICK MONDERSON

African Nationalist Poetry and Prose Photo. Mos Def.

Miscreant behaviors represented in the person of "Joe the Plumber;" "Tea party" gatherings displaying signs and sounds portraying Mr. Obama as a "witch doctor" and chanting "kill the Nigger;" putrid dribbles of the Sarah Palins, Joe Wilsons, Jim DeMints, Allen West, "Black Protester with Guns" and his "Pastor praying for Obama's death;" the "White House Protester" in shorts and with "middle finger in the air" helped perpetuate a climate of systemic racism, hatred and disrespect toward

AFRICAN NATIONALIST POETRY AND PROSE

President Obama. Let us not forget Mitch McConnell's racist and failed diatribe "I intend to make Barack Obama a one-term resident;" all aided by the obstructionist Republican "Party of No's" chokehold on the federal legislature. Much of this Donald Trump inherited and actively exploited in pursuing his agenda. What a conglomeration of persons acting negatively against an individual, a black man; extraordinary in many ways, still his superior intellect best them time and time again. And so, one has to wonder about the conspiratorial nature of their intent. Nonetheless, Obama persevered in rescuing the nation from a debilitating recession and its devastating economic impact, a besmirched nation's image abroad, and having to contend with two wars raging in Iraq and Afghanistan. The perverted state of mind disguised in racist machinations became manifest when, after the 2012 Presidential Election witnessed during October 2013, *The New York Times* newspaper published an article entitled "A strategy long in planning" that involved Mitch McConnell, Ed Meese and top Republican operatives aided by some 20-CEOs of Republican NGOs particularly targeting the Affordable Care Act, maliciously misnomered "Obamacare."

Countering the treasonous behavior and intent and unleashing religious and ethical soul-force with spiritual power because of its sincerity, resoundingly enabled grand-mothers to consistently undergird Obama and strengthen his faith in face of the many challenges and doubt. Persevering, he is today considered and has been Polled the greatest American president in modern times.

Many saw the conspiracy as early as 2008 but the 2012 actions involving the same actors was documented proof of a crime against the Presidency. These were conspirators who clearly failed in their primary effort of restricting Obama's election and re-election.

Fast forward to 2018 and in preparation for the gubernatorial mid-term election in Florida, surprises emerged in the Primary contest. Just before, President Trump appeared before Republican preachers seeking their support to counter the "coming Democratic wave" expected at the mid-term November election by saying, "If Democrats win control of Congress there will be violence." He probably referred to those anti-Obama forces who support him and will be toppled from their questionable perch to this end. This master manipulator invoked fear in the minds of these pastoral leaders creating a religious, political and ethical dilemma for them and their followers tethered to a man with such terribly negative impeccable credentials.

Today, the nation currently has 50 governors, one for each state. All of a sudden one African-American, Andrew Gillum, the Democratic contender emerged victorious in the Florida primary. He was instantly

AFRICAN NATIONALIST POETRY AND PROSE

attacked by both Mr. Trump and the Republican standard bearer for governor, Ron DeSantis. The sad thing is, practically before the final voter count was in, Mr. Trump's attack on Gillum emboldened Mr. DeSantis who referred to Mr. Gillum as "articulate." White men are never addressed as "articulate." More significant, he also used the term "monkey" in referring to the results of a potential vote for Mr. Gillum.

For years, decades and more, ill-intentioned individuals have used the term "monkey" to refer to African-Americans. Monkeys have hair on their chests and while a few African-Americans do have hair on their chests, most whites do have this monkey distinguishing physical characteristic. Early in his first tenure, the *New York Post* published a political cartoon showing two New York policemen "shooting Mr. Obama" characterized as a monkey or ape. Even more recent, Roseann Barr lost her TV show by referring to Valerie Jarrett, an Obama aide, as a "monkey." The disturbing reality, like the dog running after its master, this Trump clone DeSantis seems well-trained in "lowness." However, and significantly, as Michelle Obama laid it down, "When they go low, we go high." Gillum did just that and stuck to the issues of Health Care, Joblessness, infrastructure repairs, climate change, clean air, Women's Rights' etc. Amidst all this and unquestionably, Barack Obama can be considered an aristocrat, political, ethical and intellectual, because

FREDERICK MONDERSON

of his elegance of mind and nobility of spirit, as well as being "frighteningly prepared" to execute his extraordinary work ethic. This is a somewhat similar "presidential timber" that characterized Senator John McCain. Donald Trump, on the other hand, is a low class, billionaire with white supremacist tendencies and, as he struggles to "hold back the dawn," his world is coming apart based on the possibility of criminality linking him and his associates. That is why he will forever be a subject of historical discussion but as villain not hero.

Sadly, African-Americans who have struggled across this nation for equality in human and civil rights; consistently profiled "while Black;" been victimized through poor education, joblessness, lack of quality health care and efforts of consistent political disfranchisement; and as Ayana Pressly a new personality on the scene who spoke against the Trump "firehose of insult and assault" we must insist all persons "fight, organize and mobilize." All this, despite being misrepresented by a few Blacks who "see the world differently" and support Donald Trump unquestionably. The question then becomes, 'Will these thinking Black-Americans rush to vote, 96 percent of them, for a man described as a crook, bigot and racist?' Such is hardly the case for as John Anthony West indicated, "the snowball goes down the hill only until its momentum is expended."

AFRICAN NATIONALIST POETRY AND PROSE

African Nationalist Poetry and Prose Photo. Members of **a Panel** at **NAN's 2018 Convention**.

African Nationalist Poetry and Prose Photo. Tribute to the Ancestors – Image, 2019.

FREDERICK MONDERSON

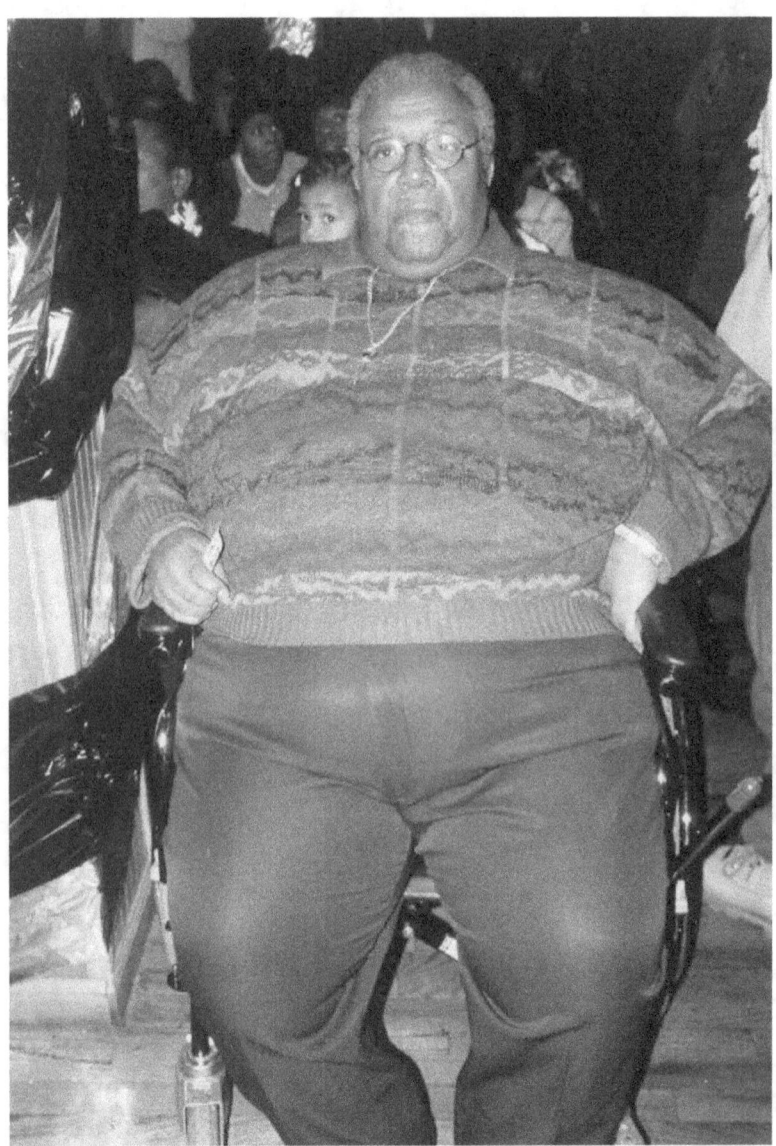

African Nationalist Poetry and Prose Photo. An "Old Warrior," Mr. Curry, spent his time wisely in service to African people.

AFRICAN NATIONALIST POETRY AND PROSE

African Nationalist Poetry and Prose Photo. "Mother Africa" in all her colorful and resplendent glory.

68. STAND STILL ... BY DR. FRED MONDERSON

"Stand still and witness the Salvation of the Lord!"

Word has it that the Trump Administration had considered revoking former President Barack

FREDERICK MONDERSON

Obama's Security Clearance, but this ridiculous and possibly vindictive idea was shelved. This act began the breech of his oath of office to serve as a model of justice and equality for all Americans. Nevertheless, such a decision comes after Donald Trump's championing the "Birther falsity" he "red herringed" that grew legs and ultimately projected him to the United States Presidency. Meanwhile, in his capacity as President during his tenure, Mr. Obama was fully-engaged at the well-known critical junction of the nation's history.

The Obama Administration was unique in a number of ways but principally as the first African-American President of the nation. Number 44 challenged failing norm practices and created economic and financial policies that placed the nation's economic structure on a sound footing. He rescued banks and "Wall Street;" the auto and housing industry as well as state and local governments shortcomings were given a tremendous "shot in the arm;" while remaining committed to the war on terror, Iraq and Afghanistan and much more. Now, while the Obama Presidency created a reservoir of pride and dignity for the Black experience at home and much goodwill to the American cause abroad, all were because of the man's elegance of mind and nobility of spirit. This and more are reasons people loved Obama.

As all this unfolded, Sunday after Sunday and intervening week-days, Saintly grand-mothers and grand-fathers, their sons and daughters and grand-

AFRICAN NATIONALIST POETRY AND PROSE

children gathered in church houses to pray for Barack Obama; a man on a divine mission to save America tottering on the brink of financial and economic ruin; joblessness; housing collapse; and managing the nation's involvement in global conflict creatively. President Obama, with his head down began turning the battleship of state away from the threatening waters of doom and he did it successfully. Yet, in challenge, he had to contend with the masquerading evil and racist implications of "I intend to make Barack Obama a one-term President" Mitch McConnel; the disrespectfully shocking "Birther King" Donald Trump consistently asking for birth certificate and college transcripts as if he never had such.

But they were not alone. After Obama orchestrated the Affordable Care Act, Senator DeMint called for his "Waterloo;" Michele Bachmann accused him of running "a gangster government" in a city where, the FBI is head-quartered along with some 22 other American security agencies including the CIA, NSA, Etc. All the while, Senator Grassley declared Obama "stupid;" Rick Santorum accused him of "poisoning the well;" "Lipstick on a Pig" Sarah Palin had charged he was "palling around with terrorists." Nevertheless, in the general society because of his policies, people were returning to work, banks began lending again, the auto industry regained its market share, housing starts picked up, then Obama

FREDERICK MONDERSON

deployed his "primary weapon" Michelle Obama on the world stage in which she "floored the Queen," "wow" the Germans; "disarmed" the French and earned the moniker "Mighty Michelle."

African Nationalist Poetry and Prose Photo. Again, the Message is clear!

AFRICAN NATIONALIST POETRY AND PROSE

Still, out of jealousy, full of racial animus, the "Tea Party" gathered in nefarious fashion; Militias paraded threateningly under false pretexts; all the while Ted Nugent sang their chorus of "The Nigger in the White House." Yet, undaunted the grand-mothers prayed and prayed for President Obama and oh, what a glorious transference of religious and spiritual nourishment and empowerment such efforts were for their hero on a mission. Nevertheless, Obama continued to swim among sharks, barracudas and piranhas but remained wary of their bite. After all, he admitted, "Politics is a contact sport." Sadly, on their knees in conversation with their god, Dylan Roof entered that Holy Sanctuary in resplendent KKK, Confederate and Nazi regalia then killed 9 in "Mother Emanuel." No less alarming, the surviving Saints, similarly as Jesus on the Cross said to the Centurion, "We forgive you. We don't want to be burdened with your hatred."

And so, as the wheels of truth, justice and righteousness - Ma'at, rolled on, President Obama "fought back to be re-elected." This come back in favorability was against the coordinated assaults, disrespect, the climate of racist animus and deceit generated as a result of McConnell's failed quest; the coordinated strategy of Ed Meese aided by from some 22 CEO's of Republican NGOs, who all mobilized against the ACA they maliciously misnamed "Obamacare." Joe Wilson could not resist

FREDERICK MONDERSON

and so injected his "You lie," as the President of the United States delivered the State of the Union message in the Hall to the Members of Congress. And the Elders prayed on for Obama and the nation, generating tons of spiritual, ethical and emotional strength and goodwill the oppressor could not counter.

Then the "Lord of Hosts" decided to intervene! Still, baffled, he began weighing the requests of Evangelicals even while noticing Blacks on their knees, enjoining to bring good into the world. These oppressed persons had good reason to engage their god, especially after the deaths of Trayvon Martin, Michael Brown, Eric Garner, Gurley and more as a climate of questionable public and private behavior unfolded. But who could question divine design and intent? Still, the black-white divide began turning into a chasm.

Who knows, perhaps the divine decided to chastise America and so allowed Donald Trump access to the Presidency in the cosmic realization, "You only get one shot." In the resulting tumultuous celebratory exuberance from under every rock came an emissary. The glitter of "new penny jewelry" blinded everyone. Moving quick under promise of hiring "the best people" President Trump began rescinding Obama's Executive Orders, engaging corporate entities on the economic and financial pedestals Obama created, while Wall Street began its historic climb. Republicans were elated and touted each success. As

AFRICAN NATIONALIST POETRY AND PROSE

they saw it, Mr. Trump boasted then, "Only I can do it!"

African nationalist Poetry and Prose Photo. "**Conscious Liberated Black**."

FREDERICK MONDERSON

And so, the base, which actually means "bottom" loved their President. It was as if relieved of "Black rule," the "Great White Hope" had arrived. And so, this "Bull in the China House" began running rough shod over everyone, insulting the media, touting "fake news" claims, and even evoking Obama at every turn trying to sully his legacy. Through it all the Saints remained on their knees praying a fallen angel will not consume all.

Meanwhile, given "Absolute power corrupts absolutely," Donald Goliath began trampling across the social and political landscape of the nation. Sowing confusion, denying everything, lying like no other, still he must have had a sense the Avenging David was on the way.

As myriad of events began unfolding the questionable Trey Gowdy chose to "run" and "fight" in another arena; "Stupid" Grassley, discombobulated and speechless, to this day, remains dumb-founded; Wishy-Washy Senator Graham is proving a master of zig-zag; and only Bob Corker stands to deliver! While Mitch McConnell and Speaker Paul Ryan, in face of 4200 Donald Trump lies, misstatements, plus insults, racist rants and more, both fail to do the manly thing as the people's representative for as John Brennan has indicated, Mr. Trump is "drunk with power." And so, the behemoth spread, like the librarian in BLADE, spewing darkness across the American moral and ethical landscape while having political implications that

AFRICAN NATIONALIST POETRY AND PROSE

continue to divide the nation. Many of the President's "best people" fell short and were removed from office or ran afoul of the law. For example, Michael Cohen – pleaded guilty – 8 counts; Paul Manafort – guilty – 8 counts; Michael Flynn – guilty – lying to the FBI; George Papadopoulos – guilty – lying to the FBI; Scott Pruitt – 14 investigations into his tenure; Tom Price – HHC boss -fired; Steve Bannon forced out; Jeff Sessions – Recluse - Omarosa Manigault-Newman – turned traitor. Then there is Rob Porter, fired for spousal abuse. Strange that every time one of these things happen, the President describe these as "good people." As David Axelrod exclaimed, Mr. Trump is "offensive to the truth."

Even as the Special Counsel Robert Muller sifts through the myriad of evidence, he has successfully brought 191 criminal charges against 35 defendants while securing 5 guilty pleas. It's a generally philosophic belief, "one man can become a majority if his truths are immutable." In light of the 2016 election claims of Russian interference, Trump making nice with Russia, one man "called out" the President and in viewing the overt evidence pronounced "the king is naked." Naturally he braced for the backlash but his many years of service to the nation made John Brennan immune to Trump's water pistol. Perhaps that water falling to earth germinated the prayers of the Saints on their knees which began the budding opposition to injustice and tarnishing of the American ideal. Perhaps their prayers will

FREDERICK MONDERSON

continue to be answered. After all, those saintly people who identified with the Black man in the White House, had suffered so much from the insults, humiliation, even racist climate directed toward President Obama.

"Whom the gods wish to destroy they first make mad." In this regard, Martin Luther King reminded, "The arc of the moral universe is long but it bends towards justice." In the streets of New York, we are told, "What goes around comes around." Perhaps the conviction of Mr. Manafort and Mr. Cohen were part of the "Big Payback" answer to prayers for the years of Obama persecution, insults to Black women, sports personalities, Mexicans and other Latinos. Mr. Trump has shown no concern for diversity, a pillar in the strength of America. Let's not forget the "Central Park 5" whom he tellingly disparaged, which all seem to indicate for Mr. Trumps, while the "Cows are not there yet," the "Chickens have certainly come home." Thus, in comparing Obama and Trump, we see Midday and Midnight. You go figure, who's who.

President Trump has his many plates full; he had many fires burning as an enormous cloud settled across the American skies. This has unsettled him terribly. This is a man in crisis. His base chose to be oblivious to such developments because in his utter contempt for the rule of law, he kept insisting, "Don't believe what you read. Don't believe what you see. That is not what is happening." In his "alternative universe" of evasions and untruths the continued

AFRICAN NATIONALIST POETRY AND PROSE

echoed repeats of "No collusion" is not correct. In that "out of this world place," his Adviser Kelly Ann Conway offered "Alternative facts" and his attorney Rudy Giuliani insisted, "truth is not truth." Such pronouncements are naturally unrealistic. In this regard, the award-winning journalist Carl Burnstein speaks of the "sewer seeping up from the White House swamp." Nevertheless, like lemmings in Trump's "alternative universe," his supporters, seem clueless and bent on following him over the cliff. What is the truth, however, is that after President Trump suspended John Brennan's Security Clearance, he then published an additional "enemies list" of ten names whose clearance he announced as considering suspending?

For a man who secured several military deferrals due to "bone spurs" and who is now Commander-In-Chief of the nation's armed forces and whose "enemies list" may have given more than 300 years of service defending this nation, the insult was unbearable. So, Admiral William McRaven (Retired), who oversaw the raid to eviscerate Osama bin Laden considered Trump's description of the press as the "Enemy of the people," as the "greatest threat to our democracy." In response, he wrote, "Suspend my clearance so I can stand next to John Brennan." Then 15 intelligence personnel penned a letter in support of Brennan and the Admiral. These were joined by 60 others and again by another 175 American service patriots, who essentially told the

FREDERICK MONDERSON

President as did Admiral McRaven "you have embarrassed us before our children, humiliated us on the world stage, and worst of all, divided us as a nation."

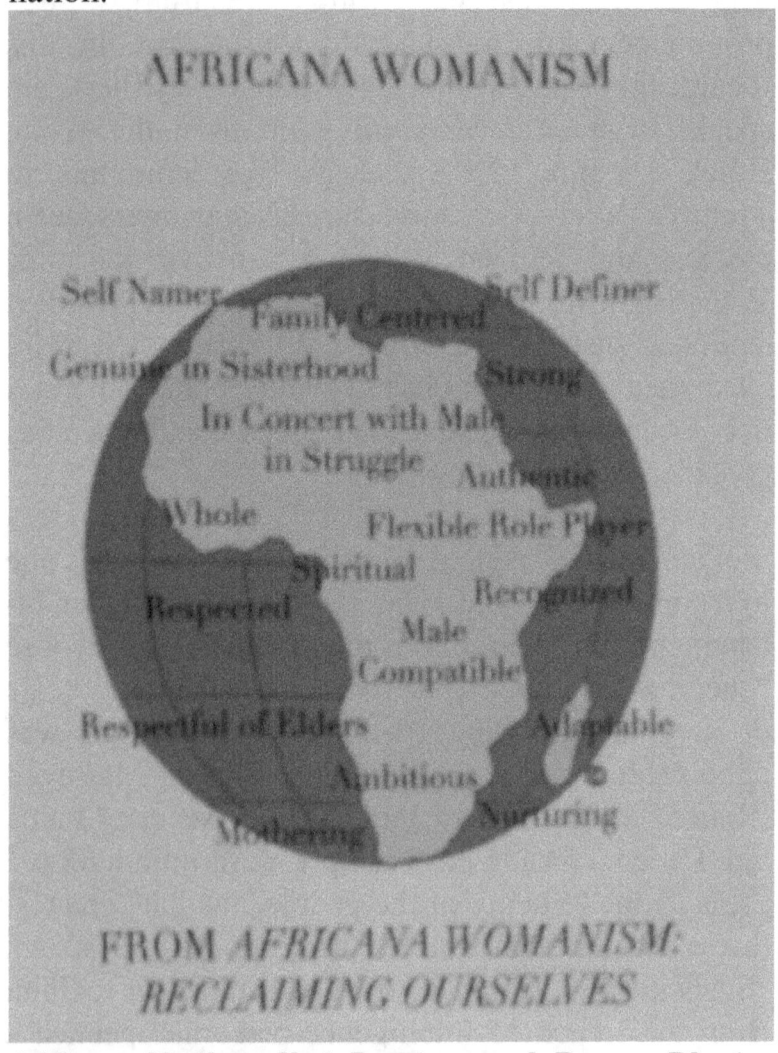

African Nationalist Poetry and Prose Photo. "African Womanism – Reclaiming Ourselves."

AFRICAN NATIONALIST POETRY AND PROSE

African Nationalist Poetry and Prose Photo. D'Shaun.

African Nationalist Poetry and Prose Photo. Still they keep coming for the 20th **MMM** Anniversary.

FREDERICK MONDERSON

African Nationalist Poetry and Prose Photo. Nelson Mandela, South African "Freedom Fighter."

Naturally, in their jubilation of false triumph, his base never saw and still does not see this coming. In fact, they fail to see the big picture facing a worried Trump who has been obfuscating in text. He faces the specter of Muller, McGhan, Omarosa, Cohen, Manafort, Gates, Stormy Daniels, Karen McDougal, Vladimir Putin, Kim Jung Un, China, Iran, and an unleashed Brennan, Clapper, Hayden, and much, much more. He must certainly be worried. Significantly, this man of spite, bigotry, racism and homophobia, in the

AFRICAN NATIONALIST POETRY AND PROSE

words of Omarosa, "Trump has met his match." Matching this, many have argued, "corruption is the feature of the Trump Administration."

African Nationalist Poetry and Prose Photo. Iconic Oprah Winfrey.

However, whatever may be said of Omarosa, she has brought home the bacon! We heard about, even speculated about Donald Trump but now she has recorded goods on him in the form of video, recordings, pictures, emails. Added to this, Donald Jr. is also in trouble for lying, even meeting with an

FREDERICK MONDERSON

American adversary's representative. In all this, Paris Dennard, Ben Carson, Kanye West, the Cleveland Pastor, Mark Burns, Kelly-Ann Conway and all the trump apologists, loyalists, his "best people," many of whom were fired for criminal and unethical activities, are now saddled with and must deny "Trump's sh-t don't stink." Fact is, these people are so far in, they're in the Perfume room."

The real question is will Donald Senior and Junior share the same cell as Muller plays on. Meanwhile, as the Saints continue praying, they "Stand to Witness the Salvation of the Lord" in all its magnanimous retribution.

African Nationalist Poetry and Prose Photo. Freedom Williams.

AFRICAN NATIONALIST POETRY AND PROSE

African Nationalist Poetry and Prose Photo. "Unbought and Unbossed" Congresswoman Shirley Chisholm.

African Nationalist Poetry and Prose Photo. Nelson Mandela and Barack Obama, iconic Global Titans.

FREDERICK MONDERSON

African Nationalist Poetry and Prose Photo.
Former President Barack Hussein Obama.

African Nationalist Poetry and Prose Photo.
AFRICANS at the 20th **MMM** Anniversary.

AFRICAN NATIONALIST POETRY AND PROSE

African Nationalist Poetry and Prose Photo. "**In the Beginning**" there was only **AFRICANS AND AFRICA**.

African Nationalist Poetry and Prose Photo. Tribute to the Ancestors – Image, 2019.

FREDERICK MONDERSON

African Nationalist Poetry and Prose Photo.
Tribute to the Ancestors – Image, 2019.

African Nationalist Poetry and Prose Photo.
Tribute to the Ancestors – Image, 2019.

AFRICAN NATIONALIST POETRY AND PROSE

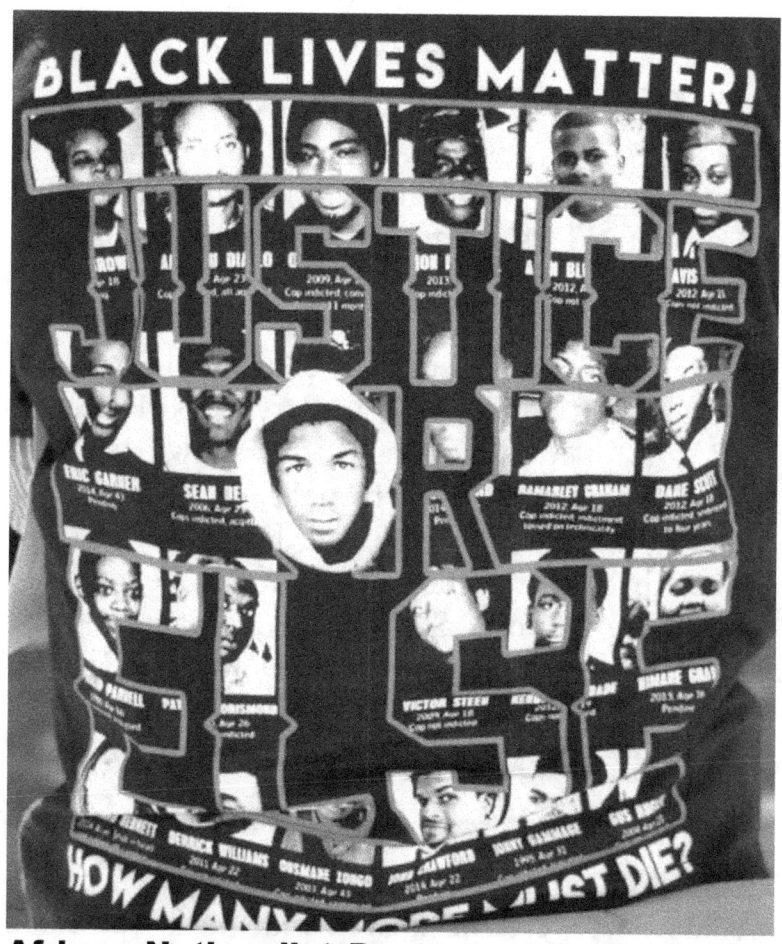

African Nationalist Poetry and Prose Photo.
BLACK LIVES MATTER! They do!

FREDERICK MONDERSON

69. JAMES BROWN: A PERSONAL VIEW
BY
DR. FRED MONDERSON

The passing of James Brown has certainly resonated on distant shores because his musical genius and showmanship as well as his principled positions were known worldwide. Watching CNN Headline News many times were repeated something Rev. Al Sharpton said about the legendary "God-Father of Soul," the "hardest working man in show business." It was that "James Brown made us Proud!" The famous song title: "Say it Loud, I'm Black and I'm Proud" had far-reaching implications beyond the shores of America. Significantly, as art lyrics, it galvanized a people and inspired them along the arduous path of social change in the dynamics unfolding in American political and cultural landscape.

Being a foreign born national in a colonial heritage, we knew we were Black, we lived Black, but Black was a closet secret. We were never taught Black History, about Black America, about Black accomplishments. It was all about the history of our colonizers; in my case British. For example, books such as J.A. Rogers' "World's Great Men of Color" and "Sex and Race" were published in the 1950s and certainly available in the 1960s, but were unknown in the Black world. There was that language, cultural, historical disconnect between American Blacks,

AFRICAN NATIONALIST POETRY AND PROSE

British Blacks, Dutch Blacks, French Black, Spanish Blacks, most important African Blacks! This is what the principal adherents to Pan-Africanism as well as Marcus Garvey struggled to combat. They created that notion of the Black Diaspora and James Brown's lyrics and affirmations filtered throughout as a rallying cry making Black men and women proud of their skin color and by extension reinforcing ties with the African cultural heritage.

In the British West Indies, Guyana to be exact, we equally never realized the potency of the cinema and the carefully regulated inculcation of a foreign cultural manifesto for control of colonized people. We were constantly fed the Tarzan movies in which Hollywood reduced the African to mere buffoons. We enjoyed John Wayne movies and the western particularly those featuring Native Americans. Then there was that movie, I don't remember its name when James Brown and the Famous flames came out of the cold and did a song and dance with the spin around the mike, those quick shuffles, the slide, a drop to his knees and had the cape thrown over him. Finally, he did the Split. He was, like, the first Black action hero to me and many others of my age group.

After that, all my young companions were doing the drop down and the split. This is how we were turned on to James Brown in the early 1960s. In fact, in high school, I remember a fellow student Scantleberry whose pants were split doing "the split" as he saw

FREDERICK MONDERSON

James Brown doing it. And we all had a good laugh. After that, we were moved and sang along and danced as the James Brown "hits" kept coming.

While "Sex Machine" and "Papa's Got a New Bag" were entertaining boasts, "Say it Loud, I'm Black and I'm Proud" was an unequivocal philosophical and principled statement right in the kisser to the powers that be, the oppressor, the establishment, racist institutions, the media, everyone with an agenda of Black suppression. This crystal-clear statement was very important for many reasons but for historical affirmation it was significant. In another somewhat similar situation, from Biblical times, the Queen of Sheba had said "I'm Black and comely" and a great deal of ink was spilled by publication media to reinforce the notion of Black inferiority. The dissenters mis-quoted the Queen saying she instead said, "I'm Black, but comely" implying sort of self-hatred, an aversion to being Black, yet affirming she was still pretty or beautiful. However, there was no mistaken what James Brown said and meant!

The significance of James Brown's song is that as a creative songster, an artist, a leader, he had the people, south and north, east and west, singing and dancing to this new shibboleth, even beyond the shores of America; all intoned with this genius, James Brown. All of a sudden Black was beautiful and we could be proud of it. Remember when he said he wanted to be a teacher but he felt like a preacher, or something like that.

AFRICAN NATIONALIST POETRY AND PROSE

Even more meaningful his creative genius was like fuel to the Civil Rights Movement as it affirmed its stance in those challenging and troubled times. Naturally, like all leaders, when he said, "Hit Me" the anti-Black forces did just that, but "Maceo" and the band played on. Meanwhile, the "God-Father of Soul" had etched his place in the minds, hearts and feet of the people. More importantly, he influenced generations of song and dance men and women, Black, Brown and white. "Mr. Dynamite," "The Minister of Superfund," "Soul Brother Number One," in his autobiography, once referred to those who did follow his lead in funk-soul, jazz, rhythm and blues, pop, and even the later original creation hip hop, """I taught them everything they knew," he said, "but not everything I know."

Strange how coincidences seem to pole one on top of the other. More than a year ago, Al Sharpton held an affair at the Apollo and James Brown was there. The Rev. carried on about how his dad had brought him to the Apollo see James Brown and nw he confessed, "Dad, today I'm honoring James Brown." His dad never believed his son would aspire to the U.S. Presidency. I also took my son Erik to the Rev. and James Brown on that occasion at the Apollo theater in Harlem. James Brown was a standard bearer of Blackness who made us all proud. Through it all, I don't think he ever used the "N" word in any of his lyrical creativity and that was significant.

FREDERICK MONDERSON

African Nationalist Poetry and Prose Photo. James Brown and his famous, "Say it Loud, I'm Black and I'm Proud" affirmation!

AFRICAN NATIONALIST POETRY AND PROSE PHOTO! "I LOVE BLACK PEOPLE!"

www.ingramcontent.com/pod-product-compliance
Lightning Source LLC
Chambersburg PA
CBHW070819250426
43671CB00036B/465